INSIGHT

INSIGHT

◆

Why We're Not as **SELF-AWARE**
as We Think, and
How **SEEING OURSELVES CLEARLY**
HELPS US SUCCEED at Work and in Life

◆

Tasha Eurich

CROWN
BUSINESS

Library of Congress Cataloging-in-Publication Data is available upon request.

ISBN 9780451496812
Ebook ISBN 9780451496829

Printed in the United States of America

Jacket design: Christopher Brand
Jacket illustration: Francesco Ciccolella

10 9 8 7 6 5 4 3 2
First Edition

To Mama, Noni, and my beloved S.P.

It is most perilous to be a speaker of Truth. Sometimes one must choose to be silent, or be silenced. But if a truth cannot be spoken, it must at least be known. Even if you dare not speak truth to others, never lie to yourself.

—FRANCES HARDINGE

CONTENTS

1. The Meta-Skill of the Twenty-First Century 1

PART ONE: ROADBLOCKS AND BUILDING BLOCKS

2. The Anatomy of Self-Awareness:
   The Seven Pillars of Insight 21

3. Blindspots:
   The Invisible Inner Roadblocks to Insight 48

4. The Cult of Self:
   The Sinister Societal Roadblock to Insight 71

PART TWO: INTERNAL SELF-AWARENESS—MYTHS AND TRUTHS

5. Thinking Isn't Knowing:
   The Four Follies of Introspection 97

6. Internal Self-Awareness Tools That Really Work 127

PART THREE: EXTERNAL SELF-AWARENESS—MYTHS AND TRUTHS

7. The Truth We Rarely Hear:
   From Mirror to Prism 157

8. Receiving, Reflecting on, and Responding to
   Difficult or Surprising Feedback 191

PART FOUR: THE BIGGER PICTURE

9. How Leaders Build Self-Aware Teams
   and Organizations 213

10. Surviving and Thriving in a Delusional World 254

   Appendices 287

   Acknowledgments 307

   Notes 309

   Index 345

1

THE META-SKILL OF THE
TWENTY-FIRST CENTURY

The men burst in with urgent news to report. A party of 35 enemy scouts had been spotted roughly seven miles away, camped out in a rocky ravine. What would the young lieutenant colonel decide to do?

The pressure was on, and he knew it. After all, this was a time of war, and he alone was responsible for the 159 recruits he'd led into the field. Despite the fact that the colonel was a 22-year-old rookie with zero combat experience, he'd somehow found himself second in command of an entire army. Not only did he have to act quickly and decisively, he needed to prove himself to everyone who was watching. This would be a crucial test of his military prowess, but he had no doubt he would ace it. The supremely self-assured young man was just *itching* to show his superiors what he was made of.

Those men in the ravine? They were clearly planning to attack, he confidently (and, as it turned out, inaccurately) concluded. So the colonel ordered a sneak assault. In the early hours of May 28, his troops descended on the unsuspecting party, who didn't stand a chance. In less than 15 minutes, 13 enemy soldiers were dead and 21 were captured.

Brimming with pride over his victory, the colonel returned to camp and began firing off letters. The first was to his commander. But before even recounting news of the battle, the emboldened leader took the opportunity—in the form of an eight-paragraph diatribe—to grouse about his pay. His next letter was to his younger brother, to whom he nonchalantly bragged about his fearlessness in the face of enemy attack: "I can with truth assure you," he wrote, "I heard the bullets whistle and believe me there was something charming in the sound."

His self-congratulatory correspondences completed, it was time to plan his next move. Convinced that the enemy was about to launch a revenge attack, he realized he would need to find a better location for their camp. After crossing a nearby mountain range, the colonel and his men found themselves in a large, low-lying alpine meadow. The grassland was surrounded on all sides by rolling hills dotted with bushes and a dense pine forest. Surveying the area, the colonel declared it the perfect defensive location and ordered his troops to begin preparations.

A few days later, he looked on proudly as his men put the finishing touches on their circular stockade, which consisted of scores of upright seven-foot logs draped with animal skins. And because it could hold only 70 men at once, he'd ordered them to dig a three-foot trench for everyone else to crouch in. The colonel thought it was marvelous, assuring his commander that "we have with nature's assistance made a good entrenchment and by clearing the bushes out of these meadows prepared a charming field for an encounter." He knew they'd be outmanned, but "even with my small numbers," he reported, "I shall not fear the attack of 500 men."

Unfortunately, not everyone agreed with the confident young leader. One of his many questionable decisions was the placement of the fort. Because it was built on such soft ground, a light shower of rain would turn the meadow into a swamp, and a downpour would flood the trenches and drench their ammunition. What's more, they were so close to the woods—just 60 yards away—that enemy marksmen could sneak up undetected and effortlessly fire on their fortress at close range. As for the fort itself, the colonel's allied commander—a seasoned battle veteran—insisted that "that little thing upon the meadow" simply would not hold.

Undeterred and convinced that he knew best, the colonel dismissed these arguments out of hand, furiously proclaiming the commander and his army to be "treacherous devils" and "spies." A minor rebellion followed, with the allied commander and his followers fleeing in fear (incidentally, this fear turned out to be extremely well-founded). In the battle that was to come, the colonel wouldn't find the bullets whistling past him to be quite as charming.

And that battle would be momentous. So momentous that the colonel's mistakes would change the course of history. In the years since, historians have attempted to explain how the operation went so tragically wrong. Many have appropriately criticized the colonel for "advancing when he should have retreated; for fighting without awaiting sufficient reinforcements; for picking an indefensible spot; for the slapdash construction of the fort; for alienating his . . . allies; and for shocking hubris in thinking that he could defeat the imposing [enemy] force."

But the colonel's downfall can't be attributed simply to tactical errors, flawed maneuvers, or the lost trust of his men. Examining them alone overlooks their root cause: at the most basic level, the colonel lacked the single most important, and yet least examined, determinant of success or failure—whether on the battlefield, in the workplace, or anywhere else. That quality is self-awareness.

While a precise definition is more complex than it first seems, *self-awareness* is, at its core, **the ability to see ourselves clearly—to understand who we are, how others see us, and how we fit into the world around us.**[*] And since Plato instructed us to "know thyself," philosophers and scientists alike have extolled the virtues of self-awareness. Indeed, this ability is arguably one of the most remarkable aspects of being human. In his book *The Telltale Brain*, neuroscientist V. S. Ramachandran poetically explains:

> Any ape can reach for a banana, but only humans can reach
> for the stars. Apes live, contend, breed and die in forests—
> end of story. Humans write, investigate, and quest. We splice

---

[*] Throughout the book, I'll set key terms, tools, and key takeaways in bold type so it's easier to refer back to them.

genes, split atoms, launch rockets. We peer upward . . . and
delve deeply into the digits of pi. Perhaps most remarkably of
all, we gaze inward, piecing together the puzzle of our own
unique and marvelous brain . . . This, truly, is the greatest
mystery of all.

Some have even argued that the ability to understand ourselves
is at the core of human survival and advancement. For millions of
years, the ancestors of *Homo sapiens* evolved almost painfully slowly.
But, as Ramachandran explains, about 150,000 years ago, there was
a rather explosive development in the human brain—where, among
other things, we gained the ability to examine our own thoughts, feelings, and behaviors, as well as to see things from others' points of view
(as we will learn, both of these processes are absolutely critical for self-
awareness). Not only did this create the foundation for higher forms of
human expression—like art, spiritual practices, and language—it came
with a survival advantage for our ancestors, who had to work together
to stay alive. Being able to evaluate their behaviors and decisions and
read their impact on other members of the tribe helped them, to use a
slightly more modern reference, not get voted off the island.

Flash forward to the twenty-first century. Though we may not face
the same day-to-day threats to our existence as our ancestors did, self-
awareness is no less necessary to our survival and success—at work, in
our relationships, and in life. There is strong scientific evidence that
people who know themselves and how others see them are happier.
They make smarter decisions. They have better personal and professional relationships. They raise more mature children. They're smarter,
superior students who choose better careers. They're more creative,
more confident, and better communicators. They're less aggressive and
less likely to lie, cheat, and steal. They're better performers at work who
get more promotions. They're more effective leaders with more enthusiastic employees. They even lead more profitable companies.

On the flip side, a lack of self-awareness can be risky at best and
disastrous at worst. In business, regardless of what we do or what stage
we're at in our careers, our success depends on understanding who we

are and how we come across to our bosses, clients, customers, employees, and peers. This becomes even more important the higher you ascend on the corporate ladder: senior executives who lack self-awareness are *600 percent more likely* to derail (which can cost companies a staggering $50 million per executive). And more generally, un-self-aware professionals don't just feel less fulfilled in their careers—when they get stuck, they tend to have trouble figuring out what their next phase should even be.

The list goes on and on. After so many years of researching the subject, I would go so far as to say that **self-awareness is the meta-skill of the twenty-first century**. As you'll read in the pages ahead, the qualities most critical for success in today's world—things like emotional intelligence, empathy, influence, persuasion, communication, and collaboration—*all stem from self-awareness*. To put it another way, if we're not self-aware, it's almost impossible to master the skills that make us stronger team players, superior leaders, and better relationship builders—at work and beyond.

Now, you'd certainly be hard pressed to find many people who don't instinctively know that self-awareness is important. After all, it's a term we tend to toss around pretty freely—about our boss, our colleagues, our in-laws, our politicians—although have you noticed that when we do, it's usually in the negative, as in "so-and-so just isn't self-aware"? But despite the critical role it plays in our success and happiness, self-awareness is a remarkably rare quality.

For most people, it's easier to choose *self-delusion*—**the antithesis of self-awareness**—over the cold, hard truth. This is particularly true when our delusion masquerades, as it often does, as insight. The colonel is one example. Let's look at a more modern manifestation. I recently picked up Travis Bradberry's best-selling book *Emotional Intelligence 2.0*, and I was astonished to learn that over the last decade, our collective emotional intelligence (EQ) has improved. (EQ is defined as the ability to detect, understand, and manage emotions in ourselves and others, and countless studies have shown that people who have it are more successful, more resilient in the face of obstacles, more tolerant of stress, better at building relationships, and more.) But in my work as an organizational psychologist, Bradberry's findings didn't match what I had observed: at least anecdotally, I've seen low EQ becoming more, not less, of a problem in recent years.

It wasn't until I took the online assessment that came with the book that I identified the stunning source of the discrepancy. While, yes, Bradberry's research involved a staggering 500,000 people, his conclusions were *based on their own self-assessments.* Think about that for a minute. Picture a few of the least emotionally intelligent people you know. If you asked them to evaluate their own EQ, how much would you bet that they'd see themselves as *at least* above average? So an alternative, and far more likely, explanation for Bradbury's findings is a **growing gap between *how we see ourselves* and *what we really are.*** In other words, what looked like an *increase* in EQ was more likely a *decrease* in self-awareness.*

Our increasingly "me"-focused society makes it even easier to fall into this trap. Recent generations have grown up in a world obsessed with self-esteem, constantly being reminded of their wonderful and special qualities. It's far more tempting to see ourselves through rose-colored glasses than to objectively examine who we are and how we're seen. And this isn't just a generational problem, or even just an American one—it afflicts people of all ages, genders, backgrounds, cultures, and creeds.

Right now, you might be mentally conjuring all the delusional people you know and chuckling—the co-worker who thinks he's a brilliant presenter but puts everyone to sleep in meetings; the boss who brags about being approachable but terrifies her team; the friend who thinks she's a "people person" but is always the most awkward guest at the party. Yet there's something else we all need to consider. As the Bible asks, "How can you say to your brother, 'Let me take the speck out of

---

* I'm often asked how self-awareness is related to emotional intelligence. The simple answer is that whereas emotional intelligence is primarily about awareness and regulation of emotions in ourselves and others, self-awareness is a much broader term: it covers our internal characteristics that go beyond emotions—our values, passions, aspirations, fit, patterns, reactions, and impact on others—as well as how we're seen by other people.

your eye,' when all the time there is a plank in your own eye?" (Matthew 7:4). Whether it's at work, at home, at school, or at play, **we're quick to accuse others of being unaware, but we rarely (if ever) ask ourselves whether we have the same problem.** Case in point: in a survey that I conducted among potential readers of this very book, a full 95 percent reported that they were either somewhat or very self-aware!

The truth is that while most of us think we know ourselves pretty well, this confidence is often unfounded. Researchers have established that our self-assessments "are often flawed in substantive and systematic ways." As you'll read more about soon, studies show that we tend to be terrible judges of our own performance and abilities—from our leadership skills to our car-driving prowess to our performance at school and at work. The scariest part? The *least* competent people are usually the *most* confident in their abilities.

And in most cases, the planks in our eyes are pretty obvious to everyone but us. A tone-deaf college student who drops out of school to become a singer. A braggadocious boss who reads scores of business books but remains a terrible leader. A parent who spends very little time with his kids but thinks he's "Dad of the Year." A thrice-divorced woman who's convinced that the end of each marriage was her ex's fault. Or a colonel who thinks he's a military genius but is really about to get in way over his head.

But being overconfident about our abilities isn't the only way that low self-awareness can play out. Sometimes we lack clarity about our values and goals, causing us to perpetually make choices that aren't in our best interests. Other times, we fail to grasp the impact we're having on the people around us, alienating our colleagues, friends, and families without even knowing it.

Now, if that's what unawareness looks like, the next logical question becomes: What does it mean to be self-aware? When I began my three-year research program on the subject, answering this question seemed like a rather straightforward place to start. Yet I was stunned to learn just how many conflicting definitions existed. Without a clear definition of self-awareness, though, how could I possibly develop an empirical method to help people improve it? So my research team and

I spent months reviewing more than 750 studies to see what patterns emerged. And in the process, we unearthed two main categories of self-awareness that, strangely, weren't always related.

Internal self-awareness has to do with seeing yourself clearly. It's an **inward understanding of your values, passions, aspirations, ideal environment, patterns, reactions, and impact on others.** People who are high in internal self-awareness tend to make choices that are consistent with who they really are, allowing them to lead happier and more satisfying lives. Those without it act in ways that are incompatible with their true success and happiness, like staying in an unfulfilling job or relationship because they don't know what they want.

External self-awareness is about understanding yourself from the outside in—that is, **knowing how other people see you.** Because externally self-aware people can accurately see themselves from others' perspectives, they are able to build stronger and more trusting relationships. Those low in external self-awareness, on the other hand, are so disconnected with how they come across that they're often blindsided by feedback from others (that is, if others are brave enough to tell them). And very often, by the time they hear this feedback, their relationships are too far gone to be salvaged.

Now, it's easy to assume that someone who is internally self-aware would also be externally self-aware—that being in touch with our feelings and emotions helps us tune in to how we're seen. But strangely, research (mine and others') has often shown *no relationship between them*—and some studies have even shown an inverse one! You probably know someone who loves to gaze at their own navel but has precious little understanding of the way they're coming across. For instance, I have an acquaintance who spends thousands of dollars each year on therapy and meditation retreats to "work on himself," but his friends see him as oblivious and insensitive—and he has absolutely no idea. The other side of the coin is also dangerous. Being too fixated on how we appear to others can prevent us from making choices in service of our own happiness and success.

The bottom line is that to become truly self-aware, you have to understand yourself *and* how others see you—and what's more, the path to get there is very, very different than what most people believe. But if this sounds intimidating or untenable, there is good news. My research has shown that **self-awareness is a surprisingly developable skill.**

◆

The colonel's epic battle finally happened on the morning of July 3. An enormous force of 700 enemy soldiers, commanded by the half brother of one of the massacred scouts, rounded on the colonel's flimsy fortress in three huge columns. Despite the size of the opposing army, the colonel was convinced he would be victorious, just as he'd been the last time.

From the cover of the forest, the enemy began to rain bullets upon them. And because their position was so utterly unprotected, the colonel's men could return fire only by popping up from their trenches and shooting blindly. Mostly, they missed their targets. And just when things didn't seem like they could get much worse, a torrential downpour began to drench the meadow, turning their fort into a mud pit and rendering their ammunition useless.

The battle lasted only a day, but the colonel would pay an astronomical price. Compared to just 30 enemy casualties, 100 of his men lay dead or wounded in the muddy, blood-soaked meadow. On July 4, the colonel surrendered, signing a document in a language he didn't speak. (In so doing, he would inadvertently admit to perpetrating war crimes, and the fallout would dog him for months.)

In a final act of humiliation, as the colonel and his remaining men marched back home, they were helpless to stop the enemy from looting their baggage as they departed. Following their narrow escape from this unmitigated calamity, the colonel's regiment was divided into 10 smaller companies. And rather than accept a demotion to captain, he quit.

But here's what I didn't tell you about this embarrassing battle and the hopelessly self-deluded man responsible for it. The year was 1754. The place was Great Meadows, located in present-day Pennsylvania. And the colonel was none other than George Washington. The events at Fort Necessity soon snowballed into the Seven Years' War, and as English author Horace Walpole writes, "The volley fired by a young Virginian in the backwoods of America [would] set the world on fire." It would also be the first—and last—time that Washington would ever surrender to his enemy.

Given Washington's reputation as a heroic general, brilliant states-man, and father of our nation, his behavior as a 22-year-old rookie is pretty shocking. But that's precisely the point: though he became a wise, restrained, self-aware statesman, he started out as a brash, ar-rogant, unaware upstart. As historian W. W. Abbott put it, "more than most, Washington's biography is the story of a man constructing himself." And if we examine that process of construction, we unearth many clues about what a successful self-awareness journey looks like.

Where Washington 1.0 couldn't see or acknowledge his shortcom-ings, Washington 2.0 reveled in searching them out. "I can bear to hear of imputed or real errors," he declared. "The man who wishes to stand well in the opinion of others must do this." Where Washington 1.0 didn't care what anyone thought of him, Washington 2.0 "studied every side of [important decisions], analyzing how his actions would be perceived." Where Washington 1.0 favored fantasy over reality, Wash-ington 2.0 believed in "consult[ing] with our means rather than our wishes." Where Washington 1.0 suffered from delusions of grandeur, Washington 2.0 tempered his ambition with humility and service to the greater good. When Congress elected him president, for instance, he modestly responded, "While I realize the arduous nature of the task which is conferred on me and feel my inability to perform it . . . all I can promise is only that which can be accomplished by an honest zeal."

Here's the key point: although there was only one George Wash-ington, there are so many others—professionals, parents, teachers, stu-dents, artists—who have made similar self-awareness transformations. I have spent the last three years researching such outliers: people who have made remarkable, against-the-odds improvements in their self-knowledge and reaped the resulting rewards. Throughout this book, you'll hear their inspiring and instructive stories.

Yet studying these outliers wasn't my original plan. When I first began my research, after reviewing every study on self-awareness my team and I could get our hands on, I decided to interview a few dozen people who fit our criteria for high self-awareness. My logic was that if I could learn what they were doing, I would unlock the secret formula for everyone else. But I hit a brick wall that, in hindsight, I should have anticipated. Interviewing people to whom self-knowledge came naturally—and who had always been self-aware, at least as adults—turned out to be surprisingly pointless. When I asked my interviewees what they did to stay self-aware, they said things like "I don't know—I guess I just try to reflect on myself," or "I've never thought about it. I just do it," or "I guess I was born this way."

Suddenly, I had an epiphany: if I wanted to hack the code of self-awareness, I wasn't going to find the answer in those who came by it naturally. Instead, I had to find people who had made dramatic, game-changing improvements in self-insight over the course of their adult lives. In other words, I needed to study self-aware people *who didn't start off that way.*

As we began our search for these self-awareness savants, my research team and I adopted two stringent and unwavering criteria. The first was that they had to be high in both types of self-awareness—internal and external—as rated both by themselves and someone who knew them well. Second, they needed to have begun their adult lives with low to moderate levels of self-awareness but dramatically improved it over time, again as rated by themselves and someone who knew them well.

After surveying thousands of people from all around the world, our team identified 50 individuals who fit our two criteria. One of my research assistants playfully but appropriately began to refer to them as *self-awareness unicorns*—after all, they were rare, special creatures that most people didn't believe even existed!—and the term stuck. Our self-awareness unicorns came from all walks of life, and remarkably, there were no patterns by job type, industry, age, gender, education, national origin, or any other demographic characteristic. They were professionals, entrepreneurs, artists, students, teachers, stay-at-home parents, executives (even a Fortune 10 CEO), and more. But this diverse group *did* have two things in common: a belief in the supreme importance of self-awareness and a commitment to develop and hone it throughout their lives.

To help you get a better understanding of what a self-awareness unicorn really looks like, let me tell you about the first time I realized I was in the presence of one.

◆

It was almost exam time at the Government Secondary School in Chibok, Nigeria, and 276 girls were deep in hard-earned sleep. In the early hours of April 14, 2014, their peace was suddenly shattered by a group of men bursting into the darkness of their dormitory. The men reassured the panicking and confused girls, "We're security guards. We're here to assist you."

Once the now-terrified students had left the safety of their dorm, they were loaded onto trucks at gunpoint and driven to a fortified camp in the Sambisa Forest. The men were, in fact, members of the Nigerian terrorist organization Boko Haram. Though at the time I'm writing this, 57 of the girls managed to escape and 23 have been released or rescued, it's hard to say whether the remaining 196 will ever be found. And though this story received worldwide attention, what isn't widely known is that the Nigerian military had four hours' warning about the attack. They also knew exactly where the girls were being held. And yet they did nothing.

Far from the Sambisa Forest, a manager at a Nigerian oil-and-gas company was in New York City when she heard the news. Initially, she dismissed it as impossible. But 34-year-old Florence Ozor soon realized that it was tragically and unacceptably real. She had to do something—but what?

Florence had always felt most comfortable at home with her nose in a book. She wasn't outgoing and had always intentionally stayed under the radar, both at work and in her community. And as someone who kept her head down to avoid being labeled self-promoting or arrogant, Florence certainly wasn't someone you'd expect to see on the front lines of the war on terror. But in a divine act of timing, she'd recently had a profound insight that would alter the course of her entire life. **If self-awareness is a journey,** *insights* **are the "aha" moments along the way.** They're the fuel powering the souped-up sports car on the highway of self-awareness: with them, we can step on the gas pedal; without them, we're stranded on the side of the road.

And Florence was about to hit the gas. Just days before the Chibok girls were abducted, she was in Washington, D.C., attending an orientation for a coveted four-week mentoring program put on by *Fortune* magazine and the U.S. State Department. One morning, Florence was sitting in a breakout session on engaging the media to create social change that was making her pretty uncomfortable. To her, the session's call to action seemed to be to hang out a neon sign for the media that said "Look at me!" She'd always stood for justice, but not publicly—Florence was more inclined to fight these battles in small circles. As an introvert, she'd feared that stepping onto the world stage would let too many people into her space, and the inevitable result would be a loss of privacy and control.

But shortly after the session ended and Florence returned to her hotel room, a dam suddenly burst inside her. Her desire for privacy, she realized, was nothing compared to the changes she wanted to effect in the world. And the day the Chibok girls were abducted, this resolve profoundly deepened. She made an instinctive and instantaneous decision: no matter what the risk, no matter what she'd have to give up, it was a moral imperative to take a stand to bring the girls home. *Never again will I run away from something just because I'm scared of the spotlight,* she vowed, *I've always been a fighter—why not let the world know it? That is who I really am.*

By the time Florence had returned home from New York, the #BringBackOurGirls movement had begun to sweep the world. But her government was still doing nothing. Around that time, a remarkable woman named Hadiza Bala Usman organized a group to demand a response from both the international community and the Nigerian government. Armed with the newfound insight that she was capable of creating a wide social impact, Florence joined the group's first protest in the capital city of Abuja. They gathered in the pouring rain near the city's Unity Fountain, an enormous cement monument with a cascade of water soaring many stories into the sky. Holding the protest here wasn't just a signal of their intent—unity—they also needed to be close to the country's national assembly.

The protesters would continue to gather there every day until their message was heard. In the process, they faced intimidation and harassment by hired thugs who chased them with sticks, stole their phones and cameras, and even broke chairs over their backs, all while indifferent police and public servants looked on. But nothing has diminished their will. Florence and her compatriots will continue to demand action until the girls are safely home.

People tell Florence all the time how surprised they are that she stepped out of her small circle and into public life. Initially, she says, she even surprised herself, but she came to realize that this resolve wasn't entirely new—it just hadn't been brought out this powerfully before.

And since that time, her growing notoriety (both online and offline) has allowed her to make a deeper and more profound mark on her country, her continent, and her world. Through her newly formed Florence Ozor Foundation, for example, Florence and her team are focused on creating opportunities, inspiring success, and fostering prosperity on the African continent. In 2014, they spearheaded a civic, nonpartisan initiative to educate and engage Nigerian citizens in the electoral process. They began a far-reaching media campaign that shaped the conversation and ensured that Nigerians knew where (and why) to vote. When the election was postponed, they partnered with organizations to organize protest marches, making the emphatic statement that the Nigerian people would not accept any more postponements. And it was thanks in large part to their efforts that, in spite of the unprecedented threat of terrorism and violence, nearly 30 million Nigerians turned out for the presidential election on March 28, 2015.

Florence's remarkable commitment to self-awareness has helped her make choices in service of her long-term success and happiness. It's helped her realize the impact she can have on the world. It's helped her find her life's calling. And with each passing day since the pivotal insight that steered her in a new direction, she has found that the more people she reaches, the bigger difference she can make. (Incidentally, as someone who knows Florence well, I have absolutely no doubt that she will accomplish her greater vision, perhaps, as I often tell her, as the first female president of Nigeria.)

But what's just as remarkable about Florence is that this particular insight was just one among many others. That's the thing about unicorns—they know that **self-awareness isn't a one-and-done exercise.** It's a continual process of looking inward, questioning, and discovering the things that have been there all along. Just like George Washington, Florence Ozor is a study in the transformative power of self-awareness.

◆

While researching this book, I was lucky enough to interview Alan Mulally, the former CEO of Ford who led one of the most successful corporate turnarounds in history—he also happens to be a personal hero of mine. At the beginning of our interview, I asked him a rather direct question: Assuming he got as many interview requests as I suspected (he did: often dozens per week), why did he agree to talk to me? As we sipped coffee on a sunny patio in Scottsdale, he smiled. And with a twinkle in his eye, he replied, "Because no one has written this book yet, and it *needs* to be written. Throughout my career and my life, there has been one essential truth: the biggest opportunity for improvement—in business, at home, and in life—is awareness."

I couldn't have said it better. Though many management thinkers and business leaders sing the praises of self-awareness, there have been few, if any, systematic attempts to scientifically examine where it comes from and how to get more of it. For that reason, the central purpose of my research has been to help people increase their self-awareness in service of their personal fulfillment and professional success. Along the way, I made more than a few shocking discoveries that challenged conventional wisdom, and learned that much, if not most, of what people think improves self-awareness can actually have the opposite effect. In the pages ahead, you'll discover these surprising myths and learn what it really takes to become self-aware.

I wrote *Insight* for anyone who wants to make the leap from self-blindness to self-insight, and in turn reap the rewards of smarter choices, stronger relationships, and a better life. My goal is to help you avoid the roadblocks and wrong turns; to give you tools to unlock a whole new level of self-knowledge; and to show you how to survive and thrive in an increasingly unaware world.

In Part I of the book, you'll learn the building blocks of and roadblocks to self-awareness. In Chapter 2, we will begin with the Seven Pillars of Insight that separate the aware from the unaware. Once we understand what it really means to be self-aware, we'll then take on the roadblocks and learn how to bust through them. Chapter 3 will examine the inner barriers that don't just hamper self-awareness, but fill us with an unwarranted confidence that we already *are* self-aware. In chapter 4, we'll move to the biggest societal obstacle to insight: something called the Cult of Self. Whether you know it or not, this tantalizing sect has been trying to recruit you and everyone you know to become more self-absorbed and less self-aware.

Part II will focus on internal self-awareness. In chapter 5, I'll overturn the many myths and follies around what it actually takes to improve it. You'll discover why introspection doesn't always lead to insight, how those who seek the absolute truth about themselves are the least likely to discover it, and why many common self-awareness approaches like therapy and journaling have hidden pitfalls. Once we've established what *doesn't* increase internal self-awareness, chapter 6 will show you what does, with several practical approaches that you can apply right away.

Part III confronts the surprising myths and truths of external self-awareness and shows us why we can't unearth it on our own. We'll discover that even when we *think* we understand how other people see us, we're often dead wrong. Chapter 7 will expose the biggest misconceptions that people have about external self-awareness. Despite the lip service given today to "feedback" in the business world and beyond, it's rare to get candid, objective data on what we're doing well and where we could stand to improve. I'll give you a few approaches to bust through these barriers and seek feedback—at work and at home—on your own terms. Finally, in chapter 8, you'll learn how to hear that feedback without fighting or fleeing, and how to act on it while remaining true to who you are.

Part IV pulls back to look at the bigger picture. Chapter 9 will examine how good leaders foster self-awareness in their teams and organizations. You'll see why trying to force team candor can be a surprisingly costly mistake—if you don't have certain building blocks in place first, your efforts will backfire, creating less insight and more silence. I'll end with a step-by-step process (one I've used for more than a decade) for your team to exchange feedback in a safe, direct, productive way.

Chapter 10 has the lofty but important goal of helping you survive and thrive in an increasingly delusional world. When I talk with people about my research, they often ask, "Can you *please* help me deal with [insert name of delusional person they know]?" We certainly can't force others to become self-aware, but there are a surprising number of strategies that can reduce their negative impact, and in a few cases, even help them be less delusional. I'll end the book with my Seven-Day Insight Challenge, a practical and battle-tested tool to help you engineer a few quick wins in your self-awareness journey. And if you're interested in a more "block and tackle" guide, I encourage you to download the workbook available at www.insight-book.com.

Ultimately, there are two types of people—those who think they're self-aware and those who actually are. My bold vision is to create a world filled with the latter. The barriers to self-awareness are numerous, but with the help of outside eyes and a few powerful tools, they are not impossible to navigate. And when we do, we're laying the foundation for a whole new level of confidence and success. After all, without insight, how can we chart a course that will bring us joy and happiness? Or create deep and lasting relationships? Or fulfill our true purpose? I'm hoping that this book will be a powerful wake-up call to three simple facts: that self-awareness is the exquisite foundation to a life well lived, that it *is* possible to make the journey, and that the courage and effort it takes to get there are well worth it.

Part One

◆

Roadblocks

and

Building

Blocks

2

THE ANATOMY OF SELF-AWARENESS

The Seven Pillars of Insight

*The beginning of knowledge is the discovery of
something we do not understand.*
—FRANK HERBERT

For thousands of years, the Mayans were the dominant society in Mesoamerica.* Yet until archeologists began to study this extraordinary civilization in the early 1800s, their ruins lay dormant for nearly a millennium. Since that time, we've unearthed remarkably specific details about the Mayan way of life. Long before the advent of what we know of as the modern calendar, for instance, the Mayans measured time using days and months. They had a complex grasp of astronomy. They cultivated crops in the unlikeliest of places. They created one of the first written languages. They built massive palaces and pavilions without metal or machines, and they are even thought to have discovered how to make rubber.

But in the midst of these groundbreaking discoveries, there was one much larger mystery that plagued archeologists for more than a century. As one of the most populous civilizations in human history, the Mayans reached an all-time high in AD 800, and yet by AD 950, 95 *percent* had mysteriously vanished. Scientists developed several theories as to why this occurred—a catastrophic event like an earthquake

---

* Which was centered around the Yucatan Peninsula, Guatemala, Belize, Mexico, and the western parts of Honduras and El Salvador.

or volcano, a virus brought by Spanish settlers, a gruesome civil war—but for many years, there were no concrete answers, and the question vexed scientists for decades.

But all along, the evidence had been staring them in the face—they just hadn't stitched the information together in the right way. Then, finally, someone did. In his 2005 book *Collapse*, geographer Jared Diamond proposed that the Mayans' disappearance was the combination of massive deforestation and prolonged drought, which caused crops to fail, trade to shift, and cities to be slowly swallowed by the rainforest as survivors moved away. Though there isn't total agreement, most scientists believe that Diamond finally solved the central mystery of the Mayans once and for all.

The science of self-awareness has followed a remarkably similar pattern. Just as the Mayan ruins lay dormant for centuries before being discovered by archeologists, the topic of self-awareness can be traced as far back as 600 BC—yet it's only been subjected to scientific scrutiny in the last 40 years. For millennia the discipline of self-knowledge was confined to philosophy and religion. Roman philosopher Plotinus believed that happiness was achieved by knowing our true self. And perhaps most famously, the seven sages of ancient Greece inscribed the phrase "know thyself" at the entry of the Temple of Apollo at Delphi, a mantra that Plato later reinforced in the teachings of Socrates.

And though most people associate self-awareness with Buddhism, nearly every religious tradition recognizes its importance. In chapter 1, we saw the Christian parable about the planks in our (and others') eyes. Confucius advised that to govern others, one must first govern oneself. The Hindu Upanishads said that "enquiry into the truth of the Self is knowledge." In the Jewish faith, self-knowledge has been called "the prerequisite for any self-improvement." Avicenna, a tenth-century Muslim philosopher, wrote that "self-awareness is essential to the soul and [our] awareness of ourselves is our very existence."

But sadly, when self-awareness researchers finally had the chance to catch up, they made many of the same mistakes the Mayan archeologists did, spending years focused on surprisingly myopic details at the expense of bigger, more important questions. The result? Piles of disjointed, often peripheral research that no one even bothered trying to stitch together. So when I set out to summarize the current state of scientific knowledge on self-awareness, I initially came up with more questions than answers, starting with the most central question: What *was* self-awareness, exactly?

As you read in the last chapter, when I initially began my research program, I was surprised to learn that one of the biggest obstacles to the study of self-awareness was the astonishing lack of agreement about how to define it. In the early 1970s, psychologists Shelley Duval and Robert Wickland were among the first to scientifically examine a construct that they called "self-awareness." But Duval and Wickland chose to define it as a *temporary state of self-consciousness* (sort of like how you feel at a party where you don't know anyone—the feeling of "everyone's looking at me and I want to go home"). Kenyon College professor Allan Fenigstein and his team's definition wasn't much better, with self-awareness being more akin to the personality trait of self-consciousness. The definitions that other researchers concocted were all over the map—from introspection to pondering how other people see us to the difference between how we see ourselves and how others see us. But in my view, most of these definitions largely missed the point.* Why? Because *focusing* on ourselves doesn't mean that we *understand* ourselves.

In my work as an organizational psychologist, one self-evident truth has always been that people who have a clear understanding of themselves enjoy more successful careers and better lives—they've developed an intuitive understanding of what matters to them, what they want to accomplish, how they behave, and how others see them. Unfortunately, though, I couldn't find *this* version of self-awareness anywhere in the scientific literature. In fact, the picture of a self-aware person that most existing research painted was less of an enlightened Dalai Lama figure and more of a neurotic Woody Allen one (no offense, Mr. Allen— I love your movies!). Clearly, there was a huge mismatch between how

---

* There have been a few notable exceptions, like researcher Anthony Grant— we'll learn more about his work in chapter 5.

researchers were defining self-awareness and what it really looked like, at least to me, in the real world.

So, my research team and I spent more than a year identifying what made up this real-world self-awareness. We arrived at the following definition: **self-awareness is the will and the skill to understand yourself and how others see you**. More specifically, we discovered that our unicorns—the people from our study who dramatically improved their self-awareness as adults—possessed seven distinct types of insight that unaware people didn't. They understood their *values* (the principles that guide them), *passions* (what they love to do), *aspirations* (what they want to experience and achieve), *fit* (the environment they require to be happy and engaged), *patterns* (consistent ways of thinking, feeling, and behaving), *reactions* (the thoughts, feelings, and behaviors that reveal their capabilities), and *impact* (the effect they have on others).

In this chapter, we will uncover the essence of these *Seven Pillars of Insight* and begin to paint the picture of the rich, multifaceted understanding that makes up self-awareness. Then we'll discuss an equally important dimension of insight: that to be truly aware, we can't just understand ourselves; we also need to know how we're seen by others.

THE SEVEN PILLARS OF INSIGHT

Benjamin Franklin was a celebrated politician and inventor and one of America's most beloved early statesmen. But one of the lesser-known achievements of this Renaissance man was the incredible self-insight he gained over the course of his adult life—indeed, because he was born nearly 30 years before George Washington, it's actually Franklin who might have been America's first unicorn.

Born in Boston in 1706 as the tenth son of a soap maker, Franklin was forced to leave school at age 10 because of his family's financial struggles. By age 12, he was serving as his brother James's bound apprentice in a printing business. But in 1723, after years of fraternal mistreatment (in today's parlance: bullying), Franklin ran away from home to start a new life in Philadelphia. Just three years later, he'd already failed in two business ventures and fathered an illegitimate son. (Just as with Washington, most history textbooks seem to gloss over such unflattering facts.)

Though Franklin was raised as a Presbyterian, he rarely attended church, declaring that he was unimpressed and frustrated that "not a single moral principle was inculcated or enforced." That depressing conclusion, coupled with his childhood struggles and ill-advised early life choices, brought about Franklin's commitment to "arriv[e] at moral perfection." So, at the ripe age of 20, he created a set of principles by which he wanted to live his life:

1. **Temperance**. Eat not to dullness; drink not to elevation.
2. **Silence**. Speak not but what may benefit others or yourself; avoid trifling conversation.
3. **Order**. Let all your things have their places; let each part of your business have its time.
4. **Resolution**. Resolve to perform what you ought; perform without fail what you resolve.
5. **Frugality**. Make no expense but to do good to others or yourself; i.e., waste nothing.
6. **Industry**. Lose no time; be always employ'd in something useful; cut off all unnecessary actions.
7. **Sincerity**. Use no hurtful deceit; think innocently and justly, and, if you speak, speak accordingly.
8. **Justice**. Wrong none by doing injuries, or omitting the benefits that are your duty.
9. **Moderation**. Avoid extremes; forbear resenting injuries so much as you think they deserve.
10. **Cleanliness**. Tolerate no uncleanliness in body, cloaths, or habitation.
11. **Tranquillity**: Be not disturbed at trifles, or at accidents common or unavoidable.

12. **Chastity**. Rarely use venery but for health or offspring, never to dullness, weakness, or the injury of your own or another's peace or reputation.

13. **Humility**. Imitate Jesus and Socrates.

Franklin called them "virtues," but one could also call them **values**, which is our first pillar of insight. Indeed, developing **a core set of principles that guide how we want to live our lives** is a first and critical step in becoming self-aware. In particular, values define the person we want to be and provide a standard for evaluating our actions. In a move that puts even the most diligent self-awareness unicorns to shame, Benjamin Franklin evaluated his actions through a "little book" he created to track his progress, filling the margins with inspirational quotes from Cicero, the *Proverbs of Solomon*, and James Thomson (along with inventing bifocals and swim fins, Franklin also appears to have been the father of the self-help journal). On every page

Temperance.						
Eat Not to Dullness; *Drink not to Elevation*						
	S	M	T	W	T	F	S
T							
S	**	*	*	*			
O	*	*	*		*	*	*
R			*		*		
F		*			*		
I		*					
S							
J							
M							
Cl.							
T							
Ch							
H							

was a red table with each virtue in its own row, and each day of the week in its own column. And though he paid special attention to one virtue every week, he reviewed the entire list at the end of each day, making a "little black spot" if the day's behavior hadn't reflected that virtue.

Though not all self-awareness unicorns are as diligent as Franklin, many employ similar techniques. One young professional, for example, has his list of values pinned to his refrigerator: each evening while he's cooking dinner, he evaluates how well his actions mirrored them that day. In addition to a studied commitment to living their own values, many also described dedicating time and effort to instilling them in their children. (For a few questions to help you explore your own values, take a look at appendix A.)

◆

Henry David Thoreau once said, "Do what you love. Know your bone; gnaw at it, bury it, unearth it, and gnaw at it still." Thoreau had it right: when we understand our *passions*—**what we love to do**—we're finding a bone we can chew on forever. My friend Jeff, a proud unicorn, can trace his passions back through the branches of his family tree. He inherited an engineer's brain and curiosity for how things work from his maternal grandfather, along with a sense of craftsmanship and an aversion to boredom from his paternal grandfather. He spent the first part of his career bouncing around various IT jobs, from computer system administrator to higher-education software designer. Then, quietly at first, he began to notice that he was becoming more interested in the design of buildings. In time, his new passion became so insistent that he could no longer ignore it. So he packed in the IT work and landed a coveted spot in a master's program in architecture.

When he finally graduated and scored a job, Jeff reveled in his accomplishment. He'd done it. He was an *architect* now. It was true that every day wasn't as perfectly fulfilling as he had imagined. There were bad clients to deal with, of course. And sometimes there were bad bosses. As an introvert, Jeff found working in an open-concept office to be pretty draining. And he had to admit, some of the projects were kind of boring. A surprising number of them, actually. Perhaps that was why he kept finding himself going home after each increasingly trying day feeling exhausted and empty. Then one day, he finally asked himself, "Can I do this for the next thirty years?" The answer was a clear and resounding "No."

Jeff spent months trying to figure out what his next step would be. On index cards, he listed as many things that he enjoyed doing as he could think of, arranging and rearranging them to find the patterns. It was at this point that Jeff finally listened to the nagging voice he'd been ignoring for years. *I'm not going to be really happy*, he discovered, *unless I'm working for myself.*

He decided to explore how that would actually feel on a day-to-day basis. And after much consideration, Jeff finally settled on his next move. He had designed software; he had designed websites; he had designed buildings—now he would form a consulting company that would help artists and entrepreneurs design their own businesses. By doing what he loved, Jeff would help others do what they loved (talk about a virtuous circle of self-awareness). And with a final jolt of glee, he realized that he'd be able to work out of his home office. The process of exploring his passions also helped Jeff understand that he isn't wired to seek the stability of a 30-year career—he's wired to follow his curiosity for design wherever it leads him. (For a few questions to get you thinking about *your* passions, take a look at appendix B.)

Entrepreneur Ben Huh experienced a similar "midlife" career crisis—only his arrived a bit earlier. At the ripe young age of 23, Ben felt like his life was over. He'd spent eighteen months, and hundreds of thousands of dollars of other people's money, on a startup that had gone up in smoke. The sense of shame and defeat was just too much for the young overachiever to bear. He spent days in bed, isolated, broke, and even haunted by thoughts of suicide. After he finally managed to pull himself out of this bleak period, Ben realized that he needed a plan. So he sat down with a blank sheet of paper and made a list of things he wanted to achieve in the life he'd come so close to ending. The task turned out not to be as easy as he thought it would be. The struggle, he has said, was in being able to see into this future and find the "evergreen shoots" that would define it.

For anyone who knows Ben, the fact that he decided to kick-start the next phase of his life with a list of life goals won't seem surprising. For as long as he can remember, he's been ambitious and goal driven. Ben was born of humble beginnings in Seoul, South Korea, and his family moved to the United States when he was 14. His parents cleaned buildings to scrape by, and Ben helped as much as he could, often fishing soda cans from the trash to recycle for pennies. The family shared a one-bedroom apartment; Ben slept in the master bedroom, his mom and dad on a mattress in the living room. He was determined to build a more comfortable future for himself, and eventually became the first person in his family to graduate from college.

And so, six years later, alone in his new home of Seattle, Ben created his list. It included things like meeting the perfect woman, selling a company for profit, and learning how to ride a motorcycle. Now I know what you're thinking: I'm about to tell you to put this book down and start making your list of life goals right away. But hold on—Ben's story comes with a surprising twist. Years later, he was the successful CEO of humor website I Can Has Cheezburger (aka the birthplace of cat memes), which he'd purchased in 2007. Yet something was still missing, and he couldn't put his finger on what it was.

One day, he was having a seemingly ordinary lunch with one of his investors, discussing some of the struggles he was experiencing. He said, "You know, I have these goals. There are all these things that I want to do." That's when his lunch companion dropped a bombshell that would ultimately trigger an explosive change. "The goals aren't important," his investor said. "What's important is the process of getting there."

That lunchtime wisdom would become the catalyst for a year-long process to, as Ben puts it, "figure out why I am here on this planet." Instead of adding more bullet points to his bucket list, he started to ask himself a far more central question: What did he *really* want out of life? He eventually came to realize that the answer was simple: to experience as much of the world as he could with the people he loved. At that point, he had the means to do something truly special with

Emily, the perfect woman he'd met (and checked off his list) in 2001. And that's exactly what he did.

In 2015, Ben made the decision to step down from Cheezburger, and he and Emily promptly embarked on a once-in-a-lifetime trip around the world. Ben doesn't yet know where the rest of his journey will take him, but one thing he can be certain of is this: it will be far more meaningful than simply checking a bunch of goals off a list.

Ben's story is a powerful example of what it *really* means to understand our **aspirations**. What's more, it shows that while setting goals is relatively easy, they don't always lead to true insight or perfect happiness. Instead of asking, "What do I want to achieve?" the better question is, **"What do I really want out of life?"** While goals can leave us feeling deflated and disappointed once we've achieved them, aspirations are never fully completed; we can get up every morning feeling motivated by them all over again. And even if we aren't in the enviable position of being able to quit our job and travel the world, we can all live better lives by understanding what we want to experience and accomplish while we're here on this planet. (By the way, there are a few questions to help you learn more about your aspirations in appendix C.)

◆

I once worked with a commercial banker (and unicorn) in the early stages of a promising career—let's call him Sam. Sam had a quiet confidence and a rare ability to connect with anyone, which would have set him on a path to success in almost any industry. But these skills were particularly useful in the world of banking, where clients appreciated the openness and confident spirit that Sam couldn't help but exude. And sure enough, right out of college, he scored a well-paying job at a growing bank.

Of course, no job is perfect, and Sam quickly realized that his manager was a major source of discomfort and frustration. Sam and his new boss seemed to have virtually opposite work approaches: where Sam listened and connected, his manager jumped to conclusions and bullied. When they met with potential clients, Sam explored what they needed, but his manager would strong-arm them to make on-the-spot decisions. Not only did this fail to bring in new clients, it made short-term ones out of the ones they had.

On the upside, the bank provided generous individual incentives for hard work, handsomely rewarding employees who met their goals. But Sam couldn't help but notice that this gave employees no incentive to work together, which was exactly the condition under which he thrived. And there was virtually no support for employees like Sam who valued taking the time to build trusting relationships with prospects—there was only pressure to make quick sales.

Unnerved by the atmosphere of friction and competition, Sam felt like a fish out of water. And with each passing day, his despair grew. He soon noticed he was taking his stress home: instead of enjoying the precious little time he spent with his girlfriend and his family, he was constantly preoccupied by everything that was upsetting him at work.

But as difficult as things became, the trials Sam faced ended up having a silver lining, because they led him to a valuable discovery about his own nature. When he began to closely examine the causes of his stress, he discovered a strong need to form deep and lasting relationships with his colleagues and clients. And in realizing this would probably never happen in his current work environment, he knew he had to leave.

Because Sam was so talented, he soon found a job with a company known for its strong client focus, and he quickly became one of his department's top performers. Something had finally clicked: his mood improved, he had more energy to serve his clients, and his life outside work became more fulfilling. Among other positive developments, Sam proposed to his girlfriend and she accepted. (It probably goes without saying that she will most certainly enjoy planning a wedding with "the new Sam" far better than with "the old Sam.")

When we determine where we *fit,* **the type of environment we require to be happy and engaged,** we get more done with less effort, and end the day feeling like our time was well spent. This involves understanding simple truths—like the fact that you're happier when you're traveling, or that you need to go for a run during your lunch hour—as well as deeper insights to help you live a happier life—like the kind of partner who will fulfill you or the type of company where you'll thrive. (To help you clarify the best fit when it comes to your job, your relationships, etc., you'll find a few questions in appendix D.)

In many ways, the pillar of fit builds on the ones before it: only by knowing what you value, what you're passionate about, and what you want to experience in life can you start to create a picture of your ideal surroundings. Just look at Sam. As difficult as it was to leave his first grown-up job, he was lucky to gain such valuable insight about where he fit so early in his career. By finding a company that shared his values and let him do what he loved, he also found an environment that energized rather than exhausted him. And whether you're thinking about your home life, your work, or the people with whom you choose to surround yourself, energy is probably the ultimate measure of fit. At the end of the day, is your environment creating energy or taking it away?

◆

If I asked you to describe your personality, what would you say? You might tell me that you're driven, or kind. Or, if you've taken a personality test lately, perhaps that you're an INTJ/Yellow/Expediter/ Analytical-Conceptual.

Psychologists often use the word "personality" to describe our patterns of behavior. Our **patterns** are **our consistent ways of thinking, feeling, and behaving across situations**. For example, if I snap at my co-worker one morning, I might just be tired. But if I snap at her most mornings, not only will she not invite me to the office happy hour, I probably have a pattern of prickliness. Psychologists have been busy trying to distill and measure the human personality since World War II, when personality tests were first developed to assist in military selection. Most people in the business world have had some experience with personality assessment, whether it's the Myers Briggs, or the Hogan, DISC, Insights, Emergenetics, Social Styles, NEO, Birkman, Keirsey Temperament Sorter, True Colors . . . and boy, could I go on, but fortunately I won't—in the United States alone, there are more than 2,500 personality assessments on the market, and some are far better than others. But even though our unicorns saw these assessments as important self-awareness milestones, they also reported that they were not sufficient for cultivating true insight on their own.

What's more, it's not enough to shine a light on our behavioral patterns across *most* situations—we must examine our patterns *in specific kinds of situations* as well. Let me give you an innocuous, if slightly humiliating, personal example. A few years ago, I was doing some work with a group of leaders in Uganda. The retreat center where we were having our meeting was in a beautiful but secluded area accessible only by water. When our group arrived at the dock, there were two boats: one for us and one for our luggage. Though I wasn't quite aware of it at the time, I instantly became anxious and spent the rather lengthy ride internally debating the foolish question of whether my luggage and I would ever be reunited. Of course, just minutes later, we were.

Flash forward to another work trip—this time in Honduras to teach a leadership workshop. My client had chartered three vans to pick everyone up at the airport: two for us and one for our luggage. When we arrived at the hotel, all of the bags had been unloaded, but this time, mine was nowhere to be found. We searched everywhere and eventually discovered that it had been left on the curb at the airport. That's when I had a complete and total meltdown. Everything in my bag was replaceable, and rationally I even knew that it probably would show up (it did)—yet there I was, crying in the hotel lobby like a bully had stolen my lunch money. It was at that point that I began to suspect a pattern: when my luggage and I are separated, I become upset. No, *irrationally* upset. Given the fact that I travel more than 100,000 miles a year, it was a pertinent epiphany.

A few months later, my husband and I were visiting his brother and sister-in-law, who were living in Costa Rica at the time. We decided it would be fun to hop a puddle-jumper to Bocas del Toro, a small island in Panama, for a long weekend. Upon our arrival at the tiny airport, which consisted of one dilapidated building where a surly woman presided over "immigration" with a tattered three-ring binder, the property manager of the house we rented was kind enough to give us a ride. He threw our bags in the bed of his pickup truck and we all squeezed into the backseat. Then, without warning, the sky opened up and a hard rain started pelting our luggage. I pressed my face against the rear window, helplessly watching my suitcase get drenched.

But this time, I instantly recognized what was happening. I looked at my husband and announced, "I am irrationally upset that my bag is getting rained on."

"I can see that," he replied.

"I think," I attempted, "I'll see if I can take some deep breaths and maybe just calm down a little." And so I did. Understanding this pattern had helped me be more mindful in the moment and measurably improved my day.

They say that knowledge is power, and that is certainly the case for this pillar. Whether it's an irrational luggage-separation anxiety or anything else, recognizing our patterns—especially our self-defeating ones—helps us take charge. For example, if you're an introvert who tends to get drained after back-to-back meetings, find a few minutes of alone time to recharge at the end of the day. If you shoot off angry e-mails when you've worked too many hours, save your late-night responses in a draft folder to review in the morning. If after a few glasses of wine you feel an inescapable urge to call your ex, give your phone to a friend (who hopefully is also driving you home) before you start boozing. The point is to first detect the pattern, then be able to identify it when it's happening, and then experiment by making different—and better—choices.

◆

Susan was doing the best she could. Her demanding boss at the growing real estate company where she worked often required that she put in 70-hour weeks. Though she was constantly stressed, she threw everything she had into her role, usually managing to keep her head above water. Or so she thought. One day, completely out of the blue, Susan was abruptly fired.

Stunned, devastated, and angry, she blamed her superiors for this shocking turn of events. She hadn't given up on them—how could they give up on her? But once her anger died down, Susan was determined to seek a silver lining in this very dark cloud. She had a sneaking suspicion that her behavior had played a role in her boss's decision—she just didn't know exactly how. As she carefully sifted through what she called the "oh, shit moments" in her now ex-job, Susan realized that her unawareness of her real-time *reactions*—that is, **the thoughts, feelings, and behaviors that reveal our capabilities**—had come back to bite her. Her reactions to her co-workers, especially under stress, were unmasking a serious weakness: her inability to control her emotions. And especially with her boss, she hadn't been doing a very good job of it. *He's got to know I'm working 70 hours a week*, she'd reasoned; *he should be able to let a few snippy comments go.* But he wasn't, and she'd paid a hefty price.

Since her shocking realization, Susan has worked to manage this weakness and better monitor her reactions. When she's stressed, she now pays careful attention. Is she cutting people off? Is her tone short? Does she seem agitated? When she feels herself becoming abrupt, she makes a point to pause, think, and soften her tone. On the rare occasion that the stress becomes too intense to manage, she will excuse herself, take a breather, and return to the conversation.

Another upside that came from Susan's ordeal was that she found a new job that was much more fulfilling and much less stressful. In her new position, she works hard not just to manage her stress, but to adapt her communication style to others' (rather than expect them to adapt to hers). This has been a total game-changer, and it's no wonder that it helped her become a bona fide unicorn.

However, it's important to point out that when we examine our reactions, we don't just uncover our weaknesses; sometimes we can discover strengths we never knew we had. Paul, a longtime operations executive, was raised in a poor town in Colorado. His shy nature, coupled with a critical family, led him to believe from a very young age that "everyone was better than me." Things became so bad that at the age of 23, he made the difficult decision to move to the big city (i.e., Denver) and try to make it on his own.

All Paul could afford was a tiny property in a rough part of town that was called, somewhat ironically, Uptown. "At the time, it was really sketchy," he told me. "The house had been foreclosed on by the bank, and it was a mess. The windows were all broken out. I didn't even get a key." But despite the dilapidated condition of his new home, there was something about the neighborhood that gave him a feeling of community, opportunity, and promise.

Not long after he moved in, Paul found himself chatting with a neighbor who wanted to form a registered neighborhood organization. He didn't know exactly what that was, but he was happy to get involved anyway, making flyers and passing them around to generate support. And when the organization was formed, he helped out where he could. For the first few years, everything seemed to be going well. Until, that is, he had a chance conversation with a friend who worked at the city planning office.

Paul learned that the organization's current president—a local attorney—had been making decisions on many important matters that the group didn't even know about, let alone have the opportunity to discuss. "The things he was signing off on, and approving on behalf of the neighborhood, were projects that would have benefited some very influential businesspeople far more than us," Paul told me.

What put him over the edge, though, was learning that plans were in motion for a 20-story high-rise just a few blocks from his house. And if it went ahead, it would change the neighborhood forever. When Paul heard this news, a hidden side of him kicked into gear. There was no way he was going to let the president get away with this. Paul called an urgent meeting and he agreed to step down.

While Paul was surprised by his swift and decisive reaction, he was even more surprised when he learned his neighbors' new choice for president. It was . . . him. He didn't want to let them down, so despite some hefty reservations, he decided to give it a try. But the new role couldn't have come at a more trying time. In exactly 10 days, the association would have its one and only chance to stop the high-rise at a city planning meeting. Paul had never given a presentation before, of any kind whatsoever, let alone to a room crammed full of people looking to him as their leader. "So here I am," he told me, "I'm twenty-five, I'm shy, I really didn't want to be president, and I'm nervous as heck." But he stood up and delivered his presentation as best he could.

When it was finally over, he wasn't really sure how he'd done. That is, until one of his neighbors, who worked for Hughes Aircraft, excitedly approached him and practically offered him a job on the spot. *Maybe,* he realized, *I'm not as inept at all this as I thought.*

Paul's gut response to the actions of a slippery attorney set forth a chain of events that opened his eyes to qualities he'd never known he had: a knack for public speaking, a gift for working through conflict, and the initiative to step up in the face of a challenge. And just like that, a new world began to open up for him. Paul went on to have a career as a successful CEO and has run businesses all over the world. And that 20-story high-rise? Naturally, it was never built. Years later, his organization managed to get the Uptown neighborhood listed on the National Register of Historic Places, and it's since become one of the most desirable places to live in Denver. (If Paul has inspired you, appendix E has some questions to help you get at the foundational aspect of this pillar—that is, your strengths and weaknesses.)

◆

So far, each pillar of insight has been about *us*—what *we* value, what *we're* passionate about, what *we* aspire to do, what environment *we* need, how *we* behave, how *we* respond to the world. But to be truly self-aware, we must also build on that to understand our **impact**: that is, **how our behavior affects others.** Over the course of our daily lives, we often encounter people who appear completely oblivious to this: the boss who assigns an arbitrary emergency project on a Friday afternoon, paying no notice to his employees' groans and sighs. The man in the grocery store blocking an entire aisle while a mother with a double stroller hopelessly waits to pass. The woman who inexplicably sits through two cycles of a left-turn arrow, seemingly unaware of the multitude of deafening honks from the cars trapped behind her.

Theoretically, these people might have a stellar understanding of their inner selves, but when it comes to the impact that they have on those around them, it's like they're completely blind.

Not surprisingly, this final pillar is especially important for leaders, as Eleanor Allen learned the hard way. She'll never forget the five little words that turned out to be the most surprising—and game-changing—feedback she has ever received: "You have got to stop."

Just a month earlier, Eleanor had stepped into one of the greatest challenges of her career. She and her family had moved to Puerto Rico, where she'd become the program manager for a large and complex water infrastructure capital improvement program. During the first few days in her new cramped but well-appointed office, it began to dawn on her that her new job was going to be considerably more difficult than she'd imagined. With a rising sense of horror, she discovered letter after legalese letter from their client explaining that the team had not been supplying what had been requested, and what they *had* been supplying was unacceptable. Eleanor's team was clearly on the verge of being fired.

But if she'd stepped into a burning building, Eleanor was also confident that her previous experience had equipped her with a fireproof suit. After all, the engineer by training had led challenging programs and projects all over the world, earning the kind of problem-solving skills that could only be developed through truly high-stakes work. She carefully triaged the situation and started firing off a stream of regular e-mail instructions to her 100-person team. Although she would have loved to have more time to build relationships in person, there just wasn't any. *I'll get to that after I put out the fire*, she vowed.

A few weeks went by. And somehow, things still weren't getting done. Again and again, Eleanor would assign a task that was due to the client on a certain date, which would come and go with no deliverable. She felt frustrated and alone, and didn't understand why she couldn't make the changes that were needed. One afternoon, as she sat fuming behind her paper-cluttered desk, Eleanor finally lost her cool. *How could these smart, capable people be this ham-fisted?!* she exploded. *No wonder we're about to get fired!* As if on cue, her office door burst open.

It was her deputy, Evelio, a bristly, energetic, and fiercely intelligent local engineer.

"What's the matter?" Eleanor asked. "What's going on?"

Evelio slammed the door behind him. "You!" he said, at a volume just a hair shy of shouting. "You have *got* to stop."

"What?" she stammered, completely blindsided. "What are you talking about?"

Evelio took a step toward her. "You are driving us crazy!" he said. "No one is reading your e-mails! No one knows what our priorities are!"

"But I . . ."

"Eleanor," he said. "*You're* the one who's going to get us fired!"

She could tell her deputy had come prepared for a fight. But in a moment of pure, brilliant, shining self-awareness, she took a breath, looked him in the eye, and said, "Okay, then. Tell me. What should I do instead?"

"Step away from your computer," he said. "Right now. Don't even think about typing another e-mail."

She did as she was told, lifting her hands from the keyboard.

"Now get up. We're going to go talk to our team. You have to build some trust with them before you issue any more orders."

Eleanor hesitated, seemingly glued to her chair.

"Come with me," he said. "I'm going to reprogram you."

That was when Eleanor realized her mistake. She'd been communicating with her team all wrong—and without seeing the impact it was having on their morale and productivity. With each e-mail, the team's resentment mounted, causing them to dig their heels farther into the already shaky ground. Apparently, the very in-person interactions Eleanor felt they didn't have time for were precisely what the team needed most.

From that moment forward, Eleanor effectively called it quits on the e-mail. With Evelio's help, she began to invest in really getting to know them, organizing Friday socials, convening a Fun at Work Committee, and, with my help, holding an offsite meeting with her leadership team. She also found every possible excuse to spend time with her client, appearing at their office just in time for coffee or lunch in the cafeteria. In weeks, she noticed a new and palpable feeling of trust. As time went on, those bonds only grew: now, when there was a hiccup, they called her to troubleshoot it instead of issuing an austere letter.

In less than six months, Eleanor and her team literally took the project from worst to first: they became the best performing program on the island, completing their work on time and under budget. (And they had fun!) Two years later, when Eleanor was promoted to another role, Evelio effortlessly stepped into her shoes. Eleanor went on to become the CEO of the global non-profit Water for People, but says that to this day she's never enjoyed socializing with colleagues as much as she did with Evelio and their team in Puerto Rico (a fact to which I can also personally attest, and not just because of the blur of mojitos I vaguely recall during my visit).

Luckily, while increasing awareness of our impact requires commitment and practice, it *is* possible (and for a few questions to help you do that, take a look at appendix F). The key skill we must develop to read our impact is *perspective-taking*, or the ability to imagine what others are thinking and feeling (this is different from empathy, which involves *actually* experiencing others' emotions).

It may seem counterintuitive that looking at the world from other people's perspectives would help us understand ourselves better. Let's look at one study that powerfully demonstrates the impact of perspective-taking on the pillar of impact. Researchers surveyed more than 100 Chicago couples every four months for a year on their feelings of marital satisfaction, intimacy, trust, passion, and love for their partner. Disconcertingly, during the period of the study, the couples, who were married an average of 11 years, showed "robust declines in marital quality."

The researchers wanted to see whether anything could turn the tide. So they asked their participants to write for 21 minutes about a conflict in their marriage. Compared to couples who simply wrote about the conflict, those who were instructed to write about how a "neutral third party who wants the best for all" would view the conflict saw the decline in marital satisfaction reverse completely over the following year. By rising above their own perspective and seeing their problems through their spouses' eyes, they could be more level-headed and less defensive. This mindset helped them better understand how their actions were impacting their spouses, and in turn, start treating them better.

But the great irony of perspective-taking is that we are least likely to do it when we need to do it most. I was recently on a Hong Kong–bound flight that, after hours of hopelessly boarding and deplaning, was finally canceled. Of course, all 500 passengers had somewhere to be—tears, anger, and a general sense of panic filled the air. A brave gate agent led our angry mob to a customer-service area manned by four airline employees. When my turn came, I hesitantly tiptoed over to an agent—his name-tag said "Bob"—fearing that I might not like what he was about to tell me. "I'm so sorry, Dr. Eurich," Bob mumbled, "but I can't get you to Hong Kong today."

Just as I was about to start foaming at the mouth, I noticed the fear in Bob's eyes. Luckily I'd recently learned about a tool developed by psychologist Richard Weissbourd called "*Zoom In, Zoom Out.*" To successfully take others' perspectives in highly charged situations, Weissbourd advises, we should start by "zooming in" on our perspective to better understand it. So I zoomed in: *I'm hungry, tired, and furious at the airline for its mechanical ineptitude.* Next, we should "zoom out" and consider the perspective of the other person. When I imagined what Bob was experiencing, I thought, *Poor Bob. I wonder what his day has been like.*

"Were you scheduled to work this evening?" I asked. "No, ma'am," he instantly responded, pointing to his colleagues, "All four of us were heading home for the evening but were called back in. I was supposed to pick my kids up from school because my wife is out of town. I'll probably be here until ten p.m." I'd been feeling pretty sorry for myself, but I now felt even worse for Bob. I asked if the other passengers had been yelling at him. He nodded and said, "People usually get so mad that they forget we're people, too."

I learned two unexpected lessons that day: first, that zooming out helped me calm down a bit and remember that I wasn't the center of the universe (always helpful). Second, that taking Bob's perspective helped me understand the impact of my behavior—which in turn helped me to control it.

FROM INSIDE OUT TO OUTSIDE IN: THE IMPORTANCE OF EXTERNAL SELF-AWARENESS

When Ben Franklin assembled his 13-point plan to arrive at moral perfection, his initial list contained only 12 virtues. But upon sharing it with a close friend, he learned that he'd completely overlooked his most significant opportunity for improvement. As Franklin later wrote:

> [My friend] kindly informed me that I was generally thought proud; that my pride show'd itself frequently in conversation; that I was not content with being in the right when discussing any point, but was overbearing, and rather insolent, of which he convinc'd me by mentioning several instances.

As we learned earlier, one of the biggest myths about self-awareness is that it's all about looking inward—that is, insight from the inside out. **But armed with only our own observations, even the most dedicated students of self-awareness among us risk missing key pieces of the puzzle.** For example, after you made that jokey comment to your colleague, was she genuinely amused or taken aback? While telling your life story to the guy you just met at a cocktail party, was he interested or did he secretly want to escape to the bar? When you gave your boss constructive feedback on her last department-wide presentation, was her "Thanks, I'll keep that in mind" grateful or dismissive?

To be truly self-aware, yes, we need to understand ourselves, but we also need to know how people perceive us—and to do this, looking inward is not enough. As we'll soon learn, other people are the only truly reliable source of information about how we come across. The bottom line is that self-awareness isn't one truth. It's a complex interweaving of information from two distinct, and sometimes even competing, viewpoints. There is the inward perspective—your internal self-awareness—and the outward perspective, external self-awareness, or how other people see you. And remember, not only is there *little to no relationship between internal and external self-awareness*, having one without the other can often do more harm than good. You've probably witnessed the folly of people who think they have themselves figured out but are completely oblivious to how others see them. At the other end of the spectrum, we all know people who are so focused on the impression they create that they don't understand or act in their own best interests.

Let's pretend that internal and external self-awareness are hydrogen and oxygen, two of the most well-known elements on the periodic table. On its own, hydrogen is dangerous because it spontaneously ignites. (Remember the *Hindenburg*?) And though oxygen is not flammable by itself, in excess, it causes many things to burn more easily. But when you combine hydrogen and oxygen in the right proportions, the two elements unite to create life-sustaining water. Self-awareness is a bit like that: when we couple a clear perspective on ourselves with the ability to abandon that perspective and see ourselves as others do, this magical combination is a tremendous force for good.

Yet given the delicate balance between internal and external self-awareness, could there be certain pillars that are better acquired through private reflection than feedback from others, and vice versa? We'll return to this question a bit later, but the answer is a qualified yes. Typically, our own views can be especially helpful for pillars that aren't as visible to others: our values, passions, aspirations, and fit. For example, if a successful accountant outwardly appears to be fulfilled in his job but secretly dreams of a career as a Broadway dancer, he is likely the sole possessor of that information. The reverse is true for the pillars that are more visible to others, like our patterns, reactions, and impact. Here, the self-awareness roadblocks we'll soon learn about can get in the way of an objective assessment, so we may need others' input to see ourselves more clearly. But the truth is that **for all seven pillars,**

it is critical to gain *both* an internal and external perspective. Then and only then can we develop a true understanding of who we are and how we're seen.

As an example, I have a friend—let's call her Joan—who recently sought feedback from her co-workers to better understand her strengths and weaknesses. Unfortunately, they not-so-delicately communicated that she needed a personality transplant (though by all objective measures, she was performing phenomenally at work, receiving frequent recognition from her superiors and team). Thankfully, Joan had the internal self-awareness to see this feedback for the workplace sabotage that it really was. When evaluated alongside what she already knew to be true about herself, the feedback helped her realize that *she* wasn't the problem—the problem was that the company's cutthroat culture wasn't the right fit for her. She's since moved to a smaller company and I've never seen her happier. This is the perfect illustration of the magic that happens when we balance internal and external awareness.

And while balancing the two types of self-awareness isn't always easy, our lives are brimming with opportunities to do so. There's a wonderful Chinese proverb that says: "When the winds of change rage, some build shelters while others build windmills." Where most people choose to hide or run for cover, self-awareness unicorns use their experiences to help power and fuel their internal and external self-knowledge. In particular, our research shows that they have a unique ability to recognize and learn from what I call *alarm clock events*: situations that open our eyes to important self-truths. Sometimes, alarm clock events boost our internal self-awareness by helping us see ourselves in a new or different light; other times, they give us new data on how we're coming across to the outside world.

I've uncovered three general categories of alarm clock events. The first is *new roles or rules*. When we are asked to play a new role at work or in life, or play by a new set of rules, it stretches our comfort zone and demands more from us, and therefore can supercharge our self-knowledge. At work, for example, this can be things like job changes, promotions, reassignments, new responsibilities, or joining a new group or organization. In particular, our first leadership experiences are especially ripe opportunities for insight—in fact, when the American Management Association surveyed 700-plus CEOs, they saw these early formative experiences as the most impactful learning events of their careers.

But it's not just work situations that challenge us with new roles and rules. The same is true in other parts of life: leaving home for college, taking on a new role in a community organization, starting a new romantic relationship, or becoming a parent. And again, the most powerful insights can often come from early experiences. For instance, Stanford researcher Seana Moran has found that when a young person has made dramatic gains in self-knowledge, it's often the result of a situation that "challenges values or norms which may have been unreflectively accepted from family and culture."

The second type of alarm clock event is an *earthquake*. Earlier, we read about Susan, a unicorn who achieved a new level of self-knowledge after being fired from her job. This is an example of the kind of event that, because of its significance and severity, shakes us to our core. Other examples might be the death or illness of a loved one, a divorce or the end of a significant relationship, or any serious failure or setback. Because earthquake events are so life-shattering, they all but force us to confront the truth about ourselves. I know someone whose husband abruptly left her, claiming that she was emotionally unavailable. She was crushed; yet she had no choice other than to face this emotionally devastating reality. It led her down a path to better understand how she was behaving—and how that behavior was getting in her way—which ultimately served her in all her relationships, romantic or otherwise.

But by definition, earthquake events also run the risk of paralyzing us, suppressing our emotional agility and making it that much harder to absorb what we've learned about ourselves, much less channel it productively. As management professor Morgan McCall observes, the emotionally laden nature of these situations tempts us to distance ourselves from them: we may get defensive, blame others, become more cynical, overcompensate, shut down, or give up. Luckily, there are steps we can take to protect against this. Our first task, as McCall and his colleagues advise, "is absorbing the suffering rather than reacting to it." Susan, for example, could have continued to blame her boss and remain in denial about her role in her dismissal. But just when she most wanted to react to the situation, she instead chose to understand it. However, absorbing the truth isn't enough; we have to put that insight into action, not just owning our mistakes and limitations but also committing to correcting them. Indeed, once Susan accepted her situation, she vowed never to let something like that happen again.

The third type of alarm clock event is something I call an *everyday insight.* One common assumption about self-awareness is that it's only earned through dramatic, earth-shattering events—but this couldn't be further from the truth. Surprisingly, by a margin of two to one, our unicorns reported having gained the most insight from more mundane situations. They mentioned instances when they suddenly saw their behavior in a new light, whether it was through an overheard conversation, an offhand comment, or even a bit of unexpected recognition. Others cited developmental experiences at work, like leadership programs, 360 reviews, and so on. Some unicorns even found "aha" moments in the midst of the most ordinary, even boring, daily activities, like exercising or cleaning.

Shortly after Susan graduated from college, for example, she and her best friend were moving into their first apartment. When they were unpacking their kitchen, Susan remembers her outrage upon noticing that her friend had stacked their plastic cups in front of the glass ones in the cupboard. "No one should drink out of plastic glasses!" she huffed. Hearing the way she came across in that moment, Susan realized, *I am having an outsized reaction to something that isn't important. Why am I being so controlling?* In that moment, she was able to see herself from a slightly different perspective, and it produced a big insight that was about far more than plastic cups.

I see our findings on everyday insights as very good news: in a nutshell, we're just as likely to earn self-knowledge during the course of our daily lives as we are during more challenging times. But in both cases, our unicorns didn't just sit around and wait for self-awareness to strike—they built windmills, turning new information into energy to effect real and lasting change.

Now that you know the pillars upon which self-awareness is based, we can dive into specific strategies for strengthening it, and therefore improve our choices, our relationships, and our success. But before we do, we need to get a better understanding of the two biggest obstacles standing in our way.

3

BLINDSPOTS

The Invisible Inner Roadblocks to Insight

It ain't what you don't know that gets you into trouble.
It's what you know for sure that just ain't so.
—JOSH BILLINGS

The toughest coaching session of my professional career began with me staring, for what seemed like an eternity, at the top of a senior executive's bald head. That head belonged to Steve, a construction company boss with a bleeding balance sheet. He'd been in the job for just four months when his CEO asked me to come in and help him.

That morning, I'd taken the elevator to the eighth floor, waited in the reception area, and was finally shown to Steve's palatial office by an assistant whose voice shook slightly when she announced me. As the door closed silently behind me, Steve didn't look up from his computer, acknowledging my presence only with a long sigh and an aggressive flurry of mouse clicks. Which left me standing there, awkwardly staring at his head and admiring the contents of a presentation cabinet. It included a large award in the shape of a demolition ball, and that really said a lot about the situation.

I'm not easily unnerved, but as the seconds dragged by, I began to feel the challenge that lay ahead of me as a sensation of mild nausea. It didn't help that I was holding a red folder bulging with interview notes that told me just how volatile this man could be.

"Should I take a seat?" I finally ventured.

"Please, Dr. Eurich," he sighed impatiently, still not looking up. "Whatever makes you comfortable."

As I sat down and opened my folder, ready to begin, Steve pushed his chair back. Finally, he looked at me. "Let me tell you a thing or two about my operation here." Then, with the restlessness of a caged tiger, he began pacing up and down behind his desk, sharing his ambitious vision for the business and his hardball leadership philosophy. I was impressed with his energy—I also knew that our work together would require all he could muster.

Steve's department, he told me, was in trouble, although I already knew that. His predecessor had been fired because of cost overruns, so his in-the-red business unit needed to drive growth while finding efficiencies wherever possible. It was your classic high-stakes, "change the engine while the plane is in the air" situation. There was no room for failure, but Steve had no doubt that he was just the man for the task. His self-proclaimed leadership skills included setting high expectations, rallying his troops, and being tough but fair. "I know I'll face challenges in this role," he confidently stated, "but I also know how to get the best out of my people."

Unfortunately, Steve was totally delusional.

What I'd uncovered when I interviewed his direct reports, and what his CEO had only begun to sense, was that Steve's reign was already proving disastrous. In the 16 weeks since his official promotion, three employees had already quit. A fourth, who had recently started taking blood pressure medication because of the "Steve stress," was halfway out the door. Though not a single member of Steve's team questioned his capabilities and experience, they thought that he was—to use a more polite term than they did—a complete jerk. He'd bark orders at them, question their competence, and scream at them in a way they found unprofessional and frightening. And they weren't a bunch of whiners, either. I found them to be seasoned, seen-it-all types who weren't looking to be coddled. Steve had simply pushed them too far.

To be fair, Steve had grown up in the rough-and-tumble industry of construction, where he'd learned that great leadership often meant "he who yelled the most." And while this hard-charging style may have been passable in the past, it was a costly miscalculation in his current role, especially against the backdrop of the company's collaborative culture.

As he paced around his new office, proudly detailing all the ways he was exactly the visionary leader his company needed during this difficult period, I marveled at how utterly oblivious he was. His behavior was hurting his employees' morale, his team's performance, and his own reputation. Even losing some of his best people hadn't shaken his self-image as an effective and respected leader. But Steve's team had had enough of his bullying. And somehow, I had to find a way to break that to him.

THE EPIDEMIC OF STEVE DISEASE

A young Haley Joel Osment is wrapped up in a pink blanket, his head resting on a soft pillow. He intensely stares at Bruce Willis. "I want to tell you my secret now," he begins. The camera zooms in tightly to his terrified face.

"I see dead people."

"In your dreams?" Willis asks. Osment stares back silently, his sad eyes indicating that's not where he sees them. "While you're awake?"

"Walking around like regular people," Osment replies. "They only see what they want to see. They don't know they're dead."

"How often do you see them?"

"All . . . the . . . time."

This scene is, of course, from the movie *The Sixth Sense*, and young Osment (spoiler alert) actually does see dead people. But substitute the word "delusional" for the word "dead" and it would be just as true of our world today. The scene reminds us that self-delusion—that is, seeing only what we want to see—is all around us. But if you prefer the radio over movies, take humorist Garrison Keillor's invented town of Lake Wobegon, where every child is above average. We chuckle at this statistically impossible trope because we see such delusion everywhere:

at work, in class, at PTA meetings, at the grocery store, even in our own homes.

And almost everyone who has spent time in the business world has encountered a boss or colleague like Steve. You know the type: people who, despite their past success, obvious qualifications, and undeniable intelligence, display a complete lack of insight into how they are coming across. The boss who thinks his detail orientation makes him a good manager, but in reality is simply infuriating his employees; the client who thinks she's a great partner but is known the office over for being impossible to work with; the father who doesn't believe he's teaching his kids to be racist, but grips his child's hand and crosses the street every time a person of color walks toward them. The common factor here? All are completely confident in their self-views, and all are completely wrong.

According to behavioral economist and Nobel Prize laureate Daniel Kahneman, human beings possess an "almost unlimited ability to ignore our ignorance." Research suggests that we tend to think we're smarter, funnier, thinner, better-looking, more socially skilled, more gifted at sports, superior students, and better drivers than we objectively are. Scientists have dubbed this the "Better Than Average Effect." But in honor of our "above average" executive, I call it *Steve Disease.*

Of course, mathematically speaking, 49 percent of us *will* be above average on any given measure. But often, where we actually fall on the bell curve has little resemblance to where we think we fall. In one study of more than 13,000 professionals in financial services, technology, nursing, and more, researchers found almost no relationship between self-assessed performance and objective performance ratings. In a second investigation with nearly 1,000 engineers in the San Francisco Bay area, more than 33 percent rated their performance in the top 5 percent relative to their peers—and only one brave soul labeled himself as below average.

Empirical evidence of Steve Disease also extends outside the walls of corporate America. In one famous study, a full 94 percent of college professors thought they were above average at their jobs. And in another—and perhaps disturbingly for anyone planning a medical procedure in the near future—surgical residents' self-rated skills had literally no relationship with their board exam performance (although, thankfully, that's probably why they have a board exam).

It's likely no surprise that the consequences of Steve Disease are as severe as the problem is pervasive. At work, for example, employees who lack self-awareness bring down team performance, reducing decision quality by an average of 36 percent, hurting coordination by 46 percent, and increasing conflict by 30 percent. In aggregate, companies with large numbers of unaware employees show worse financial performance: one study with hundreds of publicly traded companies found that those with poor financial returns were 79 percent more likely to have large numbers of employees who lacked self-awareness.

As anyone who has worked for a delusional boss can attest, Steve Disease is especially infectious—and disastrous—in the ranks of management. As we learned earlier, when leaders are out of touch with reality, they're six times more likely to derail. Being overconfident can also blind managers to their employees' brilliance, causing them to underestimate their top performers' contributions. And though people in positions of power don't usually start off any less self-aware (it requires a certain measure of self-awareness to ascend to a leadership position in the first place), their delusion often grows with their rank and seniority. Early successes give way to an intoxicating pride that blinds them to truths they can and should be seeing.

And as their power increases, so does their degree of overestimation. Compared to managers and front-line leaders, for example, executives more dramatically overvalue their empathy, adaptability, coaching, collaboration, and (ironically) self-awareness skills. What might be even more shocking, though, is that compared to their less experienced counterparts, experienced leaders are more likely to overestimate their abilities. Similarly, older managers tend to misjudge their performance relative to their boss's ratings of them far more than their younger peers do.*

---

* It's been shown that, in general, we become more accurate at self-assessing between the ages of 25 and 35, but our accuracy tends to decrease between 35 and 45. Also, and quite shockingly, business students, compared to students majoring in physical sciences, social sciences, and the humanities, most strongly inflated their self-assessments relative to their objective performance.

But wait. Shouldn't a leader's experience, age, and seniority *increase* insight? There are a few reasons why this isn't the case. First, senior positions are often complex, with murky standards of performance and subjective definitions of success. Second, above a certain level, there usually aren't reliable mechanisms to supply honest feedback sufficient for gauging performance on these more subjective measures. Making matters worse, many powerful people encircle themselves with friends or sycophants who don't challenge or disagree with them. As professor Manfred Kets de Vries put it, they're surrounded by "walls, mirrors and liars." And finally, executives are often rewarded for delusion—for example, overconfident CEOs tend to be paid more than their peers, and as their compensation packages grow, so do their levels of over-confidence. In reality, CEO compensation has less to do with talent or performance than it does with PR and perception; no board wants their CEO to be below average, so no one lets their packages lag market expectations. These companies might as well be headquartered in Lake Wobegon!

Yet regardless of our degree of overestimation—and whether we're in a position of power or not—our misguided beliefs follow us home, sometimes taking an equal toll on our personal lives. Researchers have found that one in four people has emotionally distant personal relationships because of their bullish views of their personality and behavior. Overconfidence can also affect how we parent. For example, the majority of mothers and fathers grossly overestimate the number of words they speak to their pre-verbal children (children who hear more words at home develop better vocabularies, higher IQs, and better academic performance). Eighty-two percent of parents also think that they're capable of handling their finances despite holding too much debt and neglecting to build long-term savings, and it's these same parents who fancy themselves as great financial management teachers to their kids—that's about as likely as poor Steve winning "Boss of the Year."

Now, it probably comes as no shock to hear that this delusion rubs off on our children, which just perpetuates the cycle. One study surveyed more than a million high school seniors on a number of personality characteristics and revealed that a full 25 percent placed themselves in the *top 1 percent* in their ability to get along with others. How many thought they were below average? Two percent.* And despite many parents' hopes that their kids will miraculously develop self-awareness on the first day of college, that generally isn't the case. When researchers asked university students to compare themselves to their peers on traits like "polite," "responsible," "cooperative," and "mature," students in the study rated themselves as above average on a whopping 38 out of 40 traits.

Making matters worse, the *least* competent people tend to be the *most* confident in their abilities, a finding first reported by Stanford psychology professor David Dunning and then-graduate student Justin Kruger. Their research revealed that participants who performed the worst on tests of humor, grammar, and logic were the most likely to overestimate their abilities. Those who scored in the 12th percentile, for example, believed on average that their ability fell in the 62nd. This phenomenon came to be known as the **Dunning-Kruger Effect,** and it's been replicated with dozens of other skills like driving, academic performance, and job performance.

All this being said, is it possible that deep down, people know they're incompetent but just don't want to admit it to others? Strangely, the Dunning-Kruger Effect still surfaces even when people are incentivized to be accurate about their abilities. So it seems that the incompetent are not in fact lying; the more likely possibility is that they are, according to David Dunning, "blessed with inappropriate confidence, buoyed by something that feels . . . like knowledge."

In the very nature of this phenomenon lies a troubling paradox: If you were afflicted with Steve Disease, would you even know? Researchers Oliver Sheldon and David Dunning designed a series of ingenious studies that revealed just how oblivious even the smartest, most successful people are about their delusions. They began by bringing MBA

---

* This study was conducted in 1976—when Baby Boomers were in college—providing evidence that Millennials were not the original instigators of this pattern! And I say this, totally objectively, as a Millennial.

students—intelligent, driven professionals with an average of six years' work experience—into their lab and giving them an assessment of emotional intelligence (EQ), which, as we learned earlier, is a critical skill for success at work and in life. You'd think that if you presented clever people with evidence that they needed to improve their EQ, most would want to take steps to do so. But that's not what Sheldon and Dunning found. When given the opportunity to purchase a discounted book on improving EQ, the students with the *lowest* scores—that is, those who most needed the book—were the *least* likely to buy it.

When giving keynotes to organizations, I'll often present the statistic that 50 percent of managers are ineffective. After dozens and dozens of talks all over the world, the reaction I get is always exactly the same. At first, people in the audience politely smile. So I ask them, "Do you know what this means?" Then, after an invariably long pause, I instruct them to look to their left, then their right. Nervous laughter breaks out, and they finally get it. The terrible manager is either them or the person next to them! At that point, everyone starts looking around hesitantly at each other, thinking, *Well, since it isn't me, it must be this guy next to me, right?*

The point is that it's uncomfortable to consider the possibility that we're not as smart or skilled or emotionally intelligent as we think we are—after all, to paraphrase Daniel Kahneman, identifying other people's mistakes and shortcomings is much easier and far more enjoyable than facing our own. But **when people are steeped in self-delusion, they are usually the last to find out.** The good news about Steve Disease is that it is curable, and in a moment, we'll explore how. But first, it's worth asking: Why are we this delusional in the first place?

◆

While the capacity for self-awareness exists in nearly all human beings, absolutely no one is born with it. As infants, we think we're the center of the universe. After all, at that age, we're little more than a mewling bag of constant demands that usually get met, as if the world itself was set up for the sole purpose of serving our needs. (I have a client who re-calls thinking as a young child that the world *literally* revolved around him and therefore only existed during his own waking hours!) Our first awareness milestone is therefore to gain an understanding of ourselves as separate from the world around us.

Just when we're strong enough to push ourselves off our knees, and happen to see a reflection of ourselves in a mirror, we coo at the stranger looking back. But around age two, we begin to learn that this person is actually us. We're not the whole world after all—we're just another thing that lives in it. With this knowledge, obviously, comes a potentially disappointing fall in status. And with that comes the dis-quieting onset of emotions such as embarrassment and envy.

Yet at this point, while we may have realized that we're just another "self" surrounded by other selves, our brains haven't yet developed the ability to objectively evaluate that self. Studies show that when young children rate how they are performing in school, for example, their evaluations have little to no resemblance with their teachers'. In other words, we don't yet know the difference between our wish and our reality. The mere desire to be the best and prettiest ballplayer in the room means that we *are* the best and prettiest ballplayer in the room. Adorable as that may be at this age, these inflated views persist despite repeated revelations of their inaccuracy. (You might even know a few adults who have yet to overcome this affliction, but we'll get to that.)

By our pre-teen years, the fresh, early breezes of awareness begin to blow in. Here, we start to develop the capacity to label our behaviors with descriptive traits (like "popular," "nice," and "helpful") and ex-periment with a more balanced self-view—that is, the possibility that we might actually possess a few less-than-ideal characteristics. Then comes the tempest. During our stormy teenage years, we discover a new and apparently limitless capacity for introspection. Building a coher-ent theory of who we are, with all our apparent contradictory moods and urges, can be tortuous. And just as our self-views become increas-ingly jumbled and complex, we begin to spend an almost unreason-able amount of time wondering what others think of us. As confused as we are during this period, we're just as likely to think irrationally negative things about ourselves as we are positive ones. This example, from Susan Harter's book *The Construction of Self*, should really take you back to that fun process:

> What am I like as a person? You're probably not going to understand. I'm complicated! . . . At school, I'm serious, even studious . . . [but] I'm a goof-off too, because if you're too studious, you won't be popular. . . . [My parents] expect me to get all A's and get pretty annoyed with me . . . So I'm usually pretty stressed-out at home, and can even get very sarcastic . . . But I really don't understand how I can switch so fast from being cheerful with my friends, then coming home and feeling anxious, then getting frustrated and sarcastic with my parents. Which one is the real me?

Most of us spend years wrestling with these contradictions, desperate to pin down the essence of our teenage personalities. For some, this self-seeking manifests in many hours of uninterrupted brooding behind a closed bedroom door, often accompanied by deafeningly loud music (in my case, it took the form of long-winded journal entries that are simply too embarrassing to talk about). Other times, it can lead to acting out: shoplifting, cutting class, or bullying.

Thankfully, as we approach our second decade on earth, we start to organize these conflicting self-perceptions into more cohesive theories (*Just because I'm shy around people I don't know doesn't mean I'm not mostly outgoing*). We start to understand and embrace our attributes, our values, and our beliefs, and often deepen our sense of what we *can't* do well. We also feel a new level of focus on our future selves, which can provide a welcome sense of direction.

But though most people show a predictable progression toward becoming self-aware, our pace varies wildly. The journey to self-awareness is therefore a bit like the Kentucky Derby: we all begin at the same starting line, but when the gun fires, some of us speed out of the gate, some of us progress slowly but surely, and some of us falter or get stuck along the way.

In the absence of a committed effort to build self-awareness, the average person makes only meager gains as they grow older.* Our self-awareness unicorns, however, are different. Though they enter childhood as equally or only slightly more self-aware, their pace accelerates with each passing year. In the race to insight, these Triple Crown winners break away from the pack early on and continue to widen their lead over each stage of their lives.

Remember, though, that the behaviors needed to create and sustain self-awareness are surprisingly learnable. We just have to know where to start—which, at least foundationally, means understanding the obstacles that prevent us from seeing ourselves clearly. Some exist within us, and others are imposed on us by our increasingly delusional world. For the remainder of this chapter, we'll focus on the inner obstacles to self-awareness—that is, how we get in our own way, and usually without even knowing it.

THE THREE BLINDSPOTS

One of my all-time favorite psychology studies was conducted with prisoners serving time in the south of England. Psychology professor Constantine Sedikides and his colleagues gave the prisoners, most of whom had committed violent crimes, a list of nine positive personality traits and asked them to rate themselves on each in comparison to two groups: average prisoners and average non-incarcerated community members:

- Moral
- Kind to others
- Trustworthy
- Honest
- Dependable
- Compassionate

---

* For you statistics geeks, the correlation we've found between age and internal self-awareness is only .16, and for external self-awareness, it's .05.

- Generous
- Self-controlled
- Law-abiding

Now imagine you find yourself in jail for, let's just say, armed robbery. It seems hard to believe that you'd use any of the above traits to describe yourself, right? And yet the prisoners did. In fact, not only did they rate themselves as superior to their fellow inmates on these measures, on no fewer than eight out of nine traits, they even thought they were superior to average non-incarcerated community members. The one exception? Trait number nine. According to Sedikides, inexplicably, "they rated themselves as *equally* law-abiding compared to community members." (Don't think about that for too long or your head will explode—trust me.)

This study is a stark, if somewhat ludicrous, example of just how blind we can be to the truth about ourselves. When it comes to the inner roadblocks that most limit our success, there are three main areas where we get in our own way. And the more we ignore **The Three Blindspots**, the more pernicious they become.

Professor David Dunning (who first showed us that the least competent people are also the most confident) has spent most of his career trying to understand why we're so terrible at evaluating our own performance. Though there is admittedly no satisfying single explanation, Dunning and his colleague Joyce Ehrlinger uncovered the powerful influence of something they call "top-down thinking" (I call it **Knowledge Blindness**)—which is our first blindspot. In a series of studies, they discovered that the opinions we have about our abilities in specific situations are based less on how we perform and more on the general beliefs we have about ourselves and our underlying skills. For example, participants who saw themselves as good at geography thought they'd performed particularly well on a geography test, even though as a group they'd scored no better than anyone else.

Ironically, the more expertise we think we have, the more harmful knowledge blindness can be. For an example, let's look back to 2013, when the Boston Red Sox beat the St. Louis Cardinals in a nail-biting

World Series. Before the season began, ESPN published the predictions of 43 bona fide baseball experts on the outcome of the season. How many do you think predicted that either Boston or St. Louis would make it to the World Series? The answer is zero. The same was true for the experts polled by *Sports Illustrated*. *Baseball America*'s picks performed only slightly less terribly, with one out of ten predicting that St. Louis would go the distance. So these 60 well-paid, highly respected baseball authorities showed an absolutely abysmal 0.83 percent success rate in predicting the World Series teams. Had each expert chosen two teams at random, they would have been more than seven times more accurate!

At first glance, this seems like a freak occurrence—a statistical anomaly. But as it turns out, experts are wrong more often than we think, and not just when it comes to sports. In 1959, psychologist Lewis Goldberg conducted a seemingly simple study where he compared the accuracy of expert clinical psychologists' diagnoses with those made by their secretaries (as they were then called) to demonstrate the important role of experience in such judgments. You can imagine his dismay upon discovering that the experts were no better at diagnosing psychological disorders than their inexperienced counterparts (who were actually 2 percent *more* accurate!).

Yet even for non-experts, being overconfident about our skills and talents can get us into trouble. We might choose a field or specialty for which we're poorly suited ("I'd be a great astrophysicist; I'm good at math!"), overlook mistakes in our personal life ("It's okay to let my five-year-old walk to school alone; I'm a great parent!"), or take poorly advised business risks ("We should definitely buy this failing company; I'm great at turnarounds!").

Our inner roadblocks don't just create blindness about what we think we *know*—they distort our perceptions about what we think we *feel*. To understand **Emotion Blindness**, our second blindspot, imagine the following question:

On a scale from 1 to 10, how happy are you with life these days?

How would you go about answering this? Would you go with your gut instinct, or would you thoughtfully consider the various factors in your life and made a more measured judgment?* Most people are adamant that they would use the more thoughtful approach—after all, accurately assessing our precise level of happiness is not an easy task. Indeed, studies show that when we're asked how happy we are, we have every belief that we're considering all the available data in a rational way. But unfortunately, our brains prefer to use the least possible effort and therefore don't always cooperate. So even when we think we're carefully deliberating a certain question, we're actually making more of a gut decision. For this reason, we're surprisingly awful at judging our emotions, including happiness. According to Daniel Kahneman and other researchers, our brains secretly and simplistically morph the question from "How happy are you with life these days?" into "What mood am I in *right now?*"

To illustrate Emotion Blindness in action, Kahneman describes a study by German researcher Norbert Schwarz, who set out to investigate life satisfaction. Unbeknownst to his participants, he arranged for half the group to find the German equivalent of a dime on a nearby copy machine outside the lab. Though they had no idea why, those who found the coin—a mere 10 cents!—subsequently reported feeling happier and more satisfied with their lives as a whole.

In another study, students were asked two questions: "How happy are you these days?" and "How many dates did you have last month?" When the questions were presented in that order, their love lives weren't related to their overall happiness. But when the questions were reversed, and participants thought about the number of dates they'd been on *before* evaluating their happiness, those who'd gone on more dates reported being happier.

The main danger of Emotion Blindness is that we often make decisions, even important ones, from a place of emotion *without even realizing it.* In the fall of my senior year of high school, I was deep into my

---

* In his book on the subject, *Thinking, Fast and Slow*, Daniel Kahneman calls these processes "thinking fast" and "thinking slow," respectively.

search for the perfect college. My parents and I took two separate trips, a few weeks apart, to eight schools on the East Coast. The weather during the first visit was sheer perfection. At every school I visited, happy students were frolicking outside, enjoying the cool, crisp temperature and the peak fall foliage. But my second trip coincided with one of those dreadful New England storms that dumped sheets of freezing rain and kept the sky gray for days. Naturally, when I visited *those* schools, the students weren't so much frolicking as they were helplessly running from building to building in a futile attempt to stay dry.

So which colleges do you think ended up on my list of favorites? You guessed it—all four schools from my first visit and zero from my second. Though I didn't realize it at the time, I now know how much of an impact my emotions had on my judgment. It can be disconcerting to realize that we're so ill-equipped to evaluate the thought processes that drive our decisions, but as with all blindspots, the more aware we are of their existence, the better chance we have of overcoming them.

Which brings us to **Behavior Blindness**, our final blindspot. It's also one that most of us experience far more often than we realize. A few years back, I was invited to deliver the closing keynote at a professional conference for engineers. Because of our shared practical mindset and the three years I spent working at an engineering firm, I've always gotten along famously with engineers, or "my fellow geeks," as I affectionately call them. But from the moment I set foot on stage that day, something felt off. For the life of me, I couldn't make my points cogently; my jokes were bombing; and I just didn't feel like myself.

Over the course of the hour, I became increasingly hysterical, and my inner monologue turned into a blow-by-blow account of my incompetence. *Why didn't that joke get a laugh? How could I have forgotten to mention that point? Why do they seem so bored?* Much to my horror, I remembered mid-talk that the bureau agent who had booked me was in the front row. *Well, that's it,* I concluded, *he'll never recommend me to a client again.*

When my talk was over, I rushed offstage just about as quickly as my legs would carry me and ran smack into the bureau agent who'd come backstage to find me. Ready to face the music, I asked, "What did you think?" Sure that he was going to demand his client's money back, I braced myself for the inevitable torrent of criticism that was sure to follow. But his gleeful response was literally the last thing I ever expected to hear: "Oh, my gosh. They *loved* it!"

Struggling to grasp how this could be possible, I asked, *"REALLY?"* and he nodded earnestly. At the time, I thought he was being unnecessarily polite (i.e., lying). But later that day, when I checked to see how many audience members had opted in to my monthly newsletter,* I was stunned to discover that a higher percentage had signed up than any audience I'd ever spoken to!

How could I have been so wrong? Psychologists used to think the inability to see our own behavior clearly or objectively was the result of a perspective problem; that we literally can't see ourselves from the vantage point that others can. By this account, I couldn't have accurately evaluated my speech because I couldn't see myself from the same perspective as the audience did.

But this explanation turns out not to hold water. In one study, participants were given a series of personality tests and videotaped making a brief speech. They were then asked to watch the video and identify their nonverbal behaviors—things like eye contact with the camera, gestures, facial expressions, and voice volume. Because the participants could see themselves from the same angle that others could, the researchers predicted that their ratings would be fairly accurate. But shockingly, their ratings failed to match up with those of an objective observer even when they were offered money for correct answers. (By now, we've established that money is of little help in making us more self-aware.) Though scientists are still working to definitively uncover the real reasons for our Behavior Blindness, there are, as we'll soon see, a few tools you can use to avoid falling victim to it.

---

* Which you can do at www.TashaEurich.com.

BRAVER BUT WISER: FROM BLINDNESS TO (IN)SIGHT

To understand how almost anyone can move from self-blindness to self-insight, let's turn back to my coaching client, Steve. As we got deeper into our work, it was obvious that the blindspots I've just described were alive and well. It might now make sense that **Steve Disease is actually a combination of all three blindspots.** Steve's knowledge blindness about his leadership expertise had given him an overconfidence that could only be described as epic. His emotion blindness was leading him to make decisions based on gut feelings rather than reason. And he was completely oblivious to how his behavior was going over with his staff.

With these forces at play, I knew that Steve would be one of my greatest professional challenges, though he certainly wasn't my first. After all, a central part of my job is to tell senior executives the truth when everyone else is afraid to or doesn't know how (and I'm proud to report that I've only been fired once for it). In so doing, I've found that with some effort, delusion can usually be overcome, and even the most unseeing can learn to open their eyes—sometimes they just need a little shove.

In Steve's case, I was that shove, and it was going to have to be an unusually forceful one. But before we could begin to deal with his willful resistance to self-improvement, I first had to tackle his willful resistance to letting me get a word in edgewise. I decided that a direct approach was necessary. With his diatribe showing no sign of losing wind, I locked my eyes with him until he finally stopped pacing. "Steve," I said, "there's no way around this. Your team hates you." He wouldn't have looked more shocked if I'd stood on my chair and claimed to be his long-lost daughter. Glancing at my folder of research, he asked, "What did they say about me?" I had no choice but to tell him. And since his team had warned me about his temper, I was prepared for what came next. The raised voice. The clenched jaw. The menacing stares. The vein in his neck. And right there across the desk, Steve's face was turning bright red.

"How could they SAY THOSE THINGS ABOUT ME? *HOW COULD THEY SAY THAT I YELL!?*"

Then, as if exhausted by his own delusion, he slumped in his chair and gazed out the window for a good minute. The last time Steve had been silent, it had been an attempt to demonstrate the power he believed he had over me. But this silence had an altogether different quality. "So," he said at last, swiveling his chair toward me with an expression of calm intention, "I've been doing these things for the last four months—or twenty years?—and nobody told me?" Indeed, rather than face his harsh reality, he'd chosen the path of blissful ignorance, which was easier in the moment but disastrous in the long run. That's the problem with blissful ignorance. It works just fine . . . until it doesn't.

Many people have experienced a "come to Jesus" moment like this—an alarm clock event that opens our eyes to the unpleasant reality that others don't see us the same way we see ourselves. These moments often come without warning and can cause serious damage to our confidence, to our success, and to our happiness. But what if we could discover the truth earlier and on our own terms? What if we could see our behavior clearly, before it begins to hurt our relationships and undermine our career? What if we could pair a quest for the truth with a positive mindset and a sense of self-acceptance? What if we could learn to be *braver but wiser*?

The Greek myth of Icarus is an apt metaphor. Icarus tries to escape the island of Crete using wings that his father, Daedalus, built from wax and feathers. Daedalus warns Icarus not to fly too high or too low: flying too low meant the sea would weigh down the feathers and flying too high meant the sun would melt the wax. But against his father's instructions, Icarus decides to fly too high. And sure enough, the wax melts, knocking him out of the air and sending him to his death.

When it comes to the way we see ourselves, we must be brave enough to spread our wings, but wise enough not to fly too high, lest our blindspots send us soaring straight into the sun. When we learn the truth, it can be surprising, or terrifying, or even gratifying—but no matter what, it gives us the power to improve.

This is what I had to help Steve understand, and I knew we had our work cut out for us. We reviewed his feedback for hours. At first he was resistant, searching for any excuse to counter the criticism. But to his great credit, he slowly started to accept what he was hearing. By the end of our first session, I was seeing a new side of him. "I've never questioned my leadership approach," he told me. "Not for years, anyway. Why would I? Everything's always been pretty great. But the last couple months, something's felt off. I didn't know what it was. Results haven't been what I was expecting, and the worst thing is, it's been following me home." He smiled ruefully.

"The good news is that these problems are totally fixable," I told him. "And you've just taken a major step."

"Really? What did I do?" he exhaustedly inquired.

I grinned. "You just accepted reality."

Indeed, the commitment to learn and accept reality is one of the most significant differences between the self-aware and, well, everybody else. The self-aware exert great effort to overcome their blindspots and see themselves as they really are. Through examining our assumptions, constantly learning, and seeking feedback, it's possible to overcome a great many barriers to insight. Although it would be unreasonable to expect that we can see or eliminate our blindspots altogether, we *can* gather and assemble data that helps us see ourselves and the impact of our behavior more clearly.

The first step is to **identify our assumptions**. This may sound obvious, but unfortunately, it's rare to question our assumptions about ourselves and the world around us, especially for ambitious, successful people. I witnessed a telling example of this when I used to teach a weeklong executive strategy program. On the morning of the second day, participants would enter the training room and find a small, plastic-wrapped puzzle at each table. When we told them that they'd have five minutes to assemble the puzzle, many of these powerful people would scoff at such a silly activity, wondering why we were wasting their valuable time. Humoring us, they'd open the plastic seal, dump the puzzle on the table, and begin turning the puzzle pieces, which were blue on one side, face-up (or what they assumed was face-up). After a few minutes, having assembled only about 80 percent of the puzzle, they would be scratching their heads in, for lack of a better word, puzzlement. Just as time was about to run out, one person—mind you, almost without exception, it would be just *one* out of about 20 senior executives—would realize that the puzzle could only be solved by turning some of the blue puzzle pieces "upside down."

In our day-to-day lives, we rarely even think to ask ourselves whether we should turn over any proverbial puzzle pieces. As Harvard psychologist Chris Argyris explains in his must-read book *Increasing Leadership Effectiveness*, when something doesn't go the way we want or expect, we typically assume that the cause exists in our environment. Surely there was a screw-up in the puzzle factory, or the missing pieces somehow got lost on their way out of the box. The last place we look is at our own beliefs and actions. Together with his colleague Donald Schön, Argyris labeled this type of thinking, one in which we fail to seek data that confronts our fundamental assumptions of ourselves and the world, "single-loop learning."

In contrast, the process of ***double-loop learning*** involves confronting our values and assumptions and, more importantly, inviting others to do so as well. In his work with executives, Argyris discovered that double-loop learning can be especially difficult for successful people who are used to "inventing, producing, and achieving"—after all, they've gotten this far with their current assumptions, so they must have gotten something right. But what they don't often realize is just how critical turning over the proverbial puzzle pieces is for their continued success.

So how can we learn to do this? One approach is to **get into the habit of comparing our past predictions with actual outcomes.** Celebrated management professor Peter Drucker suggested a simple, practical process that he himself used for more than 20 years. Every time he would make an important decision, he would write down what he expected to happen. Then, when the chickens had come home to roost, he would compare what actually happened with what he had predicted.

But what if you want to identify your assumptions in real time rather than in hindsight? Another tool comes from decision psychologist Gary Klein, who suggests doing what he calls a ***pre-mortem*** by asking the following question: "Imagine that we are a year into the future—we have implemented the plan as it now exists. The outcome was a disaster. Write a brief history of that disaster." This process tends to reveal potential pitfalls in a way we'd rarely consider otherwise. The same approach can be used for most big decisions, such as moving to a new city, accepting a new job, or deciding to settle down with a romantic partner. (And by the way, in appendix G, you can find a few questions to help you unearth your assumptions and discover whether you might have some, as Donald Rumsfeld might call them, "unknown unknowns" about yourself).

A second technique to minimize our blindspots is simply to **keep learning**, especially in the areas where we think we already know a lot. In their landmark 1999 study, David Dunning and Justin Kruger found that when overconfident poor performers were trained to improve their performance on a task, not only did they improve, so did their awareness of their prior ineffectiveness. A true commitment to ongoing learning—saying to ourselves, *the more I think I know, the more I need to learn*—is a powerful way to combat knowledge blindness and improve our effectiveness in the process.

Finally, we should **seek feedback on our abilities and behaviors.** Out of all the tools we've reviewed so far, objective feedback has the best odds of helping us see and overcome all three blindspots. Why? As we'll discuss later, the people around us can almost always see what we can't. And as such, we need to surround ourselves with those who will tell us the truth, both at work and at home. We need colleagues, family members, and friends who will (lovingly) knock us down a peg when we're getting too big for our britches. In the category of "amusing yet accurate observations," Stanford researcher Hayagreeva Rao believes that leaders who have teenage children are less prone to overconfidence for this very reason. As anyone with a teenager knows, they are perpetually unimpressed and will never hesitate to tell you how great you *aren't*. (And it's true that surrounding yourself with people who disagree with you is one of the most fundamental building blocks of leadership success. Great leaders have people around them who call them out, and failed leaders almost never do.)

I'll be the first to admit that seeking feedback can be one of the most intimidating and terrifying things you'll ever do. But trust me, the insight you will gain will be worth it. Just ask our friend Steve. At the end of our first meeting, he made a decision. Looking me in the eye, he bravely announced, "I don't like this information, but I accept it. And with your help, I'm going to figure it out." It was another huge step in the right direction.

At this point, Steve now had the *will* to make different choices, but he still needed to develop the *skill*. So in the months that followed, I helped him share his intentions, read his effect on his team, and seek feedback from people who would tell him the truth. In one coaching session a month or so after our initial meeting, Steve was still struggling to understand why everyone thought he was such a loose cannon. So I tried a different approach: "Do you understand how you reacted during our last meeting when I gave you the feedback from your team?" "Sure," he replied. "I don't think you do," I said, and then did my best impression of his response—aggressively staring at him, raising my voice, and clenching my jaw—so he could see just how hostile his behavior had been. "I don't think I've always been like this," he said, "but I'm pretty sure I've been scaring my family just as much as I'm scaring my team." And now that he better understood how his behavior was affecting others, he could begin to experiment with a different and more effective approach.

This process went on for months. And like anyone undertaking such a task, Steve had his fair share of setbacks, but he continued to make progress. In the months that followed, he saw an improvement in his effectiveness and felt a new level of confidence. Eventually, his team began to notice that something was different—and so did his family. They all started to talk about this wonderful person they called "the New Steve." It was also not a coincidence that his team met their aggressive business plan that year, or that his CEO started to trust his abilities and decisions.

Steve's tale illustrates both how incredibly hard it is to confront the reality about ourselves *and* why it's unquestionably worth the effort. When it comes to making the choices that guide our lives, truth is power, whether that truth is music to our ears or sounds like fingernails on a chalkboard. As Buddhist nun Pema Chödrön points out, "The most fundamental . . . harm we can do to ourselves is to remain ignorant by not having the courage and the respect to look at ourselves honestly and gently." And luckily, the difference between unicorns and everyone else has less to do with innate ability and more to do with intention and commitment. Throughout the rest of this book, we'll discuss more strategies to help us find the courage and respect to look at ourselves honestly and gently—and in so doing, become more successful in our careers, more satisfied in our relationships, and more content in our lives. But before we do that, it's critical to understand—and fight—the second big roadblock to self-awareness: something I call the Cult of Self.

4

THE CULT OF SELF

The Sinister Societal Roadblock to Insight

We have fallen in love with our own image, with images of our making, which turn out to be images of ourselves.
—DANIEL J. BOORSTIN

International Falls, MN—The Dragons' season came to a close as Paycen's pair of goals carried the Icemen to a 4-2 victory on Saturday, with five goals scored during a wild second period. The Icemen scored one minute into the second as right wing Loeden lifted the puck over goaltender Keltie's blocker. The Dragons tied the game when Kaeden and Caiden set up a power-play goal. With Jaxon in the penalty box after drawing Brecon's blood with a high stick to the nose, the Dragons were patient on the power play. Kaeden fed the puck below the goal line to Caiden, who made a pass to Constandino in the slot for an easy Dragon score.

Okay, so this is a completely made up recap of a hockey game. But the one thing I didn't make up were the player's first names. If you didn't notice them, go back and take another look: Paycen, Keltie, Brecon, Jaxon, Constandino, and yes, Kaeden and Caiden (what are the chances?). I lifted these strange and unusual monikers from the real draft roster of the 2015 Western Hockey League, made up of 68 American and Canadian high schoolers. The ones I didn't even mention? Kale (yes, like the vegetable), Lach, and *four* named Dawson (James Van Der Beek would be touched).

So many bizarre names among a single group of hockey players might sound like a simple, if odd, coincidence. But the Western Hockey League is not an outlier. A 2012 *Parents Magazine* survey reveals that these days, parents are choosing names like Blayde, Draven, Izander, Jaydien and Zaiden (for boys), and Annyston, Brook'Lynn, Luxx, Sharpay, and Zerrika (for girls). And I'm sure you've come across some doozies yourself.

In one of the largest studies to date on American naming trends, researchers Jean Twenge and Keith Campbell analyzed the names given to more than 325 million babies born between 1880 and 2007. During the early twentieth century, they found, parents consistently chose conventional names for their newborns. In 1890, 1900, 1910, and 1920, for example, the most common names were John for boys and Mary for girls. In the decades that followed, parents continued to stick with the classics like James, Michael, Mary, and Linda.

But beginning in the 1980s, Twenge and Campbell discovered a rather strange pattern: fewer and fewer parents were going with the old standbys. Between 1983 and 2007, the percentage of U.S. parents who chose common names for their children dropped sharply each and every year—most dramatically in the 1990s and continuing to decline in the 2000s. Here's a pretty telling data point: in 1880, nearly 40 percent of boys and 25 percent of girls received one of the 10 most popular names—but in 2010, that number dropped to less than 10 percent for boys and 8 percent for girls. "Parents used to give their children common names," Twenge observes, "so they would fit in. Now, they give their child a unique [one to] stand out and be a star."

I don't point this out to judge. Of course, parents can name their children whatever they want (it's a free country). I point this out because aside from being interesting, this trend is a sign of an unstoppable phenomenon that's sweeping our world. And it's a powerful roadblock to self-awareness.

Whether you know it or not, a powerful cult is trying to recruit you. Cults tend to show a misplaced or excessive admiration for a particular person or thing, and this cult has chosen an irresistible figurehead: *you*! Frankly, it's easy to see why the promise that the **Cult of Self** makes can be too tempting to resist. It lulls us into thinking that we are unique, special, and superior. That our needs matter more than everyone else's. That we're not subject to the same rules as other people are. That we're deserving of things simply because we want them. No wonder the Cult of Self has successfully recruited so many of our neighbors, friends, and colleagues—perhaps it's even succeeded in luring you. The last chapter was about our internal roadblocks; in this chapter, we'll discover this insidious societal obstacle. Perhaps more importantly, we'll learn several methods for resisting its siren song—or breaking free if you're already ensnared.

TURNING THE TIDE: FROM EFFORT TO ESTEEM

As many grouchy Baby Boomers will point out at the slightest provocation, things weren't always like this. In the broader timeline of human history, the Cult of Self is a fairly recent phenomenon. For thousands of years, traditional Judeo-Christian values emphasized modesty and humility—the polar opposites of the Cult of Self—as measures of a well-lived life. In the eighteenth century, the United States (which now boasts some of the Cult of Self's most enthusiastic members) was founded on the very principles of hard work, grit, and resilience. This **Age of Effort** lasted hundreds of years, arguably peaking with the so-called Silent Generation (born between 1900 and 1945) and the events of the early 20th century—World War I, the Great Depression, and World War II. The Age of Effort fostered a collective mentality that shunned the glorification of the self.

But with the start of the self-esteem movement in the middle of the twentieth century, the Age of Effort started to give way to the **Age of Esteem.** The seeds were first sown with the humanistic psychology movement of the 1950s and 1960s. Carl Rogers, for instance, argued that humans could only achieve their potential by seeing themselves with "unconditional positive regard." Perhaps more famously, Abraham

Maslow proposed that humans have a hierarchy of needs, at the top of which was self-actualization—that is, total happiness and fulfillment. Yet by Maslow's own admission, self-actualization was incredibly difficult to achieve. Conveniently, self-esteem was just one rung down, and all that was needed to achieve it was a change in mindset. In other words, we didn't need to *become* great; all we really had to do was *feel* great.

Not surprisingly, self-esteem began to catch on like wildfire. In 1969, psychotherapist Nathaniel Branden published the international best-seller *The Psychology of Self-Esteem*, in which he confidently concluded that self-esteem had "profound consequences for every aspect of our existence" and that he "couldn't think of a single psychological problem—from anxiety to depression, to fear of intimacy or of success, to spouse battery or child molestation—that is not traceable to the problem of low self-esteem." To say that Branden oversold his thesis is like saying that Kim Kardashian feels pretty good about herself.

Though Nathaniel Branden is often seen as the father of self-esteem, a man named John Vasconcellos took the movement to a whole new level. After he was sworn in to the California State Assembly in 1966, the first move of the law student turned politician with a childhood history of depression was to introduce legislation for the *California Task Force to Promote Self Esteem and Personal & Social Responsibility*—to the tune of an astounding taxpayer-funded $735,000 (roughly $1.7 million today).

The task force's first order of business was to empirically establish that high self-esteem reduced crime, drug and alcohol abuse, teen pregnancy, child and spousal abuse, and welfare dependency. There was just one tiny, insignificant issue: they couldn't. In fact, the task force was forced to grudgingly admit in its own report that "the associations between self-esteem and its expected consequences are mixed, insignificant, or absent" and that there was no relationship "between self-esteem and teenage pregnancy, self-esteem and child abuse, self-esteem and most cases of alcohol and drug abuse." Though no one wanted to admit it, the idea that self-esteem predicted life success was, to put it bluntly, a total and complete farce. Yet in a statement of stunning disregard for the scientific method, Vasconcellos disavowed the task force's findings, saying "we all know in our gut that it is true."

Enter psychologist Roy Baumeister, upon whom journalist Will Storr aptly bestowed the title "the man who destroyed America's ego." Baumeister began studying self-esteem early in his career and was initially one of the movement's biggest believers. Over time, however, his skepticism grew. He couldn't understand why people like Vasconcellos claimed that people with low self-esteem were violent and aggressive— his experience had been just the opposite. But never one to rely on experience alone, Baumeister dug into the science, and in 2003, he and his colleagues published an unequivocal indictment of almost three decades—and over 15,000 studies—of self-esteem research.

Their review was chock-full of evidence that the relationship between self-esteem and success was virtually nonexistent. For example, military cadets' self-esteem had no relationship with their objective performance as leaders. College students' self-esteem didn't give them superior social skills. Professionals with high self-esteem didn't enjoy better relationships with their co-workers. And in an even bigger blow to Nathaniel Brandon and his disciples, boosting the self-esteem of the unsuccessful *hurt* their performance rather than improved it. Baumeister and his colleagues' obvious conclusion was that self-esteem was neither "a major predictor [n]or cause of almost anything," least of all success and personal fulfillment.

I haven't even gotten to the *really* shocking part. Baumeister's research revealed an inconvenient truth that challenged the very assumptions upon which the entire movement was built. Low self-esteem wasn't actually an ailment from which most Americans suffered in the first place. At the same time self-esteem proponents were "bemoan[ing] the lack of self-love," self-esteem levels were steadily and almost uncontrollably rising. The real social ill was that most people felt *too* good about themselves (often without any objective reason).

And it got worse. Baumeister's review showed that people with high self-esteem were more violent and aggressive. When their romantic relationships were in trouble, they were more likely to walk away, be unfaithful, or engage in other destructive behaviors. They were also more likely to cheat, drink, and do drugs. All of this was literally the opposite of what the California Task Force had been arguing.

Though it's been decades since Baumeister and his research team uncovered the sham that is self-esteem, we can't seem to shake our obsession with getting more of it. Why? The bottom line, I believe, is that **it's far easier to *feel* wonderful and special than to *become* wonderful and special**. And just like in Garrison Keillor's fictional town of Lake Wobegon, we continue to spoon-feed our children the idea that they are just that.

◆

In the northwest of England, at the confluence of two ancient rivers, lies the enchanted town of Barrowford. In the seventeenth century, the area was known as a center of witchcraft, with 10 of the so-called "Pendle Witches" having been hanged there on a warm summer day in 1612. But today in its verdant hills, valleys, and winding cobblestone streets, another strange magic is afoot.

To the average visitor, Barrowford might look like an ordinary, if quaint, bedroom community dotted with upscale restaurants and antique stores. Little would they know that Barrowford boasts a very interesting feature: it's the town where children are never naughty. Don't believe me? Then how do you explain Barrowford Primary School, where the head teacher, Rachel Tomlinson, insists that there is no such thing as a bad child? Each one of her 350 students is, she says, "special and unique." For that very reason, teachers don't raise their voices or provide discipline of any kind. Punishment, says Tomlinson, only "robs the victim and the perpetrator of the things they need." Instead, apparently all that's needed to get the best out of these boys and girls is to remind them of their specialness—unconditionally and often.

But if, on the rare occasion that the magical praise-spell breaks and a child does misbehave, teachers are given but one method of recourse. They are permitted to send the child to another classroom, at which point they may only point out, "You know I think you're wonderful, but your mistaken behavior shows me that it would be best for you to have some time here, where these children can help you to stop making that mistake." Rather amusingly, the teachers' sole nuclear option is to tell them (ostensibly with a straight face), "you have emptied my resilience bucket."*

The children of Barrowford Primary are given this unconditional praise regardless of how they perform in the classroom, with Tomlinson's pupils telling a team of visiting inspectors that "no one minds that we don't do our best work." One year, when students received their Key Stage 2 standardized test results, the school sent them home with a letter explaining that academic evaluations can't possibly measure all of their special and wonderful qualities and that regardless of their scores, Tomlinson was proud that they had all "tried their best during a tricky week."

And such self-esteem stoking hasn't created a miracle of high achievement any more than hanging those poor women in 1612 rid the town of witches. In fact, in September of 2015, the school was handed the worst rating possible, deemed "inadequate" by British government inspectors. Other experts have labeled Barrowford's educational philosophy a "fantasy." Tomlinson's response to the criticism was priceless in its delusion: though she was disappointed, she was also "very positive and excited about the future."

Barrowford's misguided approach was designed to produce an army of children whose self-esteem is preserved at all costs. And again, in this the school is not alone. We've all heard the examples: sports teams where everyone is a winner, like one branch of the American Youth Soccer Organization that hands out roughly 3,500 awards each season (this works out to at least one award per player). Others prevent students from losing altogether, like the schools in the U.S. and Europe

---

* Journalist Allison Pearson delightfully imagines what would have transpired if such a philosophy were applied in Britain's diplomatic relations circa World War II:

Dear Mr. Hitler,
You have emptied our resilience bucket. Please give Poland back or you will have a serious impact on our well-being.
Love, Britain

that banned all competitive sports. There are the elementary schools where failing grades and red pens have been outlawed because they're too "negative," or where students spend time working on daily "I Love Me" lessons. The high schools with 30 valedictorians who ship their students off to colleges where grade inflation is an ever-increasing problem.

This gingerly treatment of young egos is even alive and well in America's most prestigious and selective institutions. For example, in 2001, a whopping 91 percent of Harvard students graduated with honors, and in 2013, at least half of all grades awarded were A's. But in 2015, 72 percent of students polled didn't think that grade inflation was a problem. As the proud sister of a Yale graduate, I found myself especially relishing this story, until I learned that Yale has experienced similar problems: a 2012 ad hoc committee on grading found that 62 percent of all grades given were an A or A–, versus just 10 percent in 1963. Entertainingly, many Yale students and faculty believed this pattern was simply the result of "a more consistently excellent student body."

This is all evidence of a sweeping problem I call the **Feel Good Effect**, though its consequences are far more pernicious than the cheery name suggests. In the workplace, for example, the best-case scenario is that people who see themselves as special and amazing annoy those who have to work with them. In the worst case, they are woefully ill-equipped to deal with the tiniest bit of criticism, crushed in the face of the smallest screw-up, and devastated by the minor setbacks on the path to their predestined greatness. Comedian George Carlin has a great bit about this. "No child these days," he says, "gets to hear these all important character building words: 'You lost, Bobby. You're a loser, Bobby.' They become used to these kid gloves and never hear the truth about themselves until they're in their twenties, when their boss calls them in and says, 'Bobby clean the s*** out of your desk and get the f*** out of here, you're a loser!'"

This is equal parts hilarious and harsh, but Carlin makes a truly excellent point. In the real world, not everyone gets to graduate with honors—and in fact, the more delusional we are about our skills and abilities, the *less* likely we are to succeed. Take one study, which found that when college freshmen were overconfident about their academic abilities, they also had poorer well-being and lower engagement in their schoolwork throughout their college experience than students who were more realistic.

The Feel Good Effect also hurts our relationships. In one of the most comprehensive studies of its costs to date, researchers assessed 100 college students' views of their personalities, comparing their self-ratings with trained psychologists' ratings of them. The psychologists viewed young men with accurate self-perceptions as honest and smart. However, for those young men who gave themselves unrealistically positive ratings, the psychologists described them as "guileful and deceitful, distrustful of people and having a brittle ego-defense system." Similarly, young women who were accurate were seen as "complex, interesting, and intelligent," and those whose self-images were unrealistically positive were seen as "defensive" and "thin-skinned." And it wasn't just trained psychologists who saw differences between the delusional and the aware. When asked to evaluate the overconfident, even their own friends thought they were "condescending," "hostile," and "self-defeating." The realists, on the other hand, were seen as "charming" and "poised."

By blinding us to the truth about our skills and abilities, the Feel Good Effect even causes us to make life choices which, as good as they may feel in the moment, can really hurt us in the long run. Take the classic reality-TV cliché: a young pre-med student skips her final exams to drive 10 hours to audition for the reality singing competition du jour. Yet rather inconveniently, she's also a horrible singer and never makes it past the first round. Here, the choice that resulted from her overconfidence got in the way of her far sounder future plans.

But what if you're not delusional but merely positive—the kind of person who sees the world through rose-colored glasses? An optimistic temperament predicts persistence, so it's not surprising that entrepreneurs and founders tend to be more optimistic than the average professional. But when optimism is unfounded, those rose-colored glasses can really obscure insight. The odds, for example, that a small business will survive for five years after being founded are 35 percent. But 81 percent of entrepreneurs believe that their odds of success are 70 percent or more, and an incredible 33 percent see their chances as "dead certain."

And alas, such unwarranted optimism persists even in the face of cold, hard truths. Management professors Thomas Åstebro and Samir Elhedhli reviewed data collected by the Canadian Innovation Centre, a non-profit that helps entrepreneurs bring their ideas to market. The program evaluates new business plans and subsequently assigns companies a grade from A to F; on average, and more or less consistent with real-world failure rates, 70 percent are given a D or F. But almost half of these entrepreneurs persisted anyway. Many even doubled their efforts, wrongly thinking that hard work could improve the viability of their unviable business. In literally every case, it didn't.

◆

We've now seen that willful blindness to our shortcomings can set us up for failure. And yet the self-awareness unicorns in our study showed a remarkable pattern: in a few specific situations, they strategically put on their rose-colored glasses, and it provided them with tangible benefits. To quote one such unicorn, a brilliant project manager who recently dealt with a devastating medical diagnosis, "You can visit denial-ville, but you can't build a house there."* She told us that when she found out she was sick, she needed a few days of blissful ignorance to store up the energy to face her new reality. But then she picked herself up, dusted herself off, and bravely and realistically began her fight.

How do we know when to put our glasses on and when they should come off? A good rule of thumb is that **when we need to bounce back from constant challenges, or where we can succeed through sheer persistence, the Feel-Good Effect can be helpful.** This is especially true in professions like acting, where rejection is part of the job description. It can also be true in the "publish or perish" world

---

* Throughout the book, unicorn quotes appear near-verbatim; I've made some small changes to improve readability without altering their meaning.

of science. As Daniel Kahneman notes, "I believe that someone who lacks a delusional sense of significance will wilt in the face of repeated experiences of multiple small failures and rare successes, the fate of most researchers." But there is one hugely important caveat: before you put on your rose-colored glasses and head down the path of persistence, make sure that your path actually leads somewhere. If, to use the above example, you're simply a terrible actor, no amount of persistence will get you to the Broadway stage. You have to read the signs that your path could be a dead end and be ready to change course if you're not getting anywhere.

There is one last type of situation where temporarily donning our rose-colored glasses can be a good idea. I was giving a self-awareness workshop to a group of professionals when I met Katie, a shy, bespectacled accountant who spent the entire class solemnly taking notes. At the end of the session, though, she seemed reluctant to commit to putting the feedback-gathering techniques she'd learned into practice. I sensed there was more going on, so I approached her after class. I learned that Katie was a partner at a professional services firm, and that the last month had been excruciating. Her firm had just brought in a new partner who seemed dead set at undermining her. Katie had also just been appointed as trustee of her parents' estate in the midst of an all-out family war. Quite simply, with all the things going on in her life, Katie didn't have the bandwidth to focus on self-improvement— she was just trying to get through this crisis and emerge unscathed.

Sometimes life can hand us challenges so difficult that we *need* rose-colored glasses to help us get through them. Our unicorns echoed this sentiment: one put his self-awareness journey on pause when he was unexpectedly fired. Another found her divorce so devastating that some strategic blissful ignorance got her through the worst parts. But if our unicorns indulged in a little self-delusion from time to time, it was only temporary. When they were ready, they bravely faced the music and resumed their self-awareness journey.

As a final point, it's worth noting that there's a fine line between feeling good and willfully ignoring the signals around us. Even though there are a few situations where keeping our rose-colored glasses on is the best option, most others—especially things like a new job, a big promotion, a company turnaround, a merger or acquisition, a blow-out fight with a loved one—require you to take them off no matter what. **Where failure is not an option, you don't have the luxury of blissful ignorance.** Unfortunately, as you're about to read, there is an epidemic afoot that is threatening to further throw that delicate balance to the wind.

ME, MY SELFIE, AND I

It was the most perfect start to a morning I could remember. After I'd worked six months straight without a break, my husband had surprised me with a birthday trip to Hawaii. Our busy schedules only permitted us three days away, but as we settled into our rented cabana with our freshly prepared omelets, we felt like we'd booked into paradise forever. The sky was clear, the warm sun was enveloping us, and the sweet scent of gardenia mixed with the salty smell of the ocean. We had nothing to do but sit and enjoy the perfectly unobstructed vista of blue sea rolling onto white sand.

I was smiling at my husband, who was basking in his quickly accumulating spousal brownie points, when suddenly a shadow fell over us. *That's strange,* I thought, *there weren't any clouds a moment ago.* Before I had the chance to squint at the sky, I heard a shriek and a giggle. An attractive young couple in their early twenties had come to a halt right in front of us. We said nothing as they laid out their towels right in the middle of the view we'd been so peacefully enjoying. As they pulled off their shorts and T-shirts, revealing toned, tanned bodies clad in designer swimwear, I shook my head in minor irritation as little kicks of sand landed in my omelet.

After blankly staring at the ocean for a few minutes, the young woman jumped up. Apparently, it was now time to commence an activity with which you may be familiar: Beach Selfies. My husband and I didn't try very hard to mask our chuckling as she dramatically flipped her hair, pushed her sunglasses to the tip of her nose, and pursed her lips into the all-too-familiar Duck Face.

Then things crossed the line from amusing to annoying. With her hips back and her chest forward, she pranced and posed, squinting at her screen every 30 seconds to review the shots. "She's got to stop soon," I whispered to my husband, attempting to skim the sand from my breakfast. "Five minutes." "Ten," he predicted. We were both wrong. When she finally finished—a full 15 minutes later—she sat back down as if nothing out of the ordinary had just happened, lay back on her towel, and went to sleep, completely oblivious to the open-mouthed stares from everyone in her general vicinity.

Beach Selfie Girl's behavior is hardly unique, and this episode is just one example of the exponential momentum that the Cult of Self has gained with the explosion of social media. One of our unicorns described a friend who routinely takes 40 to 50 selfies a day; once, when they were out to dinner, the friend spent the entire meal snapping photos of himself. At one point, he excused himself to go to the restroom—where he took even more selfies and posted them on Instagram, all before returning to the table.

We all know someone who suffers from *Selfie Syndrome*. Symptoms include a once-unthinkable level of self-absorption, resulting in delusions including (but not limited to) the belief that people care what you ate for breakfast, that today is your child's half-birthday, or that you are having the *best vacation ever*. It might even be fair to say that in many respects, for many people, Selfie Syndrome has crossed the line into a kind of widespread, low-grade narcissism. Certainly, almost all of us have encountered full-fledged narcissists in our personal or professional lives. You know, those people who are so convinced they're the center of the universe that they can't seem to see past themselves to the people around them.

But what we don't always realize is that paradoxically, **an intense self-focus not only obscures our vision of those around us; it distorts our ability to see ourselves for what we really are.** Indeed, research has shown that in general, there is an inverse relationship between how special we feel and how self-aware we are. One need not look far to find examples: the people who post the most selfies on Facebook, for instance, seem to have the least awareness of how annoying this behavior is to the rest of us.

When we examine the "impersonally personal" nature of social media, the idea of narcissism running rampant makes sense. In most online communication, we don't see the other person's reactions or facial expressions, which makes it easier to be detached, self-centered, and unreflective. Researchers call this the "moral shallowing hypothesis," where our ultra-brief online interactions lead to rapid, superficial thought, which makes us see ourselves, and others, in a more shallow manner.

Of course, this isn't to say that anyone who takes selfies or uses social media is a narcissist. But scientifically, there is no question that these things are related, and there is ample evidence that narcissism is on the rise. For example, in a study of tens of thousands of U.S. college students, Jean Twenge and her colleagues found that between the mid-1980s and 2006, narcissism increased a full *30 percent*, as measured by statements like "If I ruled the world it would be a better place," "I always know what I'm doing," and "I will never be satisfied until I get all that I deserve."

And lest you pin this trend entirely on Millennials, it's not just those of us born between 1980 and 1999 who show this pattern. Another long-running study that analyzed high schoolers' responses to the question "I am an important person" found that in the 1950s only 12 percent agreed, but by 1989 (that is, when Gen Xers were in high school), that number jumped to roughly 80 percent. And remember the study from the last chapter, where 25 percent of high-school-aged Baby Boomers put themselves in the top 1 percent in their ability to get along with others?

Selfie Syndrome isn't a generational phenomenon, nor is it confined to the arguably more self-centered cohort of adolescents. Our growing "me" focus can be found everywhere from contemporary literature to social media, even in the Oval Office. One study that analyzed State of the Union addresses between 1790 and 2012 found a decrease in the use of other-related words like *his/her* and *neighbor*, and an increase in self-focused words such as *I, me,* and *mine.* Similarly, my own Google Ngram* search of more than 15 million books revealed that while the use of the word *me* decreased nearly 50 percent between 1900 and 1974, it increased more than 87 percent between 1975 and 2008!

Right now, you're probably thinking of a particularly narcissistic Facebook friend or self-absorbed celebrity. But I encourage you to also ask how *you* use social media—whether it's Facebook, Instagram, LinkedIn, Twitter, Snapchat, or anything else that's been invented since this book was published. Ask yourself: When you post a picture of your perfect vacation, what's going through your head? What image of yourself are you trying to project? What are you hoping to achieve? Few of us think about our social media habits in such rational or analytic terms. In fact, they usually feel so natural that we *don't* think about them, which is precisely the problem.

This suggests a bigger question: Why do we use social media in the first place? Even though social media is supposed to be social, one 2015 study found that maintaining our relationships can often be the last reason we use these platforms. At the top of the list is sharing information about ourselves, which is often called *self-presentation.* Now, on its own, self-presentation isn't necessarily a bad thing. But an interesting pattern has emerged suggesting that as self-presentation increases, empathy decreases. Since the year 2000, right around the time when sites like MySpace, Friendster, and other precursors to Facebook exploded, people started becoming less empathetic and more self-centered. Research shows that compared to college students in the early 1980s, today's pupils are 11 percent less likely to agree with statements like "I often have tender, concerned feelings for people less fortunate than me" and "I sometimes try to understand my friends better by imagining how things look from their perspective."

At this point you might be wondering whether this is a

---

* Google Ngram is web-based search engine that tracks the frequencies of words and phrases found in books printed between 1500 and 2008 in eight languages.

chicken-or-egg situation. How can we conclude that social media is *causing* narcissism? Isn't it just as likely that narcissistic, un-self-aware people are simply more likely to use social media? These are important questions, and there's actually evidence that both are true. Let's start with the second question: Do narcissists use social media more? Studies from both Western and Eastern cultures show that narcissists indeed use social media as an outlet for their inflated self-views, spending more time posting self-promotional content like selfies.

Let's now go back to the first question—is social media actually *causing* our self-absorption? Here, there is also supportive evidence. One study randomly assigned participants into one of two groups, who each spent 35 minutes online. The first group spent time editing their MySpace pages (really takes you back, doesn't it?) while the other plotted the route they took to school on Google Maps. When researchers measured narcissism levels in each group, participants who had spent time on MySpace scored significantly higher, suggesting not only that social media does increase narcissism, but that it has a *virtually immediate* impact.

Of course, people who love selfies and unique baby names usually fall short of being diagnosable narcissists—a personality disorder characterized by an exaggerated sense of self-importance, a need for power and admiration, and a failure to recognize the needs of others. Research shows that narcissists tend to have brief but intense friendships and romances that end once the other person sees their true nature. They feel entitled to things they haven't earned and are unable to tolerate criticism.

In the work world, while narcissistic leaders can be confident setting a clear vision, they tend to overrate their performance, dominate decision processes, seek excessive recognition, show less empathy, and are more likely to behave unethically. And while they think quite highly of their leadership abilities, they are actually rated lowest in effectiveness by their teams. Narcissistic CEOs in particular have been found to be less responsive to objective performance feedback than non-narcissistic ones, often with devastating effects. In a fascinating study, when researchers Charles Ham and his colleagues measured the size of CEO signatures in SEC filings in S&P 500 firms (with a sizable signature being an indicator of narcissism), they found that the larger a CEO's signature, the worse the company performed on a number of indicators (lower patent counts and citations, poorer return on assets, over-investment, lower future revenues and sales growth).

In additional to its social and professional consequences, even low-level (i.e., non-diagnosable) narcissism can chip away at our self-confidence. Think about the version of yourself that you present online. If you're like most people, you might present an airbrushed, "hoped-for" version that gives an overly favorable impression of your life. These effects have been documented everywhere from Facebook status updates to dating profiles to the Twitter feeds of congresspeople during election years. For instance, we tend to use fewer negative words in social media than in other forms of communication, and half of status updates are posted with the goal of creating a favorable impression.

Paradoxically, this incessant promotion of our hoped-for self can be ego-crushing, especially when the "actual" and "hoped for" versions don't match up ("my Paris vacation photos sure look perfect, but what no one knows is that my husband and I spent the whole vacation fighting and I think I might want a divorce"). When we're trying so hard to convince everyone how successful or happy or attractive we are, not only are we often not fooling anyone; we're reminding ourselves of how unsuccessful or unhappy or unattractive we really feel.

To see how damaging social media self-inflations can be for our self-image, let's examine the case of 18-year-old Australian model Essena O'Neil. She recently became something of a poster child for the Cult of Self resistance movement when she shocked her millions of Instagram, YouTube, Tumblr, and Snapchat followers by announcing that she was shutting down her social media profiles. O'Neil told her fans that she'd spent most of her life addicted to the exposure, approval, and status that her followers gave her, and her endless pursuit of others' adoration had actually taken an enormous toll on her self-confidence. The more she posted, the more obsessed she became with perfection, and, in turn, the more frustrated she became when she never attained that ideal: "I spent hours watching perfect girls online, wishing I was them.

Then when I was 'one of them' I still wasn't happy, content or at peace with myself."

O'Neil has since launched a website called "Let's be Game Changers," where she curates resources to expose what she calls the "fakeness" of social media. At the time of writing, O'Neil's website doesn't have a single photo of the model, and only a short blurb about her, which is entitled "Me?" Sometimes the people who break with the Cult of Self are those we least expect. Let's talk about how we all can do it.

FROM SELF-ABSORPTION TO SELF-AWARENESS: RESISTING THE CULT OF SELF

It may not surprise you, given what you read in the last chapter, that most of us don't think we're narcissistic. The good news is that only 4 percent of the population actually fits the diagnostic criteria; the bad news is that the remaining 96 percent of us can display some narcissistic behaviors, at least some percentage of the time. Since this book is all about making the brave decision to confront the truth about ourselves, I've included an assessment in appendix H to help you gauge how many such behaviors you currently exhibit. But no matter what your score, if you want to move away from self-absorption and toward self-awareness, it's worth examining the following three strategies: becoming an informer, cultivating humility, and practicing self-acceptance.

As you go about your daily life, how much time and energy do you spend focused on *you*? It's probably more than you think. One study found that we spend up to 60 percent of our talking time discussing ourselves, and when we're on social media that number jumps to a whopping 80 percent. But our unicorns are different. Overwhelmingly, their conversations (online and offline) focus more on others—friends, co-workers, the events taking place in the wider world, etc. One appropriately noted that "the world doesn't revolve around me." Another explained that his approach to interacting with others involves "being curious about something outside of myself."

But is focusing on other people even possible when most forms of social media seem to exist for the sole purpose of self-promotion? Let's start by looking at the big picture. Researchers have discovered that people who use social media generally fall into one of two categories: 80 percent are so-called "Meformers," who like to post messages that are all about telling everyone about what is going on with them. The remaining 20 percent are "Informers," who tend to post non-self-related information—helpful articles, amusing observations, funny videos, etc. Informers tend to have more friends and enjoy richer, more satisfying interactions than Meformers.

It might not come as a surprise that our unicorns, to a person, were Informers. But when I began drilling down into this topic, I was shocked to learn that they also spent *more* time (almost 20 percent more) on social media than non-unicorns. They just spent that time very differently. Instead of logging on and posting a selfie, an update about their upcoming vacation, or their latest professional achievement, they used social media as a way to truly engage and stay connected with others. One unicorn, an entrepreneur in her fifties, told us: "Social media allows me to see what people I care about are up to. I don't post on Facebook often, but I do try to share something uplifting or funny or different a few times a week. If I post a picture, it's more likely to be an eagle in a tree or a sunset. Something beautiful that I can share with others." Like other unicorns, her social media goals aren't to rack up "likes," but rather to inform, entertain, and inspire. As another unicorn, a manager in his mid-forties, put it, "sometimes the Kanye Wests of the world need public validation that 'yes, you're great.' I don't find myself needing that."

The message here is clear: to move from self-absorption to self-awareness, **try being an *Informer***—that is, focusing less on you and more on engaging and connecting with others. For the next 24 hours, then, my challenge to you is to pay attention to how much you talk about yourself versus how much you focus on others—both online and offline. When tempted with a "Meformer" conversational topic or post, ask yourself: "What am I hoping to accomplish by doing this?" Be warned, this won't be easy at first. Since I began working on this book, I've used this technique and been surprised at how strong the pull toward self-absorption can be. It has unmasked a lot of behaviors that I was previously unaware of. I have since made an effort to change the way I'm showing up, especially online. When you try this exercise for a few days, I'd bet money that you'll discover something that will surprise you.

Focusing on others, however, won't help us fight the Cult of Self on its own. We also need to take a more realistic view of our own qualities, or in other words, **cultivate humility**. Because it means appreciating our weaknesses and keeping our successes in perspective, humility is a key ingredient of self-awareness.

When she was a little girl, Angela Ahrendts dreamed of being a fashion designer. She'd spend hours gazing at the gorgeous photos in her mother's magazines and sewing her own clothes. When she entered college, the place where her youthful dreams were supposed to turn into realities, she began to wonder why the other fashion design students seemed so much more talented than she was. One day, a professor took her aside and gave her some advice that, while well intentioned, must have been difficult to hear. The kind of person who can talk about fashion but isn't able to produce it? "We call that," he told her, "a merchant."

It's probably fair to say that most ambitious students, upon being told they're simply not good enough to fulfill their dreams, would disappear down a whirlpool of self-delusion. "What does my professor know, anyway?" we'd demand of anyone within earshot. "She's always had it in for me." But not Ahrendts. Growing up as one of six children in New Palestine, Indiana, she was taught to work hard and remain humble. As a result, she had the self-awareness to realize the professor was giving her great advice.

And she took it. She became a clothing merchant. By 2006, Ahrendts had become CEO of Burberry. She transformed the luxury brand's design and retail and digital presence and, in doing so, orchestrated an impressive company turnaround in the midst of a global recession. Along the way, she racked up a boast-worthy slew of honors, having landed on *Forbes*' Most Powerful Women list four times in five years, being named one of *Fortune*'s Businesspeople of the Year, and receiving the Outstanding Leadership Award from Oracle, to name a few.

But it isn't Ahrendts' style to boast about these achievements. And when Apple CEO Tim Cook was interviewing her for the role of SVP of Apple's online and retail businesses, she made a point of stressing to him that she was neither a technical guru nor someone with any experience in the world of consumer electronics. Yet Cook knew he didn't need a tech wiz or a retail expert to turn around Apple's struggling retail division. What he needed was a team player; a selfless leader who could engage and inspire.

So what did Angela Ahrendts' first few months in her new role look like? Where a more self-absorbed leader might have tried to make a splash with an aggressive vision that may or may not have been the right decision for the company, Ahrendts embarked on a tour of more than 100 stores, call centers, and back offices with one simple aim: to listen. Her next step was to begin sending weekly personal messages to her 60,000 retail employees—not with the goal of telling them about herself or her plan for the division, but rather to get them more involved in the decisions that affected their world. Ahrendts helped her employees see themselves as "executives . . . who are touching customers with the products that [Apple] took years to build."

Her surprising lack of ego and inclusive leadership style have confused some members of the press, prompting Jennifer Reingold of *Fortune* to ask, "What the heck is Angela Ahrendts doing at Apple?" But her results speak for themselves. Financially, 2015 marked the company's most successful year ever, with revenue expanding 28 percent to $234 billion while her employee retention skyrocketed to 81 percent—Apple's highest figure ever recorded. Oh, and she is now the most highly paid employee in one of the planet's most iconic and valuable companies, with an estimated annual package worth more than $25 million.

There is no question that humble people like Angela Ahrendts are objectively more successful, in part because their focus on other people makes them more liked and respected. Because they work hard and don't take things for granted. Because they admit when they don't have the answers. Because they are willing to learn from others versus stubbornly clinging to their views. As a result, people on teams with humble leaders are more engaged, more satisfied with their jobs, and less likely to leave. This is true particularly for senior leaders, where narcissism is especially dangerous if they cannot learn to temper it.

Yet the virtue of humility is often the exception rather than the rule in our Cult of Self society—both in the world of business and outside it. I see three reasons for the sad state of affairs. First, people often confuse humility with low self-worth, and thus label it as undesirable, even though the opposite is true—because it means appreciating our weaknesses and keeping our successes in perspective, humility is actually a necessary ingredient for self-awareness. The second reason humility is in short supply is that to gain it, we must tame the powerful beast at the epicenter of the Cult of Self: our ego. Finally, humility requires accepting a certain degree of imperfection, and most goal-oriented, Type A people rarely give themselves the permission to do so. (For a quick assessment to determine your level of humility, take a look at appendix I.)

But does humility mean that we should hate ourselves for our inevitable faults? Or that we should constantly harp on our weaknesses to avoid getting a big head? Thankfully, the alternative to boundless self-esteem doesn't have to be self-loathing but rather *self-acceptance*—our third approach to fighting the Cult of Self. Where self-esteem means thinking you're amazing regardless of the objective reality, self-acceptance (also called self-compassion by some researchers) means **understanding our objective reality and choosing to like ourselves anyway.** So instead of trying to be perfect—or delusionally believing they are—self-accepting people understand and forgive themselves for their imperfections.

Encouragingly, self-acceptance delivers all of the advertised benefits of self-esteem with few of the costs. Though the two are identical predictors of happiness and optimism, only people high in self-acceptance hold positive views of themselves that aren't dependent on external validation (that is, they don't need excessive praise, or hundreds of

Facebook "likes," or metaphorical gold stars to feel good about themselves and their contributions).

And self-acceptance isn't just a good idea in theory—it has very real benefits for our success and well-being. In one study, Kristin Kneff and her colleagues asked job-market-bound undergraduates to participate in a mock interview for a job they "really, really want[ed]." When the interviewer asked the students to describe their greatest weakness, those high in self-acceptance reported feeling significantly less nervous and self-conscious afterward—had it been an actual job interview, they likely would have performed much better as a result.

So how can you increase your self-acceptance? One step you can take is to **better monitor your inner monologue.** Organizational psychologist Steven Rogelberg and his colleagues showed how helpful self-accepting self-talk can be in a study of senior executives attending a weeklong leadership program. At the end of the week, each participant wrote a letter to their future self about the lessons they learned and the changes they wanted to make. The researchers coded each letter as either self-accepting (which they called "constructive") or self-critical. The executives who used self-accepting language were more effective and less stressed than the self-critical ones (and fascinatingly, the self-critical leaders were also less creative).

We'll revisit this idea in the next chapter when we talk about recognizing and stopping rumination, but for now, especially if you're feeling bad about yourself—guilty, fearful, upset, unable to cope—take notice of whether you're being self-critical ("There I go forgetting to set my alarm! What is wrong with me? Why can't I do the most basic things, like be on time?") or self-accepting ("That was a mistake—but I'm only human and these things happen"). A helpful question to ask can sometimes be, "Would I say what I just said to myself to someone whom I like and respect?"*

---

* If you're interested in learning more methods of increasing your self-acceptance, I strongly encourage you to visit Kristin Kneff's website: http://self-compassion.org/category/exercises/.

Making the decision to humbly but compassionately accept ourselves takes courage. As one of our unicorns, an architect by training who is now a global technology director, explains, "The problem is not being aware of yourself but loving the person you find out you are." Can this process be uncomfortable? Sometimes. But often, discomfort means you're making progress. Another unicorn, a mid-career marketing manager for a consumer products company, put it this way: "The more committed you are to building self-awareness, the more empathy and grace you learn to extend to yourself."

There are few better examples of humility and self-acceptance than unicorn George Washington's farewell address, arguably one of the most revered presidential speeches in modern history. As he is saying goodbye to the country he helped build in the twilight of his life, he notes that "I am unconscious of intentional error, [but] I am nevertheless too sensible of my defects not to think it probable that I may have committed many." He goes on to ask American citizens to extend him the same grace he's giving to himself: "I shall also carry with me the hope that my country will never cease to view [them] with indulgence and that . . . the faults of my incompetent abilities will be consigned to oblivion, as myself must soon be to the mansions of rest."

We've now explored the often unseen obstacles to self-insight—both the blindspots that keep us from seeing ourselves clearly and the social forces that feed the beast of delusion. Now we can start learning to improve it. As you're about to learn, this requires us to abandon many of our preexisting notions about what it really means to be self-aware. So in the coming chapter, we'll debunk some of the most common follies and misconceptions about internal self-awareness and learn what we should do instead.

Part Two

◆

Internal Self-Awareness:

Myths

and

Truths

THINKING ISN'T KNOWING

The Four Follies of Introspection

Why should we not calmly and patiently review our own thoughts, and thoroughly examine and see what these appearances in us really are?

—PLATO

It was a Tuesday evening around 11 p.m. Holed up in my dark office and lit only by the glare of my computer monitor, I sat staring at a set of freshly analyzed data. To say that I was perplexed would be an understatement. A few weeks earlier, my team and I had run a study looking at the relationship between self-reflection and outcomes like happiness, stress, and job satisfaction. I was confident that the results would yield few surprises. Naturally, people who spent time and energy examining themselves would have a clearer understanding of themselves.

But to my utter astonishment, our data told the exact opposite story. (In fact, when I first saw them, I thought we'd done the analyses wrong.) The results revealed that people who scored high on self-reflection were *more* stressed, depressed, and anxious, less satisfied with their jobs and relationships, more self-absorbed, and felt less in control of their lives—and to boot, these negative consequences increased *the more they reflected*! What on earth was going on!?

Though I didn't know it at the time, I'd just stumbled upon a shocking myth about self-awareness—one that researchers were only beginning to understand. A few years earlier, when University of Sydney coaching psychologist Anthony Grant was examining the same phenomenon, he discovered that people who possess greater insight—which he defines as an intuitive understanding of ourselves—enjoy stronger relationships, a clearer sense of purpose, and greater well-being, self-acceptance, and happiness. Other similar studies have shown that people high in insight feel more in control of their lives, show more dramatic personal growth, enjoy better relationships, and feel calmer and more content. So far so good, right?

But Grant also found that there was no relationship between introspection and insight. The act of **_thinking_ about ourselves wasn't correlated with _knowing_ ourselves**. In fact, in a few cases, he found the opposite: the more time the participants spent in introspection, the *less* self-knowledge they had (yes, you read that right). In other words, we can spend endless amounts of time in self-reflection but emerge with no more self-insight than when we started.

This capacity for self-examination is uniquely human. Though chimpanzees, dolphins, elephants, and even pigeons can recognize their images in a mirror, human beings are the only species with the capacity for **introspection**—that is, the ability to **consciously examine our thoughts, feelings, motives, and behaviors.**[*] For thousands of years, introspection was seen as a beneficial, error-free activity. In the seventeenth century, for instance, philosopher Rene Descartes argued that the only knowledge of any value emerged from examining ourselves. In the early twentieth century, pioneering psychologist Wilhelm Wundt used introspection as a central component of his research on perception and consciousness. And in a more modern albeit less scientific example, a post-takeout-dinner fortune cookie recently advised me: "Turn your thoughts within. Find yourself."

Fortune-cookie wisdom aside, introspection is arguably the most universally hailed path to self-awareness—or at least internal self-awareness, which is the focus of this chapter. After all, what better way is there to increase our self-knowledge than to look inward; to delve deeply into our experiences and emotions; to understand why we are

---

[*] I use the word "introspection" synonymously with "self-reflection" or "self-examination."

the way we are? We might be trying to understand our feelings (*Why am I so upset after that meeting?*), questioning our beliefs (*Do I really believe what I think I believe?*), figuring out our future (*What career would make me truly happy?*), or trying to explain a negative outcome or pattern (*Why do I beat myself up so much for minor mistakes?*).

But my study results—along with Grant's and others—clearly show that this kind of self-reflection doesn't help us become more self-aware. And when I decided to dive head-first into the literature on introspection, I learned that what I'd uncovered was just the tip of the iceberg. One study, for example, examined the coping style and subsequent adjustment of men who had just lost a partner to AIDS. Those who engaged in introspection (such as reflecting on how they would deal with life without their partner) had higher morale in the month following their loss, but were more depressed one year later. Another study of more than 14,000 university students showed that introspection was associated with poorer well-being. Still other research suggests that self-analyzers tend to have more anxiety, less positive social experiences, and more negative attitudes about themselves.

To help understand why, let's look at Karen, a 37-year-old real estate agent. Despite having a successful career, Karen has struggled in her personal life. When she was just 19, she fell in love with a musician whom she married just two weeks later. But one short year into their marriage, her husband abruptly left her. Eventually, Karen remarried, this time to another real estate professional whom she'd met through work. And though her second marriage lasted longer than her first, it also ended in divorce, leaving her wondering where she had gone wrong.

As she carefully examines her life, Karen keeps coming back to what she sees as the central trauma of her childhood: at just one week old, her birth parents put her up for adoption. Though she cherishes her adopted parents, Karen has never really gotten over these feelings of abandonment. Why, she asks herself over and over, did her birth parents give her up? After untold hours of reflection, Karen has come to believe that all of her current problems—in relationships and life—can be traced back to her birth parents' rejection. With this nugget in hand, Karen concludes that her relationship issues are a product of her history and thus all but inevitable.

Just like Karen, most people believe that the answers to our inner mysteries lie deep within us, and that it's our job to uncover them—either on our own or with the help of a therapist or loved one. Yet as my research revealed, **the assumption that introspection begets self-awareness is a myth.** In truth, it can cloud and confuse our self-perceptions, unleashing a whole host of unintended consequences. Unquestionably, Karen approached her introspective exercise with the earnest goal of better understanding herself. But without her realizing it, the process became what self-awareness researcher Timothy Wilson calls "disruptive." Continually asking herself why her birth parents gave her up is the wrong question: not only is it distracting, it surfaces unproductive and upsetting emotions that won't help Karen move forward in a healthy way.

Introspection can also lull us into a false sense of certainty that we have identified the real issue, as it did for Karen. But according to Buddhist scholar Tirthang Tulku, we can't always trust what we see when we look inward. Our "belief in this image," he notes, "draws us away from the true qualities of our nature . . . [and] prevents us from seeing ourselves clearly." He uses an apt analogy: when we introspect, our response is similar to a hungry cat watching mice. In other words, we eagerly pounce on whatever "insights" we find without questioning their validity or value. And even though they might *feel* helpful, on their own they're unlikely to actually help us improve our internal self-awareness.

Now if you're someone who values introspection—perhaps you have a therapist, or you enjoy taking long, reflective walks, or you simply take pride in being in touch with yourself—these findings might be concerning. But we need not despair. **The problem with introspection, it turns out, isn't that it's categorically ineffective, but that many people are doing it completely wrong.** In this chapter, I'll overturn the four biggest myths, or follies, of this practice, exposing why each doesn't work the way we think it does and how approaching introspection a bit differently can yield deeper insight about who we are.

Folly #1: The Myth of the Padlocked Basement (or Why We Can't Excavate Our Unconscious)

Betty Draper enters her psychoanalyst's office, removes her scarf and coat, and carefully collapses onto a black leather couch. Without a word, the psychoanalyst solemnly sinks into an armchair behind her, notepad in hand. Betty sighs deeply, pauses for a moment, and begins to reflect on her feelings about the upcoming Thanksgiving holiday and how stressful it is for her. Conveniently out of Betty's sight, her therapist stares at his notepad without interjecting, save for a few utterances of "uh-huh" throughout her soliloquy.

"This has helped," Betty confidently states at the conclusion of her session. But has it, really? This scene, set in 1961, is from Season 1 of the television show *Mad Men*. Betty has sought psychoanalysis to deal with her unrelenting feelings of anxiety. Yet months into her treatment, she fails to see any improvement and her husband, Don, begins to grow impatient about Betty's progress. "It's a process," the analyst reassures him, "you've got to trust the process."

The father of psychoanalysis, Sigmund Freud, would have likely told Don Draper the same thing. Underpinning his famous theory, which he developed in 1896 and practiced for the remaining 40 years of his career, was the idea that there exists a hidden part of the human psyche lurking below our consciousness—one that cleverly represses important information about ourselves. It was the psychoanalyst's job to excavate these sometimes painful insights through deep and focused analysis, which could often take many years. (In Betty Draper's case, she may have been confined to her therapist's couch for the next decade had she not learned that he was reporting their conversations back to her husband—an ethical no-no, even back then.) And as you're about to see, whether or not you're in therapy, Freud's psychoanalytic approach created arguably the strongest, most persistent myth of internal self-awareness.

While Freud's theories were mostly met with respect and reverence in the twentieth century, the twenty-first has not been so kind. Psychologist Todd Dufresne, for example, didn't hedge his bets about

Freud when he concluded that "no other notable figure in history was so fantastically wrong about nearly every important thing he had to say." Freud has been appropriately criticized for failing to scientifically test his approach, with some even accusing him of unethical behavior, like falsifying patient files to fit more neatly into his theories. Many contend that his methods were ineffective at best, and that he may have actually worsened some of his patients' mental health. Take the famous case of "The Wolfman," Sergius Pankejeff, whom Freud supposedly cured of his crippling anxiety and depression. Unfortunately, Pankejeff didn't share Freud's sentiments, enduring psychoanalysis for another 60 years and calling the psychoanalyst's impact on his life a "catastrophe."

And while much of Freud's work has been largely discredited, his enduring influence on our assumptions about introspection simply cannot be overstated. Most people still believe in the now-debunked promise that we can extract self-insight through deep psychological excavation—whether it's through therapy or any other dedicated approach to self-examination.* Though Freud was correct in identifying the existence of the unconscious, he completely missed the boat on how it worked. Specifically, where Freud believed that our unconscious thoughts, motives, feelings, and behaviors could be accessed through psychoanalysis, research has unequivocally shown that we *can't* uncover them, no matter how hard we try. It's as though our unconscious were trapped in a basement behind a padlocked door, and Freud believed he'd found the key. But modern scientists have shown that there actually *is* no key (not unlike the spoon that wasn't in *The Matrix*). **Our subconscious, in other words, is less like a padlocked door and more like a hermetically sealed vault.**

But if Freud's techniques don't produce insight, is this an indictment of all attempts to excavate our unconscious—most notably

---

* To be fair, psychoanalysis has evolved, and many twenty-first-century approaches now work to give clients a more integrated view of themselves versus trying to open the padlocked basement door. This actually resembles the Life Story approach we'll learn about in chapter 6.

therapy—as a means to do it?* Certainly, therapy serves many empirically supported purposes, like helping spouses and families better understand one another and treating disorders like depression and anxiety. But some findings should give us pause in assuming that it universally improves self-insight. First, placebo effects may explain up to half of therapy's efficacy—in other words, just *thinking* that it helps us is part of what makes it help us. What's more, as counseling psychologist Jennifer Lyke points out, the most important predictor of success isn't the technique the therapist uses, but the relationship she has with her client. However, the fact that some people—including 20 percent of our unicorns—have successfully used therapy as a path to insight means we shouldn't dismiss it completely.

So the right question probably isn't "Does therapy work?" but instead "How can we approach therapy to maximize insight?"** Because it *can* help—to a certain extent, under certain conditions, and particularly if we approach it intelligently and acknowledge its potential limitations.

The first imperative is to **choose the right approach**—one that focuses less on the process of introspection and more on the outcome of insight (i.e., each of the Seven Pillars, like our values, reactions, patterns, etc.). "The danger of too much introspection in therapy," Dr. Lara Fielding, a Los Angeles–based clinical psychologist, says, "is that we spin a story that gets us stuck." In other words, rather than getting wrapped up in how broken we are, we should be focusing on what we can learn and how to move forward. One such approach is Cognitive Behavioral Therapy, or CBT. Fielding, who specializes in CBT, explains that the goal is to use "skillful self-reflection" to unearth our unproductive thinking and behavior patterns so we can make better choices in the future. In the case of Karen, for example, this approach

---

* An important note here: when I refer to therapy, this does not include the practice of leadership and executive coaching, which is more related to the solutions-focused approach that we'll talk about in chapter 6.
** This is also assuming that you're seeking treatment for more everyday issues and general insight, as opposed to a more significant issue like abuse, depression, anxiety, etc.

might help her recognize the residual trauma from her adoption and turn her focus to loosening her grip on it, changing the patterns of behavior that aren't serving her, and moving forward with understanding and purpose.

Another tip is to **adopt a flexible mindset**, which is applicable both within and outside the confines of a therapist's office. A flexible mindset means remaining open to several truths and explanations, rather than seeking, as Freud often did, one root cause to explain a broad range of feelings and behaviors. This involves letting go of a desire for something that Turkish psychologist Omer Simsek calls the *need for absolute truth*. Unquestionably, a common motivation for introspection (or even to buy a book like this one) is to finally figure ourselves out, once and for all.

Yet paradoxically, the search for this kind of rigid and unequivocal certainty about ourselves is the enemy of internal self-awareness. Why? It blinds us to the many nuances in how we think, feel, behave, and interact with the world around us. Simsek observes that it can "hinder the search for, or creation of, alternative viewpoints to the problems [we] experience [and therefore] can undermine the usefulness of . . . self-reflection." Not only does a quest for absolute truth result in less insight, it can have unintended consequences such as depression, anxiety, and rumination (which we'll return to shortly). And, counterintuitively, my research shows that when self-aware people let go of this need, the more self-aware they become, whether or not they seek therapy. (For a quick diagnostic of your need for absolute truth, see appendix J.)

So what, then, is the role of therapy in internal self-awareness? It is probably best to see it as a tool to seek a new perspective and help us explore our own. As one unicorn put it, a therapist's value is in "holding a mirror to our thoughts, feelings and behaviors." More broadly, introspection should be a process of open and curious exploration rather than a search for definitive answers. Kelsey, a middle school science teacher and unicorn we'll meet later in the book, likens the quest for self-knowledge to space exploration: "There is so little we know, but that's what makes it so exciting." The bottom line is that it's virtually impossible to find singular causes for anything in our complicated world, let alone our own messy thoughts, emotions, and behaviors, but letting go of this need helps set the stage for self-awareness.

Folly #2: Why Not Ask Why?

Think about your favorite movie, book, or TV show. If I asked you to describe why you like it, what would you say? At first, it might be difficult to articulate. *I don't know*—The Great Gatsby *is just a really good book.* But after some thought, you'd probably come up with a few reasons. *The characters are interesting. Fitzgerald's prose is crisp and smart. And I've always really liked Long Island.* If I asked how confident you were about those reasons, you'd likely say you were pretty sure. But you'd likely be as wrong as you were confident. Though most of us think we're a credible authority on our thoughts, feelings, and behavior, there is a stunning amount of evidence showing that we're often remarkably mistaken.

In one study that's equal parts hilarious and enlightening, a pair of Harvard Business School professors showed male college students different issues of a sports magazine. They varied the number of sports covered, the number of feature articles, and the theme of the issue, which was either a "top ten athletes" ranking or photos of women in swimsuits. For half the participants, the swimsuit issue covered more sports, and for the other half, it contained more feature articles. The researchers then asked their eager subjects which magazine they preferred and to rank the criteria used to make their choice (e.g., number of sports, feature articles, etc.). In the category of "findings that surprised absolutely no one," the male students overwhelmingly preferred the swimsuit issue.

But when asked to explain why, something interesting happened: they inflated the importance of the magazine's other attributes— regardless of what they were—to justify their (clearly hormonal) preference. If their swimsuit issue covered more sports, they listed that as the reason; the same thing happened for the issue with more feature articles. And lest we label this tendency to rationalize our preferences as hilarious but innocuous, similar findings have emerged in high-stakes situations, like the tendency to hire men over women for stereo-typically male jobs.

Yet when it comes to preferring a swimsuit magazine or hiring a man over a woman, isn't it possible that we *know* the real reason for our behavior but just don't want to admit it to others? For the answer, let's turn to one of the most famous studies in psychology. Even if you've read about it before, it's instructive in showing just how clueless we are about why we behave the way we do. In the 1970s, psychologists Donald Dutton and Arthur Aron conducted a creative study in the Capilano River Regional Park in Vancouver, Canada. Their subjects were tourists visiting the park who had just crossed one of two bridges. The first was sturdy and not particularly scary-looking. The second was a suspension bridge hovering 240 feet in the air. Imagine how you would feel walking across this:

Dutton and Aron hired an attractive woman to stand at the end of each bridge and invite male passersby to take a short survey, after which she would give them her phone number in case they "wanted to talk further." In reality, they wanted to see how many men would call to ask her out after the study. The idea was that those crossing the suspension bridge would experience a rush of excitement and attribute it to the woman, making them more likely to call her. And that's exactly what happened. Versus only 12 percent of the sturdy-bridge crossers, 50 percent of the men who crossed the suspension bridge picked up the phone.

But when Dutton and Aron asked the men *why* they called, do you think anyone said, "Walking across the rickety suspension bridge led to a state of autonomic arousal, but rather than attributing the cause of my increased heart rate, dry mouth, and sweaty palms to a fear of plunging to my death, I misattributed them to the woman I saw at the end of it"? Of course not. Their comments were more like, "I called her because she was pretty." Obviously, the female confederate looked the same in both the conditions, so that can't be the whole story. More likely, it was simply the most reasonable and logical explanation, so the men latched on to it without any further questioning. As Ben Franklin once said, "so convenient a thing it is to be a reasonable creature, since it enables one to find or make a reason for everything one has a mind to do."

The bottom line is that when we **ask why**, that is, **examine the causes of our thoughts, feelings, and behaviors**, we are generally searching for the easiest and most plausible answer. Sadly, though, once we have found one, we generally stop looking—despite having no way of knowing whether our answer is right or wrong. Sometimes this is a result of something called "confirmation bias," which can prompt us to invent reasons that confirm our existing beliefs—and since our answers reflect how we see ourselves, we accept them as true. If I see myself as literary, I'll list Fitzgerald's crisp prose as the reason why I love *The Great Gatsby*, or if I fancy myself an astute study of the human psyche, I might cite the complexity of his characters. This is just one example of how asking "why" can simultaneously muddy the waters while giving us an inflated sense of confidence in our newfound "insight."

Asking why can also cause our often lazy brains to mislead us. Let's say that I ask you to list all the reasons why your relationship is going the way it is. And let's say that last night, your spouse stayed out at the office happy hour later than planned, leaving you alone to cook dinner for your visiting, and rather dull, in-laws. Because of something called the "recency effect," this could be your most salient thought about your relationship—so when you're asked why the relationship is going the way it is, your brain might misdirect you to the first available explanation—*he doesn't spend enough time at home and leaves me to deal with his parents*—even though that behavior is actually rare and out of character. Likewise, if instead of leaving you alone with your in-laws, your otherwise unavailable spouse had surprised you with a weekend getaway, your brain might mislead you to think your relationship is in better shape than it really is.

Asking why can also reduce the quality of our decisions. In one study, researchers asked self-described basketball experts to predict the outcomes of national tournament basketball games. Half analyzed the reasons for their predictions prior to making them, and half were simply asked to make their predictions. Astonishingly, those who questioned their choices predicted far fewer winners than those who didn't—once they started to overthink things, their expertise went out the window. Other investigations have shown that asking why reduces our satisfaction with the choices we make.

A final reason that makes asking why disruptive is the negative impact it has on our overall mental health. In one study, after British university students failed what they were told was an intelligence test, they were asked to write about *why* they felt the way they did. Compared to a control group, they were more depressed immediately afterward, and even 12 hours later. Here, asking why caused the participants to fixate on their problems and place blame instead of moving forward in a healthy and productive way.

So if asking why doesn't help us better understand our true thoughts and emotions, what *should* we ask? A study by psychologists J. Gregory Hixon and William Swann provides a shockingly simple answer. After telling a group of undergraduates that two raters would be evaluating their personality based on a test of "sociability, likeability and interestingness" that they'd taken earlier in the semester, the researchers asked the students to judge the accuracy of their results (which were actually exactly the same for everyone: one rater gave a positive evaluation and the other gave a negative one). Before making their accuracy judgments, some participants were given time to think about *why* they were the kind of person they were and others were asked to think about *what* kind of person they were.

The "why" students, it turned out, were resistant to the negative evaluation: instead of accepting or even considering it, they spent their time "rationaliz[ing], justify[ing], and explain[ing] [it] away." The "what" students, on the other hand, were more receptive to that same new data, and to the notion that it could help them better understand themselves. The lesson here is that asking "what" keeps us open to discovering new information about ourselves, even if that information is negative or in conflict with our existing beliefs. Asking "why" has an essentially opposite effect.

Given all of this, it makes sense that our unicorns reported asking "what" often and "why" rarely. In fact, when we analyzed the transcripts of our interviews, the word "why" appeared less than 150 times, but the word "what" appeared more than 1,000 times! One unicorn, a 42-year-old mother who bravely walked away from a career as a lawyer when she finally realized that there was no joy for her in that path, explained it well:

> If you ask why, you're putting yourself into a victim mentality. People end up in therapy forever for that. When I feel anything other than peace, I say "What's going on?" "What am I feeling?" "What is the dialogue inside my head?" "What's another way to see this situation?" "What can I do to respond better?"

So when it comes to internal self-awareness, a simple tool that can have a rather dramatic impact is one I call **What Not Why**. Let's look at an example of it in action. Recently, I was talking with my good friend Dan. Having run his own business for many years, Dan is living the good life: he makes tons of money, lives in a huge house, and works from home a few hours a week when he isn't traveling to exotic destinations. Which is why I was stunned to hear him say, "I am so unhappy. I think I need to sell my company. But I don't know what else I want to do."

This situation presented an opportunity: with geeky glee, I asked Dan if I could practice my new tool on him. He agreed. When I first inquired "Why do you want to change what you're doing?," Dan let out a huge, hopeless sigh and started rattling off all of his personal shortcomings: "I'm bored too easily. I've gotten cynical. I don't know if I'm making any difference in the world." The "why" question had the effect I'd predicted: not only did it fail to produce useful insight, but Dan became, if anything, more confused when he tried to figure out why the spark had disappeared. So I quickly changed course: "*What* do you dislike about what you're doing?" He thought for a moment. "I dislike sitting in front of my computer and remotely leading a company—and don't even get me started on the time zones. I just feel burnt out and disconnected."

"Okay, that's helpful," I replied. "What *do* you like?" Without hesitation, Dan replied, "Speaking. I really like speaking." He told me that when he was in front of an audience, he could make an immediate impact. I knew the feeling, and could see the spark right away. This realization made Dan immediately more focused and clear-headed—he began to think about whether he could adapt his current role to spend more time sharing his message.

I could have asked Dan *why* questions for hours and he'd likely have ended the conversation with no more insight, and probably in a much worse mood. But less than five minutes of *what* questions had drawn out a high-value discovery and a potential solution to his problem. Dan's experience is illustrative: *Why* questions draw us to our limitations; *what* questions help us see our potential. *Why* questions stir up negative emotions; *what* questions keep us curious. *Why* questions trap us in our past; *what* questions help us create a better future.

Indeed, **making the transition from *why* to *what* can be the difference between victimhood and growth.** When Paul, the executive, unicorn, and neighborhood association activist we met earlier, moved back to the United States after a stint in Germany, he made the decision to purchase a small ceramics manufacturing company. Despite its aging equipment, his due diligence suggested that this was a little company that could: it had weathered the recession and boasted a stable of tenured employees. But right out of the gate, Paul's employees resisted the improvements he began to make, creating delays that hurt the company's already bleeding balance sheet. He quickly learned that he'd been too optimistic with both his budgets and his cash reserves.

At this point, Paul was tempted to go down the dangerous road of *why*. Why wasn't he able to turn things around? Why didn't he do a better job with his financial projections? Why wouldn't his employees listen to him? But he knew that these questions weren't productive. So instead, he asked himself, *what now?* Paul explored three equally unattractive options: he could burn through his savings, he could take out a massive loan, or he could close the business. He chose to close the business. And here he asked *what* again. *What do I need to do to close up shop? What can I do to lessen the impact on my customers? What can I do to realize the maximum value of the business?*

Armed with these insights, Paul created a plan and began to execute it. Because he stayed clear-headed, he was even able to find creative ways to do good for others while winding things down; for example, when he had more unfinished ceramics products than buyers, he offered the inventory to nearby paint-your-own ceramics shops, who were downright overjoyed at the windfall. He did the same thing with his equipment, donating much of it to schools and non-profits. Paul turned what could have been a shattering earthquake event into a chance to show what he was made of.

In addition to helping us gain insight to our problems, the What Not Why tool can also be used to help us better understand and manage our emotions. Seventeenth-century philosopher Benedict de Spinoza observed that "an emotion, which is a passion, ceases to be a passion as soon as we form a clear and distinct idea thereof. [The emotion] becomes more under our control, and the mind is less passive in respect to it."

Let's say you're in a terrible mood after work one day. We already know that asking *Why do I feel this way?* should come with a warning label. It's likely to elicit such unhelpful answers as *because I hate*

Mondays! or *because I'm just a negative person!* What if you instead asked *What am I feeling right now?* Perhaps you'd realize that you're overwhelmed at work, exhausted, and hungry. Rather than blindly reacting to these feelings, you take a step back, decide to fix yourself dinner, call a friend for some advice about how to manage your work stress, and commit to an early bedtime.

Asking *what* instead of *why* forces us **to name our emotions,** a process that a strong body of research has shown to be effective. Evidence shows that the simple act of translating our emotions into language—versus simply experiencing them—can stop our brains from activating our amygdala, the fight-or-flight command center, and this in turn helps us stay in control. If this sounds too simple to be true, try naming your feelings for a week and see what you notice.

All this being said, however, the notion of asking *what* instead of *why* may still be difficult for some people to digest, especially if you've been to business school and/or are trained in techniques like root-cause analysis. In his book *How the Mighty Fall,* business author Jim Collins even says that when companies get wrapped up in *what* they are and don't understand *why* they got that way, they risk becoming extinct. This highlights an important exception to the rule: when navigating business challenges or solving problems in your team or your organization, asking why is critical. For example, if an employee drops the ball on an important client project, not exploring why it happened means you risk recurrences of the problem. Or if a new product fails, you need to know the reason to ensure that products are better in the future. A good rule of thumb, then, is that **why questions are generally better to help us understand our environment and *what* questions are generally better to help us understand ourselves.**

Folly #3: Keeping a Journal

Charley Kempthorne has been keeping a journal for more than 50 years. Every morning before the sun is in the sky, the professor-turned-painter carefully types out at least 1,000 words reflecting on his past, his beliefs, his family, even his shortcomings. (His long-held habit of longhand writing was put to bed in the 1980s when he impulse-purchased a Broth Word Processor during a trip to Sears.) The prolific fruits of his labor reside in an impressive storage facility in Manhattan, Kansas, where his estimated ten million words are printed, bound, and filed. This project, Kempthorne says, is an end in itself: "It helps me understand my life . . . or maybe," he hedges, "it just makes me feel better and get [the day] started in a better mood." But Kempthorne (along with any journaling junkie) might be disappointed to learn that his enduring exercise may not have actually improved his self-awareness.

At this point, you're probably convinced that I've gone completely off the deep end. *Everyone knows,* you might be thinking, *that journaling is one of the most effective ways to get in touch with our inner self!* However, a growing body of research suggests that introspection via journaling has some surprising traps that can suck the insight right out of the experience. My own research, for example, has shown that people who keep journals generally have no more internal (or external) self-awareness than those who don't, with one small but important exception that I'll reveal in a moment. In another study, students who reported keeping diaries showed *more* self-reflection but *less* insight—and to boot, the journalers were more anxious.

And yet, 35 percent of our unicorns reported keeping a journal. How can we make sense of these peculiar and seemingly contradictory findings? **The resolution lies not in questioning whether journaling is the right thing to do, but instead discovering how to *do journaling right*.**

Psychologist James Pennebaker's decades-long research program on something he calls **expressive writing** provides powerful direction in finding the answer. It involves writing, for 20 to 30 minutes at a time, our "deepest thoughts and feelings about issues that have made a big impact on [our] lives." In the 30-plus years during which Pennebaker has been guiding people through this exercise, he has found that it helps virtually everyone who's experienced a significant challenge. Even though some people find writing about their struggles to be distressing in the short term, nearly all see longer-term improvements in their mood and well-being.

Pennebaker and his colleagues have shown that people who engage in expressive writing have better memories, higher grade point averages, less absenteeism from work, and quicker re-employment after job loss. Expressive writing has even been shown to help collegiate tennis players improve their games. And fascinatingly, the physical benefits can be as dramatic as the psychological ones. In one study, undergraduates who completed Pennebaker's journaling exercise for just four days had stronger immune systems and fewer doctor's visits than a control group almost two months later.

Intuitively, one might think that the more we study positive events in our journal entries, the more psychological benefits we'll reap from the experience. But this too is a myth. In one study, participants wrote about one of their happiest times for eight minutes a day over the course of three days. Some were told to extensively analyze the event and others were instructed to simply relive it. The analyzers showed less personal growth, self-acceptance, and well-being than those who relived it. But why was this the case? As G. K. Chesterton perceptively observed, "Happiness is a mystery like religion, and should never be rationalized"—that is, by examining positive moments too closely, we suck the joy right out of them. Instead, if we simply focus on reliving our happy memories, it's relatively easy to avoid this trap. Therefore, the first take-home in seeking insight from journaling is to **explore the negative and not overthink the positive**.

When we explore our negative events through expressive writing, we'll generally get the most payoff when we see it as an opportunity for learning and growth. Pennebaker notes that journalers "who talk about things over and over in the same ways aren't getting any better. There has to be growth, change, or closure in the way they view their experiences." Mr. Kempthorne, for example, smartly evolved his approach. His self-described "pompous" early entries focused too intensely on introspection; now, he says, he writes "short narrative scenes," which help him make better sense of his feelings and experiences. Those who benefit most from expressive writing tend to start with incoherent, disorganized perceptions of their problems and finish with a coherent, meaningful narrative (we'll come back to this idea in the next chapter).* In that way, journaling is similar to therapy: if used as a means of exploration—of holding up a mirror—it can help us make sense of the past and the present and move forward more productively in the future.

Another trap journalers can fall prey to is using the activity solely as an outlet for discharging emotions. Interestingly, the myriad benefits of expressive writing only emerge when we write about both the factual *and* the emotional aspects of the events we're describing—neither on its own is effective in producing insight. Logically, this makes sense: if we don't explore our emotions, we're not fully processing the experience, and if we don't explore the facts, we risk getting sucked into an unproductive spiral. True insight only happens when we **process both our thoughts and our feelings**.

But we also need to guard against turning journaling into an exercise in self-absorption. Remember that our unicorns spent more time—on social media and in face-to-face interactions—focused on things other than themselves. The same can be said for the practice of journaling. Earlier, I mentioned that the journalers in our study were no more internally self-aware than non-journalers in every area but one: where many people see journaling as an opportunity to explore their inner workings, the truly self-aware know it can also help them understand their impact on others. Accordingly, our unicorns who journaled often reported exploring other people's perspectives in their entries. One told us a story in which she and a friend had a difficult talk, which ended in her friend crying for reasons she didn't understand. She waited a while, and when she was ready, she wrote about the conversation from her friend's point of view. The exercise gave her immediate insight that helped her understand her friend's reaction and gain a more objective perspective on her own.

The final thing to keep in mind about journaling should be welcome

---

* And when journalers use more causal and insight-related words like "infer," "reason," "understanding," and "realize" to make sense of negative events, the benefits of journaling increase exponentially.

news to everyone but Mr. Kempthorne. To ensure maximum benefits, it's probably best that you **don't write every day**. It's true: Pennebaker and his colleagues have shown that writing every few days is better than writing for many days in a row. "I'm not even convinced," Pennebaker says, "that people should write about a horrible event for more than a couple of weeks. You risk getting into a sort of navel gazing or cycle of self-pity. But standing back every now and then and evaluating where you are in life is really important." And indeed, few unicorns reported writing in their journals every day. Jeff, the architect-turned-entrepreneur we met a few chapters back, told us that he journals only when he's trying to make a difficult decision. Like other unicorns, he uses the process to make sense of his life on a broader level rather than a daily means of psychological excavation.

Of course, if you're a prolific journaler, the right approach may require some restraint. But with a little self-discipline, you can easily train yourself to write less and learn more. If you currently write daily, start by limiting yourself to every other day, then every third day, then try easing into just once a week. Mark the journal days in your calendar, and keep a few Post-it notes handy to jog your memory about what topics you want to tackle.

Folly #4: The Evil Twin of Introspection

If one of the worst things that ever happened to Marcia Donziger was being diagnosed with Stage III ovarian cancer when she was just 27, one of the best was the overwhelming love and kindness she received from her family and friends as she recovered from surgery and chemotherapy. And while Marcia couldn't have been more grateful for that support, she learned that with such love and attention came a surprising downside. Marcia felt pressure to personally thank everyone for their kindness and obligated to keep them all updated. She was exhausted from making phone call after phone call, saying the same thing over and over, when all she really wanted to do was rest. Thankfully, Marcia made a full recovery. But she never forgot the unexpected burdens she faced in keeping her loved ones informed.

A few years later, when a close friend of Marcia's was also diagnosed with cancer, her friend created a simple but effective website to communicate with friends and family. And it got Marcia thinking. What if every cancer patient had access to a free, customized service to post updates, receive messages, access resources, and organize their treatment—all in one place? Not only would such a service help patients' friends and family rally around them, it would free up their time and energy to heal.

Marcia turned her idea into reality, founding the non-profit organization MyLifeLine.org, which today boasts hundreds of thousands of registered users. She quickly learned that making a non-profit financially viable takes a serious amount of fundraising, often in the form of speeches to potential donors. Luckily, Marcia had always been excellent at talking about this deeply personal cause. That is, until one hot spring afternoon, when she was slated to speak at MyLifeLine.org's annual Kentucky Derby fundraiser. The year before, her speech had earned a thunderous standing ovation. But today, Marcia felt off her game for some reason, and her pounding migraine wasn't helping. As she stood at the podium, looking out at her 400 expectant, mint-julep-sipping guests, her mouth was dry and her mind was empty.

And if you think this is the point in the story where I tell you it was all in her head, and that her speech was in fact a stunning success, think again. It was nothing short of a disaster—she spoke too fast, flubbed her words, and at one point completely forgot what she was saying. When it was finally over, the smattering of polite applause she received felt like boos and jeers. And when Marcia mingled among the guests after her speech, no one even mentioned it. (The year before, almost everyone had congratulated her.) She felt it in the pit of her stomach: she knew she'd let the organization down.

That night, Marcia was in tears as she told her family what had happened. And for weeks, she obsessed over her public humiliation. Every morning, she'd wake up feeling embarrassed, replaying her speech—and the audience's uncomfortable reaction—over and over in her mind. Though her boyfriend kept assuring her that it hadn't been that bad, Marcia continued her endless self-flagellation.

John Milton once said that the mind "can make a heaven of hell, and a hell of heaven." At some point, I'm sure that you too have found yourself stuck in this kind of endless loop of self-scrutiny—almost everyone does. We might replay a certain conversation in our minds, beat ourselves up about something we did (or didn't do), or twist ourselves into mental knots trying to figure out why we're not the person we want to be. *How could I have embarrassed myself in front of all those people? Why am I still in this horrible relationship? Why can't I stop eating those damn cookies and finally lose this holiday weight?* And as anyone who has gotten stuck in this cycle knows, we don't ask ourselves these questions once or twice or even three times—but over and over, to the point that we can think of little else.

This single-minded fixation on our fears, shortcomings, and insecurities has a name: it's called **rumination**, and **it's introspection's evil twin**.* As you may have guessed, in addition to simply being a mental hell, rumination is also a huge barrier to insight. And just as Marcia discovered, once we fall down the rabbit hole, it's tough to claw our way out. Sometimes it even gets to the point of ruminating that we can't stop ruminating!

I believe there is a nefarious character buried deep within each of us. The Ruminator is ready at a moment's notice to second-guess our choices and remind us where we come up short. Sometimes, when this sly, stealthy creature kicks us down his evil spiral, we are fully aware that it's happening, though we feel helpless to stop it. But other times, and far more dangerously, the Ruminator tricks us into believing that we're engaging in productive self-reflection. After all, why else would we put ourselves through such mental self-flagellation if not to gain insight? In Marcia's case, for instance, it would have been easy to believe that her rumination was serving a useful purpose. If she could understand what went wrong, she'd be able to do a better job next time, right? I sometimes even hear people use the word "ruminate" as a synonym

---

* By the way, most researchers believe that rumination is different from worry; whereas rumination typically focuses on past or present events, worry focuses on our fears about the future.

for "reflect" (i.e., "that's an interesting question; let me ruminate on it for a few days"). This is why rumination is the most insidious of all the follies: not only does it effectively prevent insight, it can masquerade as productive self-reflection.* **And when it comes to self-awareness, if introspection is disruptive, rumination is disastrous.**

At this point, you may be recognizing yourself more and more in the descriptions of such behavior. We all do it, though some more than others (and by the way, you can get a read on how often you ruminate by taking the assessment in appendix K). And although we can ruminate on just about anything, research has shown that we do it most when we feel we don't measure up in an area that's especially important to us. A chronic people-pleaser might ruminate about upsetting a close friend; a workaholic might ruminate about a poor performance rating; a devoted mother might ruminate after her surly teenager tells her she's the worst mom ever.

But "normal" or not, rumination might be costing you more than you think. My own research has shown that frequent ruminators are less satisfied with their lives and relationships, feel less control over their destiny, and are generally less happy. Other research has shown that rumination is related to lower grades, impaired problem solving, worse moods, and poorer-quality sleep.

And when it comes to our mental health, rumination can be a sad, vicious cycle. For example, people who experience depression are more likely to get stuck in ruminative thought patterns, causing them to focus more on their depression and, as a result, feel even worse. Ruminators are also more stressed and anxious even in the absence of depression. In one of the largest studies on stress to date, a survey of more

---

* When we engage in "normal" self-reflection, a part of our brain called the default mode is activated. But Stanford researcher J. Paul Hamilton recently discovered that when we ruminate, another area of our brain also turns on that, among other things, is involved in processing sadness—the subgenual prefrontal cortex. The fact that both of these regions are activated when we ruminate helps explain why rumination can often masquerade as introspection, and how it blocks our brains' ability to gain insight. Though it's rather clunky, if you're ruminating, you might say, "There goes my subgenual prefrontal cortex bumming me out and preventing me from gaining insight again!"

than 32,000 people from 172 countries found that while the number and severity of negative events in people's lives were the biggest predictors of mental health problems, their rumination levels were also a significant factor in how much stress and anxiety they experienced.

Earlier we learned that introspection can be an obstacle to insight. If that's the case, rumination might as well be a 50-foot-high blockade. When we're ruminating, we're spending so much energy looking at what's wrong with us that we have no mental energy left to explore any of the pillars of insight. As one of our unicorns said, "If we spend too much time scrutinizing what's in our rearview mirror, we're certain to crash into a light post." That's why research shows that despite incessantly processing their feelings, ruminators are *less* accurate at identifying their emotions: their minds are so laser-focused on an incident, reaction, or personal weakness that they miss the larger picture.

Another reason rumination is an enemy of insight is that it's effectively an avoidance strategy. This might seem odd, given that the process involves endlessly dwelling on our problems. But in reality, when we obsess over the causes and meaning behind negative events, we keep the emotions that come with them at arm's length, which can often be even more painful for us than the act of ruminating. Indeed, there is a correlation between rumination and other avoidant coping strategies like drinking. In one study of people who had just completed a rehabilitation program for alcohol abuse, ruminators were 70 percent more likely than non-ruminators to relapse to their previous drinking levels. Ruminators have also been shown to avoid the people and situations causing them to ruminate instead of dealing with them directly.

For all these reasons, rumination clearly hurts our ability to accurately read our internal selves. But even though the process is largely an inwardly focused phenomenon, it can also hurt our *external* self-awareness. For one thing, ruminators are so busy beating themselves up that they neglect to think about how they might be showing up to others. They generally ignore or avoid feedback, lest it send them down the rabbit hole. They therefore tend not just to be poor perspective-takers, but also to be more narcissistic and self-absorbed than non-ruminators.

Now, it's tempting to assume that self-awareness unicorns are bliss-fully unencumbered by the malevolent malady of rumination. After all, they *are* unicorns, right? But even though they ruminate much less often than the rest of us, they aren't immune—only 7 percent reported never doing it. But we did find that they used two slightly different tactics.

First, unicorns were better at recognizing when the Ruminator was creeping up on them and subsequently better at stopping him in his tracks. In fact, roughly three-fourths employed specific rumination-busting strategies, which we'll discuss in a moment. Second, they had a more self-accepting attitude about rumination in general. One uni-corn, a former teacher and stay-at-home mom of four, explained that "the goal can't be rumination zero. It is a part of life. My goal is to identify it as quickly as possible, work on a strategy to get out of it, and not be upset with myself about doing it." Another unicorn (okay, it's my sister Abby, whom we'll meet in the next chapter) told us that "rumination is like a storm. It comes through, rains on everything, and then when it's done, there is blue sky. Funnily, one way I deal with rumination is to not worry about it!"

Let's circle back to Marcia's public-speaking catastrophe. What I didn't mention earlier is that Marcia is also a unicorn, and that this event was a pivotal milestone in her self-awareness journey. While Marcia was tunneling down the rumination rabbit hole, her team at MyLifeLine.org was busy tallying the amount they had raised at the event. When the number was finally in, the CEO gathered her staff in the conference room. She ominously announced, "Well, I'm going to come straight out with it." Marcia felt sick. She braced herself for the moment an actual dollar amount would be put on her failure, and in front of her entire team no less.

But instead, she heard, "This was the single most successful fund-raising event we've ever had." In that moment, Marcia had an epiph-any: while she had been obsessing about her speech, everyone else had long forgotten it—after all, they had far more important things to think about. And her less-than-awesome performance had in no way detracted from the success of the event.

Since this realization, Marcia has learned to ask herself the following question whenever she is about to fall down the rabbit hole: *Does anyone else care about this as much as I do?* When the answer is no, she tries to let it go. And in fact, **reminding ourselves that people don't generally care about our mistakes as much as we think they do** was one of our unicorns' most commonly cited rumination-busting strategies.

Another mindset that can help us combat rumination was originally discovered by child psychologists Carol Dweck and Carol Diener in the 1980s. When Dweck and Diener observed fifth-graders during a problem-solving exercise, they noticed that the children approached the task with one of two distinct mindsets. Some were more concerned with their performance (let's call them the "do-well" kids), while others placed more importance on learning and improving (the "learn-well" kids). When the children were succeeding, both groups were engaged and happy—no huge surprise there.

When the children began to fail, however, a dramatic difference emerged. The do-well kids became upset and blamed their failings on personal shortcomings (i.e., the Ruminator was out in full force). They also had various "this is stupid, I'm taking my toys and going home" reactions, like bragging about their abilities in other areas or telling the researchers they were bored. And knowing what we now know about rumination, it's not surprising that two-thirds showed a subsequent decline in their problem-solving abilities.

The learn-well children, on the other hand, reacted completely differently to their failure. In fact, they didn't see it as a failure at all. One gleefully reported, "I love a challenge" while rubbing his hands together and smacking his lips (which might also be the cutest reaction imaginable). And where the do-well kids fell into a spiral of self-loathing, the learn-well kids' self-confidence actually improved. Nearly all maintained their problem-solving abilities, with many increasing them substantially.

A *learn-well mindset*—that is, **channeling our thinking to focus on learning over performance**—is not only a great rumination-buster; it has also been shown to improve work performance in adults. In one study, for example, the mindset helped medical-supplies salespeople to persist in the face of challenges. Compared with those who had a do-well mindset, the learn-well reps had significantly stronger sales performance over a three-month period.

When things go wrong, are you a "learn-well" or a "do-well" kind of person? Do you fall down the rabbit hole, or do you pick yourself up, dust yourself off, and reattack the task? (If you're curious, I've included an assessment in appendix L to help you find out.) If you're more "do-well" than you'd prefer, there is good news: research has repeatedly shown that we have the power to change our mindset. One unicorn shared a wonderful story that illustrates how. Tim, a longtime pharmaceutical executive, had hired a high-level manager without enough due diligence. When the manager crashed and burned, Tim beat himself up about it for days. Luckily, he and his family—Tim's high school sweetheart and their two grown sons—had booked a ten-day cruise the following week.

One picture-perfect morning, Tim woke up before everyone else and decided to take a walk on the deck. But even with the fresh ocean air swirling around him, he again found himself dwelling on his mistake. Just as the Ruminator was about to hijack his day, he looked out at the ocean and realized something: *Even though I made this mistake, the world isn't going to end, and it's sure taught me not to do it again.* Then, the perfect metaphor presented itself: *I have to toss this overboard!* So he did—as a result, he was able to enjoy the rest of the week with his family, and return to work a smarter, wiser leader.

Our third rumination-buster is actually a distraction technique. Although this move—which I call **hitting pause**—feels like the last thing we should do when something is truly vexing us, it's one of the simplest rumination-busters at our disposal. Instead of replaying our self-doubt on repeat, we can walk away and do something that will take our mind off it. Research shows that the most effective distractions are those that have a fast and positive reward of some kind, like cleaning, seeing friends, or exercising. (I personally believe that few ruminative episodes can withstand a bike ride on a beautiful, sunny Colorado day.) And while I don't condone permanently running away from the hard stuff, hitting pause helps us come back to our problems later, and with a more level head. Once we get some distance, we start to see them as less upsetting and more solvable—and sometimes they cease to look like problems at all.

The fourth tool is the oddly useful method of **thought-stopping**, which is similar to hitting pause but doesn't involve actively stepping away; this pause instead takes place internally. In one study, psychiatric patients were asked to let their minds wander to whatever ruminative thought came into their mind (actual examples from the study: their teeth were decaying; they had touched vomit; they couldn't stop thinking about women's buttocks—just your average, run-of-the-mill worries). Then, their therapist yelled "Stop!" while making a sudden noise. As ridiculous as this sounds, it stopped the patients' rumination right in its tracks. If you don't have a therapist to follow you around and scream at you, it might help to picture a large stop sign, or to say to yourself *I'm not getting anything out of this, and it's time to stop these thoughts.*

Thought-stopping can be especially helpful in combating something I call **post-decision rumination** (or PDR for short). Once we've made a difficult decision, the Ruminator *loves* to taunt us with questions like "Are you sure you made the right call?" and "Do you know how disastrous it will be if you're wrong?" But by stirring up so much self-doubt, PDR can paralyze us just when we need to move forward and successfully execute our decision. As a result, it's easy to see why PDR can be especially dangerous for big decisions like selling a business unit, changing careers, or ending a marriage. So when facing a difficult decision, by all means, deliberate over it as much as you need to—weigh the pros and cons, evaluate different scenarios, seek advice. But once you make it, you have to trust it and move forward. This doesn't mean ignoring the consequences of our decisions. On the contrary, stopping PDR is what you need to do so you *can* manage them without the distraction of all that unproductive mental chatter.

Finally, allow me to introduce our last rumination-busting tool, **reality checks**, by way of an upsetting but instructive personal story. A while back, I was delivering a yearlong leadership development program for a client. Six months in, we sent out a survey to learn how people were feeling about the experience: what they liked and how we could make it better. The results were overwhelmingly positive. But thankfully, they didn't hold back on how we could improve, and we heard many productive suggestions. I was feeling pretty good, until I read this:

> My biggest learning from this program is how much money a consultant can make by presenting banal, trivial, feel-good, recycled and repackaged pop psychology and common sense concepts as innovative leadership training.

Ouch, right? My initial response was to laugh, even though I didn't actually find it the least bit funny. Then I started to feel like someone had punched me in the stomach. *Could he be right?* I began to wonder. *Has everyone else been thinking this but were too afraid to tell me?* Then came the absolute panic. *Have I been completely incompetent this whole time?!* The Ruminator had come to roost, and he wouldn't leave for weeks. I just couldn't stop replaying the comment in my mind. Whenever I met with a client or gave a speech, there it was: *Your ideas are trivial and banal. Get out of this line of work immediately. Stop embarrassing yourself.*

After weeks of mental anguish, and probably a little too late, I finally decided to call a friend who is a much better consultant than I am. "I'm sorry you had to hear that," she began after patiently listening to my story. "My first reaction is that I feel sorry for this guy. You're a phenomenal consultant, and I'd guess that his comment was more about him than it was about you." I had been so upset that this hadn't even crossed my mind. "But," she continued, "let's assume there's something productive in his feedback anyway. Do you have any objective evidence that your ideas aren't original?" (By the way, this question is another superb rumination-buster.)

Her inquiry instantly changed my mindset from *I am horrible at my job* to *Maybe there's something I can learn from this.* "Well," I ventured, "There aren't many new things under the sun when it comes to leadership, and I'm certainly not the most creative person in the world. But people tell me that one of my strengths is making fuzzy concepts accessible and actionable, not necessarily that I always tell them something about leadership they didn't already know." Then, a blinding flash of the obvious hit me. "Maybe I should just *say that* at the beginning of my programs." And ever since then, I have.

The person who wrote that nasty comment almost certainly wasn't trying to help me, but my friend's reality check helped me learn from it anyway. Almost to a person, our unicorns reported that when in the grip of rumination, one of the best things we can do is get a reality check from someone we trust. And when we do, there is usually an opportunity for both hope and learning.

You now understand the four biggest follies of introspection: that there is no key to the padlocked basement, that asking ourselves why is as pointless as it is dangerous, that journaling doesn't always increase self-knowledge, and that rumination masquerading as introspection can hurt us more than we realize. You've also learned how to carefully avoid the traps that can come along with them, as well as five rumination-busting strategies you can use right away: remembering that no one cares about our mistakes as much as we think, cultivating a learn-well mindset, hitting pause, thought-stopping, and reality checks. In the next chapter, you'll learn three more powerful and battle-tested internal self-awareness tools.

6

INTERNAL SELF-AWARENESS TOOLS THAT REALLY WORK

Few of us ever live in the present. We are forever
anticipating what is to come or remembering
what has gone.
—LOUIS L'AMOUR

After a three-hour drive from my home in Denver, my younger sister Abby and I were bumping down a narrow dirt road in the Roosevelt National Forest on our way to the Shambhala Mountain Center.

When we finally pulled into the dusty parking lot, I grouched, "I want to go home."

Abby met my sullen mood with a beaming smile. "Well, I can't wait," she said, sniffing the air. "A whole weekend with nothing to do but hang out with you and practice mindfulness in the Colorado Rockies!"

"But *I want to go home*," I repeated, this time with a dramatic whine.

"Oh God, Tasha," she said, "people come from all over the world to meditate here."

"And visit The Great Stupid." I chuckled at my own lame and oddly hostile joke.

"The Great *Stupa*," she said. "The Great Stupa of Dharmakaya." As she reached for her door handle, she solemnly stated, "I have wanted to come to a mindfulness meditation retreat for years. I am *not* going to let you ruin this for me."

As we lifted our luggage from the back of my vehicle—the sole gas guzzler in a shoal of hybrids and mud-caked Smart cars—I decided to bite my tongue and focus on the emergency Xanax I had hidden in my back pocket.

I love my sister deeply, but we are two very different souls. Abby, put simply, is the warm summer day to my raging winter blizzard. I really wasn't trying to be negative—I was just struggling to overcome my aggressive stereotypes about mindfulness and meditation. Though these days it seems as though virtually everyone in America practices it, as a hard-nosed scientist, the activity always felt a bit "woo-woo" to me (i.e., based on wild claims but lacking in scientific evidence).

Yet upon discovering that 70 percent of our unicorns practiced mindfulness in some form, I was forced to grudgingly check it out. And what better place than the Shambhala Mountain Center? Founded by Buddhist meditation master Chögyam Trungpa Rinpoche in 1971 and home to the famous 108-foot stupa built in his honor, it is, according to its website, a "contemplative refuge . . . an oasis for relaxing into our basic goodness, rediscovering a sense of balance and appreciating the sacredness of our world."

As Abby and I dragged our luggage down the long, cold path toward the registration center, we approached a gang of very attractive, very fit girls in black yoga pants. I could tell this wasn't their first meditation-retreat rodeo. They glared judgmentally at me and my designer suitcase as we passed—clearly they could tell its contents didn't include any clothing made of hemp, and they were right. In a display of emotional perspicacity that is utterly typical of Abby, who is ten years my junior, she stopped to reassure me. "Ignore the Mindfulness Mean Girls," she said. "If you give it a chance, this weekend will be amazing. It's exactly what you need."

"You're right," I finally conceded. "It's only nerves. I just have to get over myself."

"Give it twenty-four hours," she said, smiling optimistically. "I guarantee you'll be loving it."

In the last chapter, we learned about the follies of introspection and how to avoid them to increase our internal self-awareness. Thankfully, there are many surprisingly effective approaches. For example, Buddhists have practiced meditation—which has been shown to produce powerful self-awareness improvements—for thousands of years. And unless you live under a rock, you've probably noticed that it's experiencing a renaissance. But though meditation may be one of the oldest paths to internal self-awareness, it isn't the only path. In this chapter, we'll learn three separate but complimentary strategies to dramatically increase our internal insight. One is designed to examine who we are in the *present*, another to probe the patterns rooted in our *past*, and another to make sure we reap the rewards of self-examination in the *future*. Let's start with a popular tool that helps us understand the present: mindfulness, both the meditative and the non-meditative varieties.

◆

If introspection means analyzing our thoughts, feelings, and behaviors, and ruminating means unproductively dwelling on them, **mindfulness** is the opposite: **simply noticing what we're thinking, feeling, and doing without judgment or reaction.** Yet contrary to popular belief, mindfulness and meditation are not always synonymous. People tend to associate mindfulness with yogis or ashrams or silent retreats, but in recent years, it's come to encompass a much wider (and thankfully more diverse) range of activities. This is in no small part due to the work of Harvard psychologist Ellen Langer, who has been researching the topic since the 1970s. Her work has brought mindfulness "out of the Zen meditation caves and into the bright light of everyday functioning."

Where most people mistakenly see mindfulness simply as meditation, Langer provides a far broader and more practical definition: "the process of actively noticing new things, relinquishing preconceived mindsets, and then acting on . . . [our] new observations." So even though meditation is *one* way to practice mindfulness, it isn't the *only* way—and it's not for everyone. In fact, when asked about meditation in an interview, Langer once quipped, "The people I know won't sit still for five minutes, let alone forty."

I know the feeling. Truth be told, the idea of relaxing into the present moment has always kind of stressed me out. Like many of my Type A compatriots, *my* nirvana is achieved by checking off all of the items on my daily to-do list. I'm so addicted to productivity and activity that during our honeymoon, my husband literally had to pry my BlackBerry out of my hands and lock it in our hotel safe.

Of course, I am certainly not alone in my addiction. In a series of 11 experiments, researcher Timothy Wilson and his colleagues asked participants to spend between 6 and 15 phoneless minutes in a room by themselves with nothing to do but think. Not surprisingly, they didn't exactly enjoy the experience, and many found it downright unpleasant.* This prompted Wilson to wonder just how far people would go to avoid being alone with their thoughts. So he designed a follow-up experiment that gave people the choice between mental quiet time and an objectively less-pleasant activity: mild electric shocks. Incredibly, more than half the participants elected to *give themselves electric shocks* rather than endure just five solitary minutes. Wilson and his team reached the rather arresting conclusion that "people prefer to be doing something rather than nothing, even if that something is [uncomfortable or downright painful]."

Yet in spite of—or perhaps as a reaction to—our addiction to distraction, mindfulness (and particularly mindfulness meditation) is currently having a bit of a cultural moment. After all, when celebrities like Angelina Jolie, Anderson Cooper, and Ellen DeGeneres tout (or, I should say, tweet) the benefits of anything, you know it's only a matter of time before the masses jump on board. And jump on board they have. It's not just celebrities who have gone gaga over mindfulness: corporations like Google, McKinsey, Nike, General Mills, Target, and Aetna are using it to harness the improved productivity and well-being it supposedly brings. Many have also brought mindfulness into the classroom, with school programs reaching more than 300,000 students across the country, from prestigious East Coast preparatory academies to inner-city public high schools. Even the U.S. Marines and professional sports teams like the Boston Red Sox are embracing

---

* It might be helpful to point out that the participants were equally displeased regardless of age, education, income, or social media use.

meditation and other mindfulness exercises. The result is a nearly one-billion-dollar cottage industry—and it seems only to be growing.

Paradoxically, despite the trendiness of mindfulness, I don't think many people these days would agree that we're actually getting better at it. If anything, we seem to be moving in the opposite direction. As just one of many anecdotal examples, I was recently waiting in line at the airport. To amuse or perhaps distract myself, I decided to count how many of the travelers at our gate were scrolling through their smart-phones. You might not be shocked to learn that all 42 people—*every single one*—had their eyes glued to their little screens. It was a striking example of what Ellen Langer calls **mindlessness**; instead of being present, it's far easier to occupy ourselves with distractions like e-mail, texts, Facebook, Instagram, Pokémon GO, or whatever happens to be the new fad of the day. Here's a revealing data point: more than 38 million Americans admit to shopping on their smartphones while sitting on the toilet. Folks, I'd say we've got ourselves a problem.

And it's not just the computers in our pockets that meddle with our mindfulness; our own minds contribute just as much. When Langer's Harvard colleagues Matthew Killingsworth and Daniel Gilbert tracked 2,000 people's real-time thoughts as they went about their daily lives, they found that whether working, watching television, taking care of their children, running errands, or doing almost anything else, nearly half reported being distracted with other thoughts than what they were currently experiencing. In fact, for 21 out of the 22 activities they tracked, no fewer than 30 percent of participants reported thinking about other things, like the past, the future, and life's "what ifs." (The one exception, rather unsurprisingly, was sex.)

So what toll, exactly, does mindlessness take on us, and in particular on our ability to be self-aware? For one, Langer's research has found that distraction decreases happiness. What's more, we lose the ability to monitor and control our thoughts, feelings, and behaviors—and this makes self-awareness virtually impossible. In one study, researchers asked dieters to either watch a distracting video clip of bighorn sheep or watch themselves on video for 10 minutes. Then, they were allowed to eat as much ice cream as they wanted. Who went hog wild? The distracted dieters, of course. When their attention was pulled away from their actions, they were less aware and in control. This principle holds whether we are eating ice cream, responding to a difficult situation with a co-worker, making a critical career decision, or anything else. Luckily, when practiced correctly, mindfulness is a rather straightforward antidote to this problem. Let's start with the more mainstream view of this approach.

◆

As a walking prototype of distraction, I knew I'd be a fish out of water at the Shambhala Mountain Center. It was for this precise reason that I'd roped in my younger sister and token family unicorn. And rather conveniently, Abby had recently become a passionate advocate of meditation.

But precisely 24 hours after my sister "guaranteed" that I'd be "loving" the meditation course, I was trying to decide between laughing hysterically and running away screaming. Picture a group of 20 adults in a completely silent room walking in circles, very, very slowly. Our shoulders were hunched over, our hands (for reasons that were never fully explained) placed in a highly specific position, one balled into a fist with its thumb sticking up and the other curled around it, and both pressed into our stomachs just beneath our belly button.

Everyone was taking this walking meditation extremely seriously—at least, everyone besides me. We paced, heel-toe, heel-toe, heel-toe, around and around, for what was allegedly 20 minutes but seemed like two hours. All I could think of were the people I grew up secretly chuckling at, who often lived in Boulder, Colorado, and had super-earnest, super-annoying levels of commitment to their alternative lifestyles. I didn't want to become one of them!

But I was also determined to see the weekend through. As a scientist, I've been trained to follow the data wherever they lead, and to my great irritation, the results on mindfulness meditation are clear and compelling. Research shows that people who practice it are happier, healthier, more creative, more productive, more authentic, more in control of their behavior, more satisfied in their marriages, more relaxed, less aggressive, less burnt-out, and even thinner. So as ridiculous as I felt, I was at least self-aware enough to know that my biases were irrationally influencing my opinion about something I had never even tried.

Plus, I was on deadline for my book (this one), and this retreat was an important piece of my research on self-awareness. There's a growing body of evidence that mindfulness meditation can save us from the traps of introspection and rumination you read about in the last chapter. In one study, when researchers put people who had never meditated through a 10-day intensive mindfulness training retreat, the subjects were less likely to introspect compared to a control group, both immediately afterward and weeks later. In contrast, the control group's introspection levels actually increased. Participants trained in mindfulness were also less depressed and less upset, and they even had better memories and attention spans.

Although the direct connection between mindfulness and self-awareness is just beginning to be understood, initial research is telling. One investigation of mental health professionals showed that the more mindful among them also tended to enjoy greater self-insight. Some researchers have even suggested that the reason mindfulness reduces stress, anxiety, and depression is *because* it increases insight.

Of course, mindfulness on its own is not sufficient for complete self-awareness—after all, to truly know ourselves, we need to delve a bit deeper—but it does help us notice and control our reactions while avoiding the follies of introspection. When we're mindful, we experience our emotions without overthinking or overreacting, and we remember that the way we feel now isn't the way we'll feel forever. As Dr. Megan Warner, associate clinical professor in the Yale School of Medicine's psychiatry department, explains, "Mindfulness offers a strategy to disconnect from where our thoughts, emotions and pain can take us."

Mindfulness meditation can also create real impact in the hard-nosed world of business. Mark Tercek witnessed this firsthand soon after being appointed president and CEO of the Nature Conservancy. Coming from a successful career as a managing director and partner at Goldman Sachs, he thought he'd escaped the high-pressure life when he left Wall Street. Yet Mark found himself facing some tough decisions in the early months of his new job, which he began right at the start of the 2008 financial crisis. But even after the Nature Conservancy had weathered the storm, Mark still sensed that something was a bit off for him both professionally and personally. So he called our mutual friend Marshall Goldsmith, one of the world's top executive coaches, for help. Marshall interviewed Mark's executive team, his board, and even his family. Apparently, Mark's hard-charging style had been ruffling a few feathers at work, and some of that was following him home.

Mark was surprised. Even though things had been tough, he hadn't fully realized how much his tendency to make quick, impulse-driven decisions was affecting others. With Marshall's help, Mark vowed to work on three things: to be a better listener, to embrace a more positive mindset, and to stop sweating the small stuff. Things got a bit better in the months that followed, but not as much as Mark had hoped. Despite Marshall's support and Mark's commitment, Mark wasn't sure how to push past this plateau.

Around that same time, Mark became interested in mindfulness. He'd start each day with 10 minutes of meditation; and if he couldn't wake up early, he'd steal away to his office to focus on his breath and get in a more positive frame of mind. With each passing day, not only did Mark begin to feel happier and calmer, it didn't take long for him to notice a few more unexpected benefits. On the days he meditated, he found himself making measurable progress toward the goals he'd set with Marshall: he was pushing past that plateau that had seemed insurmountable just weeks earlier.

Soon, Mark realized that he could better recognize—in the moment—when he needed to override his gut and make a different choice. He was better able to stop and listen. He was less reactive, critical, and defensive. He was finally in control of the pillar of reactions. Mark was also pleased with the difference this relatively small daily ritual was making at home. On days he'd meditated, his kids would say, "Dad, what happened? You're so nice now!" "Hey, be careful," he'd playfully joke. "No, Dad, you were nice before," they would tactfully answer, "but now you're *really* nice."

Mark realized what researchers also know to be true: because mindfulness helps us be more aware of our thoughts and feelings, we can better control our behavior and make smarter decisions in real time. And though mindfulness is much loved by those seeking *internal* self-awareness, it also has surprising benefits for *external* self-awareness; by quieting our egos, we become more open to feedback from others.

Psychology professor Whitney Heppner and her colleagues discovered this effect through a rather creative experiment. They asked students to write an essay about themselves, which would supposedly be used by other participants as the basis for choosing a partner for a subsequent computer task. One-third of the students were told they had been chosen by another participant (the acceptance group), one-third were told that no one had chosen them (the rejection group, essentially the equivalent of being the last person picked in gym class), and one-third were asked to mindfully eat five raisins prior to learning that they hadn't been chosen by another participant (the mindfulness-rejection group).*

During the computer task, the researchers gave participants the choice to blast as much noise as they wanted at their competitors. They predicted that the rejected participants would be angrier and therefore aggressively punish the people who hadn't picked them. This is exactly what happened, at least for the non-mindful rejection group. Yet even though the mindfulness-rejection group had been equally shunned, they were *two-thirds less aggressive*—in fact, their reactions were statistically indistinguishable from the acceptance group. Mindfulness seemed to have guarded against the defensiveness and anger that can accompany critical feedback or perceived failure. After all,

---

* In case you're wondering, mindfully eating a raisin goes something like this: "Imagine that you have never seen a raisin before . . . next rub the raisin gently across your lips, noticing how it feels against them. Now, put the raisin in your mouth, and roll it around slowly on your tongue . . . take a very small bite . . . now chew the raisin slowly . . ." and so on.

even though it's important to understand how other people see us, those views don't completely define who we are.

MINDFULNESS WITHOUT THE MANTRAS

We've seen that mindfulness meditation can produce some pretty dramatic improvements in self-awareness and well-being. But remember, mindfulness has a broader definition than just meditation. So if you are as ambivalent about meditation as I was, you'll be pleased to learn that there are many scientifically supported mindfulness methods that don't require a single mantra. For example, a few non-meditative unicorns reported that simply spending time outdoors—things like hiking, running, biking, or going for a long walk—helped them stay focused on the present. A few even believed that these activities were among the most important tools in their ongoing self-awareness—sometimes just a few minutes of true quiet can do wonders for putting us back in touch with our thoughts and feelings. And although just writing about the following activity gives me anxiety, many unicorns achieved this quiet by shutting off their phones during certain parts of their day—most consistently in the evenings and early mornings. Other unicorns reported finding a similar peace through prayer.

Before we move to a few non-meditative mindfulness tools, an important point is in order. **Mindfulness is *not* the same thing as relaxation**. In fact, even though these two activities seem similar, their outcomes couldn't be more different. In one study, unemployed men and women either went through a three-day mindfulness meditation program or a three-day relaxation program disguised as a mindfulness one. Both groups engaged in many of the same activities, but only the first program employed real mindfulness techniques. For example, both incorporated stretching—but where the relaxation group was encouraged to chat with one another during those exercises, the mindful group was instructed to pay attention to their bodily sensations, even unpleasant ones.

At the end of the three days, both groups *felt* equally refreshed and better able to manage the stress of the job-seeking process. But when the researchers scanned their brains, their MRI results told a different story: only the mindfulness group was *actually* more focused and calm. And four months later, when researchers measured participants' interleukin 6 levels (an indication of inflammation, which is a sign of stress), the relaxation group's levels had increased more than 20 percent while the mindfulness group's decreased by the same amount. The lesson here? Whatever you do to center yourself, make sure you spend that time actively noticing new things rather than just mentally checking out.

Now, to understand how to practice non-meditative mindfulness, it might be helpful to re-review Ellen Langer's definition. The process of drawing novel distinctions is, according to Langer, "the essence of mindfulness." But what does it mean to draw novel distinctions? In a nutshell, it's seeing ourselves and our world in a new way. Langer gives the example of traveling. When we're in a strange place, we tend to notice new things in ourselves and the world around us—the sights, the sounds, the people—versus our day-to-day lives, where we tend to focus on the familiar and draw on the perspective we've always had. But we don't need to travel to far-off lands to experience these benefits. If we can get in the habit of mindfully noticing new things in ourselves or our world, it can dramatically improve our self-knowledge.

One way to do this is *reframing*, which simply means looking at our circumstances, our behaviors, and our relationships from a new and different angle. Let's look at the story of Aviana, a unicorn, mother of two, and manager in the wireless telecommunications industry whose courage in reframing her circumstances was a major force in achieving greater self-knowledge; it even played a role in saving her career. A few weeks after giving birth to her youngest son, she received devastating news. The call center where she worked—no, *loved* to work—for the past 11 years would be closing, and everyone, including her, would be out of a job. Worse yet, because her husband worked there too, her family was about to go from two incomes to zero literally overnight.

Aviana was panicked and afraid. She would lie awake at night staring at the ceiling thinking, *What am I going to do?* She decided to return early from her maternity leave for the simple purpose of stockpiling as much cash as possible. But back at the office, her co-workers' reactions didn't help her state of mind. "Isn't this *horrible?*" they'd whine. After a few days of letting everyone get her even more lathered up, Aviana wondered whether there was another way of looking at the situation. *Instead of focusing on what I'm losing,* she pondered, *what if I focused on what I might gain?* Yes, she was losing her job, but this also could be an opportunity to grow, and maybe even to get a better job than the one she had.

Armed with this new perspective, Aviana quickly realized something that should have been obvious to her before. Right out of high school, she'd taken a few semesters of college courses, but when they failed to hold her attention, she left to explore the working world and never looked back. That had been a mistake, she realized, and this was her chance to make it right—and in fact, if she didn't go back to school, she'd be seriously hurting her long-term job prospects. So, 11 years after her first attempt, Aviana re-enrolled in an online undergraduate program while simultaneously applying for other jobs in the company.

Before she knew it, her last day of work arrived. That afternoon, she learned that a co-worker was organizing a happy hour, which seemed fun but dangerous given everyone's freshly deposited severance checks. She handed in her badge and was about to head to the bar when her phone rang. It was the hiring manager calling about one of her company's open positions! Before the manager had even finished offering her the job, Aviana exclaimed, "I'll take it! And I can start Monday!"

The new position was a breath of fresh air and a net win for her career. Since then, Aviana has received two promotions. And thanks to her company's tuition-reimbursement program, she's close to finishing her degree in organizational leadership.

Aviana's flexibility in reframing the loss of her job as an opportunity—rather than staying mired in a mindset of helplessness—dramatically improved both her career and her life. But interestingly, reframing isn't just helpful when things go wrong. Quite often, we gain valuable perspective by reframing when things are going *right*. Earlier, I mentioned my friend whose husband left her for what, to her, seemed like completely out-of-the-blue reasons. If she had thought "My marriage seems to be doing really well right now—but what if it weren't?" she might have stumbled upon some of the issues before it was too late. I'm certainly not suggesting that you become a giant bummer to yourself and others—what I *am* suggesting is that **looking at both the good and the bad from multiple angles will help you maximize your insight and success.**

When in a difficult situation, ask: What opportunities can I find? What about my weaknesses could be strengths? When I look back on my life or career, what successes have I had in my most trying situations? What is one gift I've gotten from my most challenging personal or professional relationship?

By the same token, when things are going well, you might ask: What are the potential risks and how can I avoid them? What aspects of my strengths could become weaknesses? What potential challenges can I find in my past successes? What is one risk in my best personal or professional relationship, and how can I mitigate it?

If you're a theater geek like I am, you probably know that characters in plays sometimes step out of the action to speak directly to the audience or observe a scene. As many of our unicorns showed us, we can use this same technique to gain valuable insight by **reframing our experiences from a more objective angle**. One unicorn explained that when she and her husband are having a disagreement, she mentally steps outside of herself to "watch" what's going on—so instead of being an angry spouse, she becomes an observer. (This might remind you of perspective-taking; but while perspective-taking is about putting yourself in others' shoes, this is about observing things from a more detached, objective angle.) Negotiation expert William Ury aptly calls it "going to the balcony," but whatever name it goes by, this kind of reframing can be immensely valuable.

Our second non-meditative mindfulness tool is *comparing and contrasting*. When we compare and contrast, we're looking for similarities and differences between our experiences, thoughts, feelings, and behaviors over time. In particular, this can be a great way to see patterns (one of the Seven Pillars of Insight) that we might not have picked up on in the past. But, you might be wondering, if mindfulness is about noticing the present, how does examining our past help? Because comparing and contrasting past experiences *to what is happening right now* can give us immense clarity about the present. For example, "I was so happy with my job last week—what's different this week that's making me so miserable?" or "When I chose my major in college, it seems like I got the most excited in my business-related classes than anything else. Am I tapping into that same passion in my current job?" or "If I've had the same challenges across multiple jobs, what might this mean?"

Personally, I am indebted to the compare-and-contrast tool for the single most important "aha moment" of my career. I spent the first five years after college in an academic setting, working as a researcher and adjunct instructor while earning my PhD. But being a businessperson at heart, I also took on whatever consulting gigs I could—first under the supervision of my graduate professors and then as a consultant with a small firm in Denver. After I finished school, and having fallen in love with the business world, I held a series of corporate roles as an in-house organizational psychologist. Eventually, I scored what I thought was my dream job—I worked for an incredible company with a team I adored and a boss who essentially gave me free rein to do whatever I thought was most helpful for the company.

But less than two years later, a feeling of restlessness began to set in. At first, I pushed away these feelings, telling myself I was being ungrateful for the opportunity. But despite my best efforts, the restlessness grew to the point where I could no longer ignore it.

One evening, I was discussing this predicament with my husband. "If memory serves," he offered, "you felt pretty much the same way in your last job right around year two." I hadn't noticed it myself, but he was right. What I was experiencing wasn't unhappiness per se—instead, I felt trapped in the predictable routine of the people, the projects, and the politics. Often on the way to work, a feeling of dread would wash over me as I took the same route to the same office at the same time as I had the day before.

Did I experience this, I wondered, *earlier in my career?* I couldn't remember having that feeling when I was teaching and consulting; because every new semester, new class, and new client was a clean slate, I never got too settled into a routine. It was also pretty clear that I had been much happier working for myself than when I was working for someone else. (This makes perfect sense in hindsight: I come from a long line of entrepreneurs who don't like being told what to do.) But I'd never asked myself these questions in this way before. And though the answers weren't as convenient as I would have liked, they gave me a whole new level of clarity.

Never one to act impulsively, I decided to let these rather unsettling conclusions bounce around my head for a few weeks. Then one night as I was walking from my office to my car, the answer hit me like a punch in the gut. I had to start my own company—period, full stop. And I had to do it soon, lest I wake up in my 50s, still wondering why I couldn't muster the courage to take the plunge. Despite the rather uncomfortable nature of this realization, I felt a great sense of relief and purpose. It wasn't easy to leave the cushy corporate world, but I can honestly say that I never imagined I could enjoy my job as much as I do now. And I can trace this trajectory directly to the few weeks I spent comparing and contrasting the high and low points of my career.

The compare-and-contrast tool isn't just well suited for professional epiphanies; it can also help us discover patterns that are holding us back in our personal lives. Take Jed, a single 66-year-old computer programmer (and unicorn) who had just been given, in his words, "a really long paid vacation." When his company went through a large downsizing, they offered him a retirement package, which, coupled with his fortuitous social security eligibility, meant that he could finally take some time off. Early one morning a few months into his vacation, he had just awoken and was staring bleary-eyed at the ceiling. It seemed that Jed's new life had come with an unpleasant (yet ultimately positive) side effect: free time to confront the things in his life that dissatisfied him—for one, the fact that he was still single. But instead of ruminating, he began to ask himself if there was a common factor in his failed relationships.

At the time, Jed was just finishing Flaubert's *Madame Bovary*. (He'd decided that his sabbatical afforded him the opportunity to read some of the classic novels he had overlooked in his youth.) In *Madame Bovary*, Dr. Charles Bovary marries Emma, the daughter of one of his patients. At first, Emma is thrilled to be married to Charles, but she quickly becomes bored with him—and (spoiler alert) becomes so upset about it that she literally dies. One passage caught Jed's attention:

> But how to speak about so elusive a malaise, one that keeps changing its shape like the clouds and its direction like the winds? She could find no words; and hence neither occasion nor courage came to hand . . . Charles's conversation was flat as a sidewalk, a place of passage for ideas of everyman; they wore drab everyday clothes, and they inspired neither laughter nor dreams.

When he read this, something clicked. *Could the common factor in my relationships be ME?* Jed wondered. *Could I be as flat as a sidewalk?* To discover the answer, he searched for the similarities in his behavior throughout his past relationships (specifically, the pillars of patterns, reactions, and impact). In a flash of insight, Jed realized that in every relationship, he'd held in his emotions too much. When something would upset him, he wouldn't say or do anything; he'd just shut down. This denial, Jed realized, "flattened" him, blocking any kind of deeper connection.

Right around that time, he had reconnected with an old friend he'd known for 20 years but with whom he'd been out of touch for the last 10. They started taking dancing lessons together, and lo and behold, a romance blossomed. They were married a year later, and Jed has made it a point to show up differently in this relationship. If something happened that he wasn't thrilled about, for example, the old Jed would have sat on it in silence, but the new Jed knew he needed to be more open with his feelings, even if it was difficult or uncomfortable. His marriage isn't perfect (whose is?) but he's never been happier.

If you want to try comparing and contrasting for yourself, here are a few questions to get you started. You can apply each one to almost anything that you want to better understand, such as your job, your career, or your relationships. What about X is the same and what is different than it was in the past? Have there been any patterns in my mood, positive or negative, that have coincided with changes in X? Does the way I feel about X remind me of any similar feelings I've had about a past situation? How happy or fulfilled am I with X today versus how I felt about X in the past? When I think about X over the course of my life, have things gotten better or worse?

Now let's turn to our final mindfulness tool. Studies have shown that one reason we fail to learn from experience is that we rarely take time to reflect on our discoveries. Finding the time to regularly check in with ourselves can feel surprisingly difficult in our busy, distracted world. But *daily check-ins* don't have to be time-consuming (as with journaling, more is not better). In fact, the majority of our unicorns described a habit of short, focused check-ins (just as Ben Franklin did). When explaining his process, Jeff, our architect-turned-entrepreneur, reported: "I take the perspective of a critical outsider and ask, 'How did I do today and how do I feel about how today went?'"

Instead of using the time to introspect—or worse, ruminate—we should use daily check-ins to review the choices we made that day, look for patterns, and observe what worked and what didn't. This small ritual can have a big impact, not just on our mood and our confidence, but on our actions and results. For example, in one study, call-center trainees who took just a few minutes to reflect at the end of each day improved their performance an average of 23 percent.

So try taking five minutes every evening—whether it's during your drive home, while unwinding after dinner, or after you climb into bed—to mindfully ask yourself: **What went well today? What didn't go well? What did I learn and how will I be smarter tomorrow?** The answers you unearth need not be life-altering—quite often, even insights that seem insignificant at the time can help us improve incrementally. But if we can get just a bit more mindful and self-aware each day, the sum total effect of these insights can be astonishing.

YOUR LIFE STORY: CHART THE CONSTELLATION, DON'T JUST GAZE AT THE STAR

My husband just so happens to be a giant nerd, which is precisely why I married him. By day, he geeks out as an IT systems architect at an engineering firm, and by night, among other things, he geeks out about astronomy. A few years ago, he decided his hobby had become serious enough that it required an equally serious telescope. Due to the hefty price tag of such a piece of equipment, he formed a coalition of eight or so family members who each contributed to what would soon come to be known as the Best Birthday Present Ever. Every time he uses his favorite possession, he performs an evening-long ritual of setting it up, getting it configured, sometimes attaching a camera to it, looking at what times different objects are in the sky, and so on. Then, with childlike delight, he will spend hours on our rooftop deck looking at the red spot on Jupiter, or a certain crater on the moon, or the rings of Saturn.

One weekend, we were up at our cabin in the Colorado mountains. It was a crisp, clear night, and I figured the telescope would be coming out at any moment. When I heard the back door slam shut, I prepared myself for the inevitable "Hey, come look at this!" that I'd soon be hearing from our back deck. After a while, having heard no such exclamation, I decided to go out and check on him. I was surprised to find my husband just sitting there, staring up at the sky with the telescope still in its carrying case next to him.

"Is your telescope broken?" I asked in horror.

Chuckling, he reassured me that it wasn't. "Once I got out here and my eyes adjusted," he explained, "I started looking at all the constellations—do you see how beautiful the Milky Way is tonight?" Still sensing my confusion, he opined, "Sometimes it's really nice to take a step back and look at the bigger picture."

The same is true for self-examination. If the mindfulness tools you just read about will help you understand your present self, the *Life Story* approach **helps you look backward to learn how the sum total of your past has shaped you.** If each life event is a star, our life story is the constellation. And if we spent all of our time looking at individual stars through a telescope lens, we couldn't appreciate the magnitude and beauty of the constellations that dot the sky. To that end, the process of becoming, as Timothy Wilson describes it, "biographers of our lives" is a profoundly powerful but surprisingly underutilized approach to better understand who we are, who we are becoming, and who we could be.

Psychology professor Dan McAdams has been prolifically researching life stories for more than 30 years. The approach that McAdams and his colleagues use to help people compose their life stories goes something like this:

> Think about your life as if it were a book. Divide that book into chapters that represent the key phases of your life. Within those phases, think of 5–10 specific scenes in your story—high points, low points, turning points, early memories, important childhood events, important adulthood events, or any other event you find self-defining. For each, provide an account that is at least one paragraph long:
>
> 1. What happened and when? Who was involved?
> 2. What were you and others thinking and feeling, and what about this event was especially important for you?
> 3. What does this event say about who you are, how you have developed over time, or who you might become?
>
> When you are finished writing your account, take a step back and look at your life story as a whole:
>
> 1. What major themes, feelings, or lessons do you see in your story?

2. What does the story of your life say about the kind of person you are and might become?

3. What does your story say about your values, passions, aspirations, fit, patterns, reactions, and impact on others?

After collecting life stories from tens of thousands of people, Professor McAdams and his colleagues have learned that they usually have overarching themes. And identifying them can help make sense of seemingly contradictory aspects of ourselves. Take the example of Chase, an introverted non-profit fundraiser who loves his work. His pattern of introversion and passion for a job that requires him to frequently schmooze might seem incongruous at first. But when Chase examines his life story, he notices that every high point has involved "doing good" for someone who was less fortunate. So even though his job requires more mixing and mingling than an introvert might usually prefer, it allows him to live his most important value: helping others. And if that involves a little socializing, Chase is happy to do it.

Let's look at a few specific ways to become a biographer of your life in a way that generates real insight. Research shows that self-aware people tend to knit more *complex narratives* of their key life events: they are more likely to describe each event from different perspectives, include multiple explanations, and explore complex and even contradictory emotions. In many ways, this complexity is the opposite of the need for absolute truth that we learned about in the last chapter: instead of searching for simple, generalizable facts, self-aware people appreciate the complicated nature of the key events in their lives. Perhaps for this reason, complex life stories are associated with continued personal growth and maturity years into the future.

At the same time, we also want to seek something called *thematic coherence*. When we're able to find consistent themes across multiple important events of our lives, we can glean surprising self-insights—like how Chase discovered his theme of doing good. Some common themes include achievement (i.e., personal success), relationships (i.e., forming and keeping connections with others), and growth (i.e., seeing life as an opportunity to develop and improve). Another especially interesting life-story theme is one that McAdams has focused on for much of his career: the theme of redemption. Whereas people with "contamination sequences" see a pattern of good things turning to bad ones, people with "redemption sequences" believe that bad things can turn to good.

Self-awareness researcher Timothy Wilson and his colleagues demonstrated the power of the redemption sequence when they studied freshmen at Duke University who were struggling with their grades. Clearly, the students' poor academic performance was powerfully challenging their "good student, great school, bright future" narrative. Wilson and his team divided the students into two groups: one watched videos of upperclassmen explaining how their grades improved after they adjusted to college life—that is, the freshmen heard a new narrative, one that provided an alternate explanation for their struggles. A second group was not given a new narrative. The effects were dramatic: after one year, the "new-narrative" students had improved their GPAs by an average of .11 (compared to the "old-narrative" students, whose GPAs dropped slightly), and were far less likely to drop out (a mere 5 percent of the new-narrative students threw in the towel versus 25 percent of the others).

One particularly moving example of a redemption sequence involves a young man from one of McAdams' studies—let's call him James—whose life has been fraught with hardship. Entering the world as a product of rape, James faced challenge after challenge, including a near-death experience after being stabbed. But where many would see only darkness and despair, James sees hope: "I was dead, but the doctors brought me back. . . . My philosophy of life has always been to be positive instead of negative on any circumstances you deal with. If you go with the positive ideas, you'll progress. If you get involved in the negative, you'll drown." It would be easy to label James as overly optimistic. But the research on people like him paints a clear picture: if we view our challenges accurately *and* as an opportunity for redemption, even the most horrific experiences can help us learn, grow, and improve.

So when the time is right for you to write your life story, don't look at it as a neat, clean Hollywood narrative. Embracing the complexity, the nuances, and the contradictions will help you appreciate your inner reality in all its beautiful messiness.

SOLUTIONS-MINING: FROM PROBLEMS TO GROWTH GOALS

So far in this chapter, we've explored tools to help us better understand our *present* (mindfulness, both meditative and non-meditative) and our *past* (life stories). At this point, then, one important topic remains: How can we become more internally self-aware and successful in the *future?* Or as one unicorn noted, "It's not enough to know yourself. You have to set goals and make changes to really live the life you want." Quite often, the commitment to the process of self-discovery unearths disparities between where we are and where we want or need to be in the future. Let's say that after some mindful comparing and contrasting, you realize that the company you work at isn't a good fit for you. Or perhaps charting your life story reveals the importance of family in your life, but your current 80-hour workweeks aren't in line with that value. Quite often, **whether we choose to act on our newfound self-insight is the difference between success and stagnation.**

Matt, for example, was a bright, ambitious financial services professional—in addition to being a fountain of industry knowledge, he had earned accolades from bosses, peers, and clients throughout his career for his diligent, disciplined approach. When I first met him, I was running his company's high-potential development program, into which he'd just been accepted. I could see that potential instantly.

Matt had recently been hired as a long-term successor for the role of business unit president. The plan, the company's CEO told me, was for Matt to spend the next three or so years working for the president and learning the ropes, followed by a smooth and successful transition into the role when the president retired. But, as is often the case, things didn't go as planned. A year into Matt's tenure, his boss had a sudden health crisis and had to leave the company. The CEO made the decision not to hire from the outside to replace him, at least for now, which left the door open for Matt.

But as much as the CEO *wanted* to appoint his new high-potential hire to the role, he wasn't sure Matt was ready. This left Matt in a rather awkward position: his mentor was gone, no one had been appointed to run the group, and someone was going to have to step in and fill the leadership vacuum. Matt approached the CEO and offered to fill in until they could find a more permanent solution, and he agreed. Matt knew he'd feel some growing pains: in addition to facing the same challenges every leader faces, like motivating his team, managing performance, and delivering results, he had the added complication of being an unofficial boss to some of his current peers. But rather than get discouraged, Matt decided it was the perfect opportunity to turn his problems into solutions—that is, he set a goal to develop the skills he'd need to earn the permanent job.

Most people instinctively know that when faced with a challenge, finding solutions is the most productive choice—which might explain why bosses enjoy barking adages like "Don't bring me problems, bring me solutions!"—but particularly in the business world, we still spend inordinate amounts of time focused on problems and comparatively little on how to fix them. Yet not only does **focusing on solutions**—a technique called *solutions-mining*—help us reach our goals in record time; it has the surprising benefit of helping us *think* less but *understand* more. For example, in one study, participants completed a three-month life-coaching program that focused on setting goals and measuring their progress toward them. Not only did the program help participants reach their goals in record time, they showed less introspection and more self-awareness. Another study demonstrated that people sustained this progress nearly eight months later. As an added bonus, solutions-mining is a powerful antidote to rumination.

The data on solutions-mining are so compelling that the field of psychology has formed an entire discipline based on the premise that focusing on them can produce insight, well-being, and success. Developed in the 1980s by married couple Steve de Shazer and Insoo

Kim Berg, an approach called Solutions Focused Brief Therapy has produced dramatic improvements in things like depression, recidivism, stress and crisis management, and psychological and social functioning in populations such as parents, prisoners, adolescents with behavior problems, healthcare workers, and couples struggling with their marriages. And for our purposes, the approach has also been associated with greater insight and psychological growth.

If you want to increase your ability to mine problems for solutions, a simple but powerful tool is the **Miracle Question** (you might recognize it from Chip and Dan Heath's book *Switch*). Developed by de Shazer and Berg, the Miracle Question produces insight everywhere from the workplace to our home life to the therapist's couch; it's even been shown to help golfers reduce their putting yips (i.e., jerks in their putting stroke). So what is the Miracle Question, exactly?

> Imagine that tonight as you sleep a miracle occurs in your life. A magical momentous happening has completely solved this problem and perhaps rippled out to cover and infinitely improve other areas of your life too . . . Think for a moment . . . how is life going to be different now? Describe it in detail. What's the first thing you'll notice as you wake up in the morning?

Let's circle back to Matt. After getting feedback from his team that his biggest problem was delegation, he used the Miracle Question to explore what the solution might look like. If Matt's problem were magically solved, he thought, the first sign would be that he'd no longer see asking for help as a weakness. Instead, he would embrace it as a method for greater team involvement, improvement, and prosperity.

Matt proceeded to paint a poignant picture of his desired future when the problem was solved (or, as the Heath brothers call it in *Switch*, a "destination postcard"). One where he would improve his team's engagement and performance, all while feeling less burdened and more efficient. But notice that Matt's solution wasn't an oversimplified single action ("I'll do a better job delegating"). Instead, he envisioned exactly how both he and his employees would change on a far deeper level.

And indeed, part of the reason that the Miracle Question can be so effective is that it forces us to think more broadly about our aspirations, a key pillar in our self-awareness journey. One unicorn we spoke to echoed this. Emily grew up as one of eight children in a family that struggled to make ends meet. Determined not to repeat her family's mistakes, she channeled her difficult childhood into motivation to succeed in her career.

> Self-awareness can't happen without goals. I define what I need to accomplish—for example, when I was new to my company, I needed to build strong relationships and establish credibility. The only way to do that was to earn my team's trust and develop their confidence in me. Any missteps would get me in trouble. So I had to constantly ask myself, *How will this action impact my goal?*

But when it comes to improving our internal self-awareness, all goals aren't created equal. And just like Carol Dweck and Carol Diener's learn-well kids, **when we express our goals in terms of how we will learn and grow, it opens us up to a whole new level of insight and achievement**. In one study, college students were asked to write two paragraphs about a major life goal and how they were trying to accomplish it. Interestingly, when the students described goals involving learning and growth, they demonstrated improved self-awareness, maturity, and well-being *nearly four years later.*[*]

In Matt's case, instead of simply vowing to delegate more effectively, he was able to change the way he operated on a deeper level by conquering his fear of asking for help and taking action to inspire and empower his team. For the next several months, Matt continued to work on the skills he'd need to succeed as president, should he be given the opportunity. Eventually, the CEO formally promoted him. Now, more than a year later, Matt continues to exceed expectations. He is a powerful reminder that the sooner we can explore how our challenges

---

[*] And if you're a fan of the TV show *24*, you might be interested to know that the first author of this study was . . . wait for it . . . Jack Bauer.

can lead to growth, the easier it is to take charge and get what we want out of life.

◆

At this point, you might be wondering how my maiden voyage into the world of mindfulness ended, and whether I lived to tell the tale. On the final day of the meditation course, our group took a long trek through the snow to the Great Stupa of Dharmakaya. As we crossed an elegant wooden bridge strung with colorful prayer flags, I looked up to see it towering above us—two huge white arches topped with a cone of shining gold, all set in a natural amphitheater of snowy pines. I was surprisingly moved.

After a few awe-inspiring minutes experiencing the breathtaking sight from afar, we took off our shoes and winter jackets and entered the

shrine. "Oh wow," I whispered to Abby as we walked in—and craned our necks to take in a towering golden Buddha beneath an intricately painted ceiling of azure blue.

I was surprised to find myself thinking, "I really hope we get to meditate in here."

When we did, I *finally* got it. And no one was more surprised than me. It was as if all weekend, my mind had been a glass of water with dirt swirling around inside it and now, for a few awesome minutes, it was clear. My anxious, Type A, overthinking brain had stopped running at a million miles an hour and was now perfectly calm. In that moment, I understood what all the fuss was about.

On the drive back from Shambhala, I felt happy just to sit in serene silence with my sister—something that had never happened before. There was no need, I realized with a kind of fascinated delight, to fill every second with incessant babble or music. As Abby and I descended from that magical space back into the noisy city, I considered buying myself a meditation cushion and converting half my office into a mind-fulness mecca.

The day after my return, with great gusto, I sat and meditated. The day after that, I sat and meditated (though my emotionally needy five-pound rescue poodle made the entire affair pretty difficult). But the day after that, I didn't sit and meditate. Or the day after that. The day after that, I thought maybe I'd delay my office conversion for a while. I'll admit that I haven't meditated since—not because I didn't see the possibility of what it could do, but because I find that non-meditative techniques just work better for me.

The point is that there are many ways to approach internal self-awareness—life stories for probing our past, meditative and non-meditative mindfulness for noticing our present, and solutions-mining for shaping our future. Though it's worth trying each of them at some point, you may find that certain tools work better than others. After all, part of building insight is learning what methods of self-exploration work best for you.

Part Three

◆

External Self-Awareness:

Myths

and

Truths

7

THE TRUTH WE RARELY HEAR

From Mirror to Prism

*A stranger approaching you in the street will in a second's
glance see you whole, size you up, place you in a way in
which you cannot and never will, even though you have
spent a lifetime with yourself . . . and therefore ought to
know yourself best of all.*

—WALKER PERCY

There's an old science-backed adage that the words of a drunk person
are the thoughts of a sober one. Late one Saturday night in a crowded
hometown bar, I recently learned just how true this really is.

It all began, innocently enough, in a trendy restaurant in down-
town Denver. My husband and I, along with six of his oldest friends,
had just had a magnificent meal with a surplus of food and wine. Despite the fact that I (as designated driver) had been soberly sipping club
soda, I was in a wonderful mood. I'd known everyone around the table
for more than 10 years, and it was just one of those nights when everything clicked. My friends were at their witty best and my stomach was
sore from laughing. When the check came, we decided we were having
far too much fun to go home.

"What about the Celtic?" said my friend Teresa. "We haven't been
there in forever!"

"That old Irish pub?" said my husband, wide-eyed. "I love that
place!"

An hour later, my already intoxicated friends had been quickly overcome with an even more intoxicating level of nostalgia. (The Celtic, it turned out, was where they used to hang out more than 20 years earlier.) We pushed a few high-top tables together, and with loud music blaring in the background, they began to reminisce. I chuckled to myself, picturing these now buttoned-up, middle-aged professionals engaging in youthful shenanigans.

As we broke into smaller conversations, Teresa pulled her chair closer to mine. "Tasha," she said dreamily, "we are so glad Dave brought you into our lives." *How lovely!* I thought, feeling equally grateful that he had brought them into mine. But before I could respond, she continued, "And boy have you come a long way since we first met you."

I paused, instantly puzzled. "Wha-what do you mean?"

I'll never forget what happened next. In the noisy ruckus of that crowded bar, Teresa stood up, clasped my skull with her powerful hands, and then proceeded to twist my head, agonizingly, all the way around. Well she didn't do that, of course—but that's what it felt like. I'll spare you the finer details, but apparently 26-year-old me, a freshly minted PhD who thought she knew everything, had been rather arrogant and high-maintenance.

"Thank you," I sputtered. "Thanks for your candor, Teresa. How very illuminating."

"You're totally welcome," she said, beaming.

It was all I could do to stop myself from kicking her off her stool.

Once I composed myself, I recognized that this was a true alarm-clock moment that actually presented a valuable opportunity. That opportunity, I hoped, would be to prove that Teresa didn't know what the hell she was talking about. But either way, I had to probe further.

So in the car on the way home, with my very merry husband in the passenger seat, I recounted the conversation.

"What do you think?" I asked him.

"What do you mean?"

"Is she right?"

"Um, is this a trick question?"

"No—go ahead," I assured him, trying to sound as nonchalant as possible, "I really want to know if you saw what Teresa saw."

He paused for a moment and began, "Yeahhh . . . I can see where she's coming from." I bit my tongue and took a deep breath as he continued. "I mean, remember when you asked for a hard-walled office after you'd been in your job for less than six months?"

"Did I?" I said, feigning ignorance.

"No, actually, you demanded it," he said. "That seemed pretty over-the-top to me."

At the time, I'd been of the staunch opinion that it was totally unfair that all of my peers had offices and I didn't. But suddenly, I saw things from another perspective: there I was, newly hired Dr. Smarty Pants, demanding an office like a petulant child. Now, in retrospect, I could see how this must have come across. And I was mortified.

For weeks, a sea of emotions swirled in my mind. Was I surprised to hear this truth about my younger self? Absolutely. Embarrassed at my behavior? You bet I was. But most of all, I was disappointed that no one—*no one!*—had said anything to me about it for almost 10 years. Mercifully, I have apparently improved in the intervening decade, but the fact that 26-year-old me had these tendencies is still a red flag for present-day me. And since gaining this valuable insight, I've kept it in the back of my mind, bouncing my behavior off it to be more objective about how I might be coming across. Those drunken words had revealed one of the most sobering truths about myself I have ever learned.

If internal self-awareness means gaining insight by looking inward, external self-awareness means turning our gaze outward to understand how we are seen. And no matter how hard we try, we simply cannot do this on our own. Unfortunately, though, **learning how others see us is usually thwarted by one simple fact: even the people we're closest to are reluctant to share such information**. We might pick up an observation here and there (with or without the aid of lip-loosening booze), but without concerted effort to uncover it, we're usually not getting, as they say in the courtroom, the whole truth and nothing but the truth.

In fact, we live in a world where people usually *don't* tell us the truth about ourselves. Stir in our uneasy reluctance to ask for it and we have a recipe for blissful ignorance. Indeed, for many people, the mere thought of finding out how others see us can conjure up many fears and insecurities ("You really *do* look fat in those jeans" or "Your presentation was incoherent and underwhelming" or "You were insufferably arrogant when you were 26"). Though finding out how others see us can be scary, intimidating, or downright painful, it's far, far better than the alternative.

Imagine for a moment that it's a Monday at your office. After a quick mid-morning bathroom break, you return with a long strip of toilet paper stuck to the bottom of your shoe, a fact to which you are completely oblivious. As you make the long walk back to your office, your co-workers begin snickering. "Did you see that?" they ask each other—yet to you, they say nothing. And little do they know that you're headed to a meeting with an important client.

When you and your unintentional accessory enter the conference room, your client smiles bemusedly, and also stays mum. Then, despite an otherwise successful meeting, she concludes that you're scatter-brained and slovenly and decides not to give you more of her business. If just one of your co-workers had pulled you aside, you'd have been spared the whole embarrassing and costly ordeal.

Of course, that was an intentionally ridiculous example, but the truth is that whether it's a gruff managerial style, poor people skills, a tendency to stutter when nervous, or something else, we *all* have some kind of metaphorical toilet paper stuck to our shoe. And more often than not, we are the last to see it.

Now, it's rare not to wonder, at one point or another, what people are saying about us when we leave the room. But rather than indulge this urge, most people stubbornly cling to their blissful ignorance. *Since no one has told me otherwise,* we decide, *I must know everything I need to know about [my job performance/my marriage/my leadership abilities].* Of course, this instinct is understandable—as we've seen, the cold hard truth can be hard to hear. But by avoiding it, we risk two equally unappealing outcomes. The first is that we don't learn the truth about the behaviors that are holding us back and are doomed to walk around with metaphorical toilet paper stuck to our shoe while people snicker behind our backs. The second is that we *do* eventually learn it—through an accidentally overheard conversation, a "come-to-Jesus moment," or a beer-fueled admission at a dive bar—in a way that blindsides us, or at a time when it's too late to do anything about what we've learned.

The saying that "feedback is a gift" is such a painful cliché that we often forget how true it really is. And we need this gift for one simple reason: **other people generally see us more objectively than we see ourselves.** Psychologist Timothy Smith and his colleagues powerfully demonstrated this in a study with 300 married couples in which both partners were being tested for heart disease. They asked each participant to rate both their own and their partner's levels of anger, hostility, and argumentativeness—all strong predictors of the illness—and found that people's self-ratings were infinitely less accurate than those of their spouses. Another study asked more than 150 Navy officers and their subordinates to rate the officers' leadership style, and found that only the subordinates could accurately assess their bosses' performance and promotability. Other people have even been shown to anticipate our future behavior better than we can (a fact to which you can attest if you've ever met a friend's new, obviously ill-suited love interest and correctly predicted that the relationship wouldn't last).

In fact, even complete strangers—that is, people we have never met face-to-face—can see us disconcertingly accurately. Researcher David Funder and his colleagues compared how undergraduates were rated by those who knew them well (parents, friends, and roommates), those who knew them casually (college and hometown acquaintances), and people they'd never met (strangers shown just a five-minute video of them) on roughly 70 personality traits. The three groups' ratings were astonishingly accurate: a match for all but three traits! The groups also tended to see similar qualities in the participants, regardless of how well they actually knew them. The surprising take-home is that **even people you don't know well can be a valuable source of feedback**.

Yet given all this, it's still tempting to think that *we* know us better than anyone could ever know us (after all, we live with ourselves every day, right?). To use a metaphor from earlier in the book, when we see our reflection in a mirror, it's easy to conclude that this is the only, and therefore the most accurate, representation of ourselves. It's far easier and safer to gaze at our reflection than face the possibility that others might not see us the same way. But gazing inward is a necessary but not sufficient condition for true insight.

When I'm speaking to managers in organizations, I'll often ask, "Who is confident that your employees have the same opinion about your leadership as you do?" About half the hands go up. So I up the ante. "Keep your hand up if you'd bet your retirement savings on it." At this point, I usually see a lot of pensive looks, and most people tentatively lower their hands. But when I ask whose opinion is "correct" (theirs or their employees'), perhaps because they want to seem more self-aware, many confidently shout out "My employees'!" Unfortunately, the answer isn't that simple. Just like we can't glean total insight just from gazing at our own reflection, looking at ourselves *only* through the eyes of others doesn't show us the complete picture, either.

A better metaphor for complete self-awareness than a mirror might therefore be a prism. As you may remember from elementary school science class, when you shine a white light into a prism, it comes out the other side in the form of a rainbow. Indeed, every time we seek a new perspective on how someone sees us, we're effectively adding another color to the picture. Instead of just looking at a flat white light, we begin to see ourselves in a richer, more complete and multidimensional way.

Jeremiah, one of our self-awareness unicorns, recently discovered how important those other colors really are. Many of his earliest self-awareness milestones were more internal in nature—for instance, discovering that his initial career choice wasn't a good match and returning to school to pursue his passion of brand management. And though Jeremiah believed he understood himself quite well, he didn't realize the value of an outside perspective until he had the opportunity to attend a coaching certification program through his company.

In his career to date, Jeremiah had always approached things—be it

a business decision, a career choice, or a conversation with a colleague—
with the mentality that he was doing them either the "right way" or
the "wrong way." But as he learned to coach others, he saw that there
was rarely one right answer. His greatest tool in helping clients find the
best path, he discovered, was understanding how *he* was influencing
the dynamic. If he was frustrated with a client for talking in circles,
for example, unintentionally expressing these feelings could make her
feel defensive and prevent her from doing her best thinking. And more
generally, to truly understand how he was showing up, Jeremiah realized that he had to seek out—and value—input from others. As he
told us:

> When you learn what other people think of you, they're
> holding up their mirror, which may have a different reflection
> than *your* mirror. All of our realities are a bit different, but it
> doesn't mean that any one of them is the reality.

Put simply, **self-awareness is not one truth**. It's a complex interweaving of our views and others' views of us. Indeed, according to studies on this topic, these two different perspectives, rather than capturing
redundant information, may simply capture different aspects of who we
are. And as we learned earlier, if we have only internal or only external
self-awareness, we're missing a huge piece of the puzzle. So even though
we should take others' opinions seriously, they also shouldn't define us
or completely override our self-image; the key, as we'll see, is learning how to evaluate the feedback we receive and determine how—and
whether—to act on it.

In this chapter, you'll learn a few approaches to help you get honest,
actionable feedback and develop a richer picture of how you are seen
by others. First, we'll explore the two biggest barriers to developing
external self-awareness. Then I'll show how to tackle these obstacles
using three methods to help you seek the right kind of feedback, both
at work and in your personal life.

THE MUM EFFECT (OR WHY WE LEAVE GLEN LESTER IN THE DARK)

Imagine that you've been recruited to participate in a study on consumer preferences. When you arrive in the lab, you're mildly amused to learn that you'll be providing your opinions about men's deodorant. The researcher, let's call him Dr. Rosen, leads you to a table with various brands, grandly announcing that today, you'll be evaluating each one on several factors like color and odor. Dr. Rosen finishes explaining the task, thanks you, and leaves the room.

A few seconds later, he bursts back in and asks, "Excuse me—are you Glen Lester?" (or if you're a woman, "Gwen Lester"). You shake your head. Dr. Rosen says, "Well, Glen is supposed to be here any minute. He just got a call—I'll see if there's a message." A few moments later, Dr. Rosen returns and solemnly says, "Glen should be told to call home as soon as he comes in. Apparently there is some very bad news about his family that he needs to get right away." You wonder what that news could be, feeling sympathy for this man you've never met and thinking how terrible it would be to get blindsided by horrible news in public. But here's the million-dollar question: When Glen eventually arrives, what would you do? Would you tell him he has an important message? And if you did, would you tip your hand that it was in fact bad news?

This clever experiment was designed by University of Georgia psychologists Sidney Rosen and Abraham Tesser back in 1968, and as you've probably surmised, it wasn't really about men's deodorant preferences. What Rosen and Tesser really wanted to know was whether people would be more reluctant to communicate bad news than good news. And that's exactly what they found. When Glen's news was good—there was a second group where participants were told that his family had called with a positive development—more than half eagerly spilled the beans as soon as Glen entered the room. But when the news was bad, five times fewer people passed along the complete message. In fact, even when "Glen" (who was really working with the researchers) prompted them by asking what kind of news it was, a full 80 percent refused to answer his question. Even after multiple requests, roughly a quarter never shared the nature of the news, and poor Glen Lester was left totally in the dark.

To describe this tendency, Rosen and Tesser coined the term **MUM Effect,** which stands for **keeping Mum about Undesirable Messages**. Their findings—confirmed by many subsequent studies—show that when we're in possession of information that might make someone uncomfortable, we tend to choose the path of least resistance: we simply decide to say nothing.

And the MUM effect doesn't just apply to the kind of personal news people withheld from Glen Lester. It also applies to the delivery of uncomfortable or unwanted information about our failings or weaknesses. I recently heard about a work group whose manager abruptly resigned. Upon learning the news, each of his five employees fancied themselves his successor and eagerly awaited their near-certain promotion. Not only did the promotion never come; the group's senior manager hired someone from the outside. Apparently, unbeknownst to all five employees, none were doing their current jobs acceptably in the eyes of their employer, let alone being considered for a promotion. But had the leader—or anyone—told them? Of course not! If the employees had received feedback, though, they each would have had the chance to improve. Their manager's avoidance of social discomfort didn't just hurt their promotion prospects; it hurt the functioning of the team as a whole.

Making matters worse, while people are reluctant to tell us the truth about how they see us, they don't seem to have the same problem sharing those opinions with others. In 1972, Herb Blumberg, then a graduate psychology student at Johns Hopkins University, conducted a study to investigate this phenomenon. He instructed female undergraduate students to think about four people in their lives—their best friend, their next two closest friends, and someone they disliked—and to list each person's positive and negative traits. Blumberg then asked whether they had mentioned each trait to any of the four people they were rating (for example, "you think your best friend Gina is conceited. Have you ever shared your observations with Gina?").

His findings were startling. Participants reported freely sharing their opinions, say, that Gina is conceited, with others—even people they didn't like—*but they almost never shared them with that person.* Blumberg perceptively concluded that our social world is "devised to keep people from learning too much about what others think of them."

This study is disconcerting evidence of something many of us secretly fear: that our employees, co-workers, friends, and family probably *are* sharing what they think about us—they're just not sharing it with us!

And this grim reality can get grimmer at work. When was the last time your boss sat you down to tell you how you could do better? The last time your colleagues gathered—willingly, voluntarily, and of their own initiative—to critique one another so they could improve? The last time you got honest, critical feedback outside an HR-mandated performance review (or sometimes even in one)? Wait, you can't think of a time where that happened? You're not alone.

Chances are that the following scenario sounds a bit more familiar. Barb is making a presentation to her team on a new, clearly ill-conceived initiative. When she finishes, the room is surprisingly silent, save a few unconvincing utterances of "Good job," "Nice plan," and "Can't wait to hear more." Later that day, the unofficial meeting after the meeting (sans Barb) takes place, where her team discusses, often unkindly, what they *really* thought of her presentation. This scenario is all too common because, despite modern organizations' lip service to things like feedback and performance management, very few people actually get timely, honest opinions about how they're doing.

Our inclination to be MUM actually makes sense from an evolutionary perspective. In the early days of the human race, when survival depended on belonging to a group, upsetting the social apple cart often meant being ostracized and having to go it alone—a fate that could literally mean death. So just as we instinctively pull our hand away from a hot stove, we instinctively avoid doing anything that might jeopardize our social standing. (Fittingly, social rejection activates the exact same parts of our brains as physical pain does.)

We've already seen that people prefer to stay MUM rather than share tough information—but are they willing to out-and-out lie?

Earlier we met Eleanor Allen, the program manager turned non-profit CEO who improved her self-awareness with the help of her deputy, Evelio. But in spite of her impressive trajectory, like many engineers, Eleanor is an introvert, and has struggled with public speaking for much of her career.* In her early years in particular, she'd agonize over every presentation—and once it was over she'd usually get stuck in a ruminative loop about her performance.

After her time in Puerto Rico, Eleanor and her team were bidding on another large water-infrastructure program. When she learned they'd been named one of the two finalists, her first thought was, *Oh no . . . I have to make a presentation during the final interview.* But she prepared and delivered it as best she could, and even remembers feeling uncharacteristically calm afterward.

But much to her disappointment, Eleanor's team lost the job. As a big believer in external self-awareness, she decided to get some feedback on her presentation to see whether it had played a role in the loss. Maybe she was missing something and her colleagues could help her understand what it was. So Eleanor asked one of her project team members—let's call him Phil—what he had thought of her final presentation. "Oh, you did *great!*" Phil enthusiastically replied. "I don't know why we didn't get it." Eleanor breathed a sigh of relief and concluded that there must have been another reason for the big loss.

That is, until a few days later, when she received a totally out-of-the-blue call from a colleague to express her condolences that they'd lost the project. Whispering, she asked Eleanor, "So what happened in that interview?" Eleanor told her that the presentation had gone fine. "Well, that's not what Phil told me," she replied, "He said it was *horrible!*"

Eleanor was so taken aback she almost dropped the phone. She had specifically asked Phil what he thought and *he had flat-out lied* to avoid the awkwardness of telling her the truth. And unfortunately, Phil is

---

* This is certainly not to suggest that being an introvert automatically makes anyone a poor public speaker, but rather that for some introverts, public speaking can be especially challenging.

not unique in this tendency. Research shows that **people are perfectly willing to tell white lies when they're easier than the cold, hard truth**. In one clever study, researchers Bella DePaulo and Kathy Bell invited participants into their lab and asked them to evaluate a series of paintings. Afterward, the researchers brought in the artists who created them and asked participants to share the feedback they had just given. Lo and behold, they sugar-coated their true feelings, and many outright lied—especially when the artist said that a painting was personally important. One participant tellingly went from exclaiming in private, "It's ugly. Just *ugly!*" to saying to the artist, "I like it. It's my second-favorite of the group."

As DePaulo and Bell conclude, not only are we "practitioners of politeness," we are especially likely to lie when the other person is personally invested in whatever it is we're giving them feedback about. So, we lie for the same reason our tribal ancestors did: we don't want to upset the social apple cart. Instead, we politely accept the "face" people present to the world (that is, who *we* think *they* think they are) and avoid putting forward information that may challenge it—even if doing so would ultimately be useful.

For Eleanor, Phil's white lie was an alarm-clock event that catalyzed a critical insight. With the realization that just casually asking "How did I do?" isn't enough, she's since made the commitment to proactively seek specific and focused feedback from people who will tell her the truth. And she's grown by leaps and bounds as a result: as just one example, as the CEO of global non-profit Water for People, Eleanor recently gave a phenomenal TEDx Mile High talk that would have made poor Phil's head spin! It seems that nowhere is the adage "You don't get what you don't ask for" more true than when it comes to seeking the truth about how others see us.

But as Eleanor and others like her usually discover, self-awareness becomes particularly critical, yet infinitely more difficult, when you're the boss. Studies show that self-aware leaders are more successful and promotable, and some research has even shown that self-awareness is the single greatest predictor of leadership success. The problem is, the higher up you are on the corporate food chain, the less likely you are to be self-aware, an affliction that's been labeled **CEO Disease**. After all, who really wants to tell the boss that his management style is alienating people, or that her latest staffing choices are causing friction, or that his clients find him controlling? Complicating matters, as we saw with Steve from chapter 3, the overconfidence that results from past successes can make it challenging for leaders to hear and accept difficult feedback—and thus make their employees more reluctant to give it.

Pixar president Ed Catmull has witnessed this reluctance to speak truth to power firsthand. Years before he co-founded his company and became president of Disney Animation Studios, he was a young PhD student at the University of Utah's nascent computer graphics program. He adored the comradery he had with his professors and fellow graduate students—there were no strict hierarchies, they worked independently, and everyone generally got along. Catmull liked this environment so much that he created a similar structure in his first job out of school. As the head of a small computer animation research team at the New York Institute of Technology, he hired smart people, treated them as equals, and let them do their thing. As a result, they told him pretty much everything that was going on. He was involved in social activities and was basically one of the guys—it felt good.

But when Catmull was hired to lead Lucasfilm's brand-new computer division, he realized that he'd need to rethink how he managed people. His new team would be bigger, better resourced, and have a much higher profile. To achieve George Lucas's ambitious vision of bringing computer technology to Hollywood, Catmull reasoned, he would need to adopt a more formal, hierarchical structure with a manager running each of the graphics, video, and audio groups. And when he did that, nearly instantaneously he noticed that something was different. Casual chatter had a habit of going silent whenever he entered the room. He was getting mostly good news and hardly any bad news. And his team was no longer inviting him to their social gatherings.

Catmull didn't like this very much, nor could he figure out why it was happening. He didn't *feel* like a different person than University of Utah Ed or New York Tech Ed. But after wrestling with this question for months, he finally realized that his new role as The Boss, coupled with his increasing prominence in the academic community, had changed the way people *perceived* him. "Even though I hadn't changed," he told me, "I recognized that, okay, this is the way it is, and it will probably get worse over time." In Catmull's case, the "it" was the MUM effect, and it was presenting a giant obstacle not just in his own performance, but to the collective self-awareness of his team. As we'll see later in the book, Catmull has made it a top-tier priority to combat the MUM effect and seek the honest truth, not just about himself as a leader, but about the challenges and issues his company is facing. And it has made quite a difference. Yet as we'll soon see, for leaders in particular, overcoming the MUM effect is only half the battle.

THE OSTRICH TRINITY

If the first barrier to external self-awareness is other people's reluctance to tell the truth, the second is our reluctance to ask for it. Most of us, at least intellectually, know we should be seeking more feedback than we are currently. Yet even when we have a rational reason to do something, our emotions can still stop us in our tracks; in this case, because asking for feedback makes us uncomfortable, we instead find ways to justify our willful ignorance.

In my experience, there are three primary excuses we make, and because they are designed to help us feel better about keeping our heads in the sand, I call them the **Ostrich Trinity**. But luckily, pushing past these excuses is absolutely possible, and it requires just one simple decision: to seek out the truth on our own terms rather than leaving it in other people's well-meaning (but MUM) hands.

Let's start with the first excuse: *I don't need to ask for feedback.* Having learned about the MUM effect, we already know that this is flat-out wrong—and especially wrong for leaders. For proof, we need not look further than the annals of business history. When Pehr Gyllenhammar took over as executive chairman of Volvo in 1971, the future for the automaker looked as bright and shiny as their freshly

THE TRUTH WE RARELY HEAR **171**

painted cars. The 36-year-old wunderkind had been born into business royalty; his father, Pehr Gyllenhammar Sr., was the CEO of Scandinavia's largest insurance company, Skandia. Educated at Sweden's prestigious Lund University and Switzerland's Centre d'Etudes Industrielles, Pehr Gyllenhammar Jr. was hardworking, confident, and a master at leveraging his connections. In fact, he'd only just succeeded his father as the CEO of Skandia when, months later, he replaced his father-in-law at the thriving Swedish car company.

From the outset, Gyllenhammar had little interest in maintaining a low profile. He'd proudly roll into the office each morning in his custom-built 1979 244 Turbo; or his 1980 240 Series with a B21ET engine; or his 1981 262 Coupe—each tailor-made creation was painted bright red with a matching interior. Though no other Volvo sported that color scheme, Gyllenhammar required that his cars be "cheeky" and "provocative" and have "nerve." That was also how he ran his company.

And it seemed to work. At least at first, as he basked in the success of creating Volvo's innovative team-based craftsmanship model. But this success would soon sow the seeds of his undoing. In the years that followed, Gyllenhammar's head grew in lock-step with the company's profits, earning him the nickname "The Emperor." His hubris, overconfidence, and refusal to take advice from anybody led him to pursue risky deals with paltry returns, and inexplicably, he often bragged about them to the press. In later years, as Volvo was reporting losses and closing plants, Gyllenhammar was Scandinavia's highest-paid executive. And because he had seeded Volvo's board with personal friends he knew would never confront him about his mistakes, it seemed all but certain that his decisions would go unchallenged.

In September of 1993, Volvo announced a merger with the French state-owned automaker Renault. It was a move that would make the new entity the world's sixth-largest automaker. And who fancied himself as the chairman of the majority owners? Pehr Gyllenhammar, of course! Together with Renault CEO Louis Schweitzer, they proudly outlined their plan for a new borderless business.

But from the moment Volvo's managers and employees heard the news, they were decidedly not on board. Convinced that it was both a bad business move and an attempt to sell them down the river, one anonymously called the situation "an impenetrable mess." Yet Gyllenhammar ignored their pleas and remained stunningly confident in the deal. At one point, he issued an updated prospectus that upped the deal's projected savings from $4.8 billion to $7.4 billion, despite having no new information to support such inflated estimates.

When it was abundantly clear that Gyllenhammar had no interest in listening to his employees' opinions, they decided to leak them to the press. At this point, minority shareholders began to speak up about their opposition to the deal. Similar announcements from larger shareholders like Skandia Insurance (yes, his father's own company) followed. As one large shareholder remarked, "We didn't realize Mr. Gyllenhammar had so many personal enemies."

In what must have come as an utter shock to the oblivious "Emperor," Volvo investors eventually banded together and the board withdrew its proposal for the merger. On that same day, Gyllenhammar resigned; his unwillingness to listen to his employees' feedback, his refusal to seek input from his closest advisors, and his inability to question his own assumptions would eventually wipe out $1.1 billion in shareholder wealth. The company was acquired by Ford just five years later, and Gyllenhammar's bright and shiny career tanked along with the company he had so epically mismanaged.

Though companies of this size rarely fail because of one factor alone, Gyllenhammar's hubris and lack of self-awareness were significant contributors. Case in point: years later, in a comical display of his sustained delusion, Gyllenhammar attributed the failed deal to an "envious vendetta" against him.

Whether or not we run a multibillion-dollar company, protecting our fragile egos by deciding we are right and others are wrong can be risky at best and devastating at worst. The good news is that pushing past the first excuse of the Ostrich Trinity is fairly simple: we must decide to pull our heads out of the sand and recognize that **others' opinions are just as important for insight as our own.**

Sometimes, though, we *do* want to ask for feedback, but we're worried that doing so would convey weakness or come at a cost. This second excuse, however—*I shouldn't ask for feedback*—is equally unfounded. One study showed that 83 percent of top-performing leaders regularly solicit feedback, compared to just 17 percent of the worst-performing ones. If anything, **we are socially and professionally rewarded for seeking critical feedback**; leaders who do are seen as more effective, not just by their bosses, but by their peers and employees (interestingly, those who seek primarily positive feedback are seen as less effective). And not surprisingly, nearly three-quarters of our unicorns reported having a proactive strategy to get information from people who will tell them the truth. So if we take a page from their book and muster the courage to do so, we'll be rewarded with self-insight and a new perspective on how we can improve.

The final excuse in the Ostrich Trinity is perhaps the most understandable: *I don't want to ask for feedback.* It doesn't take a degree in organizational psychology to know that feedback can be painful; even though we intellectually understand its value, we fear it simply because it might be a bitter pill to swallow. Over the course of my career, I've done hundreds of presentations and workshops, and to this day, every single time I sit down to read audience evaluations, I get a huge pit in my stomach. I'm sure you know that feeling—it's the dread that overtakes you when walking into your performance appraisal with your boss, or sitting down for a marriage counseling session, or having the first conversation with a friend or colleague after you'd had a conflict.

But while most people are afraid of feedback, surely the ease with which our unicorns hear it should serve as inspiration for the rest of us, right? As it turns out, they have the same reactions that we do (despite their mythical moniker, they *are* still human). One sales executive quipped, "Are you kidding me? I *hate* hearing that I'm not perfect!" But what makes unicorns truly special is the fact that they push through this fear, defensiveness, and vulnerability and go for it anyway. As U.S. President Franklin Delano Roosevelt once opined, "Courage is not the absence of fear, but rather the assessment that something else is more important than fear." In our case, that "something else" is insight.

Clearly, falling prey to the Ostrich Trinity is a dreadfully dangerous barrier to external self-awareness. Yet it is one that can be overcome. Instead of waiting for feedback to come to us, risking being blindsided, or worse, sticking our heads in the sand, we **can choose to learn the truth on our own terms.** So let's turn to three actionable strategies to do that. (I also suggest taking the quick assessment in appendix M to get a baseline on how much you're currently asking for feedback.)

360-DEGREE FEEDBACK

The first method, *360-degree feedback*, is seemingly ubiquitous in modern organizations. With a rich history dating back to the 1950s, it's designed to provide insight into how we're seen not only by our managers, but by a variety of groups, like direct reports, peers, clients, or board members. (It's called a 360 because we're getting data from all directions.) Recent technological advances have made 360s more accessible for workers in companies large and small, while the simultaneous growth of my field, organizational psychology, has made them increasingly popular. And nowadays, depending on who you ask, anywhere from 30 percent to 90 percent of organizations use this tool in one way or another. But 360s aren't just for businesspeople: they can be used with great success in families, schools, and community organizations, to name a few examples. In one study, undergraduates in a science and technology program that received 360-degree feedback (from their friends, parents, and teachers) turned in higher-quality homework and even received better grades in the course.

So much has been written about 360 reviews—and chances are you've had at least one over the course of your career—that I won't retread too much ground other than to briefly mention their advantages and disadvantages when it comes to increasing our external self-awareness. (And if you haven't yet taken one, see appendix N for a few free resources.) One of the biggest upsides of 360s is their anonymity. Because responses are averaged across respondents, people can provide their feedback without fear that it will come back to bite them. This is particularly true for leaders whose subordinates fear the repercussions of being brutally honest; luckily, the MUM effect usually disappears when feedback can't be traced back to us.

The second advantage of 360s is that they show us how our self-views stack up against others' views of us. For example, you might discover that while you believe yourself to be conscientious and hard-working, your boss doesn't share that opinion. Or that your peers consider you to be a great communicator and connector even though you don't see yourself that way at all. However, no matter what we learn, when multiple people are telling us the same thing, it's difficult to explain it away—that "Oh, he's just jealous because I got promoted before him," or "She wouldn't know what good communication skills looked like if they punched her in the face." As one manager who'd recently taken a 360 described, "[If my 360 tells me] anything critical . . . my first . . . reaction is 'What the hell are they talking about?' but if it's repeated . . . and you find several people have said it, you've got to face the facts: either it's simply true, or it's their perception of you, which is just as important."

Despite the clear benefits of 360s, they also come with a few disadvantages that prevent them from being the "be-all, end-all" route to external self-awareness. First and foremost, because most 360s are numeric, it can be difficult to interpret our results in a meaningful or actionable way. *Okay, so I got a 2 out of 5 on relationship-building,* we might think, *but what does that actually mean? And what should I be doing differently?* No one loves data and numbers more than I do, but this kind of information isn't always easy to translate into insight. One way to get around this is through a variation that I prefer to use in my executive coaching work, something I call a "qualitative 360." Instead of just sending people a survey, I track them down and talk to them. Then, when I report the findings, I can provide my clients with specific themes and examples that paint a richer picture.

Of course, these disadvantages don't mean we should abandon the practice of 360-feedback altogether. Instead, we should use it in conjunction with other approaches. In particular, a 360 can be an extremely helpful first step in learning about pillars like our patterns, reactions, and impact on others. Let's now examine a complementary approach that I have found to be one of the most powerful feedback tools at our disposal.

THE RIGHT FEEDBACK

One chilly winter afternoon, I sat in a cacophonous coffee shop waiting for Kim, my newest client, to walk through the door. Her boss, Greg, had hired me to work with her in the wake of a rather strange series of events. According to Greg, Kim, who ran his compliance function, was struggling to deal with some difficult feedback she'd received in a recent 360. Her behavior was becoming increasingly concerning—in the past month alone, Greg had received two complaints about her from managers in other departments.

Knowing there are always two sides to every story, I was eager to hear Kim's perspective. When the door opened with a whoosh of cold air, I looked up to see a tiny, impeccably dressed woman with a wild mop of brown hair impatiently scanning the room. Her intense eyes eventually locked with mine. "Tasha?" she mouthed. I nodded, waving her over. We exchanged a few pleasantries, but I could see she wasn't thrilled to be there.

"Let's get down to business," I said. "Why don't you tell me a little more about how I can best help you."

Kim took a deep breath and launched into her tale. A few months after Greg was hired to lead her business unit, he had decided to hold a team development session. As part of the process, he asked everyone to take a 360-degree assessment to get feedback on how they were seen by their colleagues and employees. As is almost always the case, there were plenty of surprises, and for Kim, they were not the happy kind. What she learned had in fact turned her world—and her self-perceptions—upside down. "I'm grateful that Greg hired you to help me," she said, "but I have to tell you . . . it's been devastating and I'm having trouble dealing with it. Maybe we can start by just trying to make sense of everything."

To kick off with something positive, I asked Kim if there was anything in her results that was a pleasant surprise. Her gloomy expression broke into something that almost resembled a smile. "Well, I was happy to hear my team say that I empower them," she said, "because that's really important to me. And more generally, people see me as a strategic thinker who's dedicated to doing the right thing for the business."

"I know people who would kill for just one of those qualities," I replied. "Now, what did you learn that shocked you?"

Kim fished out a pristine manila folder labeled "My 360 Results" from her purse. She removed her report, placed it gingerly on the table, and proceeded to glare at it accusingly for a good 30 seconds. She opened to a page where she'd scribbled notes all over the margin. "It seems that the people I work with think I'm acerbic, aggressive, and overconfident. One mentioned a meeting where I apparently lashed out at someone when they made a bad choice for the business. Someone else said that I assault people with questions, make snap judgments, and am too blunt."

I asked if she'd ever gotten that type of feedback before. "Never," Kim said. "The reason this is so shocking to me is that I've always been pretty insecure—the fact that *anyone* could perceive me as full of myself is . . . well, it breaks my heart." I could see tears welling up in her eyes. "I have no idea what I'm doing to create this impression," she said despairingly.

I truly felt for Kim. Having worked with so many clients in the same position, I know how difficult it is to learn that others don't always see us the way *we* see us. Indeed, the reason she'd been so blindsided was that she hadn't been asking for the right kind of feedback—or, to be frank, any feedback at all. Clearly, we had our work cut out for us. But I commended Kim for the huge step she was taking—it was a step I was sure she'd soon look back on as a turning point in her career.

After Kim had a bit of time to process our first conversation, we met again to define a few goals she'd work on over the next few months. But I could tell that something was still nagging her and asked what it was. "It's clear to me now," she told me, "that I spend so much time driving results that I'm forgetting about the relationship part. But I still don't

understand what I'm doing to create this perception. How am I supposed to improve if I don't understand what I need to do differently?"

It was an astute question that illustrated an unfortunate truth about
feedback: **if we don't understand the behavior we're getting feedback
about, we don't yet have the power to make better choices.** Luckily, I
had a solution in my hip pocket—I was just worried Kim would dismiss
it out of hand.

"I think we need to get you some better data," I began, "and the
only way to do that is for you to ask a couple of people a little more
directly." As I predicted, Kim worried that doing this would be a show
of weakness (remember the second excuse of the Ostrich Trinity?). But
after a little convincing, she agreed to try it.

To help her gain more insight about how she was seen, Kim and I
used an approach that I call the **RIGHT Feedback Process**. The idea
is that all feedback (and all sources of feedback) are not created equal:
we have to choose the *RIGHT people*, ask them the *RIGHT questions*,
and use the *RIGHT process* to get the kind of valuable information
that leads to actionable insight.

When I first started studying our unicorns, I expected that they
would report seeking feedback from everybody: their colleagues, their
friends and neighbors, the person next to them in line at the grocery
store. But to my amazement, they reported the opposite approach. One
unicorn, a bright young customer-service manager in the Philippines,
noted, "I get feedback *all* the time, but not from *all* the people. I rely on
a small, trusted group that I know will tell me the truth." And as we'll
see, she's not alone. In fact, as a group, our unicorns showed remarkable
consistency in just how selective they were. They recognize that quality trumps quantity and that not all input creates true insight—which
is why they always work to choose the **right people.**

Now, before we look at who we should turn to for feedback, let's
start with who we *shouldn't* turn to. The first category, **unloving critics**,
are the type of people who would criticize everything we do: a jealous
co-worker, an ex with a grudge, or an irrationally uptight boss. Whatever their motives—they don't want us to succeed, they don't trust

us, or they're just unreasonably critical people—their feedback rarely objectively reflects reality.

On the other end of the spectrum, the second source to avoid are **uncritical lovers**. While unloving critics hate everything we do, uncritical lovers wouldn't criticize us if their lives depended on it. This group can include both people who think we walk on water and can do no wrong (e.g., our moms) and those who are afraid to tell us the truth (e.g., people-pleasers or fearful employees). And while uncritical lovers' feedback will invariably be easier to hear, it can't always be trusted. As leadership professor John Jacob Gardner observed, "Pity the leader caught between unloving critics and uncritical lovers."

So if we shouldn't ask for feedback from unloving critics or uncritical lovers, who *should* we ask? The answer is **loving critics**: people who will be honest with us while still having our best interests at heart. But the ideal people for this job aren't always the most obvious. It's easy to assume that those we're closest to—a spouse, a best friend, etc.—would make the best loving critics. But just because someone knows us best doesn't mean they will serve us well in this role. There are a few additional factors you'll want to consider.

The first is a **level of mutual trust**. A loving critic doesn't need to be someone who would help you bury a body or bail you out of jail at 2:00 a.m. (though hopefully you'd never need this kind of friend), but they should be someone you implicitly know has your best interests at heart. Remember that *closeness* and *trust* aren't always the same thing. Often, the longer we've known someone, and particularly if we're related to them, the more complex our relationship can be (I believe the word "frenemy" was invented specifically for this situation). Choosing someone with whom we have a long and convoluted history won't necessarily preclude helpful feedback, but it might make the conversation more complicated or emotionally charged than it needs to be.

By the same token, there might be someone you don't know nearly as well, such as a co-worker or casual acquaintance, who genuinely wants you to be successful and is eager to play a greater role in helping you succeed. In Kim's case, one of her loving critics—the one I'd argue gave her the most helpful feedback—was a peer whom she'd worked with for years, but with whom she wasn't particularly close. They didn't hang out socially, but Kim knew her well enough to know she was invested in her success.

Identifying loving critics isn't easy, but here, actions speak louder than words. Does she go out of her way to help you improve? Does he invest his time and energy to help you grow and succeed? A story from the early days of Pixar president Ed Catmull's career is a perfect example of how to spot a loving critic.

As I mentioned earlier, long before Catmull founded Pixar, he was a PhD student in the University of Utah's computer science program— and when it was time to write his dissertation, he was a *nervous* one. Even though he had made the groundbreaking discovery of the z-buffer, an algorithm that allows computers to track the depth of three-dimensional objects, he had never written much of anything in his life.

When Catmull finally finished his tome, he submitted it to his dissertation committee and eagerly awaited their reviews. The first committee member to respond was overwhelmingly complimentary. *Maybe my writing isn't so bad after all*, Catmull concluded. Later that week, more feedback came in from another committee member, who also happened to be the chair of the department. But his feedback wasn't so kind, communicating in no uncertain terms that the thesis was, in fact, horribly written. For days, Catmull scratched his head trying to square these two seemingly contradictory responses.

Then one afternoon, the complimentary committee member suddenly appeared in Catmull's office and proceeded to trash his thesis, providing a laundry list of all the things that were wrong with it. And even though *that* feedback was nearly identical to what he'd heard from the department chair, Catmull's reaction couldn't have been more different. *What is wrong with this guy?* he angrily wondered. He wasn't denying that the feedback was accurate; the issue was the committee member's motive for giving it. *He doesn't want to help*, Catmull thought. *He just wants to impress the department chair.* It didn't take much deliberation for Catmull to decide to remove him from his committee.

Although his now-former committee member clearly didn't have his best interests at heart, Catmull had a hunch that the department chair did. His instincts proved to be correct when the very busy chair invited him to his home to discuss how to improve the manuscript, and proceeded to spend an entire day with him reviewing and revising. The finished product was impressive. Not only did Catmull pass his defense with flying colors; the work is widely considered one of the most historically significant contributions to the field of computer graphics. But the more important lesson Catmull learned from the experience was that anyone can give critical feedback and then cut and run—it's the people who stick around to help you see it through you can really trust.

However, when it comes to feedback, good intentions aren't always enough. (You know what they say about the road to hell . . .) To produce truly useful insight, the person must also have **sufficient exposure to the behavior you want feedback on and a clear picture of what success looks like**. For example, one of my closest friends is a lawyer. Because she has demonstrated time and again that she has my best interests at heart, she would be a great loving-critic contender— but not for everything. If I asked her to give me feedback on my public speaking skills, for example, we'd run into two problems. First, she almost never hears me speak, so she wouldn't have enough data to really comment on how I'm doing. The other problem is that, since she isn't very familiar with the world of public speaking (current trends, dos and don'ts, etc.), the feedback she gives me may be candid and sincere— but perhaps not especially helpful. However, an area where she *could* add tremendous value might be helping me understand how I show up in social situations. She has plenty of exposure to my behavior in this realm, and because she's one of the most socially savvy people I know, her observations would carry a lot of weight.

The third and final factor in selecting a loving critic is whether they will be **willing and able to be brutally honest with you**. The best yardstick here is whether they've ever told you a tough truth. But even if they haven't, you can examine their behavior in other situations. Someone who isn't afraid to speak his or her mind, even when doing so may cause social discomfort, is likely to be a good loving critic. Part of the reason Kim selected the peer I mentioned earlier was that she had seen her raise tough issues in meetings.

However, while keeping all of this in mind, you should also listen to your instincts. As Malcolm Gladwell points out in his book *Blink*, our gut reactions can be surprisingly informative. In this case, I tend to agree: if a loving-critic candidate doesn't quite *feel* right to you, they probably aren't.

Once you've chosen your loving critics, it's time to figure out the **right questions** to ask them. At this point, you're not yet having the actual feedback conversation (we'll get to that soon)—right now you're simply getting your thoughts together regarding how you want the conversation to go and how you'll use it to better understand the "you" that you're projecting to the world.

The most important characteristic of the right questions is specificity. A good way to think about this is to look at the scientific method. When scientists—chemists, physicists, and yes, even psychologists—build theories, we test specific hypotheses about the phenomenon we're studying. By the same token, if you can come up with a working hypothesis or two about how other people see you—for example, "I think I have a tendency to come across as timid and non-authoritative when I meet with clients; is that your experience?"—it will give you a focused framework for the conversation and help you either confirm or deny your suspicion.

This emphasis on specificity might be counterintuitive if you've become accustomed to the common open-ended approaches to feedback in many organizations, like the Start/Stop/Continue Model.* While this method has merits, for our purposes, it's far too broad. First off, asking your loving critics for general feedback with no parameters or specifics could be confusing for them and unhelpful to you. For example, if

---

* If you're not familiar with this model: you're asking what you should start doing that you're not doing, what to stop doing that isn't serving you well, and what to continue doing to be successful.

I said to a client, "I'd love any observations about how I'm doing"—that client won't know what's on the table. Do I want feedback on whether I ask good questions during coaching sessions? Whether my jokes are funny? Whether I'm a snazzy dresser? This ambiguity could make the feedback conversation uncomfortable for both of us. Imagine if I went in wanting to learn how I'm doing on my project but come out of it with feedback that I wear the wrong color of makeup (incidentally, that actually happened to a friend of mine during a conversation with one of her graduate professors). The bottom line is that it's on you to ask the questions you want answered—and in general, the more specific you are, the more seamless and successful the process will be for both you and your loving critics.

So we've established that the right questions come from a specific working hypothesis—but how do we develop that hypothesis? One way is to consider how you see certain pillars (like your aspirations, patterns, and impact), or to remember feedback you've received in the past. Let's look at how Kim did it. Given her aspirations to take on more responsibility in the future, she knew that she couldn't be successful if she was seen as abrupt or aggressive. Her 360 results made it clear that she had some work to do in these areas, but she needed more information. So here was Kim's working hypothesis: *I behave abrasively at work, particularly in meetings.* Since we already had inside information that her colleagues felt this way, we expected to confirm this hypothesis, but we really wanted to learn *what* she was doing to create that impression. (You'll also notice that Kim's working hypothesis wasn't an indictment of her personally, but rather a specific behavior that she wanted to better understand.)

In general, **it's a good idea to focus on just one or two working hypotheses at a time**. As with most things, when you try to do too much at once, you can get overwhelmed—and defensive—pretty quickly. ("You mean not only is my makeup the wrong color, but I'm also seen as a misanthrope who makes everyone uncomfortable in meetings?!") In general, when it comes to self-awareness and self-improvement, I'm a big proponent of realism. You can't—and shouldn't—try to transform yourself overnight. And in fact, the people I've seen make the most dramatic improvements are usually the ones who were laser-focused on one thing at a time.

Let's turn back to Kim. She was armed with her target list of loving critics (the right people) and her working hypothesis (the right questions), so it was now time to build the **right process**. Kim started by approaching her three desired loving critics: me (an easy sell) and two of her peers. She set aside 15 minutes for each conversation, which she began by giving them some context—sharing what she'd learned during her 360 and why she wanted to know more. Specifically, she requested that they observe her in meetings (plus any other notable interactions) and tell her when she *was* and *wasn't* being abrasive. And despite her enthusiasm to get started, she acknowledged that what she was asking for wasn't a small favor and suggested that they think about it before accepting. This ensured that they weren't just agreeing out of politeness—and after thinking about it, both enthusiastically agreed the very next day.

At this point, all that was left to do was implement a solid process to extract the golden egg: their feedback. First, the gestation period. Kim's loving critics would need a window of time to watch her in a few meetings and record some good observations—a month seemed sufficient. Second, the harvesting of the data. Kim requested one 30-minute phone call every month with each loving critic for the next three months. As we'll soon see, this mere four and a half hours would yield a priceless return.

Over the course of those three months, Kim diligently held her feedback meetings with her peers, and she and I continued to meet monthly. Because she'd set it up so carefully, the conversations went like clockwork. This isn't to say that the feedback was easy to hear. Kim made many shocking discoveries, but the important thing was that she was committed to working through them. For example, in the first meeting I observed, I noticed that Kim spent most of her time focused on the negative (complaining, pointing out what wasn't going well, etc.). I gave her the feedback, reading the specific examples of the behavior I'd noticed. And instead of getting defensive, she said

"I never noticed I was doing that." By the next meeting I attended, she was already approaching things more neutrally and calling out the positive.

Another loving critic pointed out a time when Kim had been unnecessarily blunt with someone, which resulted in another "aha moment." Kim had grown up in an unusually direct family, and she was now seeing that what felt normal to her was often uncomfortable for others. She needed to meet people on their terms rather than hers.

With the help of her loving critics, Kim built a better picture in her mind of how her behavior was coming across. As she experimented with new choices, she began to see that being more diplomatic didn't just improve her relationships; getting her points across without the collateral damage actually made it easier to get work done. She sure could communicate a lot better, she found, when people weren't scared of her.

Perhaps Kim's biggest turning point came when she discovered the "trigger" that sent her into a downward spiral: the feeling that her knowledge was being questioned. And with that discovery came control. She started experimenting with approaches to tame her reactions when she'd been set off, and noticed that simply giving her inner voice the opportunity to express itself helped. Merely thinking *I feel attacked or criticized right now* helped her rise above the temptation to instantly act upon that feeling (naming our emotions to the rescue!). She also found that a few moments of preparation could help her stay calm. Before walking into a meeting that she thought might trigger her, she now takes, in her words, a "mental valium." This metaphorical medication gives her the power to stay calm and open-minded, and to ask people questions to better understand where they're coming from instead of jumping down their throats.

About a month after Kim and I had completed our work together, her boss summoned me to his office for a discussion. I was worried that she'd started to slide back into her old behaviors. But when I walked into Greg's office, the normally taciturn man gave me a giant hug. In addition to sharing the dramatic changes he'd noticed personally, Greg reported that the complaints from other departments had disappeared.

(It's since been more than two years, and he's never gotten another call.) Kim's prickly relationships began to soften and deepen. She felt less frustrated, more confident, and happier at work and at home. Once Greg came to trust her, he began to give her more opportunities and more challenges—and she was nailing them. In fact, Greg recently shared that Kim is now his most valued team member. It was one of the most remarkable transformations I've ever seen—a truly inspiring example of insight in action.

THE DINNER OF TRUTH

In my experience, the RIGHT feedback process is probably the most powerful booster of external self-awareness that you have at your disposal—one that's especially well suited for the workplace. But work isn't the only place where external self-awareness matters. Aren't most of us equally curious about how we're seen in our personal lives—by our friends, our neighbors, our community, and our family? While the RIGHT method can certainly be applied to this sort of feedback, there is another slightly simpler method for learning how we show up in the personal realm. I call it the *Dinner of Truth*, and if that sounds slightly ominous, that's because it is. Yet for those who make the brave choice to try it, the Dinner of Truth can have an astonishing impact not just on our external self-awareness, but on our most important personal relationships.

It was an unusually sunny afternoon in the Pacific Northwest, and professor Josh Misner was driving his kids home from school. As they sat squished together in the front bench seat of his old Ford pickup, the trio cheerfully reported on their respective days. This was one of those everyday joyful moments that Misner loves to revel in. A prominent member of the Good Men Project, Misner is a special breed of amazingly modern father, perfectly in touch with his feelings and proud to make it known that he takes the job of raising his kids even more seriously than he does his job as an accomplished and hardworking communications professor.

Once his children had finished, he told them about an exercise he'd been tinkering with for one of his communication classes. The topic, as it so happens, was self-awareness. Suddenly, Misner realized that the perfect opportunity to test the exercise was staring him in the face. After all, he couldn't think of anyone on this earth with whom he'd rather have solid communication than his children. And even though they were young, he figured he'd get some good data—kids have a knack for saying exactly what they're thinking.

"Hey," he said, "Do you guys want to help me try out this new exercise?"

"Sure, Daddy!" his seven-year-old son Parker and ten-year-old daughter Bella enthusiastically responded.

"OK, great!" he smiled. "So . . . what bugs you the most about me?"

Misner was concerned when they started squirming uncomfortably in their seats. "Um, you're good, Dad!" said Bella. "Yep, nothing bugs us about you, Dad!" echoed Parker.

Misner loved being a father. He knew he was good at it. What could possibly be making them so uncomfortable? *It can't be anything serious,* he reassured himself.

"Guys, I understand that you don't want to tell Daddy something mean, but you're not going to get in trouble. I really want to hear what you think. Tell me anything."

A long, pregnant pause filled the car. "Dad," his seven-year-old weakly ventured, "I don't like it when you yell so much."

Parker's voice was cracking. Misner glanced from the road to see tears welling up in his son's eyes. "It makes me feel like you don't love me anymore," he continued, "and it makes me want to go hide in my room."

Misner was shattered. Desperately trying to control his expression, he looked at his daughter, who added, "I don't like it when you get mad at me, either. It hurts me and makes me cry."

As I mentioned earlier, the relationships we have with those closest to us—our spouses, our kids, our parents, our dearest friends—tend to be messier, more complicated, and more emotionally charged than those we have with our co-workers. And as Misner realized, constructive feedback has the chance of cutting far deeper when it's from the people we love. But I'd argue that this is exactly what makes it so important. (We'll pick this thread back up in the next chapter when we talk about how to deal with tough feedback.)

Painful as it was, Misner pressed on, determined to stick to the exercise that he had devised. He took a deep breath and started asking questions: "What do you hear me yelling about the most?" "What impact does it have on you?" "What can I do differently?" Then he listened to their answers without getting upset or defensive—though, as he recounts, it was not easy.

That conversation marked the beginning of a new journey, one that first transformed his relationship with his children and then, inevitably, changed him. Their feedback served as a profound reminder of the importance of listening and being patient. He felt more empathy for his kids—and now when he becomes frustrated with them, he remembers how hurtful it is when he flies off the handle. Now he watches his words and his actions much more closely. This ingenious exercise inspired Misner to make many positive changes in his own life, and the Dinner of Truth has proven time and again to produce radical insight.

So what, exactly, does the Dinner of Truth entail? Here are the instructions:

> Contact a close friend, family member, or mentor—someone who knows you well and with whom you want to strengthen your relationship. Invite this person to share a meal with you. During the meal, ask them to tell you the one thing that annoys them most about you. But first, tell the person why you're doing this, that nothing is off-limits, and that you aren't allowed to answer defensively—only to listen with an open heart and mind.

Now, as someone who has actually tried this (let this be proof that there is nothing I will not do in the name of research), I can tell you that the answer isn't easy to hear. I did it twice, and both times I dreaded the conversation more than a trip to the dentist—and I really, really don't like going to the dentist. Misner's students generally react the same way. "As soon as I present the exercise," Misner told me, "I can see the blood drain out of their faces and their mouths drop open." He fully recognizes that it requires courage—but thousands of students have lived to tell the tale and are wiser for it.

On a related note, there's a reason Misner suggests having the conversation over a meal—ideally dinner. "There's something magical about breaking bread with someone," he says. "Eating is intimate. It involves trust." Plus, let's be honest: painful truths go down a whole lot easier with a nerve-diffusing adult beverage.*

And if you set yourself up for success, the conversation will probably go more smoothly than you think. Over the years, Misner has assembled valuable list of dos and don'ts to guide his students in completing this exercise. First, he says, **mental preparation is key**. Spend some time trying to anticipate what might be said and bracing yourself for the worst-case scenario. Second, **make a decision about how "deep" you want to go**. The closer we are to the person we choose, the more insight we stand to gain, but the scarier the conversation might be.

Third, Misner warns his students that the person you ask might not be ready to open up to you right away; if that's the case, he suggests **reminding them that this is intended to help you grow**, and that all you want to do is check your perceptions against theirs. This gives them permission to be honest and candid rather than cautious and polite. Then, once your dinner companion starts sharing the feedback, Misner says, your job is to keep the conversation going. Yes, I know it will be tempting to shut down this line of inquiry as quickly as humanly possible. But to get the most out of this exercise, Misner recommends **asking questions to clarify** as necessary, just as he did with his kids during his maiden voyage of the exercise.

As scary as the Dinner of Truth might feel at first, you might be surprised at how truly exhilarating—and immeasurably helpful—it is to learn how someone you deeply care about really sees you. And I

---

* Though with more than one, you may risk a *Real Housewives of New Jersey*–style table-flipping incident.

probably don't have to tell you that this is true for all of the tools we've reviewed in this chapter. Although it usually feels safer to train our gaze inward, we can get so comfortable in our safe, warm cocoon of delusion that we don't even realize we're in it. That's precisely the reason we need feedback. So choose your loving critics, make a plan, and get ready to bask in your newfound insight.

But learning how other people see us—whether it's through a 360, the RIGHT Feedback Process, or a Dinner of Truth—is only the first step on the path to external self-awareness. As eye-opening as feedback can be, if we want to turn it into the kind of insight that makes our life better, we need to develop a few more equally critical and rewarding skills: to receive it with grace, to commit to reflecting on it, and to intelligently respond to it. Let's now look at how to put feedback to work.

8

RECEIVING, REFLECTING ON, AND RESPONDING TO DIFFICULT OR SURPRISING FEEDBACK

If you wish information and improvement from the
knowledge of others, and yet at the same time express
yourself as firmly fix'd in your present opinions, modest,
sensible men who do not love disputation, will probably
leave you undisturbed in the possession of your error.

—BEN FRANKLIN

If there's one thing I've learned over the years, it's that sometimes the greatest minds in psychology are also the minds in greatest need of psychology. One semester, I worked as a teaching assistant for an esteemed psychology professor. Unfortunately, she hadn't gotten off on the best foot with her students. They saw her lectures as vague and confusing and her aloof demeanor as an impediment to their learning. And I had to agree. Time and again, her students begged me to bring their concerns to her, but I couldn't imagine having such a conversation without breaking out in hives. It would've probably proven pointless anyway—and perhaps even made the situation worse.

As the weeks turned into slow, painful months, I helplessly watched the situation unfold. She soldiered on, apparently without thinking, and the students became more alienated and disenchanted. Then, one bright spring morning, I was sitting in my office when I received the following e-mail from her:

As we're winding down the year, I wanted to reach out to a few key people I've worked with to ask for your feedback. I'd like your candid observations on what I'm doing well and what I can do better. Please schedule a meeting where we can review your feedback.

I was amazed. Up until this point, she had appeared completely oblivious about how she was coming across in the classroom—and yet here she was, making the brave choice to actively seek feedback. So when my shock eventually subsided, I felt truly hopeful. My professor was giving me an opportunity that, if I responded appropriately, could improve the learning experiences of generations of future students. This would probably be my one shot to do it, so I put everything I had into preparing for our meeting. In the week leading up to our appointment, I spent no small amount of time combining what I'd heard from her students with my own observations. When I finally hit "print," the finished document was, if I do say so myself, finely crafted, specific, and fair.

The morning of our meeting, I woke up with a pit in my stomach. I still remember standing outside my professor's office, clutching my handout as I waited for her to call me in, my excitement quickly turning to terror. With sweaty palms, I pushed the document across the table and began my carefully planned monologue.

"All the students really value the depth of your knowledge and experience, but there are times when you can be perceived as unapproachable," I told her.

Her brow furrowed. "Of course," I quickly continued, "I have no doubt at all that you'd do anything in your power to help your students in any way you can. But I also think there are a few presentational barriers that are preventing you from getting the very best out of them." The furrow had become a deep frown. "For example, one student I spoke with mentioned a time when he asked for clarification on something you said in your lecture and you just gave him the page number of the textbook. When he checked it out, he was still confused, but was reluctant to bring it up again. In the end, he just left it and ended up missing two items on the exam."

By now she looked visibly uncomfortable, shifting back and forth in her chair as if she was sitting on a porcupine. But seeing how much she was struggling with the process made me admire her all the more. So I pressed on, trying my hardest to be respectful but candid, sharing my carefully documented examples. When I finally finished, I breathed a sigh of relief and awaited the words of gratitude that would undoubtedly follow.

What happened next gives me flashbacks to this day. My professor slid my handout back to me and flatly stated, "Well that's nice. But isn't all of this just *your opinion*?"

That's when it hit me. She had never really wanted my honest feedback in the first place—she wanted the Kabuki-theater version of honest feedback: the kind where I told her she was doing a great job and that all the students loved her, even though that was far from the objective reality.

The point here is that seeking out the truth is a necessary but not completely sufficient step in becoming externally self-aware. **To gain true insight, we also have to learn how to hear that truth—not just listen to it, but really *hear* it**. Now I'm not claiming that this is ever easy. Indeed, in my coaching practice, I've since seen just about every possible negative reaction to feedback—yelling, crying, silence, denial, you name it. In a misguided attempt to cling to the comfortable mental image we have of ourselves, it's tempting to react by getting angry and defensive (remember Steve?) or trying to run away (either literally or by not listening, shrugging it off, or pretending it never happened). Even our unicorns get tripped up. But when we make excuses, explain feedback away, or blame it on bad moods or biases, we're only hurting ourselves. After all, when we stubbornly hold tight to our perspective— looking only in the mirror rather than letting light pass through the prism—we can't always trust what we see.

In this chapter, we'll focus on how to successfully receive, reflect on, and respond to feedback. Through a tool called the 3R Model, we'll learn how to resist the siren song of denial and hear difficult or surprising feedback with open ears and an open mind. As we'll learn in this chapter, what we hear can take a few possible forms: it might be critical and surprise us. It might be critical and support our preexisting beliefs. Or, it might even be positive, either confirming or opening our eyes to a strength we didn't know we had. And it's not until we've received feedback that the real challenge begins: to carefully weigh the source, find the valuable elements, and decide what we're going to do about them. (It would, of course, be overly simplistic to imply that we should blindly accept and act on whatever we hear.) But whatever the case, successfully responding to feedback depends on understanding what we've heard—and then lining up the other person's perspective on our pillars of insight with our own. So let's start there.

◆

We first met Florence, the Nigerian businesswoman, political activist, and unicorn in the first chapter of this book. In her role as a manager at an oil and gas company in the Nigerian capital of Abuja, she is lucky to have a strong and supportive relationship with her boss. But one day, he gave her some rather unwitting feedback that rocked her to her core.

As part of the prep work for an upcoming training that Florence was attending, the school had asked her boss to fill out a survey describing her work approach. The day it was due, she was sitting in his cozy office waiting for him to arrive for a meeting. As Florence gazed at the family pictures hung with care on the warmly colored wall behind his desk, something caught her eye. It was the feedback form. And he had completed it.

Florence forced her gaze back to the family portraits and tried very hard to focus on the adorableness of his children rather than read something she knew she wasn't supposed to. When that didn't work, she checked her phone. When that didn't work, she closed her eyes and started humming to herself. Worried now about how strange she might look to anyone passing by, she opened her eyes again. And finally, she did what almost anyone in her position would have done: she peeked at the form. Florence saw a question, "How would you describe the participant?" and below it was her boss's reply—just two words: "Very ambitious." Her jaw hit the floor, and not in a good way.

Now, to the average Westerner, this feedback wouldn't be a problem. In fact, it would likely be a compliment. But in Nigeria, there are powerful social rules that govern who is "allowed" to be ambitious, and that set of behaviors is only reserved for men. For a woman, being ambitious—that is, wanting to succeed professionally, to support herself, to make her own money—runs counter to her expected place in society, as a mother, a wife, and a homemaker. Therefore, a woman who is ambitious is also seen as arrogant, proud, overbearing, and deliberately shunning the role she is expected to play in the world.

Florence was so shocked that she wasn't even going to pretend she hadn't been reading the feedback form. In all her years, she'd never thought of herself as arrogant or overbearing. But in this alarm-clock moment, she realized she had a choice. She could go into defensive mode, or she could use it as an opportunity for insight. Though it wasn't easy, Florence was determined to explore this surprising new data and come out the other side braver and wiser. And ever the unicorn, she approached this process in a way that's a perfect illustration of the **3R Model**, which I've used for many years to help others (and frankly, myself) stay in control of how we **Receive**, **Reflect** on, and **Respond** to feedback. The process helps put our egos and preconceived notions about ourselves aside and focus only on the information directly in front of us, to resist our "fight or flight" instinct, and to turn that feedback into a chance to gain self-awareness.

The process starts with **receiving feedback**, and Florence had just been given that gift whether she wanted it or not. And though she was shocked to hear that she was seen as ambitious, she was also determined not to let her emotions get the better of her. Pausing for a moment and taking a deep breath, she asked herself what she was feeling. *I am upset*, she admitted to herself, *but there might be something valuable for me in this feedback anyway.* Florence's simple but powerful decision to **mine the insight potential** in her boss's feedback led her to wonder, *What am I doing that's causing him to see me that way?* This question instantly moved her from the passenger seat to the driver's seat and changed the conversation from a trial by fire to a fact-finding mission.

But to receive feedback doesn't mean to listen passively; it means to actively seek understanding by asking questions. Not only does this give us better information to go on; it prevents us from flying off the handle or inadvertently lapsing into denial. Accordingly, Florence summoned the will to calmly ask her boss a series of questions: "Can you tell me more about what you mean when you say 'ambitious'?" "Can you give me a few examples?" "When did you first notice this behavior?" As he answered, she scribbled down his exact words in her notebook to refer to later. She thanked him and returned to her office.

For the next few days, Florence let her boss's feedback rattle around in her head. After all, she would be in no condition to figure out what it meant, let alone what to do about it, when her emotions were still getting the better of her. Interestingly, when it comes to **reflecting on feedback** (the second step in the 3R Model), unicorns wisely avoid the temptation to jump in right away. Most reported giving themselves days or even weeks to bounce back after hearing something truly surprising or upsetting.

Soon, Florence was ready to figure out what this strange feedback meant and how to respond to it. To do this, she asked herself three questions. First, **do I understand this feedback?** Although she wasn't as upset as she'd been when she heard it, she was just as perplexed. So Florence decided to talk to a few loving critics, collecting more and more insights until she began to understand what her boss had actually been trying to tell her. Although Florence's gut reaction had been to label this feedback as "negative," she soon learned that her loving critics had a more nuanced view. Her confidence did sometimes create friction with people, at least initially, but when they got to know her better, they realized that she was neither bossy nor pushy—and that her self-assurance gave her a unique edge.

This then led Florence to ask, **how will this affect my long-term success and well-being?** Remember, not all feedback is accurate or important, and as I mentioned earlier, unicorns are surprisingly picky about what they let in. After all, as Roman philosopher Marcus Aurelius reminds us, "Everything we hear is an opinion, not a fact. Everything we see is a perspective, not the truth." To figure out what is worth listening to, a good rule of thumb is to look at how pervasive a particular behavior is. Feedback from one person is a perspective; feedback from two people is a pattern; but feedback from three or more people *is* likely to be as close to a fact as you can get. Florence had clearly heard she was "ambitious" from so many people that she had to listen. But, she realized, despite the unfavorable cultural connotations, it wasn't actually having a negative impact on her long-term success—if anything, it was helping her accomplish her goals.

This realization propelled Florence to her final question, **do I want to act on this feedback, and if so, how?** Sometimes, even when we understand feedback and determine that it matters, we might decide not to respond to it right away. Ultimately, it's up to us to figure out whether making a particular change will provide a sufficient return for the effort and time it requires.

Florence did decide to **respond to the feedback** (the final step in the 3R Model), but not in the way you might expect. This process had led her to discover that even as a woman in her culture, she didn't *have* to be timid. She'd begun to realize that her unique combination of humility and confidence was not, in fact, a weakness: it was precisely what would help her achieve great things. And though she would always consider other people's feelings and emotions, she was going to live her life on her own terms.

So instead of **changing herself**, Florence decided to **change the narrative**, starting with her own. With a newfound understanding that her ambition wasn't a flaw, she cast aside her cultural preconceptions about the term and embraced it. "There will always be people who say 'Don't climb that high—you will fall,'" she says. "But I don't listen to them anymore."

Florence's chance peek at two words on a piece of paper set in motion a series of discoveries that didn't just increase her external self-awareness, but helped lay the foundation to make a more powerful mark on the world. This is a compelling lesson: if we can receive feedback with grace, reflect on it with courage, and respond to it with purpose, we are capable of unearthing unimaginable insights from the most unlikely of places.

SELF-AFFIRMATION: NOT JUST FOR STUART SMALLEY

When you picture a chess grandmaster, what image comes to mind? Probably someone who is quiet and serious; perhaps a Bobby Fischer–like image hunched over a chessboard, or a studious-looking type in a turtleneck and tweed blazer facing off against a supercomputer. But whatever your mental image, which gender did you assign to your grandmaster? In all likelihood, your grandmaster was male, and in this you wouldn't be alone. This is just one of many unconscious stereotypes that even the most enlightened people involuntarily possess. But while many of us are at least somewhat aware of the stereotypes we have about others, we often lack insight into a more surprising sort of stereotype: **the self-limiting beliefs we hold about ourselves and how others see us.** And whether we know it or not, we all have them.

But how do these stereotypes relate to dealing with feedback and improving our external self-awareness? Put simply, when we receive difficult feedback in areas that play into our existing insecurities, it can cut like a knife. Whereas the feedback Florence received from her boss was (at least initially) critical and surprising, sometimes feedback can be critical and confirming—in other words, it backs up a weakness we already believe is there. And unfortunately, the confirmation of those beliefs can cause us to shut down, feel helpless, or give up altogether. In a minute, we'll learn a simple tool to inoculate ourselves against such responses. But first, let's see just how harmful our self-limiting beliefs can be.

In 2014, psychologists Hank Rothgerber and Katie Wolsiefer wanted to learn whether the stereotype of chess players as being male influenced the performance of female chess players. Using data from the United States Chess Federation, they analyzed the stats from a dozen elementary, middle, and high school scholastic chess tournaments, looking for patterns in how male and female students fared depending on the gender of their opponents. Just as they predicted, females paired with male opponents performed significantly worse—a full 20 percent worse—than those paired with other females.* Why? When we hold negative stereotypes about our abilities—in this case, it was the girls' belief that boys were better at chess—our fear of confirming them can become a self-fulfilling prophecy, even before we receive any sort of feedback.

This effect was dubbed *stereotype threat* by psychologists Claude Steele and Joshua Aronson, and it's been demonstrated for a variety of stereotyped groups and in a wide swath of areas. In one of Steele and Aronson's studies, when African American students were told that a standardized test was a measure of intelligence (playing into the prevalent stereotype that they'd underperform their European American counterparts), that's exactly what happened. But when the students *weren't* told that the test measured intelligence, both groups scored similarly. In another study, when researchers reminded collegiate athletes, who are often stereotyped as poor academic performers, of their "jock" identities, they scored 12 percent lower than non-athletes on a Graduate Record Examination (GRE) test.

Stereotype threat doesn't just hurt performance on individual tests or tasks; it can seriously limit our long-term success. For many decades since women entered the workforce en masse, there has been a persistent gender gap in the sciences. (Despite no inherent differences in ability, women hold only 22 percent of the science and engineering jobs in the United States.) Many explanations focus on things like cultural expectations or norms. But a full decade before Sheryl Sandberg published *Lean In*, Joyce Erhlinger and David Dunning uncovered another contributing factor. They asked male and female university students to rate their ability to reason about science. Several weeks later, they invited those same students to participate in a supposedly unrelated study of scientific reasoning. Results revealed that women's views of their abilities were an average of 15 percent lower than men's,

---

* However, for this effect to emerge, she had to be matched up with a moderately to highly competent (as opposed to an incompetent) male opponent.

regardless of how they performed on the test. These findings suggest that women's self-limiting beliefs, and the subsequent choices they make about which profession to pursue, are likely significant contributors to the gender gap in the sciences.

Thankfully, there's a simple intervention we can use to inoculate ourselves against these self-limiting effects: a process Claude Steele dubbed *self-affirmation*. When faced with feedback in an area that plays into our self-limiting beliefs, merely **taking a few minutes to remind ourselves of another important aspect of our identity than the one being threatened** shores up our "psychological immune system." Let's say that you're about to walk into your performance appraisal after a tough year where you haven't met your numbers. One way you can defend yourself against this looming threat is to remember that you're a loving parent, or a devoted community volunteer, or a good friend.

This might sound simplistic or pie-in-the-sky, but I can assure you that the research supports it. For example, psychologist Geoffrey Cohen instructed a group of African American seventh-graders who were at risk of stereotype threat to take just 10 minutes at the beginning of the semester to write about their most important values. At the end of the semester, 70 percent earned higher grades relative to a group who did not perform the exercise, an improvement which resulted in a 40-percent reduction in the racial achievement gap. Fascinatingly, there's even evidence that self-affirmation buffers our *physical* responses to threat—it reduces our levels of the stress hormone cortisol, which helps us think more rationally and not lose sight of the bigger picture.[*]

If you've ever seen Al Franken's character Stuart Smalley on *Saturday Night Live*, the self-affirmation process might conjure images of a pudgy man in a yellow sweater standing in front of a mirror repeating in a calm, monotone voice, "I'm good enough, I'm smart enough, and doggone it, people like me." Indeed, on the face of it, isn't saying

---

[*] In one study, Stage I and II breast cancer patients who completed a self-affirmation exercise coped better with stress—and even showed fewer physical symptoms—a full three months later compared to those who hadn't done the exercise.

that we're great no matter what tantamount to the Feel Good Effect? Might self-affirmation simply result in our trivializing tough feedback or explaining it away?

This couldn't be further from the truth. And though the Stuart Smalley character probably did a lot for the ratings of *Saturday Night Live*, he did a disservice to the science of self-affirmation by portraying it in such a comical light. The rigorous scientific research on the practice clearly shows that, rather than causing us to trivialize what we hear, it actually helps us be more open to difficult feedback. And though self-affirmation for its own sake might veer into Feel Good Effect territory, strategically using it to shore ourselves up can help us hear tough truths. According to researcher David Sherman, self-affirmation makes us "more open to ideas that would otherwise be too painful to accept." After all, when we remember the greater picture of who we are, we can put seemingly threatening information in its proper perspective.

I learned this lesson myself a few years ago. Right around the time I started working on this book, I was getting ready to attend a holiday party thrown by an old high school friend. And to put it mildly, I'd had a pretty bad day. Like many authors I know, when I'm writing a book, I cycle between two polar-opposite emotions: euphoric excitement and crippling self-doubt (my husband has dubbed it ABD, or Author Bipolar Disorder). I had been working on a few central sections and struggling to synthesize some of our study's findings. Earlier that week, after what felt like a million false starts, I had finally cobbled a few thoughts together. But I was worried that they weren't working, so I'd shot them over to a friend of mine who works in publishing to get his take.

Much to my horror, he was even less impressed than I thought he would be. Because I was already feeling deeply insecure, his comments sent me into a spiral of even greater self-doubt. What's worse, I received my friend's feedback less than an hour before I had to leave for the party. Naturally, I spent that hour sulking around and wondering if I should even go. *To hell with it*, I thought, *if I do, at least I can forget about my book for a few hours.*

As I arrived at the warm, cozy restaurant with fogged-up windows and Christmas carols playing on the jukebox, I was elated to see many familiar faces I hadn't seen in years. For context, my high school experience was an uncommonly positive one. (Luckily, you didn't get stuffed in lockers for getting good grades or doing theater, otherwise I would have really been in trouble.) An evening reminiscing with my old friends was just what I needed. And to my surprise, I didn't think about the book even once.

When I returned home later that night, a dull, sweet pang of nostalgia washed over me. *Things were so easy back then*, I wistfully recalled. But at the same time, I noticed that I also felt a welcome sense of perspective on my writing struggles. My high school self never shrank in the face of a challenge. Why would my current self be any different? I drifted off to sleep that night with a feeling of peaceful resolve—tomorrow I *would* figure out my vexing book problem, no matter what—and slept better than I had in a long time.

The next morning, I dragged myself out of bed and, coffee in hand, padded to my office. I felt the same sensation of dread that I'd felt most mornings that week. *I will figure this out*, I kept repeating to myself. And just as I was about to fall into another ruminative pit of despair, something clicked. All of a sudden, I saw the material in a new way—a way that made much, much more sense. By the end of the day, I'd sent my revisions to my friend to review, and to my utter relief, he loved them. I realized that the party had been more than just an enjoyable night with old friends; it had provided powerful self-affirmation that helped me put my friend's feedback—feedback that tapped into my deepest fears and insecurities—into perspective. That affirmation kept my self-limiting beliefs at bay, and inspired me to tackle the challenge anew.

My own anecdotal experience aside, researchers have recently discovered that **reminiscing can indeed be a powerful mechanism for self-affirmation**. For instance, researcher Matthew Vess and his colleagues asked undergraduate psychology students to recall a positive memory from their past before receiving negative feedback about their performance on an analytical reasoning test. Those who reminisced weren't just less defensive; counterintuitively, they were also less likely to hold delusional beliefs about their abilities. Other studies have shown that reminiscing reduces rumination and increases well-being.

So whether you self-affirm by evoking the past or remembering your most important values, you *can* inoculate yourself against threatening feedback and hear it less defensively. Regardless of the approach you use, though, research has shown that **self-affirmation is most effective when you do it *before* getting threatening feedback**. And though it can sometimes sneak up on us, as it did in Florence's case, there are times when we can anticipate this kind of feedback, especially when we've sought it out on our own terms. So when you know difficult feedback might be coming, spend a few minutes shoring yourself up first. Think of self-affirmation as an insurance policy: what you hear might not be a catastrophe, but if it is, you'll be covered.

THE FLAWS IN OUR FABRIC: WHEN CHANGE ISN'T AN OPTION

Entrepreneur Levi King was born and raised on a farm in rural Idaho. After paying his way through college by working at an electric sign manufacturing company, he started a sign business of his own shortly after graduation. He sold it for a healthy profit when he was just 23 years old, and then went on to start a financial services company. But a few years later, a seemingly innocuous action sent Levi down the road to one of the most difficult—but important—insights of his career.

He had just fired a new sales rep for what he thought were extremely clear-cut reasons. But his business partner, who'd hired the now-ex-rep, disagreed. Naturally, both men believed they were right and the other was wrong. Eventually the conflict morphed into an all-out argument about who was the better leader. The partners decided to settle the question empirically: they would each take a 360 assessment, learn the truth from their teams, and compare their findings. When the results came in, Levi was sure he'd be vindicated.

But the truth wasn't so rosy. His team rated him lower on many measures than he'd expected, and worse yet, all of the things he fancied himself to be best at, like communication, were the things his team thought he did most poorly. This was a turning point for Levi. He realized that he could either, in his words, "double down and become an even bigger asshole, or learn what the heck I was doing wrong." He chose the latter and embarked on a process to better understand his communication style and leadership behaviors.

Yet after reading many books on brain science and communication, Levi came to the informed conclusion that he might *never* truly be successful at being personable, no matter how much work he put in. It just wasn't, he discovered, how he was wired. At this point, you're probably assuming that I'm about to tell you about how he pushed through this barrier, worked on himself, and emerged from the process a master communicator. But that's not what happened. Instead, Levi accepted that communication would never be his forte. And he was okay with that.

But was this wise? After earning these hard-won insights, shouldn't he have worked harder to turn them into action? Here's the truth: in the process of moving from mirror to prism, we will sometimes uncover things that will be difficult to change—flaws that are woven throughout the fabric of who we are. **The best way to manage our weaknesses isn't always clear-cut, but the first step is to openly admit them to ourselves, and then to others.** Sometimes we can make small changes that have a big payoff. Occasionally, we can completely transform. But in a few cases, the right response is, as they say in Alcoholics Anonymous, to **accept the things we cannot change**. That's exactly what Levi did.

Now armed with this insight, it was time for him to come clean to his team. Because his employees had given input to his 360, he knew they were wondering what came of it, and he wanted to be open about the whole thing anyway. So he called a company meeting, which he began by thanking them for their feedback. He then explained how he'd come to the conclusion that working on his social skills wouldn't yield meaningful returns. "In the future, it's unlikely that I will tell you good morning," he told them. "I'll forget your birthday. You'll have a baby and I won't remember to say anything to you about it." A sinking feeling engulfed the room—his employees wondered why on earth their boss was telling them all this, and what it could possibly mean.

As if he was reading their minds, Levi continued, "But I *do* care about you—deeply—and I want to tell you how I am going to show you that. I'll show you by giving you a safe place to work. I'll show you by confirming that your paychecks clear. I'll show you by making sure you find meaning in what you do. Those are things I can promise you."

To Levi's great surprise, the act of openly acknowledging these new truths paid off in ways he could have never imagined. Now that his team knew that *he* understood his biggest weakness, they no longer saw him as a too-big-for-his-britches, 25-year-old punk. They could even see the humor in situations where he was behaving badly. One day not long after his bare-all meeting, he was trying to make small talk with his head of HR and finance. He wanted to say something nice to her and noticed that she was wearing a shirt with a flower detail on the sleeves. "That's a nice shirt," he attempted.

"How weird," she replied, "you don't normally compliment me on what I wear."

"That's because you don't wear nice things—normally you just wear plain old T-shirts." And instantly, she burst out laughing.

It's been 10 years (and five more successful start-ups) since Levi's 360. And he's found that admitting—and often letting his team playfully joke about—his weaknesses has helped him reach a new level of success. Case in point, his current business credit and financing company, Nav, is growing profitably. And as a testament to Levi's leadership, it boasts unheard-of retention figures for the tech world. This is all to say that **when it comes to surprising and critical feedback, though changing is often a good option, it's not the *only* option.** Sometimes being self-aware simply means admitting these flaws to ourselves—and to our colleagues, our employees, our friends, and our families—while setting expectations for how we are likely to behave. And as they say, when we let go of the things we cannot change, it frees up the energy to focus on changing the things we can.

◆

So far in this chapter, we've seen many examples of people who learned how to cope with disquieting feedback. But it's worth mentioning that building our external self-awareness isn't always about learning all the things we're doing poorly. It's also about better understanding our unique strengths, skills, and contributions—and leveraging these insights for greater personal success. In the process of learning the truth about how we're seen, we're just as likely to encounter pleasant surprises as unpleasant ones.

I had an experience a few years ago that serves as a perfect example of what happens when we get positive and surprising feedback. I met Tom when I was teaching a strategy course to a group of corporate leaders. Tom was a self-professed "engineer's engineer"—a classic introvert who wasn't "very good with people." Tom told me that even though he loved engineering, he was feeling stalled and unfulfilled in his current role. I asked what he'd be doing if he could have any job in the world. He thought for a moment and replied that he didn't know, but that he was sure it wouldn't involve another promotion. "I just can't get anyone to listen to me," he explained matter-of-factly. "I'm not very influential." When I asked why, he simply shrugged and said that engineers aren't usually very good at "people stuff."

"Why don't I observe you this week and tell you whether or not I agree?" I offered. He consented, and we shook on it.

During our last evening together, the class was beginning an elaborate team-building activity. They were gathered in an immense hotel ballroom, surrounded by tables piled high with building supplies—PVC pipes, wood, hammers, ladders, etc. Their task was to construct a device that moved a marble from one end of the room to another. But things had gotten off to a bad start. Accustomed to always being the smartest one in the room, these leaders were having a hard time listening to each other's ideas. Naturally, they weren't making progress on the task at hand, and I could see them getting more frustrated by the minute.

All of a sudden, I heard a loud, confident voice break through the cacophony—and to my utter surprise, it was Tom. He had climbed almost to the top of one of the ladders and was smiling ear to ear, clearly fired up about the engineering problem they'd been asked to solve. But given what he had told me about his people skills, I braced myself for a disaster. "OK, gang," he began, "many of you know my background is in engineering. I don't have all the answers, but I have a few ideas. Tell me what you think about this . . ."

Just like that, the tone of the conversation changed. All of a sudden, people were listening instead of talking. They were cooperating instead of arguing. They were engaged instead of checked out. And they finished their task far faster than I would have predicted.

I sat there watching, completely dumbfounded as Tom's exuberant team members showered him with handshakes and high-fives. Afterward, I rushed up to him, grabbed his shoulders, and shouted, "Tom! Do you know what you just did?! That is the single most powerful example of influence I've seen this whole week!" I was even more astonished to see him looking back at me blankly, unsure of what he'd just done to warrant such an effusive compliment.

Tom and I spent the rest of the evening talking. Seeing him wrestle with this new, positive data about himself was an important reminder: **surprising feedback can often open our eyes to strengths we never knew we had**. And though this new information initially threw Tom's whole self-image into question (after all, he had spent essentially his entire career believing in his ineffectuality at influencing others), by looking through the prism rather than just at his own reflection, he could now see a richer, more complete image of who he was. He had always been a natural leader—he just needed a bit of help to see what was already there. Tom felt a renewed focus, not just in his career, but in his life. "You know what? I *am* going to apply for that promotion," he told me, "I think I'll do well." And that he did.

While Tom's strength came as a surprise, sometimes an outside perspective can reaffirm a positive quality that we *hope* we have in a way that helps us make more confident decisions. Kelsey, a unicorn, worked as a geologist for the first eight years of his career. But with each passing month, his interest in leaving to become a teacher grew stronger. Eventually, the urge was too powerful to resist, and he left his job and applied to a master's program in education.

When Kelsey announced the decision to his friends and family, he was surprised and gratified by their response. They gushed, "You're going to be a *great* teacher! You're so patient! I'd be lucky to have my kids in your class." As if that wasn't enough validation, when word of his choice spread around his tight-knit community, neighbors Kelsey didn't know particularly well came out of the woodwork to tell him what a smart choice he was making. Even though they'd never seen him teach, it seemed that his reputation had preceded him.

When he'd initially made his decision, Kelsey wasn't sure if he'd made the right choice—he suspected he might have it in him to be an effective teacher, but how could he be sure? His neighbors' and friends' feedback had given him the boost of confidence he needed. What's more, he figured, if people saw him this way, he now had an obligation to live up to their expectations. Fast-forward to today: he's thriving as a middle-school science teacher, his students love him, and he's proven to be a powerful force in the classroom.

At the end of the day, as Ben Franklin put it at the beginning of this chapter, when we "seek information and improvement from the knowledge of others," there are quite a few outcomes and a few potential courses of action. When we learn something **critical** and **surprising**, we can work to change, like Steve; to reframe the feedback, like Florence; or to embrace it and be open about it, like Levi. When we learn something **critical** and **confirming**—that is, something that reinforces our prior insecurities or vulnerabilities—we can use self-affirmation to channel it productively and work to minimize the impact of that weakness on our careers and our lives. With **positive** and **surprising** feedback, we can acknowledge and further invest in our newfound strengths, like Tom. And finally, as we saw with Kelsey, **positive** and **confirming** feedback gives us the confidence we need to continue on our chosen paths.

And regardless of how surprising or upsetting or gratifying that feedback may feel, reflecting on it and responding to it are far, far better than the alternative. As author Marianne Williamson once said, "It takes courage . . . to endure the sharp pains of self-discovery rather than choose . . . the dull pain of unconsciousness that would last the rest of our lives." The most successful, fulfilled, and self-aware people are simply not content with this dull pain. They take charge, bravely seeking out the truth on their own terms, making sense of it, and using it to improve where they can—all the while knowing that the occasional sharp pains of self-discovery are absolutely worth it.

Part Four

◆

The Bigger Picture

9

HOW LEADERS BUILD SELF-AWARE TEAMS AND ORGANIZATIONS

The truth is incontrovertible. Malice may attack it,
ignorance may deride it, but in the end, there it is.
—WINSTON CHURCHILL

As Mike appeared in the doorway, his boss smiled warmly. Not only was Mike a brilliant and talented aeronautical engineer; he was the 25-year-old manager's very first employee—and in a very short time, Mike's boss had grown quite fond of him.

"Mike!" he said. "Great to see you. Come in. Do you have your latest coordination sheet for me?"

"I do," said Mike, slapping the sheet onto the desk with surprising force. "But before you suggest any more changes, I just want to let you know that I'm quitting."

Mike's boss was stunned. He had worked hard to instill his attention to detail and commitment to excellence in this eager engineer, sparing nothing in helping Mike tackle all of the challenges their work presented. "Wh—what? Why are you quitting?" he stammered, his smile now replaced by a look of abject panic.

"Because you are driving me *nuts*!" said Mike. "This is my fourteenth round of revisions."

"But I just want—"

"We're at the point of diminishing returns here, sir." said the young engineer. "I just think that it would be better for both of us if I moved on."

Mike's boss was shaken to the core. He could barely speak. "I would hate to see you go," he pleaded. "Is there anything I can do to change your mind?"

But before his boss could even finish asking the question, Mike shouted, "No! I have to get away from you!" and left abruptly. *My management career sure doesn't seem to be off to a very good start*, the rejected leader realized as he stared helplessly out the window.

A few days passed, and Mike's now former boss asked if he would be willing to share what had gone wrong. And Mike did—in excruciating detail. Apparently, the young leader had a big problem. His nitpicking went beyond micromanagement: he seemed to think that his way was the only way. He'd been trying to teach Mike to think exactly like him, work exactly like him, and *be* exactly like him. Though Mike wanted to learn from his manager, he certainly didn't want to become him.

Mike's boss never forgot that feedback. Though it was hard to hear, it turned out to be the alarm-clock moment that marked the beginning of his incredible journey as a leader. You see, Mike's boss was 25-year-old Alan Mulally, the unicorn and future CEO who would go on to save not just one, but two of America's most iconic businesses: Boeing Commercial Airplanes and the Ford Motor Company.

In a 2012 commencement speech at his alma mater, the University of Kansas, Mulally coined a term for those moments of unexpected insight that challenge our beliefs about who we are. "A gem," he explains, "is a learning that enables us to reevaluate what we're doing." And the gem he received from Mike that day was that it was wrong to try to make employees in his own image. That as a leader, his role wasn't to control their every move, but instead to help connect them with the bigger picture, to give them the right tools, and to provide them the space to make mistakes but still hold them accountable.

Grabbing my arm and grinning as he recounted the story, Mulally exclaimed, "I was *so lucky* that Mike made me aware of this behavior so early in my management career! Can you imagine if no one had told me for years, or for decades? What a *gift!*"

Up until now, we've focused on self-awareness at an individual level. In this chapter, we'll explore what self-aware teams and organizations look like, and what you as a leader can do to get yours there. As Alan Mulally learned at a young age, such teams start with a self-aware leader who makes a commitment to instill insight into the very fabric of the team and organization. Indeed, Mulally believes that this passion for creating collective awareness was one of the key factors in his immense success. As he told me, "Every time you learn something that isn't working in yourself, your team, or your organization, you have a gem on your hands. Here is something we know now, that we can work on. I really can't think of anything more exciting. If you don't know what's going on, that's what's really terrifying."

This chapter will help you discover these kinds of "gems" in the team or company you lead, too. And even though we'll focus on teams in a business setting, you'll likely find other applications outside the workplace: your immediate and extended family, religious or community groups, school projects, PTA, garage bands, beer-league hockey teams, etc. (And by the way, if you're not in a formal or informal leadership position, I'll show you how to deal with unaware bosses and peers in the next chapter.) You'll discover that no matter what kind of team you're leading, whether you have one direct report or a thousand, you can't create awareness by just waking up one day and deciding that everyone should be brutally honest with each other. In fact, without laying the foundation, you might find yourself with more trouble on your hands than you had to begin with. But while teams rarely start out self-aware, with the right ingredients, most can get there and reap the substantial rewards that such insight brings.

◆

It was a chilly November morning in Dearborn, Michigan. As Ford executive Mark Fields walked into the Thunderbird Room on the 11th floor of the company's world headquarters, he had, by his estimation, a 50-50 chance of walking out without his job as president of the company's Americas region.

The year was 2006, and Ford was on the brink of bankruptcy.

Saddled with sky-high cycle times, plummeting quality levels, astronomical labor costs, and rising fuel prices, Ford's business model had become untenable. Unable to compete domestically or internationally, the company had lost a whopping 25 percent of its market share over the last 15 years. But these failings most certainly weren't due to a lack of effort by the man in the top job.

Forty-four-year-old chairman and CEO Bill Ford had taken the reins four years earlier to try to save his great-grandfather's company. He was sharp, self-aware, and possessed a humility and work ethic that belied his privileged upbringing. When he assumed his role in 2001, he'd promised that the company would hit $7 billion in profit in five years. But though he briefly got Ford back in the black that same year, by 2006, the company was facing its worst yearly loss in its history—almost $17 billion. After five years of herculean efforts (during which he never took a salary), Ford was finally forced to come face-to-face with the reality that he couldn't save his beloved company on his own.

In truth, the organization's problems ran far deeper than it appeared. It wasn't just their flawed business model or inability to grapple with increasing global competition; these things were certainly issues, but they were merely symptoms of a larger ailment. As journalist Bryce Hoffman described in his superb book about Ford's turnaround, *American Icon*:

> [Bill] Ford found himself unable to overcome an entrenched, careerist culture that resisted all change and put individual advancement ahead of corporate success. In their dark-paneled offices, executives plotted ways to undermine one another's efforts, while on the factory floor, union bosses jealously defended their members' rich benefits and scoffed at attempts to boost productivity.

The company's culture, in other words, was completely broken. And in July of 2006, Bill Ford announced to the board that he wasn't up to the challenge of fixing it: "This company means a lot to me. I have a lot tied up in it. But the one thing I don't is my ego . . . help me find a solution."* Although his successor is credited with one of the most impressive turnarounds in corporate history, it was Bill Ford's unflinching self-awareness that made it possible.

That help would come in the form of 61-year-old Alan Mulally, the then-president and CEO of Boeing's Commercial Airplane division, a spirited, red-haired Kansan with a track record of technical excellence, bottom-line results, and most importantly, dramatic turnarounds. After 37 years at Boeing, Mulally had not only saved the company from near-bankruptcy in the aftermath of 9/11; he'd led their program to design the 777—the five-year, $5 billion project that single-handedly propelled Boeing ahead of its competition for years to come.

From the moment he arrived at Ford's world headquarters on September 5, 2006, it was clear that Mulally was radically different from his predecessors. In an industry plagued by megalomania, secrecy, and paranoia, he was open, approachable, and completely unpretentious. He ate in the employee cafeteria and greeted strangers with a hug, a kiss, or a pat on the back. But those who confused Mulally's agreeableness for weakness were quickly disabused of that notion. A friend of his once remarked, "Don't mistake Alan's smile for a lack of purpose or awareness. The man has a backbone of titanium."

Mulally knew that the foundational challenge of Ford's turnaround wouldn't be improving fuel efficiency standards, or simplifying their product mix, or getting costs under control (though he would certainly do all of those things). Rather, it would be to start transforming the company's secretive, change-resistant, siloed culture into a more open, collaborative, transparent one. And in his very first press conference as CEO, Mulally made it clear that under his leadership, the truth would be king: when asked what model of car he drove, he stunned reporters by replying, "A Lexus. It's the finest car in the world." (It's worth noting that Ford's executives didn't drive Fords, either, stealthily parking their

---

* One board member called this brief but stirring speech the most moving one he'd ever heard in a boardroom.

Jaguars and Land Rovers in the garage beneath the company's world headquarters. They just weren't admitting it to reporters.)

One thing was clear from the outset: if Mulally was going to transform his new company's culture, he had to start with his executive team. The first change he introduced was a weekly meeting to review the status of the business, which he called the Business Process Review, or BPR. Replacing all other pointless and inefficient corporate-level meetings, the purpose of the BPR was awareness—**to ensure that everyone knew the plan, the status of that plan, and the reality of the challenges the company was facing.**

The BPR would be held on the same day and at the same time each week—Thursday mornings at 7:00 a.m.—and it would be mandatory for all members of the executive team. They'd review 320 metrics on everything from vehicle launches to revenue streams to productivity. Each metric would be assigned a color: green if it was on track, yellow if it had potential problems, and red if it had definite ones. Each of Mulally's nine executives would have 10 minutes to deliver a succinct report on, as Mulally puts it, "their respective progress toward creating an exciting, viable, profitable, and growing Ford for the good of all stakeholders." Mulally emphasized that this meeting would be safe— that no one should hesitate to surface problems and no one would be punished for telling the truth. There would be a learning curve, he told them, so if they didn't know something, that was okay. "We'll all be here again next week . . . and I *know* you'll know it then."

Ford's first BPR took place on September 28, 2006. Mulally's team had no idea what to expect as they nervously streamed into the Thunderbird Room, many with lieutenants in tow and all toting heavy three-ring binders. They took their seats at the large round wooden conference table, and Mulally called the meeting to order. First, he repeated his vision: *People working together as a lean global enterprise for automotive leadership.* To get there, he reminded them, everyone would have to be open about everything that was going on in their area of the business. "This is the only way I know how to operate," he said. "We need to have everybody involved. We need everybody to be aware. And we'll work together to turn the reds to yellow and then to green."

Although early BPRs took as many as seven hours, by October, the team had settled into a rhythm. Unfortunately, however, the process still left something to be desired. Despite the fact that the company was at the risk of extinction, *every* chart that *every* executive presented in *every* meeting was green. This was, as Bryce Hoffman quips, "nothing short of bovine scatology." Things weren't "green"; they were far from it, and Mulally knew it.

One week, after being presented with yet another forest of verdant charts, he decided he'd had enough. "Guys," he said, interrupting the meeting. "We're going to lose seventeen billion dollars this year and all the charts are green." No one said anything. "Do you think there's *anything* that's not going well? Maybe even just one little thing?"

The meeting room filled with a thick and itchy silence. Seats were shuffled in, throats were cleared, and eyes darted toward patent-leather shoes. The executives smelled danger. And they knew exactly what would happen to the first fool to show a red slide: the framed family portrait on their desk would be at the bottom of a cardboard box before lunch. This whole exercise was surely a trick.

Mulally tried to allay their fears. "We're not going to be able to manage a secret," he said. "The idea is that we can share what the situation is and help each other." He looked around the room once more. Yet again, seats were shuffled upon, throats were cleared, and eyes darted toward shoes. The executives hadn't felt safe bringing up problems under the previous leadership, so why should this new hotshot CEO be any different?

The days passed and the drill remained the same. Green slides, green slides, and more green slides. The truth, of course, was far less rosy. Take, for example, what was happening with the company's much-hyped first crossover vehicle, the Ford Edge. It was in full production and just weeks away from its much-anticipated launch when mechanics at the factory in Oakville, Ontario, discovered a problem with an actuator on the lift gate. This left the executive responsible for the Edge, Mark Fields, with no option but to call the entire operation to a halt.

As 10,000 lonely Ford Edges languished on the halted assembly lines, Fields was rather on edge himself. This, he figured, was the catastrophe that would cost him his job. After all, he'd been the man in charge of Ford's turnaround strategy before Mulally's arrival and he suspected he was seen as a threat to the new CEO. For longer than he cared to think about, the entire company had been buzzing with rumors of his imminent dismissal. This business with the Edge couldn't have come at a worse time. But he figured he could do his colleagues one final favor: he'd call Mulally's bluff. *Somebody has to figure out if this guy is for real,* he thought. *If I go out, it might as well be in a blaze of glory.*

And with the fearlessness of a man who had nothing to lose, as Fields and his team prepared for the next day's BPR, he decided to list the product-launch metric as red.

"Are you sure you want to do that?" asked one member of Fields' executive team.

Fields answered with a question, "Is the launch on track?" The executive shook his head.

"Well then," Fields told him, "we're going to make it red." Everyone skeptically looked at him as if to say "Good luck with that."

So when Fields walked into the BPR on that chilly November morning, he really had no idea of how things would play out. He figured the best-case scenario was that he'd get reamed out but keep his job. Worst case, he'd get reamed out and be shown the door. Never did it dawn on him that there was another possible outcome.

That week's BPR began as it always did. His colleagues presented their slides—and as usual, it was a veritable forest of green. Then it was Fields' turn. As Mulally recalls, "Up came the red slide. And WHOOM—the air went out of the room."

Fields cleared his throat. "On the Edge," he said, "we have an actuator issue, so we had to delay the launch." The entire room cringed as one. "We don't know the solution, but we're working on it." As Mulally recalls, this was the moment when people thought, *Well, that's that. Two large men are going to burst into the room, grab Mark, and cart him off, and we'll never see him again.*

And then, in the midst of that heaviest of silences came a surprising sound: Alan Mulally's exuberant applause. "Mark, this is great visibility!" he grinned. Turning to his team, he asked, "What can we do to help him out?" Right away, one of the executives suggested a solution, and they were off and running.

After all this, Mulally was optimistic that finally, the executive team would have their first successful BPR. Yet the next week, to his great disappointment, all the slides were still green. But Mulally's team saw something that day that spoke volumes. When they entered the Thunderbird Room, Mark Fields was sitting right next to a smiling Mulally. Not only had he not been fired, he had actually been commended. This was evidently the final proof that the cynical and battle-weary executives needed. They actually believed it now—they *were* in a new world. The following week, the decks they brought to the BPR were a glorious rainbow of red and yellow gems.

According to Mulally, if there was a single defining moment in Ford's turnaround, this was it. Up until that point, Ford's executives had been afraid to surface problems; to tell each other the truth; to give and receive honest feedback. The same mentality that had kept them MUM about the realities of the business also kept them MUM about their individual failures, team dysfunctions, and cultural challenges. But now, for the first time, the team was confronting reality.

From that point forward, they were on the open road (no pun intended) to self-awareness, on many levels. As individuals, they understood expectations and were facing their limiting beliefs and behaviors; as a team, they knew the business environment, the plan, and the status of that plan. But it wasn't just the executive team who possessed this information. Everyone in the company was trusted and expected to know the direction, the role they played, and how things were going. This information also flowed to their stakeholders outside the organization—their customers, investors, dealers, suppliers, and the public.

And the results speak for themselves. By 2009, in the midst of the biggest economic crisis since the Great Depression, Ford was back in the black, and it was the only one of the "Big Three" American carmakers who didn't take a cent of taxpayer bailout money. By 2011, their profit had swelled to more than $20 billion. It was their second-most profitable year in history.

If being individually self-aware means understanding who you are and how others see you, a self-aware team commits to that same understanding at a collective level. More specifically, there are five things that self-aware teams regularly assess and address: I call them the *Five Cornerstones of Collective Insight*. First, their **objectives**: what are they trying to achieve? Second, their **progress** toward those objectives: how are they doing? Third, the **processes** they're employing to achieve their objectives: how are they getting there? Fourth, their **assumptions** about the business and their environment: do they hold true? And finally, their **individual contributions**: what impact is each team member having on the team's performance?

As a result of their collective insight, self-aware teams are more efficient, more effective, more innovative, and more rewarding to be a part of. Unfortunately, as many can attest and studies often show, few teams are naturally self-aware. After all, it's hard enough to cultivate self-awareness in ourselves without the added challenge of our pesky peer relationships. And while our boss is theoretically required to tell us the truth once a year in our performance appraisal, our teammates have no such obligations. Though the people who work alongside us every day are often the ones with the most critical information about how we're doing, they're usually the most likely to stay MUM. This constant ambiguity doesn't just sap our confidence and stoke our paranoia (remember, your peers are probably sharing what they think about you with everyone but you); it can also be damaging—even fatal—to a team's collective success.

The Five Cornerstones of Collective Insight can admittedly be difficult to achieve. Not only does the MUM effect make people reluctant to share this information, they often see individual feedback as a "nice to have" rather than an essential ingredient for success. Yet though leaders should take their team's tentativeness to tell the truth seriously, they needn't be disheartened by it. With the right approach and a true ongoing commitment, you can foster a culture that encourages communication and feedback at all levels; one where honesty trumps hierarchy and even the lowest-ranking member feels safe putting problems on the table.

Specifically, there are ***Three Building Blocks*** that must be in place for a leader to drive a self-aware team. First, if the team doesn't have a **leader who models the way**, the process will be seen as insincere or even dangerous. Second, if there isn't the **psychological safety** to tell the truth, the chance of candid feedback is almost zero. But even with all this in place, you also need an **ongoing process**—not unlike Mulally's BPR—to ensure that the exchange of feedback isn't just a one-time thing but rather is built into the team's culture.

In a moment, we'll look at each of these building blocks a bit more closely. But before we do so, it's worth mentioning a critically important point. If your team doesn't have a clear and compelling direction, you are missing the reason to become self-aware in the first place. Imagine if Alan Mulally's team at Ford had started having BPRs without a solid, mutually understood set of goals. As Mulally explains, "If you don't have a vision, a smart strategy, and a detailed plan to get there, the process of self-awareness is just talking." In other words, **if a team doesn't know where it's headed, they are missing the "because" of self-awareness**, and trying to get there would therefore be both frivolous and pointless!

Building Block #1: A Leader Who Models the Way

When Doug Suttles first stepped onto the platform of the 250-by-200-foot oil rig in the middle of the North Sea, he recognized that his new assignment would test both his technical and interpersonal skills. What he didn't know was that he was about to learn one of the most important leadership lessons of his career. Suttles, a mechanical engineer by training, had just been appointed BP's offshore installation manager of the Miller platform in the North Sea, just off the coast of Scotland. On top of their number-one objective, which was keeping everyone safe, Suttles had been tasked with improving the rig's operating performance. And not only was he the sole non-Brit on the rig, he was also one of the youngest people there.

This unique situation presented Suttles with a few unique challenges. For one, he would be living with his 196 new teammates—in
close quarters and many miles out at sea. He quickly discovered that
in this multifaceted role of boss/ship captain/counselor, he wasn't just
on display during working hours—his team had eyes on him virtually
around the clock. Even the smallest choices spoke volumes: Would he
sit with managers or technicians at dinner? Would he participate in
their weekly TV game show? How well would he help them deal with
the interpersonal problems that such close quarters tend to breed?

Though Suttles had always been a big believer in cultivating self-
awareness, his time on the rig provided him with a new and critical
insight. Whether or not he was living in close quarters in the middle
of the ocean, because he was a leader, each and every choice his people
saw him make would serve as a model, profoundly influencing their attitudes, their behaviors, and their overall effectiveness.

Many years later, this lesson would help Suttles manage an absolutely unthinkable crisis. On April 20, 2010, the crew of the Deepwater
Horizon, an oil rig located in the Gulf of Mexico just off the coast of
Louisiana, was settling in for the evening. Earlier that day, BP officials
and workers had gathered to celebrate seven years of operation without
a single injury. At around 9:45 p.m., 23-year-old Andrea Fleytas was
monitoring the computer system that maintains the vessel's position
in the water when she felt a sudden jolt. A few minutes later, the crew
heard a loud hissing sound. Then came the massive explosion that
would ultimately kill 11 people, injure 17 others, and spout an estimated 4.9 million barrels of crude oil into the Gulf of Mexico.

Suttles was chief operating officer of BP's exploration and production division when he was tapped to lead the company's response to
the largest oil spill in history. In the midst of this massive emergency,
it would certainly be easy to incite panic, to place blame, or to speak
without thinking. (Many BP leaders fell prey to these traps, none more
notably than CEO Tony Hayward, who made headlines by calling
the spill "relatively tiny" and telling the press that he'd "like [his] life
back.") But recalling his time on the North Sea rig, Suttles reminded
himself to model the way, no matter how difficult things became.

Suttles' response team of BP employees, private contractors, and government workers faced a cacophony of criticism—both legitimate and spurious—from the government, the media, and the public. Which made it even more important for him to ensure that each of the Five Cornerstones of Collective Insight was in place: awareness and communication about their objectives, their progress, their processes, their assumptions, and their contributions, starting with his own. Suttles was self-aware enough to know that in such a complex and emotionally charged situation, there would inevitably be mistakes. He also knew they would need to fix them quickly. To do so, the team would have to remain cool-headed and not take criticism personally—and the only way that could happen was if Suttles was willing to acknowledge his own missteps, model emotional control, and handle the crisis calmly.

His team faced what seemed like every possible obstacle until finally, on July 15, they stopped the leak. By September 19, they'd managed to seal it completely. The lesson is that no matter what challenges you're facing, self-aware teams must begin with **a self-aware leader who models the way**. "It's easy to get isolated at the top," Suttles told me, "But if your team isn't performing as you'd like, the first place to look is at yourself. If I glance over my shoulder and there's nobody back there, that's called feedback. If I glance over my shoulder and people are following me, that's probably a good sign."

Or, as Alan Mulally once told me, "How far the team gets is completely dependent on the leader's level of self-awareness."

So how can leaders model the way? At the most basic level, as Doug Suttles and Alan Mulally have shown us, a leader must communicate her principles and act in accordance with them. Psychologists often refer to this constellation of behaviors as "authentic leadership," and their business value is unmistakable. For example, when researcher Joanne Lyubovnikova and her colleagues surveyed teams in a variety of industries across the United Kingdom and Greece, they found that those led by authentic leaders were more self-aware and, in turn, more productive than those with less self-aware leaders.

And these effects aren't just confined to the corporate world; they also extend to our homes and families. In one study, when mothers could successfully identify and manage their emotions, their children were happier and more self-aware a full year later. Having seen self-awareness modeled through a parent, they were more likely to develop this valuable skill themselves.

On the flip side, it doesn't take a degree in psychology to know that human beings have amazing BS detectors. When we sense that leaders aren't being authentic—whether they're intentionally misleading us or simply behaving in opposition to their values—we can smell it a mile away. This causes team members to avoid bringing up issues for fear of retribution, as Mulally's executive team initially did, and reality gets buried under a torrent of excuses and finger-pointing.

However, when a leader commits to confronting his flaws while also striving to improve, his team is motivated to do the same. In fact, this is a great example of preeminent psychologist Albert Bandura's theory of social learning, which suggests that followers tend to imitate the attitudes and behaviors of their leader. **When a leader is authentic, team members learn that it's not just okay but *expected* to honestly reflect** on the Five Cornerstones of Collective Insight (and the Seven Pillars on an individual level, for that matter).

So whether you are leading hundreds of employees or a handful of kids, the actions to model self-awareness are the same. First, you have to go all-in and make a total commitment to your team's self-awareness, starting with your own. As Mulally explains, "My role is to ensure awareness for everybody. To *watch* all the time—watch myself, watch others, watch the organization." Equally important is to know and communicate your credo—that is, the values that define the behaviors you expect from yourself and your team. At Ford, Mulally's credo—something he calls his *Working Together Principles and Practices**—didn't just help his team understand *him*, it drew a line in

---

* "Our expected behaviors and culture: People first; Everyone is included; Compelling vision, comprehensive strategy, and relentless implementation; Clear performance goals; One plan; Facts and data; Everyone knows the plan, status, and areas that need special attention; Propose a plan, positive "find a way" attitude; Respect, listen, help and appreciate each other; Emotional resilience . . . trust the process; Have fun. Enjoy the journey and each other."

the sand for what he expected of *them*. It's not enough just to ask for feedback and encourage your team to bring up problems; you need to listen—really listen—to what they have to say. When I asked Doug Suttles, who is now the CEO of oil and gas company Encana, the secret to a successful team, he replied:

> A lot of people use the word "trust"—I'm not big on that because it's too emotive for us engineers, and the meaning is set too wide. What really matters is: Do they have confidence in you? Not just that you'll point the ship in the right direction, but do they believe you'll listen? Do they believe you want an open and transparent environment where successes and failures are talked about? When the team is challenged, are you baiting them or actually giving them support and help?

Remember, as we've seen throughout this book, most leaders are fighting an uphill battle when it comes to their own self-awareness. And since unsolicited critical feedback rarely flows freely, leaders who want to change often have to take rather direct measures. Unfortunately, this creates a bit of a catch-22: If employees are reluctant to provide their opinions to begin with, won't they feel even more stressed when you ask them for it point-blank? Can leaders really overcome the MUM effect and elicit raw, candid feedback from those they lead? Fortunately, there is a way: something I call the **Leader Feedback Process**.

Modeling the Way: The Leader Feedback Process

A few years ago, I was approached by Jamie, the president of a hospitality and property-management company. As only the third president in its 40-year history, he'd been brought on a year prior to break the inertia that was starting to threaten the organization's very survival. His long career had given him a wide range of experience, but this was his first time in the top job.

Jamie had set the audacious goal of doubling the size of the company in the next five years, and in order to succeed, he would need to instill a sense of urgency and insist on excellence in every area of the organization. For this to happen, his executives had to feel safe voicing problems, confronting the brutal truth, and having tough conversations with one another about each of the Five Cornerstones—their objectives, progress, individual contributions, and so on.

On the surface, Jamie's executive team had all the right ingredients. They were committed to his vision. They were aligned on how they would achieve it. They were generally comfortable working together. But since Jamie arrived, there had been obvious posturing, and he never felt like he was hearing the complete truth. When I interviewed each member of his team, their responses confirmed those suspicions. They believed he was the right person for the job, but many were struggling to trust and connect with him.

Jamie and I agreed that we needed to address these issues directly—to rip off the Band-Aid, so to speak—and provide a forum for a confidential but candid discussion. We decided to devote two days to an off-site retreat that would begin with an exercise that has become a gold standard in my consulting work. Jamie would later tell me that it gave him some of the most powerful feedback he's ever received.

The process was famously pioneered in the early 1970s at General Electric and has been described as "a super-intensive getting-to-know-you meeting [where] team members raise candid observations and questions" about their leader. Though it was originally developed to help new managers and their teams get to know one another, the so-called "New Leader Assimilation Exercise" has been shown to be valuable regardless of a leader's tenure—that's why I call it the **Leader Feedback Process.** It helps managers earn nearly instantaneous insight into their team's perceptions and expectations of them while improving their leadership, communication, and well-being. What's more, empirically, their teams experience better, more trusting relationships and a greater sense of commitment to their mission.

So on a stifling summer day a few months after our first meeting, Jamie, his team, and I gathered in a mercifully air-conditioned meeting room at a local country club. "Thank you all for making the time to be here," Jamie began. "We have one goal: to become a better team. And I'm up first. Over the next three hours, you'll have the chance to give me feedback about my first year on the job. The ground rules are simple. No comment is out of bounds and everyone participates. Can we all agree to that?"

He paused, surveying their reactions. A few people hesitantly nodded, but there was a palpable sense of uneasiness. Attempting to allay their fears, he added, "To help you be comfortable being completely candid, I'm going to leave the room and have Tasha lead the discussion. I've asked that under no circumstances should she tell me who said what. Does that sound like it would work?" The fear now significantly abated, they responded with a chorus of surprisingly eager yesses.

After I (gently) kicked Jamie out of the conference room, I stood up and gestured toward seven flip-charts covering one long wall. On the top of each sheet was a question written in blue marker:

1. What do we know about Jamie?
2. What do we want to know about Jamie?
3. What should Jamie know about us as a team?
4. What concerns do we have about Jamie?
5. What expectations do we have of Jamie?
6. What do we want Jamie to stop doing, start doing, and continue doing?
7. What feedback do we have about our vision, our strategy, and our plan?

"This part of the discussion will last about forty-five minutes," I told them. "And we'll answer each question in order. Your job is to give me as many ideas as you possibly can, and my job is to write down everything you say." Positioning myself in front of the first flip-chart, I removed the cap of a large black marker. "Let's start by discussing what we know about Jamie." Three answers came instantly: "We know he has been working in the industry for twenty-five years." "We know that he has insanely high expectations." "We know that he must be really brave, because he's doing this exercise!"

And just like that, we were off and running. The comments were flowing so freely that I started to write smaller just to fit all of their replies on the giant sheet of paper. We moved to the second question, and the third, and so on. Forty-five minutes later, all seven flip-charts were covered with their comments.

I gave the team a 10-minute break and went to find Jamie. As we walked back to the room, I asked him, "Are you ready?" He grinned confidently. "Ready as I'll ever be!" But when we approached the wall of flip-charts, his grin faltered and his eyes grew wide. I gave him a few minutes to read his team's answers and helped clarify the meaning of a few comments. Before I fetched the team, I reminded Jamie how important it was to remain calm and non-defensive in the next part of our discussion.

Soon everyone was assembled around the conference table. But before we dove into the feedback, I asked Jamie to spend a few minutes giving his team some background on his life: favorite things to do growing up, number of brothers and sisters, funniest childhood memories, most important values—I've found that in the right context, sharing such information has a near-immediate impact on the team's level of trust even if they've known the leader for many years.

Next, Jamie responded to their feedback one question at a time. For some comments, a simple acknowledgment was sufficient ("Yes, I *do* have insanely high expectations." "I am glad you think we're headed in the right direction even if this first year hasn't been easy."). Others required more discussion, and in some cases, a commitment on his part to try a different approach. For example, many members of the team were frustrated that Jamie would sometimes go around them and approach their staff directly. Exploring that feedback helped him understand that this was embarrassing for his executives and confusing for their employees.

During the course of our 90-minute discussion—which Jamie started to refer to as his "proctology exam"—his insight into how the team was perceiving his behavior grew exponentially, as did their understanding of his expectations. And when Jamie and I sat down a month or so later, he told me that he was absolutely awestruck at the improvements he had seen—both in his own effectiveness and the overall functioning of the team. The retreat, he said, had accelerated their trust. They were talking more openly about real, substantive issues. And though some had occasionally slipped into their old habits, they were more engaged and collaborative than they had ever been. Not coincidentally, less than one year later, the company's revenue had jumped more than 20 percent.

Jamie and his team had certainly reached an important milestone in their journey toward collective self-awareness. In showing them that he was truly open to hearing the truth about himself, they felt safer sharing it even without being directly asked. But to create a truly self-aware team, this is only the first step. Even once leaders have opened up these channels, they must also work to ensure that they *stay* open, and not just between employees and the leader but among members of the team.

Building Block #2: The Safety (and Expectation) to Tell the Truth

In 1996, doctoral candidate Amy Edmondson began what has since become a landmark study on the science of team self-awareness. Edmondson, now a professor at Harvard, wanted to better understand the reasons for medical errors among hospital-care teams; a pressing issue given that the average hospital patient is exposed to between 480 and 960 potential errors, which kill hundreds and injure more than a million people each year in the United States alone.

Edmondson followed eight hospital-unit teams in two urban teaching hospitals over the course of six months. At first, she was puzzled to find that teams with better unit performance (quality of care, collaboration, efficiency, leadership, etc.) reported *more* errors. But as she examined the data further, she discovered the reason for these surprising findings.

The poorer-performing units weren't making fewer medication errors—they just weren't reporting the ones they'd made. The reason? These nurses, quite simply, were terrified to do so, telling Edmonson that those who did got "put on trial" and "blamed for mistakes." (When I worked in a hospital, I personally experienced the challenges of raising an issue that might negatively impact a closely watched metric.) In contrast, in the highest-performing units in Edmondson's study—that is, those with the most reported errors—the nurses were comfortable openly discussing mistakes. On these teams, they weren't afraid to tell the nurse manager that something had gone wrong.

Edmondson coined the term *psychological safety* to describe the shared belief that it's safe to ask one another for help, admit mistakes, and raise tough issues. "The term," Edmondson explains, "is meant to suggest neither a careless sense of permissiveness, nor an unrelenting positive affect but rather a sense of confidence that the team will not embarrass, reject, or punish someone for speaking up." Though somewhat counterintuitive, her comment about "unrelenting positive affect" is particularly important: in highly cohesive teams, members might be *less* likely to challenge one another, often because of a misguided desire to maintain group harmony. But as "good" as this might feel, it's detrimental to the team's self-awareness and therefore to its success.

Google's People Operations Department reached a similar conclusion after a five-year research program examining what it took to build the perfect team. Early on, after the team of organizational psychologists, engineers, sociologists, and statisticians had reviewed thousands of studies on what made teams successful, they couldn't isolate any specific patterns. So they tried a different approach, studying hundreds of Google teams on factors like personality, background, and work style. Still no answers. It seemed that the team makeup—the "who"—didn't matter, whether they were introverts or extroverts, subject experts or polymaths, worker bees or queen bees, or any combination of the above.

Interestingly, the Google team reached a breakthrough only once they began to examine the "how"—or the unwritten rules that governed the way a team worked. Their findings were consistent with what Edmondson had discovered in her hospital study 15 years earlier: psychologically safe teams consistently outperformed those that aren't.

But how does psychological safety relate to team self-awareness? A few years after her study with hospital teams, Edmondson began another investigation—this time, with a company that manufactured office furniture—extensively studying more than 50 teams via interviews, surveys, and direct observation (i.e., she essentially followed people around with a clipboard, which is also one of my favorite pastimes). Again, when team members felt psychologically safe, they were more comfortable raising issues, more likely to deal with reality, and more likely to speak the truth. They were also infinitely more successful. In fact, the precise reason that psychologically safe teams performed better was *specifically because of their higher levels of self-awareness.*

It's worth noting that for high-profile companies, a psychologically safe culture isn't just good for morale and productivity, but also for the company's public image. According to Ed Catmull, because Pixar's executives tell employees the truth, they naturally appreciate the importance of confidentiality. As a result, Pixar has never had a *single* leak to the press—not even during the dramatic due diligence period when they were being acquired by Disney. Even when Catmull, John Lasseter, and Steve Jobs announced the deal to employees, not one spoke to reporters camped outside their headquarters.

Let's look at an example of how leaders can create the safety—and the expectation—for telling each other the truth. As a new day was about to dawn during an especially stressful week, Levi King (the entrepreneur we met in the last chapter) was clearing out his inbox before attempting to catch a few futile hours of sleep. The last e-mail he sent before his head hit the pillow was an exasperated rant to his business partner about an issue that had been bugging him at their company, Nav. But the second he sent it, he knew it had been a mistake. The tone was unnecessarily rude—borderline hostile, even. Levi knew he had really messed up when his normally lightning-quick-to-respond partner waited a full 24 hours to reply. The response was measured but direct, pointing out Levi's incendiary language and politely asking whether he really felt that way.

First thing that next morning, Levi found his partner. "I am *so sorry*," he said, "I don't know what I was thinking. It was late. I was tired. I was an asshole." Thankfully, his partner accepted his apology, but instead of patting himself on the back and moving on, Levi was self-aware enough to see the larger opportunity in his gaffe. During the company's next monthly meeting, Levi hooked up his computer to the conference room projector and pulled up the offending e-mail. He watched his employees' eyes grow wider with disbelief as they scanned his message. "Is anyone proud of this?" Levi asked. They shook their heads. "Okay, then. Let's talk about what I did wrong here." They then engaged in a frank post-mortem to deconstruct exactly why the e-mail had been rude and agree on what Levi could have done differently. And though the conversation was certainly uncomfortable, he pushed through it because of the learning opportunity it provided to his team.

It should come as no surprise that the first step for leaders wanting to cultivate psychological safety in their team is to work on building trust. But though it's important, **trust alone isn't sufficient for psychological safety**. More than merely trusting that team members have one another's best interests at heart, psychologically safe teams go a step further to show each other respect, sensitivity, and caring. And to do this, they have to see one another as real human beings with weaknesses and flaws. In fact, Google's research program found that the single most powerful contributor to psychological safety was *vulnerability*, or a willingness to openly admit our failings. And it has to start at the top. "Many leaders," says Levi King, "say 'Yes it's safe [to be vulnerable,]' but they're not willing to go there themselves. I can't just talk about this figuratively. I have to show that at our company, it's okay to make mistakes—because we forgive each other and assume positive intent."

To be sure, as research professor and author Brené Brown demonstrates in her book *Daring Greatly*, doing so can often feel scary and even wrong, especially for people in positions of power. I once worked with a successful executive who saw vulnerability as a weakness earlier in his career. "If I even hinted," he told me, "that I had made a mistake, I thought my team would lose respect for me." But as time went on, he realized that the truth was actually the exact opposite. As Doug Suttles observes, "I've learned over time that being a bit vulnerable deepens people's respect for you, particularly when you're willing to acknowledge it. They walk away and say 'Holy smokes! I'm going to screw up someday. But maybe it's okay and it's a good idea to talk about it openly.'"

In addition to modeling vulnerability, leaders can foster psychologically safer teams by working together to *create clear norms*. Years ago, I was asked to help a leadership team that oversaw women and children's services at a preeminent hospital with their strategic planning process. Their newly promoted director, Tracee, along with her four nurse managers, had been tasked with keeping the department competitive. Because the facility was recognized as the city's "baby hospital," many people, including countless celebrities, traveled from all around the country to deliver there. But in recent years, local competitors had stepped up their game, offering then-unheard-of amenities like luxury suites, personal chefs, and sparkling new facilities. Tracee's team had to keep up, not just by ensuring compassionate and world-class medical care, but by offering the kind of top-notch service found in a five-star hotel.

While some managers might have simply thrown money at the problem—say, by upgrading the accommodations or trying to one-up the competition on amenities—Tracee and her team took things a step further. Understanding the direct link between their willingness to tell one another the truth and achieving their aggressive goals, they decided to focus on making their department a safer, more supportive place for their nurses and techs to work.

So before we even dove into business planning, our first step was to have a frank discussion about how Tracee's team was functioning (i.e., the cornerstone of processes). They admitted that while they usually worked well together, there was sometimes an undercurrent of tension that no one was willing to call out. For that reason, I suggested that we create a set of team norms. "The objective," I told them, "is to agree on your rules of engagement as a team. What behaviors will help you achieve your strategy? What kind of environment do you want to create? What do you need to do to make this a safe and supportive team?" To define these behaviors, we used the Start/Stop/Continue Model that we learned about in chapter 7 (while I don't think this model is particularly effective at the individual level, it can give teams a common framework to discuss what's working and what isn't).

Tracee's team's final list of norms looked something like this:

- No gossip: open, honest, safe communication.
- Always go to the person: have difficult conversations with each other in the spirit of support.
- Business is business: have crucial conversations and still be on good terms.
- Assume the best: support each other in front of staff, patients, and physicians.
- Practice forgiveness: we're human. We make mistakes. Address it and move forward.

To ensure that their norms became a living, breathing document rather than something they stuffed in a drawer and forgot, they plastered their offices and meeting agendas with them so they stayed top-of-mind. When the team members demonstrated the principles, they commended one another; when they didn't, they called one another out. Eventually, they took their norms to their own teams, and in turn started to hold the entire department accountable. The increase in performance was undeniable: employee engagement jumped from 71 percent to 86 percent in less than a year; they were among the top 10 performing hospitals out of 163 national facilities; and they even managed to grow their service line in a shrinking market. As Tracee and her team discovered, the time and energy they invested in creating a few simple norms to support psychological safety among their leadership team had paid off in spades.

Building Block #3: An Ongoing Commitment and Process to Stay Self-Aware

As the bright afternoon sun streamed in through the window, I surveyed the cluttered, colorful office I'd just entered. To my right was a long, neat desk with a huge Apple computer monitor as its centerpiece. To my left, a wall of bookcases crammed with action figures, family photos, awards, and other tchotchkes, including the cast of a hand that has become world-famous in the computer animation community. Just minutes before, I had stepped onto the 22-acre campus in Emeryville, California, traversed a long, shady walkway, and entered the atrium of the Steve Jobs Building. Flanking the front desk were life-sized versions of *Monsters, Inc.* characters Sulley and Mike on one end and a giant sculpture of *Toy Story*'s Woody and Buzz on the other. On the back wall was a giant print of Scottish princess Merida from *Brave* riding through the forest on her noble steed.

It was a Thursday afternoon at Pixar headquarters, and I was sitting in the office of its brilliant president, Ed Catmull. Like many people, I had adored his 2014 book, *Creativity Inc.* But because I am a self-awareness researcher, there were a few elements of it that had piqued my interest so much that I simply had to talk to him. Among other things, I wanted to learn more about Pixar's now-infamous "Notes Day," which Catmull chronicled in the last chapter of his book.

The year was 2013, and despite a series of record-breaking box-office hits, Pixar was experiencing a frustrating sense of inertia. On top of surging production costs, Catmull and his team had noticed a subtle but worrisome trend, especially for Catmull, for whom a core tenet is what he calls "leading by being self-aware." In recent years, as the company had grown, the culture had also changed. Instead of sustaining the "unhindered communication" that made them so successful, employees seemed to be censoring themselves more and more. Catmull wanted to know why people were so hesitant to speak the truth and, equally importantly, what to do about it.

Clearly, it wasn't enough just to encourage feedback: they needed a dedicated process to generate it. So on March 11, Pixar closed to hold a "day of honesty," which they called "Notes Day." In the weeks leading up to Notes Day, Pixar executives posed a question to employees: "The year is 2017. Both of this year's films were completed well under budget. What innovations helped these productions meet their budget goals? What are some of the specific things we did differently?" They received more than 4,000 responses about more than 1,000 unique topics, ranging from reducing the amount of time required to make each film, to developing a better workplace, to reducing implicit gender bias in their films. The executives had chosen a few more than 100 of those topics for employees to tackle in 171 separate sessions spread out across the three buildings of their campus. Employees chose which sessions to attend, and all were led by a trained internal facilitator. Each one concluded with a series of "Exit Forms"—red for specific proposals, blue for brainstorms, and yellow for best practices, as well as assignments of "idea advocates" who would help advance suggestions that came out of the conversations.

Pixar co-founder and chief creative officer John Lasseter kicked off the day by reminding everyone how important candor was to their success. He underscored how difficult it was to give and receive tough feedback, but implored everyone to do their best to be honest anyway. "This is going to feel like it's directed at you personally . . ." he said, "but put your tough skin on, and for the sake of Pixar, speak up and don't stop the honesty."

In the months following Notes Day, Catmull received many e-mails from employees applauding its concept and execution. The experiment seemed to have, as Catmull put it, "broke[n] the logjam that was getting in the way of candor" and "made it safer for people to say what they thought." It also served as a reminder for everyone that "collaboration, determination and candor never fail to lift us up."

But now that a few years had gone by, I wanted the final verdict. Had this exercise just been a one-off success, or had it truly had an ongoing impact on their culture? Were leaders still hearing the truth from their employees? Were employees actually more comfortable giving and receiving candid feedback?

With these questions swirling around in my head, as if on cue, Catmull appeared in the doorway. Dressed in a black short-sleeved button-down shirt and jeans (and, naturally, sporting an Apple watch), he hobbled over to the chair across from mine. Gesturing to the cast on his right foot, he quipped, "I got drunk in a biker bar and did a round-house kick." I chuckled, sensing that that probably wasn't how he'd actually gotten the injury.

As our conversation progressed, I was struck by Catmull's depth of thought. He was focused and professorial, eschewing simplistic or neat explanations at every turn. This was especially true when I asked him about what had happened after Notes Day. He sat back in his chair and adjusted his glasses. I smiled, expecting him to regale me with tales of how Notes Day had solved all of their candor problems and now everyone was telling the truth about everything.

But Catmull chose a slightly different path. "It was definitely a valuable exercise," he stated. "But a few big things slipped through the cracks." He explained that a few months after Notes Day, they were having a "major meltdown" with one of their films. Both their traditional channels and their back channels for feedback to leaders had failed, to the point where the film was in danger of not even being made.

Catmull paused as I connected the dots. "So these issues were there on Notes Day?" I asked, furrowing my brow. Catmull nodded. "And everyone knew they were there?" He again nodded. Flabbergasted, I asked, "And no one said anything about them on the *day of honesty?*" Catmull nodded a third time, looking at me with an expression that said *bingo.*

He went on, "We realized that we had a deeper issue that we needed to figure out. Notes Day originated from a very successful process we'd developed with our Braintrust, which is a group of our directors and best story people. That group had done a great job of making their meetings safe for notes and criticisms. We had been trying to model this style of safety for the whole company."

However, he told me, there were two problems. The first was that not every manager had the skills to solicit ongoing feedback. "People take their cues from what they see and observe," he said, "not from what we say." No matter how often the executives assured everyone that this was a safe organization for criticism, if their team didn't feel safe, they would be cautious about what they said.

The second problem, as Catmull described it, was that notes are well-intended criticisms, but they are not solutions. "Solutions," he said, "require a great deal of effort, both in understanding them, and then working out how to act on them." At the end of Notes Day, they had thousands of "notes" but still needed to sort through the information, find patterns, set priorities, and *then* develop solutions.

But the biggest shock of all was that a few big problems still went completely unmentioned. Catmull is convinced that no one brought them up because they assumed someone else would. And since the leaders didn't know about these problems, they hadn't created the right opportunity to discuss them. "It's hard to make a safe venue for a problem that we didn't even know existed," he noted. In other words, they didn't have the right data to be questioning their assumptions about how the company was functioning (i.e., assumptions being one of the trickiest of the Five Cornerstones).

Clearly, if the Pixar executives wanted to further open the floodgates of feedback, an ongoing process was needed—though it would take some adjustment to reap real rewards. Two employees, one technical and one artistic, proposed a system: if people didn't feel comfortable talking to their manager about something that wasn't working, they could approach a designated **Peer Pirate** for help. Catmull explained that "in the days of real pirates, the crew would elect one of their peers to take issues and complaints to the captain with the agreement that he wouldn't be killed for what he said."

Pixar implemented Peer Pirates as a back channel to reveal the kinds of problems that were still going unmentioned. But after eight months, it still wasn't yielding valuable information. That's when Jim Morris—Pixar's general manager at the time, and now the president of Pixar—suggested that each Peer Pirate select four to six colleagues from their departments who could communicate feedback to Catmull and Morris together. Each department assembled a group that was diverse, comfortable with each other, and therefore more likely to be comfortable with Catmull and Morris.

With this, they were onto something. The Peer Pirates took their presentations very seriously, and many issues that had gone unmentioned on Notes Day were brought to the surface. "Now we had a mechanism for finding deeper insights and patterns within and across departments," Catmull said, beaming. "Now we had gold." These insights set in motion a few significant organizational changes that are now bearing fruit.

But Catmull is quick to point out that the process wasn't a silver bullet, either. Some issues have been easy to fix, others took a lot of work, and others they're still wrestling with. "It would be a grave mistake for us, or people on the outside, to somehow think that we've got it figured out," he said. Yet the great value of the Peer Pirates was that they uncovered a few systemic problems that were getting in the way of ongoing honesty. And by addressing the underlying reasons for why employees weren't telling the truth, they helped their already smart and talented managers create a culture where they could.

Pixar's approach is just one example of how leaders can instill an ongoing process and therefore a culture of awareness. Let's look at another slightly more extreme case. In 1975, 26-year-old Harvard graduate Ray Dalio founded Bridgewater Associates in his New York City apartment. The company would go on to become the world's largest hedge fund, and Dalio credits their success to the principles of "radical truth" and "radical transparency."*

At Bridgewater, employees are encouraged to call out unproductive behavior, and criticizing others behind their backs is a fireable offense. All conversations, unless they are personal or proprietary, are tape-recorded and accessible to anyone in the company. Bridgewater has even invested in technology to support the free flow of feedback. Using company-issued iPads, employees publicly record problems and failures in an "issues log." Each person, including Dalio, also has a "digital baseball card" where they score each other on behaviors like creativity and reliability on a scale of 1 to 10—the average of which is then displayed on the card for all to see. Through another app, employees give one another "dots"—"good dots" are awarded for behaviors that support the team, and "bad dots" help employees understand how they might be hurting it. Of such processes, co-chief investment officer Bob Prince observes, "What we're trying to do here is to pursue the truth at all costs."

But what *are* the costs? And are Bridgewater's extreme practices something that other companies should emulate? Their financial

---

* Dalio codified his credo in a 123-page document containing 201 of his most strongly held life and management principles. The tome is required reading for new hires, and Dalio often uses it as the basis for nightly homework assignments for employees.

results are certainly impressive—they've returned more money than any other hedge fund in history. And indeed, many employees say they love working there so much that they can't imagine being anywhere else. But other insiders believe that the company is successful not because of this "constant drumbeat of criticism," but in spite of it. One former employee explained, "What you see at Bridgewater [is] people practicing armchair psychology. You have a bunch of 23- and 24-year-olds running around supposedly diagnosing problems that I wouldn't trust someone with a PhD in psychology to do." It is perhaps for this reason that a shocking 30 percent of new hires leave—either voluntarily or involuntarily—within two years of being hired.

So is Dalio a brilliant visionary or an Orwellian autocrat? It depends on whom you ask. Though I certainly don't disagree with his unflinching commitment to the truth, my view is that Bridgewater's methods may be unnecessarily costly, and that most teams can achieve a feedback-rich environment without such extreme measures. Let's look at one way to do that: the **Candor Challenge**, a process I have refined over many years to instill ongoing self-awareness in teams.*

The Commitment to Ongoing Team Self-Awareness in Action: The Candor Challenge

"We're . . . we're going to do *what?*" asked one indignant vice president.

"With respect, I honestly don't see why this is necessary," said another. "Business is booming. Our year-over-year growth is busting all projections."

"I agree," said Sarah, the VP of finance. "We all respect your work, Tasha, believe me. The morning session was great. But you must understand, we're already the most self-aware team I know. We have a clear direction as a company. John's a fabulous president and does a great job modeling the way for us. Everybody knows they can speak up without

---

* The seeds for this process came from Patrick Lencioni's excellent book *The Five Dysfunctions of a Team*, which I consider required reading for all current and aspiring managers.

getting in trouble. Honestly? We like each other. We trust each other. We hang out together. So, thank you, Tasha, but I really don't think we need to spend three hours exchanging feedback."

In all my years as an organizational psychologist, I'd never experienced such a brilliant and well-informed pushback. These executives not only knew exactly what to say; they were right—mostly. Theirs was a successful company that already had most of the building blocks of self-awareness in place. But, perhaps ironically, their success had created a new problem. When things are going well, people are more apt to ignore the reality of potential issues, suppress difficult conversations, and put up with bad behavior. In recent months, John had noticed an increased prevalence of turf wars—his team members had hunkered down in their departments, seemingly popping up only to squabble about minor cross-functional issues, and sometimes bringing in John himself to arbitrate.

"They're bickering like siblings!" he moaned.

"I've seen this so many times," I told him. "It's far easier for the VP of sales and the VP of marketing to lock horns in a budget battle than talk about the deeper, subtler issues getting in the way of their working together." We needed to figure out what those issues were.

Back to the retreat, and the team's well-intentioned pushback. "Okay," I said to Sarah, "I definitely hear you." I took a deep breath, knowing that what I said next would either make or break the rest of the afternoon. "Let me ask a question. How many of you are nervous?" Every hand shot up.

"Nervousness is understandable and totally normal," I said. "But the level of fear in the room suggests to me that something's still stopping you from being truly open with one another. Maybe some of you are afraid to rock the boat when the waters are so calm. Maybe some of you prefer to avoid conflict or are just keeping quiet because everyone else is. Could it be, I wonder, that you guys are missing the final building block? Have you truly made an ongoing commitment to staying self-aware as a team?" Before anyone had the chance to respond, I continued, "It would be unfair for me to tell you this will be easy, but I can promise two things. First, the process works. And second, this will be one of the most important conversations you've ever had." Nine sets of eyes stared back at me, each as wide as saucers.

I'd made my promises. Now all I had to do was keep them.

Working in my favor was the fact that we'd already had a great start. This was the afternoon of a one-day retreat that John and I had designed to look at how the organization was functioning and lay the foundation for the open exchange of feedback on an ongoing basis. The morning had been devoted to briefly verifying their strategic direction, creating team norms, and, most importantly, participating in a Leader Feedback Process for John. This exercise had gone quite well, with John discovering a few strengths and weaknesses he'd never known he had. As we just saw, seeing him model the process of receiving feedback was an important prerequisite for his team to feel more comfortable giving feedback to each other—which was what we were about to spend the next three hours doing.

The Candor Challenge takes place over a period of months or years, but most notably begins with a **Team Feedback Exchange,** in which every team member gets the chance to give their peers feedback on their strengths, their weaknesses, and what they can do to increase their contribution to the team's success. And if that isn't intimidating enough, each team member delivers that feedback in front of the entire team. To lead the exercise, leaders can enlist an outside facilitator (in John's case, it was me) who has expertise in group dynamics, like an organizational psychologist or HR professional. Alternatively, they can appoint a team member to facilitate the process. Beyond the essential requirement that this person be both trusted and socially savvy, he or she should also be neither the team's most senior nor its most junior member. (And as a general rule, the larger the team, the more helpful it is to engage a skilled facilitator; with groups larger than five or six, this is absolutely invaluable to ensure an efficient and effective process.)

John's team had been warned that the Team Feedback Exchange was coming. Three weeks ago, he'd asked them to start thinking about each of their colleagues' contributions—what they were doing that was helping the team, what could they be doing differently, and what they personally needed from each person to be successful. Now it was time for them to speak up. I stood up and walked over to a flip-chart where I'd outlined the process. It looked like this:

Process (20 minutes per person)
- Prepare feedback
- Deliver question 1 feedback (30 seconds per question)
- Deliver questions 2 and 3 feedback (30 seconds per question)
- Questions for clarification

Then I explained how it would work: each person would give feedback to each other person at the table by answering three questions—and everyone would have the chance to ask for clarification on the feedback they'd been given at the end of their turn. The nine participants would be randomly assigned to one of three groups, and the exercise would progress in rounds, with short breaks in between. At the end, we would take some time to process and debrief.

After confirming that the executives in the first group felt comfortable kicking things off, I turned to another page of the flip-chart where I'd written the three questions they would be answering about their colleagues.

1. What, behaviorally, does this person do that most contributes to our success?
2. If this person could change one behavior to be more successful, what would it be?
3. What behavior do I need from this person to help me be more successful?

"Okay," I said. "Now it's time. You have a few minutes to prepare your feedback for the first group. Remember, though, that the purpose isn't to tell your teammates everything you think about them—we're looking for one piece of feedback for each question, a thirty-second response or less."

I stressed that their feedback should focus on behaviors rather than generalities. "By behavioral feedback, I mean focusing on specific examples of **what they said, how they said it, or what they did** rather than generalities or interpretations," I said. "For example, telling someone, 'You're being aggressive,' is not behavioral; it's an interpretation of their behavior. Alternatively, if I said, 'During our last team meeting, you interrupted me three times and raised your voice each time,' that is about behavior. Focusing on what people are doing rather than our interpretations or judgments not only helps us better understand the feedback, it helps you hear it openly and non-defensively."

Just as I thought they were finally getting with the program, Sarah once again raised her hand with the enthusiasm of a straight-A student. "I understand what you're saying," she said, "but this all seems a little bit over-the-top. Is there a reason that we have to give each other our feedback verbally? Can't we just write it down and give it anonymously?"

Her colleagues began nodding and hmm-hmm'ing around the table. "I'll give you three reasons why it's always better to give it verbally, Sarah," I said. "First, the richness and detail you get in a conversation is unmatched by written feedback. Second, believe it or not, anonymous feedback can often be more hurtful. When people's comments can't be traced back to them, they're not as careful with how they word things. And third, delivering feedback out loud offers the opportunity to practice this habit in a safe, controlled environment, which makes you more likely to continue it in the future."

Sensing their continuing disquiet, I gave them the ground rules that would ensure that everyone stayed honest, open, and respectful of one another throughout the process. They were:

Getting feedback ground rules[*]:
1. No pushback or defensiveness: be curious and remember that perception is reality.

---

[*] If your team isn't already familiar with the 3R Model for getting feedback from chapter 8, I strongly suggest that you briefly review this process when presenting the ground rules.

2. Take notes and ask questions only for clarification.
3. Be open-minded and assume good intentions.
4. Thank your team members. Giving feedback isn't easy!

Giving feedback ground rules:
1. Avoid generalities ("you always" or "you never").
2. Focus on the behavior rather than the person.
3. Don't give your interpretations of others' behavior—just the behavior itself.
4. Provide examples.

With that, it was finally time to get started. I gave them a few minutes for everyone to prepare their answers for group 1: first up would be an executive named Doug. We went around the table, with each person sharing their answers to question 1, then 2 and 3.* Doug wisely took notes to capture the feedback, and when everyone was finished, they looked at him expectantly. He smiled, thanked them, and asked a few clarifying questions. And because he appeared to have made it through unscathed, they all seemed a little more at ease. The team was now getting into a rhythm. We moved to the rest of group 1, and after a quick break, we continued with groups 2 and 3.

When we finished, they broke into a loud, exhausted round of applause at what they'd just accomplished. The team had followed the ground rules perfectly and, in my eyes at least, unearthed some incredibly powerful issues. And just as important, I could tell that each one of them had managed to hear and absorb the feedback without defensiveness, denial, or hysterics. Were there some tears? Sure—there

---

* I'm often asked why I suggest this structure (i.e., all team members answer question 1, then everyone answers questions 2 and 3) rather than having each team member deliver all their answers at once. First, hearing every team member's answer to the same question at the same time, versus answers to multiple questions at once, is the best way to spot patterns. Second, I find that the urge to deliver all answers at once often stems from a misguided desire to "soften" the negative feedback ("If I tell Doug what I like about him first, it will be easier to tell him what I don't like.")—but this isn't the way to build a lasting culture of candor. Self-aware teams bite the bullet, follow the ground rules, and give it to each other straight!

often are. Interestingly, though, after years of using this exercise, I've seen just as many shed during the positive feedback as I do with the constructive feedback.

Our three hours almost up, I issued a challenge. "To close out the exercise, we're going to go around the table. I'd like each person to make one commitment based on the feedback they just heard."

"I'm going to play devil's advocate and share the voice of the customer more often," said one executive.

"I'm going make more time to meet with each of you instead of charging ahead without your input," said another.

"I guess I'd better stop harping on what's wrong and be solutions-oriented," said a third.

It had been a long afternoon. All that was left was to agree on the plan to keep the process going—something I call **Accountability Conversations**. The team decided to circle back monthly and devote 30 or so minutes to a discussion: each person would provide an update on what they were doing to make good on their commitment. Then, they'd ask the team for their feedback, support, or anything else that would help them stay on the path toward improvement. But Accountability Conversations, the team astutely realized, weren't an excuse to sit on feedback for days or weeks. So they also agreed to point out, in real time, when they saw behavior that either supported or contradicted each team member's commitment.

Before bidding John and his team farewell, I gave them a crucial reminder. "Now that this feedback-rich culture has hopefully started to take hold, try to resist the temptation to think your work is done," I told them. "Your work is not done. In fact, this is only the beginning. Staying on top of the truth requires an ongoing commitment." This is why I recommend that at a minimum, all teams should hold a Feedback Exchange at least once per year—after all, there are always new behaviors, new challenges, and new team members, and keeping the feedback flowing is crucial to addressing new issues as they crop up.

With that, John's team filed out, exhausted, exhilarated, and, yes, deeply relieved. But did I live up to my promise of giving them one of the most important conversations they'd ever had? A few months later,

I found out. If the Feedback Exchange was successful, the progress they made after it was equally hard-earned and equally extraordinary. Like any team comprised of mere mortals, they had a few slips into old behaviors here and there, but the difference was that they were now brave and committed enough to call each other out. When I asked John what the net effect of all of this was, he said, "As a team, we're getting more done in the same amount of time. We're surfacing critical business issues and fixing them before they get out of hand. And what amazes me most is that the silos are basically gone—we're working together as one team."

And while the Candor Challenge is designed primarily for the work setting, all teams can use it to cultivate and sustain a culture of self-awareness—whether they're executives running a business, families trying to get along, or volunteer groups working to change the world. (Accordingly, if you would like to implement this process in your own team, you can download a workbook to help you do it at www.insight-book.com.) Indeed, no matter what your goals are, the commitment to the process of getting and staying self-aware can be the difference between failure and energizing, spectacular success. The good news is that candor creates a virtuous cycle: the more honest you are with one another, the easier it becomes to be honest in the future. Of course, it takes work and courage to get there, but the results are well worth it. You'll deepen your relationships, foster real collaboration, and dramatically improve your progress toward fulfilling your mission.

FROM SELF-AWARE TEAMS TO SELF-AWARE ORGANIZATIONS

In 1888, while visiting his mother at his childhood home, 34-year-old George Eastman was tinkering with an anagram set, trying to conjure a name for his new company. He wanted something short, unique, and easy to pronounce. Eastman loved the word they finally invented—especially the first letter, K, which he saw as "strong [and] incisive."

Later that year, he leased the third floor of a building at 343 State Street in his hometown of Rochester, New York, and an American icon was born. Eastman's business model was almost immediately profitable, in part because his relatively inexpensive cameras required customers to repeatedly purchase high-margin items like film, chemicals, and paper. For nearly a century, Kodak thrived, gobbling up 90 percent of the film market. By the late 1970s, they made 85 percent of cameras sold in the United States. And the brand wasn't just profitable—it seemed to capture the ethos of the American Dream. As just two examples, Neil Armstrong famously took a roll of Ektachrome film to the moon, and Paul Simon paid tribute to Kodachrome, the company's 35mm film, in a song of the same name.

But Kodak's failure to grasp the changing realities of its consumer base—specifically, the birth of digital photography and the subsequent death of film—would be the company's undoing. In 1975, when Kodak electrical engineer Steven Sasson assembled a prototype of the first digital camera, management scrapped it because they believed the product would hurt their film business. In a textbook example of delusion, Sasson described the managers' reaction as something akin to, "That's cute—but don't tell anyone about it."

In the late 1970s, as Paul Carroll and Chunka Mui reveal in their book *Billion Dollar Lessons*, Kodak's challenges soon mounted on the back of increasing pressure from its partners—from photo finishers to film retailers—to evaluate the long-term viability of traditional film. Their 1981 report concluded that their current business model would remain competitive only until 1990 (not because customers preferred film, but because digital cameras and photo printers were initially prohibitively expensive). Yet instead of using the results as a rallying cry to reinvent their business and tell their stakeholders the truth, Kodak executives burrowed their heads deeper into the sand. And though they made a trivial foray into the digital space, their languid pace meant they were undercut by competitors who had already responded to this new reality. The final nail in the Kodak coffin came in January of 2012, when the company filed for Chapter 11 bankruptcy.

This is a chilling tale of what happens in the absence of self-awareness at an organizational level. If team self-awareness means confronting reality by fostering candor among team members, *organizational self-awareness* means confronting market realities by **actively seeking feedback from all stakeholders**—employees, unions, customers, shareholders, suppliers, communities, legislators—and **keeping those stakeholders informed** about how the company is adapting to serve their changing needs. Alan Mulally calls this "awareness for everybody"—where everyone knows the goal, the status, and the plan, and has a voice in deciding on the steps needed to get there. And as technology and social media open up new channels for communication and the demand for transparency in business increases, the importance of organizational self-awareness will only continue to grow.

But this practice flies in the face of the way most companies function. Paradoxically, as we saw with Kodak, **it's not always that organizations don't have the information, but rather that they can't or won't accept it**. Specifically, unaware companies fail to ask the rather arresting question that my colleague Chuck Blakeman likes to ask his clients: "What are you *pretending* not to know?" Put simply, companies who fail to appreciate their market realities are fostering a collective delusion that will almost always sow the seeds of their undoing. Though there are many reasons for this kind of delusion, it is often due to what Chuck calls "Quarterly Report Syndrome"—prioritizing short-term results over long-term success.

Organizational delusion, however, isn't just confined to ignoring external realities—the same can be true for internal truths. When Alan Mulally first arrived at Ford, it seemed that every day he would open the *Detroit News* to find some horrible story about his new company—engineering issues, manufacturing problems, harassment claims—that had been leaked by internal sources. Previous leaders may have reacted by finding out who leaked the story and reading them the riot act. But for Mulally, this was an opportunity to learn why employees were airing the company's dirty laundry in the first place.

So he called up reporter Bryce Hoffman. "Bryce, I want to talk to you about these pieces you keep publish—"

Hoffman interrupted, "Mr. Mulally, they're all true."

"I know they're true," Mulally replied. "That's not why I'm calling. What I want to know is how you're getting such accurate and detailed stories."

"Well . . . it's pretty simple," Hoffman explained. "I walk into my office every morning and I push 'play' on my answering machine. Most employees even leave their name and number in case I want any clarification."

Mulally was speechless. "Bryce, why are they doing that?"

"Mr. Mulally, they love this company," Hoffman told him. "And they're scared to death because no one is telling them what's going on. The issues they're leaking are so serious that since management isn't talking about them, they figure calling me is the safest way to bring them up!"

Mulally couldn't believe it. He was reeling. He now had no choice but to push even harder to ensure that all of Ford's stakeholders knew everything—the good, the bad, and the ugly. He would personally respond to every employee e-mail he received. He'd wander the halls and factories and *really* talk to people. He'd send frequent company-wide updates. Mulally and his executive team also began inviting guests to their BPRs—engineers, analysts, technicians—as well as soliciting their feedback on the meetings.

But that wasn't all they did. In a sweeping move to ensure that all employees understood the company's path forward (i.e., "awareness for everybody"), Mulally and his team worked with Ford's head of Human Resources to design a small blue card they gave to every employee in the company. On the front was the company vision, under the headings of "One Team," "One Plan," and "One Goal." On the back were the expected behaviors that would get them there. It would be easy to dismiss this as mere optics, or a superficial HR stunt aimed at artificially engineering employees' loyalty, but for Mulally, these weren't just words on a laminated card—they were a way of life. As Hoffman explains in *American Icon*, "it was all there, everything he wanted Ford employees to know and understand." As Mulally passed them out, he made a joke that wasn't really a joke: "Take two of these and call me in the morning. It's the cure for what ails you."

Just months after Mulally asked Bryce Hoffman about the stories being leaked to the *Detroit News*, they stopped completely. Mulally again called Hoffman. "Bryce, there are no more nasty articles about Ford in your newspaper."

"I know," he replied. "That's because there are no more messages on my answering machine."

"Why do you think that is?"

"Well, it's pretty obvious," Hoffman replied. "You're listening. You're including them. They know what's going on. They don't need to call me anymore."

By opening up the channels of communication, Ford had fundamentally transformed its relationship with employees. By the time Mulally retired in 2014, morale was at an all-time high of 87 percent (for comparison, the average engagement level in the United States that year was 31.5 percent). Thankfully, his successor was committed to sustaining a culture of awareness for everybody—a culture where leaders modeled the way, where it felt safe to share the truth, and where a rigorous, ongoing process supported the free flow of feedback throughout the organization. But wait—who was Alan Mulally's successor? You guessed it. It was none other than Mark Fields.

10

SURVIVING AND THRIVING IN A DELUSIONAL WORLD

Someone told me I was delusional.
I almost fell off my unicorn.
—SOMEECARDS.COM

A tadpole is swimming in a pond. All of a sudden a frog appears in the water next to him.

"Where did you come from?" the tadpole inquires.

"Somewhere dry," replies the frog.

"What is 'dry'?" the tadpole asks.

"It's when there is no water," says the frog.

"What is 'water'?"

The frog is speechless. Emphatically gesturing at the abundant substance surrounding the tadpole, he asks, "Water? You mean . . . you can't see it?"

"No."

"But how can you not see it? *It's all around you!*"

This little allegory perfectly captures how it feels to be around an un-self-aware person. Whether it's a spouse who doesn't pick up on social cues, a boss who seems utterly incapable of seeing her behavior through her employees' eyes, or a friend who is oblivious to how miserable his job is making him, the experience can be downright maddening. *How can this smart, otherwise reasonable person, we wonder, be so utterly blind to the "water" they are swimming in—to who they are, how they behave, and what impact they have on those around them?*

After surveying thousands of people, I've come to the obvious but nevertheless empirically based conclusion that one doesn't have to throw a rock very far to hit a delusional person. In fact, only two of our unicorns reported *not* knowing such an individual. (Comically, one decided that since he couldn't think of any, the most likely explanation was that *he* was delusional. He seemed relieved when we assured him that this wasn't the case.) Of course, not all unaware people are created equal; sometimes they are innocuous or amusing, like an oblivious person sitting next to us on the train or a character on a reality TV show. Other times, they sap our energy and try our patience: like a hopelessly self-involved in-law or a delusional boss or co-worker. And still other times, when they're as close to us as a partner, a parent, or a child, they can be a seemingly endless source of stress and heartbreak.

In the workplace, delusional people aren't just annoying and frustrating; they can significantly hinder our performance. Scarily, being on a team with just one unaware person cuts the team's chances of success in half, and unaware bosses have a detrimental impact on their employees' job satisfaction, performance, and well-being. When reporters at the *Washingtonian* asked 13,500 employees in the Washington, D.C., area about their worst boss ever, they were regaled with mind-boggling tales of bad behavior. As just a few examples, one manager made employees who said anything "particularly stupid" stand on their chair as punishment. Another added up the time people spent in the bathroom and deducted the corresponding number of vacation hours each pay period. But perhaps the most unbelievable example came from an employee who tried to take a day off to attend his father's funeral. His boss' response? "We need you now. What difference does it make to him?"

Now, it would be easy to just dismiss these three bosses—and others like them—as simply bad people. Malicious jerks. Sociopaths, even. While these things may or may not be true, most people in the unenviable position of working with them don't often stop to think about the role that self-awareness—or a lack thereof—is playing in the equation. After all, most people, even horrible bosses, don't wake up every morning and say, "Today, I'm going to humiliate and upset everyone I talk to!" Instead, they may just be completely delusional about their behavior and its impact. But this puts us in a difficult position. Upon learning the truth, the delusional might very well be horrified and even want to take action to change. But is it really our responsibility to shock others into awareness? And even more fundamentally, is it even possible?

The truth is that challenging a delusional person can be risky at best and disastrous at worst. Remember, almost everyone thinks they're above average, morally upstanding, and supremely self-aware—and the most delusional can be the *least* receptive to hearing otherwise. After all, as we've seen in previous chapters, when we hear feedback that suggests we're not what we think we are, as renowned psychologist William Swann puts it, not only do we feel incompetent, we "suffer the severe disorientation and psychological anarchy that occurs when [we] recognize that [our] very existence is threatened." Pretty heavy, right?

We've already heard the stories of so many ordinary people who have radically improved their own self-awareness, so it must at least be possible to help the delusional become more self-aware. But not everyone will want to change. (You know what they say about leading a horse to water, right?) Given this reality, what *is* the best way to deal with delusional people? Is it to understand them and perhaps help them change? Or is it better to simply minimize the collateral damage of their delusion on our success and happiness? In this chapter, I'll address these questions with the goal of providing you a few actionable strategies for dealing with the three specific types of unaware people you may encounter in your life—the *Lost Cause*, the *Aware Don't Care*, and the *Nudgable*—and keep them from draining your energy, enthusiasm, and happiness.

ACCEPTING WHAT WE CANNOT CHANGE AND CHANGING WHAT WE CAN (OR HOW TO SOLVE A PROBLEM LIKE MARIA)

Robert was happy in his new job as development manager at a small IT security company. He was passionate about the work he did, had a great boss, and trusted and genuinely liked his co-workers. In fact,

Robert loved everything about his new job—with one giant exception. That exception was named Maria.

Maria, like most un-self-aware people, seemed to inhabit her own reality. As the long-time manager of the company's support desk, she stubbornly clung to the mistaken assumption that her colleagues shared her every opinion and disparaged them when they deigned to disagree with her. She used intimidation and bullying to control her team, and it was hurting morale to the point that they couldn't muster the motivation to go out of their way to help their customers. On top of all that, Maria never let an opportunity slide to remind her colleagues about her academic credentials and years of experience.

Even Maria's conflict-avoidant supervisor seemed scared of her. After an earnest but ineffective attempt to confront the behavior a few years back, he'd thrown up his hands and effectively given her worst qualities free rein to grow. Rather unsurprisingly, Maria's behavior was a constant source of tension and conflict in the office—and if she had any vague awareness of how it was affecting the people around her, she certainly wasn't showing it.

As the days and months dragged on, Robert felt Maria's impact on the team growing like a cancer. Her co-workers were afraid to disagree with her lest she bite their heads off. They were frustrated that her boss wasn't doing anything to hold her accountable for her bad behavior. Over time, Robert found himself waking up each morning less and less excited to come to work.

Then, one day, his prayers were answered in the form of an announcement from their human resources director. Each member of the company's leadership team (of which he and Maria were members) would get the chance to receive anonymous written feedback from their colleagues. *This is our chance to put it all on the table!* Robert thought.

When it came time to put pen to paper, Robert decided that he had nothing to lose by being brutally honest about the specific behaviors that were driving everyone insane. "Maria takes her role very seriously and puts the hours in," he wrote. "But she doesn't realize her harsh tone, over-policing of staff, and constant references to her qualifications and experience combine to create a toxic atmosphere that is really hurting team morale and performance." When Robert finished recording his feedback, he felt oddly optimistic. *She's really not a mean person*, he decided, *she probably just has no idea how much her behavior is damaging our team.*

The human resources director collected and compiled everyone's feedback. And a few days later, the eight members of their leadership team—Robert, Maria, and their peers—gathered in a conference room to discuss what each person had learned from the process. Robert found himself nervous but hopeful that today would be the day they finally addressed the elephant in the room.

The morning moved at glacial pace. For some reason, Maria had asked to go last, and the team was holding its collective breath with nervous anticipation. When it was finally her turn, the air in the room was like hot marshmallow.

"I was really shocked to hear how you all see me," she began. "It was not a pleasant experience going through your feedback." For a moment, she looked upset. The team was now on the edge of their seats. Would this be the moment that she'd see the error of her ways? Would Maria's bad spell finally be lifted? "But honestly, I just didn't recognize myself in any of these comments."

Even though it felt like the walls were crashing in, the room was utterly silent. No one was quite sure how to respond to the level of delusion to which Maria clearly still clung. Robert cleared his throat and tentatively asked, "Maria, what did you hear from the team?"

"One thing's for sure. I didn't hear anything I actually need to change," she flatly replied.

"What makes you say that?" he probed, trying to remain calm.

"Well, someone said that I was full of myself—always talking about my qualifications and experience. That person was obviously just jealous of my success."

"Can you think of any other reason someone might have said that?" he carefully asked.

"What other reason is there?" Sensing an opening, Robert opened his mouth to speak. But before he could get a word out, Maria continued her thought. "There *is* no other reason."

Robert looked back at Maria, blinking. In a split second, he weighed the pros and cons of coming clean that he had written the comment and pointing to any one of the many examples of the behavior that had inspired it. But despite his initial optimism, Robert suddenly realized that no good would come of it.

Unfortunately, he was right. A full year passed since Robert's team completed this exercise, and a lot of things are different at work—a lot of things, that is, except for Maria. While each and every other team member had made a concerted effort to respond to the feedback they received, Maria continued to remain willfully ignorant; not only dismissing all of her colleagues' comments, but repeatedly reminding them how wrong they'd been.

Maria represents the first of three categories of delusional people: the **Lost Cause**. Lost Causes cling to their delusion with a righteous, indignant, and unshakable zeal. Because they can't (or won't) consider any other opinion besides their own, anyone who attempts to shine a light on their less desirable characteristics will get the proverbial flashlight thwacked out of their hand. Because they already see themselves as pretty close to perfect, they're rarely if ever willing to entertain the notion that they might have room to improve. Although you can occasionally get them to listen to feedback by appealing to their self-interest ("This behavior is hurting your reputation"), it is usually pointless to challenge their self-views.

When you discover that someone in your life is a Lost Cause, it's easy to feel hopeless. The good news is that although we can't impose insight on Lost Causes, it doesn't mean that we can't take action to minimize their impact on our success and happiness. Indeed, there is much to learn from how Robert learned to peacefully coexist with Maria—primarily by working to manage his own reactions and better understand her impact on him and the rest of the team.

Once Robert realized that Maria had no desire to improve her self-insight, he challenged himself to adopt the mindset of **compassion without judgment**. Rather than getting constantly bent out of shape about her deficits, he realized that they were simply on different journeys. If we revisit our "horse race of awareness" analogy from chapter 2,

Robert was picking up speed while Maria was dead last—but with this realization, he was able to view her as someone who was simply struggling, rather than as a malicious megalomaniac. It was actually freeing to realize that Maria's self-awareness was not his problem to fix—it was hers and hers alone.

Robert isn't the only one to adopt such an approach; when surveyed about how they deal with the Lost Causes in their lives, only about half of our unicorns reported directly intervening, but nearly all used strategies to control their own reactions. In his superb book *The No Asshole Rule*, Stanford professor Bob Sutton shares an instructive metaphor for managing our reactions to Lost Causes. (And for that matter, to the second type, the Aware Don't Care, whom you'll read about in a minute.) Imagine you're white-water rafting. Your boat is calmly floating down a picturesque river, when all of a sudden you see a rough patch ahead. As you paddle through the rapids, you're abruptly thrown into the violent waters.

Most people in this situation try to fight it: kicking and flailing to get back to the boat; trying to swim toward the shore; futilely clinging to a slippery rock. But those strategies are actually more likely to kill us than save us, and the less we battle the current, the sooner we'll find ourselves in calmer waters. Robert liked this metaphor—it reminded him that he was actually more in control than it seemed. If Maria said something antagonistic to him, for example, rather than standing up to her or trying to make her see the error of her ways, he would simply imagine *floating feet-first*, and getting out of the rough waters as quickly as possible.

When dealing with a delusional person like this, it's easy to write him or her off as simply a bad person. But what if we challenged ourselves to name a few of their positive characteristics? This is an example of another tool; one that draws on the mindfulness tool of *reframing*, or looking at our problem from a different perspective. When Maria brought her 13-year-old daughter to work, Robert was genuinely struck by how Maria treated her: she was unbelievably kind, fiercely loyal, and demonstrably proud. To stay in control of his reactions when he was working with Maria, Robert kept that image in his mind and forced himself to conjure it when she wasn't behaving quite as magnanimously toward him.

Another technique that's equally applicable to Lost Causes is one that Robert originally learned in elementary school. In fifth grade, the class bully set his sights on Robert, who would come home every day crying and fearful of the next day's abuse. This went on for weeks, until his mother said something that he never forgot. "Honey," she told him, "this kid is a bully. He's mean, he's cruel, and I know how much he's hurting you. But have you ever asked yourself, **what can he teach me?**" Initially, young Robert thought his mother was a bit nuts—what in the world could he learn from that malevolent monster?—but soon he realized that perhaps he'd been too hasty. Perhaps the experience was an opportunity to learn something about himself. *Maybe*, he thought, *he's showing me that I need to do a better job sticking up for myself.* And so he did.

Robert was reminded of this a few months after his failed showdown with Maria. Since that day in the conference room, she was aiming an inordinate amount of ire his way. And one evening, after a particularly hellish day, he'd finally had enough. He was going to quit. But as he began drafting his resignation, he remembered his mother's words. Maria, he realized, was just a different kind of bully. So Robert asked himself the question his mother had asked all those years before. Was this actually an opportunity to learn a few lessons about dealing with difficult people and therefore improve himself?

When he gave this new perspective a trial run, it worked almost instantly. He began to view the situation not as a soul-eroding marathon, but as an interesting and beneficial challenge. Though she had no idea, Maria was helping Robert increase his self-awareness and turn those lemons of delusion into lemonade.

Lost Causes aren't the only type of delusional people out there. Let's now look at a second variety, who, as we'll see, can seem indistinguishable from Lost Causes, but in reality suffer from a much, much different problem.

WHEN A LITTLE SELF-KNOWLEDGE ISN'T ENOUGH

I was once hired by a manufacturing company to coach Jerry, a VP who was a successor for their chief operating officer role. From our first meeting, I was impressed with Jerry's intelligence, instincts, and insight. But these characteristics couldn't have been more different from those of his boss, Daniel, whose behavior was the stuff of legend. The current COO's "leadership" techniques included yelling at his direct reports when they disappointed him, humiliating them in front of their colleagues, and causing even the most composed professionals to lose their cool. Unsurprisingly, Jerry's department had the highest turnover rate in the company, along with the lowest morale.

Naturally, I had lots of questions about this mysterious Daniel. Did he have even an inkling about how ineffective his approach was? Had anyone ever mustered the courage to confront him? And if they had, did he at any point even *try* to change his behavior? I would soon learn the answer, and it wasn't what I expected.

After Jerry had set his own goals for our coaching process, the two of us decided to sit down with Daniel to make sure he was on board. Jerry and I made a plan for the conversation as we waited in the cavernous seating area outside Daniel's office. When we were ushered in, I stuck my hand out to introduce myself to Daniel. Now, for some context, I've often been accused of having an unusually firm handshake (when I first met my graduate advisor, for example, his first word to me was literally "OW!"). But when I shook Daniel's hand, his grip was so aggressive that I felt like he was trying to get me to drop to the floor. That was my first clue about what was really going on.

Luckily, Jerry had a gift for dealing with Daniel that bordered on magical, and the meeting got off to a great start. Jerry's first goal was to delegate more effectively so he could focus more on the strategic aspects of his role. Daniel was on board. But he didn't quite feel the same way about Jerry's second goal, which was to work on better engaging his employees. Before Jerry could finish explaining his plan to do so, Daniel held his hand up as if to say, "Stop talking right now." Jerry obliged.

"Jerry, this one's a waste of your time."

"Why is that, Daniel?" he calmly asked, as if he had anticipated this question from his rather predictable boss.

"Because it doesn't matter if your employees are 'engaged.' The most effective management tool I've ever come across is fear. If they fear you, they will get the work done. It's really that simple."

I was so shocked that I almost fell out of my chair. I have heard executives say a lot of ridiculous things over the years, but I had never met someone who openly admitted to a strategy of intimidation. And Daniel didn't just *admit* to this strategy; he was *bragging* about it. That's when I realized that, unlike so many of the delusional bosses I've encountered in my coaching work, Daniel knew exactly how he was behaving—and it didn't bother him in the slightest. Though many of his actions screamed Lost Cause, his was an entirely different problem. Daniel was a textbook case of the second type of delusional person: one I call **Aware Don't Care**.

Whereas a Lost Cause's primary issue is a lack of insight and no motivation to acquire it, the Aware Don't Care know exactly what they're doing—and the negative impact they're having on others—*but they act that way anyway.* Why? They truly believe that their counterproductive (often borderline-abusive) behavior will help them get what they want. And therein lies their delusion. From Daniel's perspective, he (wrongly) believed that cultivating fear helped him do his job better.

I have an uncle who recently retired from a long career as a surgeon. During his residency, one of his attending physicians was an avid marathon runner; this starkly contrasted with the residents, most of whom rarely left the hospital, let alone found time to exercise. Every morning, rounds began on the fifth floor. But rather than meeting his residents there, the attending required them to gather on the first floor and march up five flights of stairs together. One day, my breathless uncle asked him if he knew how hard it was for everyone to climb the stairs. "Of course I do," the attending replied. "I do it so none of you will ask me questions." There we have it, folks. Aware, and definitely didn't care.

But since the behaviors of the Aware Don't Care can so closely resemble those of a Lost Cause, how can we tell the difference? Sometimes, we learn the answer only when we confront them—as Robert did with

Maria, and as my uncle did with his attending. Other times, though, there can be clues. Lost Causes usually show inconsistency between what they say about themselves and how they behave. Remember Steve, the construction executive from chapter 3? When I first met him, he waxed poetic about what a great leader he was and how much his employees respected him; both claims were in direct contradiction to his actions. The Aware Don't Care, on the other hand, show a different pattern. They are likely to acknowledge their behavior, but brush it off or defend it (i.e., "Yeah, I know I yelled at her, but she deserved it" or "Of course I'm pushy with clients—that's the only way to make the sale"). Like Daniel, they might even take to bragging about their unsavory characteristics.

Another way to tell Lost Causes from the Aware Don't Care is to look at their perspective-taking abilities. Lost Causes tend to believe that their way of thinking is the only way—like Maria, who assumed that everyone else shared her opinions and freaked out when they didn't. The Aware Don't Care, on the other hand, often show that they understand their behavior from other people's perspectives—like the hospital attending who knew just how onerous those five flights of stairs really were—but they also demonstrate the belief that the behavior is productive. And for that reason, it's usually not worth the energy to try to change them.

When we learned about the Cult of Self earlier in the book, we saw that narcissists—people characterized by grandiose levels of self-admiration—are an especially delusional bunch. But while a lack of self-insight has traditionally been a cornerstone of narcissism, recent research has indicated that they possess something called "pseudo-insight." For example, and rather shockingly, one of the best ways to identify a narcissist is to simply ask them whether they are, in fact, a narcissist—more often than not, they'll reply in the affirmative. But why on earth are they so willing to admit to toxic traits, like egotism, selfishness, and vanity? Just like Daniel, they are aware that they possess these characteristics, but *don't see anything wrong with them*. In fact, they tend to view them as positive! As social psychologist Brad Bushman observes, narcissists "believe they are superior to other people and are fine with saying that publicly."

There is also evidence that narcissists have at least some awareness of the (generally inevitable) erosion of their personal relationships, but they don't seem to recognize their role. Instead, they blame others and cling to their overly positive self-assessments. One fairly amazing way they do this is to conclude that others are just too dim to appreciate their brilliance. And while narcissistic leaders think extremely highly of their leadership performance, they are rated lowest in effectiveness by their teams—the only people they are impressing, in other words, are themselves.

While the two techniques mentioned above (floating feet-first and asking "what can they teach me?") will also work with the Aware Don't Care, there is another that's particularly well suited for them. I first came up with the **laugh track** when I had the misfortune of working for an Aware Don't Care boss many years ago. After a series of public humiliations, including being reamed out for a relatively small mistake in front of our entire leadership team, I was at the end of my rope. I figured I had two choices: I could quit, or I could find a better way to deal with my manager. Because I adored every other aspect of my job, I decided to try the latter. One day, after a particularly unpleasant encounter with said boss, I happened to recall my favorite TV show growing up, *The Mary Tyler Moore Show*.

Mary's boss was a surly man named Lou Grant, played by the incomparable Ed Asner. On a good day, Lou Grant was grumpy and hotheaded; on a bad day, he was nasty and downright abusive. But because his outrageous comments were often followed by a canned laugh track, to the viewer, they seemed comical and surprisingly endearing. I decided that the next time my boss said something so cruel that it made me want to cry, I'd imagine a laugh track behind it instead. Now, it would be inaccurate to say that this completely transformed my experience of working for him, but the tool did make it that much more bearable (and occasionally, hilarious).

These stories are proof that when it comes to delusional people who refuse to change, **by managing our own reactions, we often have more control than we think**. But unfortunately, changing our mindset is not always sufficient. There are times when we'll need to proactively assert ourselves and set boundaries, and there will be times—if all else fails—when the only tool we have at our disposal is to remove ourselves from the situation.

I have a good friend who, in addition to having a successful coaching practice, is a rather prolific writer. A few years back, Scott was hired by a well-known entrepreneur—let's call him Joe—to perform some initial research for a book he wanted to write. In their first meeting, Scott was blown away by how down-to-earth Joe was for a multimillionaire. Seconds after they met, Joe enveloped Scott in a huge bear hug, and throughout their conversation, he seemed positively enraptured by everything Scott had to say. *This is going to be a blast!* Scott thought excitedly.

The contract Scott drew up was simple and unambiguous—or so he thought. He would perform in-person interviews with 10 CEOs who shared Joe's management philosophy, write a report for each, and submit it, along with his travel expenses, to get paid for that portion of the work. The day before his meeting with the first CEO, which was taking place in New York, Scott's assistant Jenna had set up a final call to review the interview questions. Jenna dialed in at the top of the call to make sure everything was on track and then left Joe and Scott to proceed with their conversation.

As the call came to a close, Joe asked, "You're good on the subject areas I need covered tomorrow?"

"Yeah, I'm good," said Scott. "If you think of any others while I'm in the air, just pass them along to Jenna. She'll make sure I get them the moment I land."

"Sure," said Joe. "She seems very efficient."

"Oh, Jenna's the best," Scott replied enthusiastically. "I call her my right-hand woman. We've built the whole business together. I don't know what I'd do without her."

Initially Scott thought nothing of this portion of the conversation. But then, just a few minutes after hanging up, his phone rang again. It was Jenna.

"Is everything okay?"

"Sure," she said. "But you'll never guess who just called me? Joe!"

"Is there a problem?"

"I don't know how to say this, exactly . . . but he offered me a job."

Scott was stunned. "Wh-what?"

"He offered to double my salary. And he didn't even ask what my salary *was*!"

"You must be kidding," said Scott, suddenly choked with feelings of anger and panic.

"I turned him down, of course," she quickly added. "But I thought you should know."

That night, Scott struggled to sleep. How could Joe *do* that just minutes after he'd shared how valuable Jenna was to his business? He knew Jenna was happy and fairly compensated, and he felt lucky that she'd had the loyalty to turn Joe down. But the whole incident had left him feeling belittled and betrayed. He decided to confront Joe the next morning and **state his needs.**

"Joe, I wanted to talk to you about what happened yesterday after our call."

There was a long pause as Scott waited for Joe to realize he'd been found out and apologize for his completely unprofessional behavior. "Jenna told me that you tried to hire her away from me."

"Yeah," Joe sighed. "And she turned me down on the spot. But that's okay. You know, I have to be honest, most people in her position would crawl over broken glass to work with me. Frankly, the fact she turned me down makes me question her judgment. It's really no loss to me."

Scott couldn't believe what he was hearing. It almost seemed as if Joe thought he was calling to apologize to *him*. The multimillionaire was clearly clueless about the impact of his actions—not just on their relationship, but potentially on the success of the very project he'd hired Scott to complete. "Look, Joe, can I ask you a favor?" said Scott. "Can you please refrain from hiring my people?"

Another long pause followed. Apparently, Joe had to think it over. But finally, he agreed to Scott's request.

Though Scott was understandably unsettled by the whole encounter, he hoped it would be a minor bump in the road. He toiled over the report for his first interview, and a few weeks later, he submitted a

15-page product to Joe, accompanied by receipts for his travel expenses, just as they had agreed. Later that day, Scott received a phone call.

"Scotty," said Joe. "I got your report. I've got to tell you, I've decided I don't want this guy or his company anywhere near my book. The stuff he was saying about staff feedback? One-hundred-percent Texas horseshit."

Scott was naturally disappointed to hear that he'd wasted three weeks of work. But his disappointment was nothing compared to the fury he was about to experience.

"I'll reimburse your travel expenses, of course," Joe continued. "So don't worry about that. Just send your receipts to my office."

Scott's heart felt like it had frozen in his chest. "And, uh . . . my fee?" he said. "I'll send the invoice for the fee at the same time?"

"Scotty, no," said Joe, suddenly impatient. "I just told you. This thing is of no use to me. I'm not paying for horseshit."

Hardly containing his anger, Scott decided he had no choice but to assertively state his needs. "Joe, this is not reasonable at all. You approved the interviewee and the questions. The report is exactly what you asked for. I have to be paid."

After a long discussion—and Scott's repeated insistence that Joe honor their agreement—the irascible entrepreneur finally agreed to pay up. But Scott was still (understandably) quite perturbed. Of course, at this point he seriously considered taking the money and running. But because he believed in the project—and was getting paid quite handsomely—he decided to try one more thing before he threw in the towel. This time, he would create better guidelines for their relationship. What they needed were *clear boundaries* they could both agree on.

Scott added about four pages of specifics to the contract, spelling out the exact requirements for the work product, and just in case, the exact travel expenses that Joe would reimburse him for. After a few back-and-forths, he was able to get Joe's signature and set out to schedule his second interview. Now, even for someone as narcissistic and delusional as Joe, there could be no doubt as to where they stood. Or so he thought.

Unfortunately, Joe's behavior persisted. At one point, and in direct opposition to their contract, he even refused to pay for Scott's expenses because he'd taken a short taxi ride instead of the subway. Up until now, Scott had been doing everything he could to deal with his unaware client. He'd assertively stated his needs and aggressively clarified his boundaries. And he'd attempted to manage his own reactions. But his concern continued to grow. *How bad is this going to get?* Scott wondered. He decided to pick up the phone and call a few mutual acquaintances to get more information.

The most concerning data came from Candace, one of Joe's longtime executives. In the last two years, Candace had been diagnosed with a serious autoimmune disease, and despite knowing about her diagnosis and what it meant, Joe had apparently continued to summon her into the office at all hours of the night and on weekends. "He's killing me," Candace half joked, "and he has absolutely no idea."

As he hung up with Candace, Scott finally decided that enough was enough. It was time to **walk away**. This cruel and unfeeling behavior was proof positive that Joe simply was never going to change, and the money Scott was sacrificing was minimal compared to the sanity he would be regaining. And in case you're doubting Scott's decision, this might be a good time to tell you the topic of the book Joe was writing. It was a book on . . . wait for it . . . *emotional intelligence*. It just doesn't get any more delusional than that, does it?

Granted, not everyone dealing with a delusional person has the luxury of walking away. But as Scott discovered, when someone is as thoroughly mired in delusion as Joe, the problems they create in our lives don't magically disappear. In many cases, they intensify over time. If we've exhausted all of our options—changing our mindset, stating our needs, and reinforcing our boundaries—but still can't manage, we must face these situations with unflinching honesty about who they are and the true probability that they will ever change. Sometimes, after weighing those factors, we may indeed decide that whatever the sacrifice—whether it's leaving a job we love, cutting ties with an impossibly unaware friend or family member, or giving up a lucrative contract—our best option may be to pick ourselves up, dust ourselves off, and move forward.

HELPING THE DELUSIONAL DECODE THE FLASHING LIGHTS

Mercifully, though, not everyone is unreachable. Indeed, the third type of delusional person, the **Nudgable,** is one whose behavior we absolutely *can* have an impact on, at least to a degree. What sets the Nudgable apart from their more hopeless counterparts is that they genuinely *want* to be better; they just don't know that they need to change their approach. And unlike Lost Causes and the Aware Don't Care, they are generally surprisingly receptive to receiving this information—that is, when it's delivered in the right way.

The day I turned 16, I joyfully experienced the classic rite of passage of getting my driver's license. Eager to exercise my newfound freedom, I begged my mother to let me drive to school and back the next day. She hesitated, understandably, because I had a play rehearsal that went late into the evening and little practice driving in the dark. But eventually she relented. That evening, I got into my car, turned on my headlights, and headed home. Exhilarated to be behind the wheel, I thought everything was going great. Then I noticed that almost every car I passed was blinking their lights at me. *Why is everybody doing that?* I wondered.

I soon found out. As soon as I made it home and pulled into the driveway, my mother burst out of the garage, frantically waving at me to turn off my brights, "Honey, you're blinding the entire neighborhood!"

All of a sudden it made sense. Completely unbeknownst to me, I had been shining my brights directly at Denver drivers for miles—and what's more, they'd all been trying to tell me as much. I just couldn't, quite literally, read the signals I was getting. This is a good metaphor for what life is like for unaware people. Though they can't decode what the flashing lights in front of them mean, other people usually can. And if they're open to it, we can help the unaware see themselves through our eyes.

Call me an optimist, but I believe that more often than not, **most unaware people are at least somewhat Nudgable**. Many times, rather than representing a deep disconnect from reality, their unawareness results from far less pervasive and sometimes even situational causes. For example, research has suggested a positive correlation between stress and unawareness: that is, the more stress we are under, the more unrealistic we tend to be about our abilities, characteristics, and behaviors. This makes intuitive sense. Have you noticed that people seem to be most delusional about their behavior in times of stress? Unawareness isn't always an indictment of someone's potential to develop insight—they may just need a bit of a nudge.

My friend Lisa has been on the board of a local non-profit for nearly a decade. A few months ago, they brought on new a board member, let's call him Phil, who was more than a touch delusional. In no time at all, Phil was annoying everybody, constantly bragging about his successes in the private sector with no apparent understanding of how he was alienating those around him. That is, until he realized that the other board members were giving him the cold shoulder. When he had tried to join a few committees, he'd been effectively shut out.

One evening after a board meeting, Phil approached Lisa with a frustrated look on his face. He asked her if, as the longest-serving board member, she might give him some advice. He shared his frustration and asked if he was doing anything that was contributing to the problem. As is often the case with the Nudgable, Phil knew *something* was wrong, but he couldn't quite read the signs. Lisa suggested that he pay closer attention to his language: instead of telling everyone everything he had done, she gently suggested, perhaps he could ask his colleagues questions to get to know them better. Phil was taken aback as he processed the information. He then proceeded to announce that he would change his approach starting at that very moment. Though it took a little longer than Phil may have hoped, he was eventually able to win over his fellow board members, and was invited to join more than one committee.

In Phil's case, Lisa had the perfect opening to deliver her feedback. Unfortunately, though, not every unaware person is savvy enough to seek it out. After all, **the big catch-22 of self-awareness is that the people who need it most are usually the least likely to know they need it**. So is it ever a good idea to confront an unaware person more directly? And if so, how can we guard against the inevitable risks? How can we deliver these important insights without the recipient shooting the messenger (i.e., you)? As we'll see from the following story, when it comes to the Nudgable, a little compassion, coupled with some thoughtful preparation, can really go a long way.

◆

It was the week before Christmas in a picture-perfect mountain hotel. Sophia and Emma, who'd been best friends since kindergarten, had been having a fantastic time in Vermont, courtesy of Emma's generous and successful father. He'd treated them to seven days of private snowmobiling lessons, lavish shopping trips, and pricey dinners. But sitting in the luxurious suite they'd been sharing as the gold December sun shone through the windows, Emma suddenly looked anxious.

"What's up?" asked Sophia, sitting on the edge of the bed with a freshly made cup of coffee.

Emma was peering around the open door. "Is my dad around?" she whispered.

"What, Frank?" said Sophia. "He went to the gym to find your mom. Why?"

"It's the ski lesson he booked for tomorrow," said Emma, rubbing the back of her neck. "I don't think I want to go."

"Really?"

"Really!" she replied, wide-eyed. "Why would anyone strap slippery wood planks to their feet and slide down a mountain at a high speed . . . voluntarily? I want to live to see Christmas."

"So don't go!" laughed Sophia. "Just kick back in the spa. What's the big deal?"

"It's Dad," she said. "He'll chew me out for sure."

Sophia (who also happens to be a self-awareness unicorn) did her best to reassure her old friend that she was worrying too much. After all, Sophia had known Emma's father for years. Frank was an extraordinary man. He'd overcome a difficult childhood to put himself through college and then medical school, and he had since become a world-renowned surgeon. She knew him to be physically imposing, at nearly seven feet tall with broad shoulders and a Hemingway beard, but also extremely kind. For a long time, Frank had supported Sophia's dream of becoming a doctor, and been something of a mentor, arranging informational interviews with his colleagues, taking her to lunch to talk about her plans, and even helping with her medical school applications earlier that fall.

Of course, she'd heard about Frank's "other side" from Emma for years, who'd often complained that he could be domineering, cruel, and controlling. For example, Emma had struggled with her grades in college, and at one point announced to her parents that she was going to take a year off from school to "regroup." Frank had apparently lashed out at her, complaining about how much money he was wasting on her education and how ungrateful she was. This, of course, was devastating to Emma. "He wields his wealth and success like a weapon," she'd bemoaned, more than once.

"I know you guys locked horns when you were growing up," said Sophia. "But he's not going to want to ruin Christmas making an issue of something dumb like a ski lesson."

"Maybe," replied Emma, hesitantly at first. "Yeah, maybe you're right."

Minutes later, Frank returned.

"Go on!" mouthed Sophia, gently pushing her friend toward the lounge space.

"Dad?" said Emma, leaning on the door frame. "Would you mind if I sat out skiing tomorrow? Would that be okay?"

As he walked to the wardrobe to hang his wife's coat, Frank's expression barely changed. "Sure," he said flatly, his shoulders shrugging ever so slightly. Pleasantly surprised by her father's non-explosive reaction, Emma put the whole thing out of her mind.

The next morning, as they were all heading back to the suite after breakfast, Frank ran into a colleague in the lobby. They made pleasant conversation as an open fire crackled and popped and sweater-clad guests milled about.

But when the woman asked about Frank's plans that day, his warm demeanor instantly dissipated. "Well, *we three*," he said, gesturing wildly toward himself, Emma's mother, and Sophia, "are going to be taking a private skiing lesson. But someone," he pointed at his daughter and dramatically rolled his eyes, "is too *afraid* to go skiing and decided to cancel at the last minute—and it's too late to get my money back. Can you believe how ungrateful she is?" Frank bellowed, at a volume that reverberated through the lobby so loudly that he might as well have made an announcement on their PA system.

A long, awkward silence followed. Suddenly, Emma, choking back tears, stormed off without a word. As she went, Frank watched her with a look of genuine confusion. He turned at Sophia as if to ask, "Was it something I said?" Clearly, he had no idea how his brutish words had injured his sensitive daughter.

For the rest of that day and long into the evening, Sophia couldn't stop thinking about what she had witnessed. And the more she pondered Frank's behavior, the more incensed she became on her friend's behalf. She knew she had basically two options: to confront Frank or stay painfully MUM and see his behavior continue. Sophia felt compelled to talk to him, but she didn't know whether it would do any good. And she was pretty sure that either way, she'd be putting herself right in the firing line of his outrageous temper.

To help her decide what to do, Sophia asked herself several questions. The first was, **do the benefits of having this conversation outweigh the potential risks?** Sophia started with the benefits: first and foremost, she cared about Emma. If she could do anything to minimize the hurt that Frank caused her in the future, she'd do it in a second. Sophia also cared about Frank and knew that if this behavior continued, it could effectively end his relationship with his daughter.

She imagined the worst-case scenario if their conversation went south. The most painful thing that could happen was that Frank would never want to speak to her again, but while that was possible, she had a hunch that the more realistic worst-case scenario was that he would yell at her and sulk for the rest of the vacation. So, given these two options—a better Frank or a worse vacation—she was happy to risk the latter in service of the former.

But even once Sophia decided that the benefits outweighed the costs, she still had another angle to consider. She asked: **Does he know there's a problem?** Sophia believed (and the research confirms this) that if someone isn't feeling any pain or frustration, they might not have enough motivation to change. In Frank's case, though, he clearly knew something was wrong—his pained look when Emma ran away was proof enough—he just didn't know *he* was the reason.

A related question was: **Is his behavior counter to his best interests?** When someone is acting in a way that's inconsistent with their values and priorities, pointing out the discrepancy can be quite motivating, if a little jarring. Research has shown that human beings have a desire for congruence—that is, they want their behaviors and beliefs to match—and when they don't, they experience an uncomfortable sense of cognitive dissonance. In Frank's case, Sophia knew that he cared deeply about being a good dad to Emma. She even remembered a recent conversation where he had mentioned that the reason he worked so hard was to give Emma a better childhood than he'd had. Pointing out how his behavior was impeding those goals, Sophia reasoned, was likely to create an alarm-clock moment.

The answer to Sophia's final question—**Do I think that he will listen to me?**—wasn't as straightforward. Power differentials, like the one she had with Frank, make conversations like this very difficult. (Remember how hard it is to speak truth to power?) Indeed, for a 21-year-old pre-med student to think she should tell a successful 52-year-old surgeon how to act might seem silly on the face of it. But Sophia thought that the trust they shared would tip the balance. Frank respected her, trusted her motives, and recognized what a good friend she was to Emma; he had often remarked that she was his daughter's most mature and responsible friend. What's more, she reminded herself that he had been open to smaller pieces of feedback—albeit of a very different type—from her in the past, recalling a recent conversation in which she had playfully corrected his grammar. He'd seemed annoyed for a moment, then grinned and said, "You know, you're the only person I would ever let correct me on something like that."

After carefully weighing all sides of the issue, Sophia decided that she was going to talk to Frank. Instinctively knowing that the longer she waited, the more likely he'd be to minimize or even forget the inciting event, she decided to do it the very next day. Luckily, she had a window of opportunity already built in: Sophia and Frank were both early risers, and in the first few days of their vacation, they'd settled into an early-morning coffee routine. Tomorrow, Sophia would invite him to breakfast instead.

Later that night, as Sophia lay in bed sleeplessly staring at the ceiling, she figured she's try to channel her nerves to make a plan for the conversation and think through a few contingencies. When morning finally came, she marched to their suite's small kitchen and came face-to-face with Frank. "Frank, I'm starving," she said as nonchalantly as possible. "Do you want to grab breakfast at the restaurant downstairs?" "Sure!" he replied, and off they went.

The hostess walked them through the nearly empty restaurant and gestured toward a table in the back. Once they ordered, the pair had an uneasy chuckle about the unnerving number of stuffed animal heads on the wall above them, then discussed Sophia's plans for medical school the following year. "Frank," she told him, "I really can't thank you enough for everything you've done to help me get here. I don't think I've ever told you how grateful I am for your advice. You're an incredible doctor and an even better friend."

Sophia could literally see Frank puffing up across the table. But she wasn't just buttering him up. Not only was her gratitude authentic, Sophia know that expressing it had another benefit. She'd just learned about self-affirmation in her social psychology course and thought that affirming Frank's positive qualities as a doctor and friend would prepare him to hear about his less-than-ideal parental characteristics. (Incidentally, Sophia was right: affirmation has similar benefits with others as when we use it with ourselves.)

Smiling, Frank replied, "Wow, Sophia, thank you. It's so nice to feel appreciated! And so rare for me," he said, winking at her in a not-so-subtle reference to yesterday's episode. Sophia didn't think her opening would come this fast, but she decided to go with it.

"What do you mean?" she innocently inquired.

"I've just had it up to here with Emma. I mean, I'm sorry, I know she's your friend and I probably shouldn't be telling you this. But can you believe how ungrateful she was yesterday?"

Emma mentally reviewed the plan she'd come up with the night before. She'd decided to begin by asking questions to see if Frank could reach a place of insight on his own, without her having to forcibly drag him there.

"What was going on there, do you think?" she asked.

"The sad fact is, my daughter can be ungrateful." He lifted a croissant from the basket at the center of the table. "All my life, I've spent, I mean, my God, hundreds of thousands of dollars trying to make her happy. And all my life, she's thrown it back in my face. Skipping out on the ski lesson? I should've expected it." He ripped the croissant in half and studied it with an air of faint disgust. "I was kind of hoping that she was finally starting to grow up."

"Fair enough," Sophia remarked, "but what do you think was going on from Emma's perspective?"

"She was acting like a baby!"

Sophia tried again. "Frank, I can completely understand how mad that made you. But from Emma's perspective, why do you think she was so hurt?"

"I have absolutely no idea."

Sophia paused. She was waiting for an "aha moment," but all she got was an old man angrily chewing a pastry. "Okay, you were both really upset, right?" she said. Frank nodded. "And you don't want that to happen in the future?" More nodding. "So don't you think it's important to figure out why Emma reacted that way?"

Frank cocked his head, seemingly curious. Then, as if on cue, he punted Sophia's question back to her. "What do *you* think was going on with Emma?"

Though this was a signal that he was open to an alternative version of the events, Sophia was worried that if she came right out with Emma's perspective, he'd think she was taking sides, or wrongly conclude that his daughter had sent her friend to do her dirty work. Sophia carefully began, "Frank, I haven't talked to Emma about this yet, so I can only infer, but think about it for a minute. She was obviously really scared to go skiing." Frank rolled his eyes. She continued, "Then you lashed out at her for it, and in public, no less."

"What do you mean? I was just making polite conversation."

"Well, it was a conversation," she said. "But it definitely wasn't polite." Frank seemed taken aback by Sophia's candor. There was a tense silence. But then his shocked expression evolved into a small smile. She plodded on, "Did you notice the exact moment Emma got upset?"

"Was it when I was talking about how she didn't want to come with us to the ski lesson?" Sophia nodded. "But I still don't understand why."

Emboldened, Sophia offered, "I think Emma was humiliated. She was already embarrassed about being so afraid, and you put it out there for everyone to see. And as for the fact that she walked away, she was probably trying not to get in a fight with you in front of a stranger."

Finally, a faint glimmer of understanding came over his face. "So what I said made Emma feel like she was being punished for not wanting to go skiing?"

"Well, maybe. And Frank, if I may, there was one more thing I think Emma might have been reacting to. But let me ask you first: How did the issue of money factor into that whole situation, in your mind?"

Reaching for another croissant, he replied suspiciously, "I already told you. I was mad because Emma was wasting my money."

"I understand. But how do you think money factored into the situation for Emma? Do you think it's possible that she felt like you were holding the money you spent on the ski lesson over her head?"

Frank's arm paused in midair. The croissant fell back into the basket. "Oh, wow," he said, sitting back and exhaling. "I never thought about it that way. Is that something I do?"

Suddenly, the floodgates of insight burst open, and Frank was on a roll. He started connecting his behavior to his childhood experiences—how his family had trouble with money; how it was a frequent source of conflict; how helpless and frustrated it used to make him feel. "I don't want to repeat that pattern. I had no idea I was doing this," he pleaded. "There's nothing in the world more important to me than being a good dad. But if I didn't know I was acting this way, how am I going to know when I do it again?" Sophia thought for a moment. "Frank, why don't you ask Emma to help you?"

And so he did. It took Frank a few weeks to muster the courage to sit down with his daughter. But when they finally talked, he was surprised to find out how good it felt to get things out into the open. Though Frank and Emma's relationship didn't heal overnight, of course, Sophia noticed a palpable difference in how they were interacting just weeks later. He was doing a much better job of listening to her and staying calm, and Emma told her that he'd virtually stopped talking about money. As time went on, Frank would lapse back into his old behavior perhaps more than was ideal—after all, he was unlearning decades of ingrained habits—but the difference was that now he was more aware of it when it happened. As a result, he was able to stay focused and improve a little every day, which over time created a stronger bond between them.

As Sophia's story shows, it *is* often possible to help others to increase their insight, and it's never too late to begin. For that reason, when dealing with a delusional person, it's not a bad idea to be optimistic and assume that a person is Nudgable until it's proven otherwise. But at the same time, we must also be practical—honestly assessing their level of openness and examining whether the benefits of such a conversation outweigh the costs, wisely choosing our timing and our words, and above all, keeping our expectations reasonable. Sometimes, a single conversation can be a game-changer, as Sophia found with Frank. Other times, the person might need a few more nudges. (Research has shown that on average, the more unaware a person is, the more likely they are to require repeated evidence over time, sometimes from several sources.)

But often, if we keep the tone of the conversation positive and constructive and show that we come from a place of genuine support, we *can* help the unaware see themselves more clearly. When we **confront with compassion**, we can often nudge them to make powerful changes that don't just improve their life and happiness, but ours as well.

THE LIFELONG QUEST AND THE SPECKLED AX

A man once purchased a hand-forged ax from a blacksmith. Affixed atop its sturdy wooden handle, as the centuries-old story goes, was an iron head covered in opaque gray carbon, save for the blade, where the blacksmith had sharpened off the soot to reveal the smooth silver underneath. The man liked the look of the blade so much that he asked the blacksmith to sand the entire head to match. The blacksmith agreed, but only if the man would help him power the sharpening wheel. As the blacksmith pressed the head of the ax hard against the stone, the man began to turn the wheel. But the task was far more difficult than he had imagined, and after just a few minutes, the man stopped. And when he checked his progress, he didn't see the bright, smooth silver surface he hoped for—the carbon had only been sanded away in a few areas, and the ax was a gray-speckled mess.

The man announced that he'd take the ax home as it was anyway.

"No! Turn on, turn on," the blacksmith said. "We shall have it bright by and by; as yet, it is only speckled."

"Yes," replied the man, "but I think I like a speckled ax best."

This story, penned by America's first unicorn, Ben Franklin, perfectly illustrates how unexpectedly difficult the twin goals of self-awareness and self-improvement really are. We might strive for an ax that is shiny, smooth, and flawless, but feel intimidated by the effort and commitment it takes to get there. Rather than keep sanding away, we find it far easier to convince ourselves that we wanted an imperfect ax all along.

While a perfect silver ax—i.e., total insight and absolute truth—is not a realistic or even productive goal, that doesn't mean we should throw in the towel when the going gets tough. Without a doubt, the lifelong pursuit of self-awareness can be long, difficult, and messy. We will hit obstacles or setbacks and feel daunted by the work it takes. And just when we think we've finally sanded off all of the proverbial soot, we might discover that we actually still have a way to go.

But the fact that we are never truly "finished" becoming self-aware is also what makes the journey so exciting. No matter how much insight we've achieved, there is *always* more to be gained. Few understand this better than our unicorns, who see self-awareness as a state of being that they consistently prioritize. And for the rest of us, no matter how self-aware we start out, we can all work to continuously broaden and deepen our insight throughout the course of our lives.

As we go about that process, we will learn things that surprise us, gratify us, and challenge us. And with each new insight will come the inevitable question of "Now what?" At the beginning of this book, I called self-awareness the meta-skill of the twenty-first century—that is, it's a necessary but not sufficient condition for a life well lived. Another way of saying this is that **insight is pointless if we don't put it to use.** Imagine how differently things would have turned out if George Washington hadn't curbed his pride, restrained his fiery emotions, and learned to think before he acted; or if Florence Ozor hadn't followed her heart and joined the #BringBackOurGirls movement; or if a young Alan Mulally hadn't re-invented his management strategy after his first employee gave him a much-needed wake-up call. As we've seen from these and other examples, the most successful among us don't just work to gain self-awareness—they act on it and reap the rewards.

Undeniably, this can feel easier said than done. Most leaders I know who have completed the Leader Feedback Process, for example, come away with a long, overwhelming list of strengths to hone and weaknesses to address. And the longer the list, the more daunting and paralyzing it can feel. Yet this need not be the case. Just one thing separates people who successfully act on insight from those who don't: the ability to take things one step at a time. When Ben Franklin, for example, set out to practice his 13 virtues, he initially tried to tackle all of them at once. Unsurprisingly, this didn't go so well; it took more energy than he'd imagined to break bad habits and build better ones in their place. So he changed his strategy to focus on one virtue at a time.

In one of my all-time favorite movies, *What About Bob?* Bill Murray's character Bob has a codependent relationship with his therapist, Leo Marvin, played by Richard Dreyfuss. During one of their sessions,

Leo tells Bob he'll be going on vacation for a month. When Bob begins to panic, Leo gives him a book he wrote called *Baby Steps* to read while he's away. Leo explains, "It means setting small, reasonable goals for yourself, one day at a time." In an example of Murray's classic comedic brilliance, his character follows this advice literally, taking hundreds of baby steps out of the office and into the elevator. "I'm in the elevator!" he gleefully exclaims. "All I have to do is take one little step at a time, and I can do anything!" A silly example, of course, but research confirms that both Benjamin Franklin and Leo Marvin were onto something.

Franklin likened this approach to weeding an overgrown garden: if you just walked up and started pulling weeds willy-nilly, you wouldn't feel like you were making much progress. But instead, if you tackled just one bed at a time, you'd be surprised at how quickly you'll end up with a better-looking garden. And although by Franklin's own admission he never quite arrived at the moral perfection he set out to achieve (a typical unicorn comment), he was "a better and happier man than I otherwise should have been if I had not attempted it."

The same is true for the rest of us. The truth is that you could spend a lifetime applying and refining the concepts from this book. But as most people instinctively know, we also need quick wins to help us create and sustain momentum. To help you do this, I've created a simple exercise to catalyze your self-awareness journey, no matter where you are on that path. During each day of the *7-Day Insight Challenge*, you'll focus on one element of self-awareness. And since the point is to provide you with quick hits of insight, I designed each day's challenge to be completed in 15 to 30 minutes. To help you to record and process your learnings from the Insight Challenge, you can download a workbook at www.Insight-Book.com. And if you'd like a more scientific baseline of your current level of self-awareness before you begin, you can find a free 360 assessment at www.Insight-Quiz.com.

Day 1: *Select Your Self-Awareness Spheres*

On a piece of paper, list the three most important spheres of your life: work, school, parenting, marriage, friends, community, faith, philanthropy, etc.

1. For each sphere, write a few sentences about what success looks like using the Miracle Question: If you woke up tomorrow and everything in that area of life was near-perfect, what would that look like?
2. Then, given your definition of success, rate how satisfied are you are now on a scale of 1 (*completely unsatisfied*) to 10 (*completely satisfied*).

Your biggest opportunities for self-awareness are those where you're not as satisfied as you want to be. Circle the one or two spheres that you most want to improve (these are your target self-awareness spheres). Think about what is keeping you from achieving your definition of success and what changes you could make to get there.

Day 2: *Study the Seven Pillars*

Find a trusted friend, family member, or colleague. Go through the Seven Pillars of Insight together (chapter 2, p. 24). For each pillar, describe how you see yourself (e.g., what are your values?) and then ask the other person to share how they see you (e.g., what do they think your values are?). (And please, be a good friend and help your partner examine his or her own pillars!) After your discussion, reflect on the similarities and differences between your answers about yourself and your partner's answers about you. What did you learn from this exercise, and how will you build on it moving forward?

1. *Values*: The principles that guide how we govern our lives
2. *Passions*: What we love to do
3. *Aspirations*: What we want to experience and achieve

4. *Fit:* The environment we require to be happy and engaged

5. *Patterns:* Our consistent ways of thinking, feeling, and behaving across situations

6. *Reactions:* The thoughts, feelings, and behaviors that reveal our strengths and weaknesses

7. *Impact:* How our actions are generally perceived by others

Day 3: *Explore Your Barriers*

Think back to chapters 3 and 4 and pick one or two barriers to self-awareness that you suspect might be at play in your own life (i.e., Knowledge Blindness, Emotion Blindness, Behavior Blindness, the Cult of Self, the Feel Good Effect, Selfie Syndrome). For the next 24 hours, try to spot the barrier(s) occurring in real time, either by questioning your own behavior and assumptions or spotting them in others. At the end of the day, think about what you learned and how you can apply the strategies you've read to help you shift your thoughts and your actions.

Extra credit: For the next 24 hours, pay attention to how often you are focused on yourself versus interested in other people, both online and offline. When you're tempted to post your recent vacation photos or regale your dinner party guests with a story about your latest professional accomplishment, ask yourself, "What am I hoping to achieve by doing this?"

Day 4: *Boost Your Internal Self-Awareness*

Choose one of the internal self-awareness tools below to experiment with today. At the end of the day, spend a few moments reflecting on how it went, what you learned about yourself, and how you can build on this insight moving forward.

1. What Not Why (p. 109)

2. Comparing and contrasting (p. 139)

3. Reframing (p. 137)
4. Hitting pause (p. 123)
5. Thought-stopping (p. 124)
6. Reality checks (p. 124)
7. Solutions-mining (p. 149)

Day 5: *Boost Your External Self-Awareness*

Identify one loving critic within each target self-awareness sphere (chapter 7, p. 179). Ask them to share one thing that they value or appreciate about you and one thing that they think might be holding you back. As you're hearing the feedback, practice the 3R Model (chapter 8, p. 195).

Day 6: *Survive the Delusional*

Think of the most delusional person you know (ideally, that you'll see today). Which category from chapter 10 (Lost Cause, Aware Don't Care, Nudgable) do you think the person falls into, and what leads you to this conclusion? Practice using one tool below to better manage your relationship with this person the next time you see him or her.

1. Compassion without judgment (p. 259)
2. Float feet-first (p. 260)
3. Reframing (p. 260)
4. What can he/she teach me? (p. 261)
5. Laugh track (p. 265)
6. State your needs (p. 267)
7. Clarify your boundaries (p. 268)
8. Walk away (p. 269)
9. Confront with compassion (p. 279)

Day 7: *Take Stock*

Review the notes you took over the course of the challenge and answer the following questions:

1. What do you now know about yourself—and about self-awareness in general—that you didn't know a week ago?
2. What one goal can you set for yourself over the next month to help you continue the momentum you have now?
3. And once you've completed the challenge, be sure to join the Insight Challenge Facebook group. Just visit www.Insight-Challenge.com and you'll be automatically re-directed to a dedicated group where you can share your successes and best practices!

◆

If this book has convinced you of anything, I hope it's that self-awareness isn't just for unicorns. Truly, we are all capable of gaining insight and reaping the resulting rewards; of recognizing our self-limiting behaviors and making better choices; of knowing what's most important to us and acting accordingly; of understanding our impact so we can improve our most important relationships. The lifelong journey to understanding who we are and how we're seen can be a bumpy one, full of obstacles and roadblocks. It can be difficult, painful, and slow. It can make us feel imperfect, weak, and vulnerable. But this road is also paved with the greatest of opportunities. Author C. JoyBell C. articulated this far better than I ever could when she wrote:

> I think that we are like stars. Something happens to burst us open; but when we burst open and think we are dying; we're actually turning into a supernova. And then when we look at ourselves again, we see that we're suddenly more beautiful than we ever were before.

Self-awareness transforms us into supernovas—more beautiful, better, and brighter than we ever were before.

What Are Your Values?

Understanding our values—that is, the principles that guide how we want to live our lives—is the first pillar of insight. Values help us define the person we want to be, as well as set the stage for the other six pillars. Here are a few questions to help you better understand yours:

1. What values were you raised with? Does your current belief system reflect those values, or do you see the world differently than you were brought up to see it?
2. What were the most important events or experiences of your childhood and young adulthood? How did they shape your view of the world?
3. At work and in life, whom do you most respect and what do you respect about them?
4. Whom do you least respect and what makes you feel this way?
5. Who is the best (and the worst) boss you've ever had, and what did she or he do to earn that moniker?
6. When it comes to raising a family or mentoring others, what behaviors would you most and least want to instill?

To help you further identify or narrow your most important values, below is a fairly exhaustive list:

Acceptance	Authority	Change
Accuracy	Autonomy	Comfort
Achievement	Beauty	Commitment
Adventure	Caring	Compassion
Attractiveness	Challenge	Contribution

Cooperation	Humility	Purpose
Courtesy	Humor	Rationality
Creativity	Independence	Realism
Dependability	Industry	Responsibility
Duty	Inner Peace	Risk
Ecology	Intimacy	Romance
Excitement	Justice	Safety
Faithfulness	Knowledge	Self-Acceptance
Fame	Leisure	Self-Control
Family	Loved	Self-Esteem
Fitness	Loving	Self-Knowledge
Flexibility	Mastery	Service
Forgiveness	Mindfulness	Sexuality
Friendship	Moderation	Simplicity
Fun	Monogamy	Solitude
Generosity	Nonconformity	Spirituality
Genuineness	Nurturance	Stability
God's Will	Openness	Tolerance
Growth	Order	Tradition
Health	Passion	Virtue
Helpfulness	Pleasure	Wealth
Honesty	Popularity	World Peace*
Hope	Power	

---

* W. R. Miller et al. "Personal values card sort." Albuquerque: University of New Mexico, 2001.

What Are Your Passions?

Understanding our passions—the second pillar of insight—is key to making choices and decisions that line up with what we love to do, both in our careers and in our personal lives. Here are a few questions to help you get started in exploring your passions:

1. What kind of day would make you leap out of bed in the morning?
2. What types of projects or activities do you never seem to get sick of?
3. What types of projects or activities do you find least enjoyable?
4. If you retired tomorrow, what would you miss the most about your work?
5. What are your hobbies and what do you like about them?

If you're looking for more guidance to unlock your passions, there is no shortage of "What color is your parachute"–like assessments, and I certainly encourage you to take them. But not all are created equal, so make sure you're taking a test that's been well validated. Two of the best are:

1. The Holland RIASEC Model (you can find a free version at: http://personality-testing.info/tests/RIASEC/ or http://www.truity.com/test/holland-code-career-test).
2. The Strong Interest Inventory (you can purchase the test at http://www.discoveryourpersonality.com/strong-interest-inventory-career-test.html or http://careerassessmentsite.com/tests/strong-tests/about-the-strong-interest-inventory/).

What Are Your Aspirations?

Steve Jobs once said, "I want to make a dent in the universe." This is the essence of the third pillar of insight: our aspirations, or what we want to experience and achieve. Here are a few questions to help you identify *your* dent:

1. When you were younger, what did you want to be when you grew up and what drew you to this profession?
2. Is the way you're currently spending your time meaningful and gratifying to you? Is there anything you feel is missing?
3. Imagine that you are an impartial party reading a list of your values and passions. What might a person like this want to do and experience in his or her life?
4. What legacy do you want to leave behind?
5. Imagine that you only had one year left on earth. How would you spend that time?

What Is Your Ideal Environment?

Understanding where we fit—that is, the type of environment we require to be happy and engaged—is the fourth pillar of insight. Fit can help guide us in making major life decisions: what city to live in, what kind of life partner will fulfill us, what career or company will help us thrive, etc. Here are a few questions to help you understand your ideal environment:

1. In the past, when have you performed at your best at work, and what were the characteristics of those settings?
2. In school, what type of learning approach or classroom setting helps/helped you learn the most and the least?
3. Have you ever left a job because the environment wasn't a good fit for you? If so, what about it didn't work for you?
4. If you had to describe your ideal work environment, what would it be?
5. What types of social situations and relationships tend to make you the happiest?

What Are Your Strengths and Weaknesses?

The sixth pillar of insight is our reactions—that is, our thoughts, feelings, and behaviors in any given moment. Such reactions, at their core, are often a reflection of our strengths and weaknesses. Here are a few questions to help you begin to understand yours.

Your Strengths
1. In the past, what have you picked up easily without a lot of training?
2. What do you seem to do faster or better than other people?
3. What type of work makes you feel most productive?
4. What type of work do you feel the most proud of?
5. What have you accomplished that's genuinely surprised you?

Your Weaknesses
1. What are your biggest failures and what commonalities exist between them?
2. When have you been most disappointed with your performance?
3. What piece of constructive feedback have you heard from others most often?
4. What tasks and activities do you dread most?
5. What qualities do your loved ones playfully tease you about?

Remember, when it comes to gaining real-time insight on our momentary reactions to the world, the trick is to *reflect* less and *notice* more—so instead of pondering these things, you might examine the tool of mindfulness in chapter 6, which is arguably the most effective approach for actually gaining insight about our reactions.

What Is Your Impact on Others?

As we've seen throughout the book, it's easy to lose sight of the effect that our behavior has on others—the seventh pillar—yet examining people's reactions and responses to us is a critical part of becoming more self-aware. Here are some initial questions to help you start to reflect on the impact you might be having on others:

1. In your life and work, who are the people in whom you have a vested interest (employees, spouse, kids, customers, etc.)?
2. For each of these people or groups, what is the impression that you would *like* to create?
3. Think about your behavior in the last week with each person or group. If you were a neutral party observing that behavior, would you see it as having the impact you're aiming for?
4. In the last week, what reactions have you observed from each person or group? Think back to your interactions and try to recall not just how they responded to you verbally, but also their facial expressions, body language, and tone. Do these match up with your intentions? If not, what changes could you make?
5. If you see an opportunity to change your approach in ways that would help you to achieve the impact you desire, what could you experiment with starting tomorrow, and how will you assess your impact?

Do You Have Unknown Unknowns?

U.S. Secretary of Defense Donald Rumsfeld is famous for his statement about "known knowns," "known unknowns" and "unknown unknowns." When it comes to self-awareness, the "unknown unknowns" are what can hurt us most. It's uncomfortable to consider the possibility that we don't know ourselves as well as we think, but it's absolutely essential.

Read the statements below and circle the ones that apply to you. The more statements you've circled, the more you should be questioning your beliefs about yourself and getting feedback to calibrate those beliefs.

1. Has your job or career made you feel unhappy or unfulfilled for a prolonged period of time?
2. Have you ever been surprised that you didn't get a promotion or a job you applied for?
3. Have you ever failed at a task or project when you were sure that you'd succeed?
4. Have you ever been surprised by the results of a performance evaluation or a 360 assessment?
5. Have you ever been blindsided by negative feedback from a boss, peer, employee, or loved one?
6. Has a work colleague or loved one ever been angry with you without your knowing why?
7. Have any of your romantic or platonic relationships taken a sudden turn for the worse for reasons you didn't completely understand?
8. Have any of your romantic or platonic relationships ended unexpectedly?

What Are Your Assumptions?

One way to avoid the Three Blindspots is to identify your assumptions before you make critical decisions. Here are a few questions to help you surface your assumptions in a work context:

1. How will this decision impact the various stakeholder groups within and outside your company? Are there any stakeholders that you haven't considered?
2. What are the best and worst cases if you implement this decision?
3. What consequences for this decision have you failed to consider?
4. How would a smart and savvy competitor view this decision and how might they respond?
5. What would someone totally unconnected to this decision like and dislike about it?
6. What developments might change the thinking you've used to arrive at this decision?
7. What sources of information or data might you have overlooked in arriving at this decision?

Are You a Member of the Cult of Self?

For each item below, circle which of the two options (the left or right) best describes you:

1	I think I am a special person.	I am no better nor worse than most people.
2	I like to be the center of attention.	I prefer to blend in with the crowd.
3	I like having authority.	I don't mind following orders.
4	I always know what I am doing.	Sometimes I am not sure of what I'm doing.
5	I expect a great deal from other people.	I like to do things for other people.
6	I am an extraordinary person.	I am much like everybody else.
7	I am more capable than other people.	There is a lot that I can learn from other people.

The test you just took is a sampling of items from the Narcissistic Personality Inventory.[*] The more items on the left you circled, the more narcissistic qualities you may possess. Don't worry—having a few narcissistic tendencies doesn't necessarily mean you *are* a narcissist. But it might mean you have some work to do in resisting the Cult of Self.

---

[*] Daniel R. Ames, Paul Rose, and Cameron P. Anderson. "The NPI-16 as a short measure of narcissism." *Journal of Research in Personality* 40.4 (2006): 440–450.

How Humble Are You?

Although it's in increasingly rare supply in our Cult of Self world, humility is a necessary ingredient of self-awareness. Being humble means having an appreciation for our weaknesses, keeping our successes in perspective, and acknowledging the contributions of others.

For each item below, choose the number that best describes your behavior in general. Try to look at how you're actually behaving, rather than how you wish to behave. Because others can often see what we can't, it may be helpful to have a trusted advisor weigh in as well. When you're finished, average your responses and review the guide on the next page.

1	2	3	4	5
Very Rarely	Rarely	Sometimes	Often	Very Often

_____ 1. I seek feedback, especially critical feedback.

_____ 2. I admit when I don't know how to do something.

_____ 3. I acknowledge when others know more than I do.

_____ 4. I take notice of people's strengths.

_____ 5. I compliment others on their strengths.

_____ 6. I show appreciation for others' contributions.

_____ 7. I am willing to learn from others.

_____ 8. I am open to others' ideas.

_____ 9. I am open to others' advice.

Average	What It Means
1–2	Your current level of humility is low, and others might perceive you as arrogant or self-centered, which may be harming your relationships and preventing you from getting the most out of your team. The good news is that if you dedicate time and energy to focusing on and admitting your weaknesses and recognizing others' strengths, it will pay off in spades.
3–4	Your current level of humility is moderate. Though others may not see you as completely arrogant or self-centered, you can likely improve your relationships and effectiveness by honing your humility. You might start by focusing on the behaviors where you rated yourself lowest. And by the same token, for the items with the highest ratings, consider whether you can focus on them even more often.
5	Your current level of humility is high. Because other people see you as down-to-earth and easy to work with, these behaviors give you a significant advantage. But as you well know, you're not perfect! Take a look at the items above and ask yourself whether you can turn up the volume on any of those behaviors. You might also think about how you can create a culture around you that inspires others to be humble—be it at home, at work, or in your community.

What Is Your Need for Absolute Truth?

As you read in chapter 5, a need for absolute truth is an enemy of insight because it blinds us to our many complexities, contradictions, and nuances. To find out whether a need for absolute truth is closing you off to a multifaceted understanding of yourself, for each item below, choose the number that best describes your behavior in general. Try to look at how you're actually behaving, rather than how you wish to behave. When you're finished, average your responses and review the guide on the following page.[*]

1	2	3	4	5
Very Rarely	Rarely	Sometimes	Often	Very Often

_____ 1. I always try to find "the facts" about myself.

_____ 2. I think that the existing and real me are different.

_____ 3. I hope I will find myself as I really am one day.

_____ 4. I always think about "the facts" about myself.

_____ 5. I try to understand what my experiences actually mean.

---

[*] Omer Faruk Simsek. "Self-absorption paradox is not a paradox: Illuminating the dark side of self-reflection." *International Journal of Psychology* 48.6 (2013): 1109–1121.

Average	What It Means
1–2	Your need for absolute truth is low. Rather than overanalyzing your experiences and characteristics, you recognize their inherent complexity. Though you're committed to self-awareness, you rightfully recognize that you might never completely figure yourself out–and, counterintuitively, because you've removed that pressure, you're likely to gain powerful insight into who you are and how you're seen.
3–4	Your need for absolute truth is moderate. Though you don't always overanalyze your experiences and characteristics, you often try to identify their causes and meaning. But doing so is more likely to create anxiety than insight. To better manage your mindset, try to notice when you find yourself searching for absolute truth, and when you do, remember that this is not, in fact, a real path to insight. Instead, focus on the tools in chapters 5 and 6!
5	Your need for absolute truth is high. You enjoy self-reflection and frequently analyze the causes and meaning of your behavior. However, not only are these absolute truths hard to pin down; searching for them can make you more anxious, more depressed, and less successful, not to mention less self-aware. Give yourself a break and remember that you don't need to completely figure yourself out to know yourself. It might also be helpful to practice mindfulness–that is, to simply be aware of what's going on in the moment rather than trying to find the deeper meaning behind it.

How Often Do You Ruminate?

As you read in chapter 5, we all have a Ruminator buried inside of us—a nefarious character lying in wait to sabotage our attempts at insight by second-guessing our choices, reminding us of our failings, and sending us down an unproductive spiral of self-criticism and self-doubt. To see how much power the Ruminator is exerting over you, for each item below, choose the number that best describes your behavior in general. Try to look at how you're actually behaving, rather than how you wish to behave. When you're finished, average your responses and review the guide on the next page.[*]

1	2	3	4	5
Very Rarely	Rarely	Sometimes	Often	Very Often

_____ 1. My attention is often focused on aspects of myself that I wish I'd stop thinking about.

_____ 2. I always seem to be rehashing in my mind recent things I've said or done.

_____ 3. Sometimes it's hard for me to shut off negative thoughts about myself.

_____ 4. I often find myself reevaluating something I've done.

_____ 5. Long after an argument/disagreement is over, my thoughts keep going back to what happened.

---

[*] Paul D. Trapnell and Jennifer D. Campbell. "Private self-consciousness and the five-factor model of personality: Distinguishing rumination from reflection." *Journal of Personality and Social Psychology* 76.2 (1999): 284.

_____ 6. Often I'm playing back over in my mind how I acted in a past situation.

_____ 7. I spend a great deal of time thinking back over my embarrassing or disappointing moments.

Average	What It Means
1–2	You rarely ruminate. And though you might not be at "rumination zero," you can successfully stop it in its tracks, which improves both your self-awareness and your well-being. Because you don't have as much work to do in the rumination department, you might dedicate this energy to improving other aspects of your internal (and external) self-awareness.
3–4	You are a moderate ruminator. Sometimes, you are able to notice and stop it. At other times, the Ruminator takes over, clouding your self-insight and hurting your well-being. To ruminate less, start by looking for patterns: Are there certain people or situations that cause you to ruminate more? Are there certain techniques that are most useful than others in stopping your ruminative thoughts? Start by applying what's working to more situations and experiment with the tools in chapter 5.
5	You are a frequent ruminator. Though you may recognize when you've fallen down the rabbit hole, it's difficult for you to stop ruminating, which is considerably harming your self-insight and well-being. A first step might be to gain a better understanding of your triggers: Do certain situations or people set you off more than others? Once you've identified these situations, you can begin to apply the rumination-busting tools from chapter 5.

Do You Have a Learn-Well or Do-Well Mindset?

As you read in chapter 5, when faced with a challenging task, seeing it as an opportunity for learning (a "learn-well" mindset") rather than performance (a "do-well" mindset) can stop us from ruminating in the face of failure—and at the same time help us improve our performance. To see which mindset you gravitate toward, read the statements below and circle the ones that apply to you. When making your selections, try to look at how you're actually behaving, rather than how you wish to behave.

1. I like it when my colleagues know how well I'm doing on a project.
2. I am willing to select challenging work assignments that will help me improve my skills.
3. I'd be more likely to choose to work on a project I know I can do well than experiment with a new project.
4. I often look for ways to improve my knowledge.
5. I tend to avoid situations where I might not perform well.
6. I like to set challenging goals I might not meet versus easy goals I know I can surpass.
7. When others are trying to solve a problem, I enjoy it when I already know the answer.
8. I prefer to work in environments with extremely high expectations.

If you found yourself circling more odd-numbered questions, you're more likely to have a do-well mindset, and if you circled more even-numbered ones, you probably have a learn-well one.

How Much Feedback Are You Getting?

As you've seen throughout the book, getting honest, objective feedback from others is the best tool we have for becoming more externally self-aware. To see if you are using this valuable tool to its fullest advantage, for each item below, choose the number that best describes your behavior in general. Try to look at how you're actually behaving, rather than how you wish to behave. When you're finished, average your responses and review the guide below.

1	2	3	4	5
Very Rarely	Rarely	Sometimes	Often	Very Often

_____ 1. I have asked for feedback on my performance or behavior in the last week.

_____ 2. When I finish an important project/task, I conduct a "personal post-mortem" to learn how to do it better in the future.

_____ 3. When meeting with my boss, I frequently ask for feedback on how I'm doing.

_____ 4. I've asked my direct reports or team for feedback in the last month.

_____ 5. I thank my direct reports or team for telling the truth—even when it's tough to hear.

_____ 6. When I ask for feedback, I am clear about what behaviors I want feedback on.

_____ 7. I feel comfortable asking my peers for their perspective on how they see me.

_____ 8. When someone offers to give me feedback, I feel curious and upbeat.

_____ 9. When I hear feedback, I don't justify my behavior, interrupt, or blame.

_____ 10. When I hear feedback, I ask for ideas on how I can improve in the future.

Average	What It Means
1–2	Whether it's due to fear, overconfidence, or the belief that you're perfect the way you are, you're missing a huge opportunity to arm yourself with the truth about how you're seen. To start, try asking for feedback from one or two people whom you trust and practice the tools in chapters 7 and 8.
3–4	You seek feedback somewhat regularly, but if you did it more often, you'd have an even better understanding of how other people see you. Compare the tools in chapters 7 and 8 with your approach, and think of one tangible step you'll take to implement something new.
5	You're seeking frequent feedback from many sources, and you're generally able to hear that feedback with a curious and open mind. To continue to develop, you might consider how you'll keep up—or even strengthen—this habit by experimenting with any of the tools in chapters 7 and 8 that you might not have tried before.

Free 360 Feedback Resources

If your company doesn't have institutionalized 360s, it doesn't mean you can't take one. Though many can cost upwards of $500, here are a few "forever free" options:

1. PersonalityPad.org was developed by Eric Papas and his research team at the University of Virginia. Their noble goal is to make multi-source feedback available to everyone. The 10-question assessment is easy to complete, and the results are high-level but enlightening.
2. SelfStir.com is more comprehensive: it's longer, includes open-ended responses, and even spits out a detailed report.
3. BankableLeadership.com is one I created for the launch of my first book, *Bankable Leadership*. The 12-item survey will help you learn how you see yourself, and how others see you, with regard to your "people" and "results" behaviors.

If you decide to use one or more of these tools, I suggest that you contact the people you want to rate you in advance. Just explain that you're doing a 360, that you'd love to have them anonymously participate, and that they'll be getting an e-mail with a link to a survey so they can provide their observations of your behavior. Not only does this ensure the survey e-mail doesn't get lost in their junk folder; a personal appeal will help them understand the context and how important their participation is for your continued growth and development.

ACKNOWLEDGMENTS

First and foremost, thanks to the self-awareness unicorns across the globe who participated in our study. Each and every one of you is proof that becoming more self-aware is not just possible, but well worth the time and energy it takes to get there. We're all a work in progress, and it's heartening to know that you're out there, making yourselves—and the world—better.

To my study collaborators Apryl Broderson, Haley Woznyj, and Eric Heggestad, and my research assistants Uma Kedharnath, Sean Thomas, Julie Anne Applegate, Lacy Christ, Mike Jacobson, and Lauren Tronick (unicorn and matchless interviewer). When our team asked the adorably naive question "How hard could it really be to define and measure self-awareness?" we had no idea what we were getting into. Three years later, we now know the answer, and your dedication, wisdom, and can-do spirit made it possible. I'd also like to extend my gratitude to the friends, family, and clients who opened their networks to help us recruit study participants.

Thank you to the incredible colleagues who make my speaking, writing, and consulting career possible. To the team at Fletcher & Company: Grainne Fox, Veronica Goldstein, Melissa Chinchill, Erin McFadden, Sarah Fuentes, and especially my superlative literary agent Christy Fletcher: thank you for taking a chance on me, for your steady hand, and for your incomparable support. To Michelle Longmire, my partner in crime at The Eurich Group: every time I think I've fully come to grasp your all-around awesomeness, you do something even more awesome. I am privileged to work with you every day. To my fabulous speaking management team at SpeakersOffice: Holli Catchpole, Michele Walace, Cassie Glasgow, and Kim Stark: it's been quite a ride, ladies, and I can't wait to see what the future holds.

I owe an immense debt of gratitude to the outstanding professionals who shepherded this book at every stage of the process. Lari Bishop, you helped me turn a feeble musing into a full-fledged idea. Michael Palgon, you believed in this book long before I believed in it myself, and I'm forever grateful for your partnership and friendship. Will Storr, thank you for helping me tell my stories, for your gift of humor, and for convincing me to nix the bank-robbing clown. Thank you as well to my reviewers for their invaluable comments on the manuscript: Chuck Blakeman, Alan Mulally, Michele Walace, Michael Palgon, Chip Heath, and Lynda Spillane.

To the exceptional team at Crown: Talia Krohn, Tina Constable, Campbell Wharton, Ayelet Gruenspecht, Megan Schuman, Julia Elliott, Tal Goretsky, and Roger Scholl: working with you on this book has been a dream come true. Your professionalism, dedication, and kindness are beyond measure. Talia Krohn, my editor extraordinaire, kindred spirit, OCD compatriot, and true friend: thank you for your unparalleled abilities and problem-solving skills, for cheerfully responding to my incessant after-hours e-mails, for being my accomplice in the frog-prince practical joke of 2016, and most important, for being the best partner I could possibly imagine.

To my friends, colleagues, and mentors who provided their wisdom and assistance throughout the process: Alan Mulally, Marshall Goldsmith, Adam Grant, Ed Catmull, Tommy Spaulding, Lynda Spillane (love you, gal!), Michelle Gielan, Constantine Sedikides, Herb Blumberg, Ari Hagler, Cindy Hammel, Dana Sednek, Sarah Daly, Elisa Speranza, Florence Ozor, Eleanor Allen, Robin Kane, Roger Burleigh, Stephen Ladek, Mike Herron, Dana Graber Ladek, Linda Henman, Robin Kane, Mike Walker, Teresa Gray, Barry Nelson, Bill Whalen, Doug Griffes, Ted McMurdo, Scott Page, and most especially Chip Heath (without whom quite literally none of this would have been possible).

And last but not least, I want to thank the wonderful souls who help me stay grounded and self-aware—and who love me in spite of my many faults. To Gibson, Coles, Allie, Abs, Marita, Rogey, Dana, Ray Ray, Jason, Ang, Kristin, Apryl, Marc, G$, Mike, Sue, Rob, Teresa, Kristen, and Lynda for being my most valued and cherished loving critics. To my friends at Orange Theory Fitness for providing a safe haven during my frequent bouts of writer's block (Kaitlyn, Lindsay, Daniel, Eric, Jason, Jose, and Mia). To my writing companions, Fred and Willow. To MamaRichie (and all my family) for your unending love and support. Most especially, thank you to Dave (aka HB) for diagnosing and enduring my ABD (Author Bipolar Disorder), for forcing me to be self-aware (whether I want to be or not), and for your boundless love, encouragement, optimism, help, humor, and generosity. ILYVVM.

Chapter 1: The Meta-Skill of the Twenty-First Century

2 **"I heard the bullets whistle":** George Washington. Letter to John A. Washington. May 31, 1754. MS. N.p.

2 **"I shall not fear the attack":** George Washington. Letter to Robert Dinwiddie. June 3, 1754. MS. N.p.

3 **"advancing when he should":** Ron Chernow. *Washington: A Life*. Penguin, 2010, p. 49.

3 **"Any ape can reach":** Vilayanur S. Ramachandran. *The Tell-Tale Brain: A Neuroscientist's Quest for What Makes Us Human*. W. W. Norton & Company, 2012, p. 4.

4 **Some have even argued:** Mark R. Leary and Nicole R. Buttermore. "The evolution of the human self: Tracing the natural history of self-awareness." *Journal for the Theory of Social Behaviour* 33.4 (2003): 365–404.

4 **it came with a survival:** Donna Hart and Robert W. Sussman. *Man the Hunted: Primates, Predators, and Human Evolution*. Basic Books, 2005, pp. 159–164.

4 **people who know themselves:** This finding comes from our self-awareness research program.

4 **They make smarter decisions:** D. Scott Ridley, et al. "Self-regulated learning: The interactive influence of metacognitive awareness and goal-setting." *Journal of Experimental Education* 60.4 (1992): 293–306; Saundra H. Glover, et al. "Re-examining the influence of individual values on ethical decision making." *From the Universities to the Marketplace: The Business Ethics Journey*. Springer Netherlands, 1997. 109–119.

4 **They have better personal:** Stephen L. Franzoi, Mark H. Davis, and Richard D. Young. "The effects of private self-consciousness and perspective taking on satisfaction in close relationships." *Journal of Personality and Social Psychology* 48.6 (1985): 1584–1594.

4 **and professional relationships:** Clive Fletcher and Caroline Bailey. "Assessing self-awareness: Some issues and methods." *Journal of Managerial Psychology* 18.5 (2003): 395–404; John J. Sosik and Lara E. Megerian. "Understanding leader emotional intelligence and performance: The role

of self-other agreement on transformational leadership perceptions." *Group & Organization Management* 24.3 (1999): 367–390.

4 **They raise more mature children:** Heather K. Warren and Cynthia A. Stifter. "Maternal emotion-related socialization and preschoolers' developing emotion self-awareness." *Social Development* 17.2 (2008): 239–258.

4 **They're smarter:** Vladimir D. Shadrikov. "The role of reflection and reflexivity in the development of students' abilities." *Psychology in Russia: State of the Art* 6.2 (2013).

4 **choose better careers:** Chris Brown, Roberta George-Curran, and Marian L. Smith. "The role of emotional intelligence in the career commitment and decision-making process." *Journal of Career Assessment* 11.4 (2003): 379–392; Romila Singh and Jeffrey H. Greenhaus. "The relation between career decision-making strategies and person-job fit: A study of job changers." *Journal of Vocational Behavior* 64.1 (2004): 198–221.

4 **more creative:** See Paul J. Silvia and Maureen E. O'Brien. "Self-awareness and constructive functioning: Revisiting 'the human dilemma.'" *Journal of Social and Clinical Psychology* 23.4 (2004): 475, 480–481.

4 **more confident:** Anna Sutton, Helen M. Williams, and Christopher W. Allinson. "A longitudinal, mixed method evaluation of self-awareness training in the workplace." *European Journal of Training and Development* 39.7 (2015): 610–627.

4 **better communicators:** Ibid.

4 **less aggressive:** Peter Fischer, Tobias Greitemeyer, and Dieter Frey. "Unemployment and aggression: The moderating role of self-awareness on the effect of unemployment on aggression." *Aggressive Behavior* 34.1 (2008): 34–45.

4 **less likely to lie:** See Paul J. Silvia and Maureen E. O'Brien. "Self-awareness and constructive functioning: Revisiting 'the human dilemma.'" *Journal of Social and Clinical Psychology* 23.4 (2004): 475, 479–480.

4 **better performers at work:** Allan H. Church, "Managerial self-awareness in high-performing individuals in organizations." *Journal of Applied Psychology* 82.2 (1997): 281–292.

4 **get more promotions:** Bernard M. Bass and Francis J. Yammarino. "Congruence of self and others' leadership ratings of naval officers for understanding successful performance." *Applied Psychology* 40.4 (1991): 437–454.

4 **more effective leaders:** Bass and Yammarino, "Congruence of self and others' leadership ratings"; Malcolm Higgs and Deborah Rowland. "Emperors with clothes on: The role of self-awareness in developing effective change leadership." *Journal of Change Management* 10.4 (2010): 369–385.

4 **more enthusiastic employees:** Kenneth N. Wexley, et al. "Attitudinal congruence and similarity as related to interpersonal evaluations

in manager-subordinate dyads." *Academy of Management Journal* 23.2 (1980): 320–330.

4   **lead more profitable:** Atuma Okpara, et al. "Self awareness and organizational performance in the Nigerian banking sector." *European Journal of Research and Reflection in Management Sciences* 3.1 (2015); Harry Schrage. "The R&D entrepreneur: Profile of success." *Harvard Business Review,* November–December, 1965, 56–69; Korn Ferry Institute. "Korn Ferry Institute study shows link between self-awareness and company financial performance," kornferry.com, June 15, 2015, http://www.kornferry.com/press/korn-ferry-institute-study-shows-link-between-self-awareness-and-company-financial-performance/.

5   **600 percent more likely:** PDI Ninth House. "Accurate self-insight decreases derailment risk," *Leadership Research Bulletin,* January 24, 2013, http://www.kornferry.com/institute/565-accurate-self-insight-decreases-derailment-risk.

5   **a staggering $50 million:** J. Evelyn Orr, Victoria V. Swisher, King Y. Tang, and Kenneth De Meuse. "Illuminating blind spots and hidden strengths," kornferry.com, September 2010, http://www.kornferry.com/media/lominger_pdf/Insights_Illuminating_Blind_Spots_and_Hidden_Strengths.pdf.

5   **trouble figuring out:** University of Phoenix School of Business. "Nearly three-fourths of US workers in their 30s want a career change," *University of Phoenix News* release, July 29, 2015, http://www.phoenix.edu/news/releases/2015/07/uopx-survey-reveals-three-fourths-us-workers-in-their-thirties-want-career-change.html; http://www.bls.gov/news.release/pdf/nlsoy.pdf.

7   **"are often flawed":** David Dunning, Chip Heath, and Jerry M. Suls. "Flawed self-assessment implications for health, education, and the workplace." *Psychological Science in the Public Interest* 5.3 (2004): 69–106.

10 **"more than most, Washington's biography":** W. W. Abbot, "An Uncommon Awareness of Self," Prologue: *Quarterly Journal of the National Archives and Records Administration* 29 (1989): 7–19; repr. in *George Washington Reconsidered,* ed. Don Higginbotham (University Press of Virginia: 2001).

10 **Washington 2.0 reveled:** Chernow, p. 603.

10 **"I can bear to hear":** Ibid., p. 603.

10 **"studied every side":** Ibid., p. 521.

10 **"consult[ing] with our means":** Ibid., p. 378.

10 **"While I realize the arduous nature":** Ibid., p. 560.

11 **After surveying thousands:** If you're wondering whether a sample of 50 people is enough to glean meaningful conclusions about self-awareness, it may be important to point out the difference between quantitative and qualitative research. Though much of our research was quantitative—

that is, giving people numeric surveys—our examination of our self-awareness unicorns was qualitative in nature. Qualitative research delves deeper into each participant—in our case, with extensive interviews—in order to look for themes and patterns. And for a qualitative study, 50 is actually a pretty high number, especially considering that the unicorns were so difficult to find!

14 **nearly 30 million Nigerians:** "INEC Officially Announces Buhari as Winner of Presidential Race," pulse.ng, April 1, 2015, http://pulse.ng/politics/nigeria-elections-2015-inec-officially-announces-buhari-as-winner-of-presidential-race-id3619743.html.

Chapter 2: The Anatomy of Self-Awareness

21 **They built massive palaces:** History.com staff. "Mayan scientific achievements," History.com, 2010, http://www.history.com/topics/mayan-scientific-achievements.

21 **Mayans reached an all-time high:** Michon Scott. "Mayan mysteries," earthobservatory.nasa.gov, August 24, 2004, http://earthobservatory.nasa.gov/Features/Maya/.

21 **by AD 950, 95 *percent*:** Ibid.

22 **combination of massive:** Billie L. Turner and Jeremy A. Sabloff. "Classic Period collapse of the Central Maya Lowlands: Insights about human–environment relationships for sustainability." *Proceedings of the National Academy of Sciences* 109.35 (2012): 13908–13914.

22 **survivors moved away:** Joseph Stromberg. "Why did the Mayan civilization collapse? A new study points to deforestation and climate change," smithsonianmag.com, August 23, 2012, http://www.smithsonianmag.com/science-nature/why-did-the-mayan-civilization-collapse-a-new-study-points-to-deforestation-and-climate-change-30863026/?no-ist.

22 **Diamond finally solved:** Brian Wu. "Blue hole of Belize may explain what happened to the Mayans," sciencetimes.com, December 30, 2014, http://www.sciencetimes.com/articles/2257/20141230/blue-hole-of-belize-may-explain-what-happened-to-the-mayans.htm.

22 **topic of self-awareness:** Greg C. Ashley and Roni Reiter-Palmon. "Self-awareness and the evolution of leaders: The need for a better measure of self-awareness." *Journal of Behavioral and Applied Management* 14.1 (2012): 2–17.

22 **happiness was achieved:** D. Brett King, William Douglas Woody, and Wayne Viney. *History of Psychology: Ideas and Context.* Routledge, 2015.

22 **"enquiry into the truth":** Manfred F. R. Kets de Vries. *Telling Fairy Tales in the Boardroom: How to Make Sure Your Organization Lives Happily Ever After.* Palgrave Macmillan, 2015, p. 28.

22 **"the prerequisite for any"**: Rabbi Shlomo Wolbe, *Alei Shur, Volume 1.* Bais Hamussar, 1968, p. 141.

22 **"self-awareness is essential"**: Deborah L. Black. "Avicenna on self-awareness and knowing that one knows," in S. Rahman et al. (eds.), *The Unity of Science in the Arabic Tradition.* Springer, 2008, pp. 63–87, http://individual.utoronto.ca/dlblack/articles/blackselfknrev.pdf.

23 **"everyone's looking at me"**: Paul J. Silvia and T. Shelley Duval. "Objective self-awareness theory: Recent progress and enduring problems." *Personality and Social Psychology Review* 5.3 (2001): 230–241.

23 **self-awareness being more akin**: Allan Fenigstein, Michael F. Scheier, and Arnold H. Buss. "Public and private self-consciousness: Assessment and theory." *Journal of Consulting and Clinical Psychology* 43.4 (1975): 522–527.

23 **from introspection**: Paul D. Trapnell and Jennifer D. Campbell. "Private self-consciousness and the five-factor model of personality: Distinguishing rumination from reflection." *Journal of Personality and Social Psychology* 76.2 (1999): 284–304.

23 **pondering how other people**: Arthur I. Wohlers and Manuel London. "Ratings of managerial characteristics: evaluation difficulty, co-worker agreement, and self-awareness." *Personnel Psychology* 42.2 (1989): 235–261.

23 **difference between how**: John T. Kulas and Lisa M. Finkelstein. "Content and reliability of discrepancy-defined self-awareness in multisource feedback." *Organizational Research Methods* 10.3 (2007): 502–522.

25 **"not a single moral principle"**: Benjamin Franklin. *The Autobiography of Benjamin Franklin.* Garden City Publishing Company, 1916, 1179 out of 2559 in eBook.

26 **along with inventing**: The Independent Hall Association. "The electric Benjamin Franklin," ushistory.org, http://www.ushistory.org/franklin/info/inventions.htm.

29 **"evergreen shoots"**: Ben Huh. "I cheated on my life goals and life actually got better," medium.com, August 27, 2015, https://medium.com/@benhuh/i-cheated-on-my-life-goals-and-life-actually-got-better-78121bdf1790#.a11gu1kan.

32 **2,500 personality assessments**: Lucy Ash. "Personality tests: Can they indentify the real you?" *BBC News Magazine*, July 6, 2012, http://www.bbc.com/news/magazine-18723950.

40 *perspective-taking*: Jeffrey A. Joireman, Les Parrott III, and Joy Hammersla. "Empathy and the self-absorption paradox: Support for the distinction between self-rumination and self-reflection." *Self and Identity* 1.1 (2002): 53–65.

40 **"neutral third party"**: I'd like to thank Chip Heath for informing me

about this study! Eli J. Finkel, et al. "A brief intervention to promote conflict reappraisal preserves marital quality over time." *Psychological Science* (2013): 1595–1601.

41 *"Zoom In, Zoom Out"*: Richard Weissbourd. "The children we mean to raise," huffingtonpost.com, July 16, 2014, http://www.huffingtonpost.com/richard-weissbourd/the-children-we-mean-to-raise_b_5589259.html.

42 **"[My friend] kindly informed"**: Benjamin Franklin. *The Autobiography of Benjamin Franklin*. Garden City Publishing Company, 1916.

45 **early formative experiences:** Charles Margerison and A. Kakabadse. "How American chief executives succeed." *New York: American Management Association* (1984).

45 **"challenges values or norms"**: Seana Moran. "Purpose: Giftedness in intrapersonal intelligence." *High Ability Studies* 20.2 (2009): 143–159.

45 **Because earthquake events:** Morgan W. McCall, Jr., Michael M. Lombardo, and Ann M. Morrison. *Lessons of Experience: How Successful Executives Develop on the Job*. Simon and Schuster, 1988, p. 96.

45 **"is absorbing the suffering"**: Ibid., p. 91.

Chapter 3: Blindspots

51 **"almost unlimited ability"**: Daniel Kahneman. *Thinking, Fast and Slow*. Macmillan, 2011, p. 201.

51 **we're smarter:** Linda A. Schoo, et al. "Insight in cognition: Self-awareness of performance across cognitive domains." *Applied Neuropsychology: Adult* 20.2 (2013): 95–102.

51 **funnier:** Justin Kruger and David Dunning. "Unskilled and unaware of it: How difficulties in recognizing one's own incompetence lead to inflated self-assessments." *Journal of Personality and Social Psychology* 77.6 (1999): 1121–1134.

51 **thinner:** Pew Research Center. "Americans see weight problems everywhere but in the mirror," pewsocialtrends.org, April 11, 2006, http://www.pewsocialtrends.org/2006/04/11/americans-see-weight-problems-everywhere-but-in-the-mirror/.

51 **better-looking:** Nicholas Epley and Erin Whitchurch. "Mirror, mirror on the wall: Enhancement in self-recognition." *Personality and Social Psychology Bulletin* 34.9 (2008): 1159–1170.

51 **more socially skilled:** Paul A. Mabe and Stephen G. West. "Validity of self-evaluation of ability: A review and meta-analysis." *Journal of Applied Psychology* 67.3 (1982): 180–196.

51 **more gifted at sports:** Richard B. Felson. "Self-and reflected appraisal among football players: A test of the Median hypothesis." *Social Psychology Quarterly* (1981): 116–126.

51 **superior students:** Paul A. Mabe and Stephen G. West. "Validity of self-evaluation of ability: A review and meta-analysis." *Journal of Applied Psychology* 67.3 (1982): 180–196.

51 **better drivers:** Half of drivers believe themselves to be in the top 20 percent of driving ability, and 92 percent believe they're safer than the average driver! Ola Svenson. "Are we all less risky and more skillful than our fellow drivers?" *Acta Psychologica* 47.2 (1981): 143–148.

51 **almost no relationship:** Paul A. Mabe and Stephen G. West. "Validity of self-evaluation of ability: A review and meta-analysis." *Journal of Applied Psychology* 67.3 (1982): 180–196.

51 **nearly 1,000 engineers:** Todd R. Zenger. "Why do employers only reward extreme performance? Examining the relationships among performance, pay, and turnover." *Administrative Science Quarterly* (1992): 198–219.

51 **94 percent of college:** K. Patricia Cross. "Not can but *will* college teaching be improved?" *New Directions for Higher Education,* 17, (1977): 1–15.

51 **surgical residents' self-rated:** D. A. Risucci, A. J. Tortolani, and R. J. Ward. "Ratings of surgical residents by self, supervisors and peers." *Surgery, Gynecology & Obstetrics* 169.6 (1989): 519–526.

52 **employees who lack self-awareness:** Erich C. Dierdorff and Robert S. Rubin. "Research: We're not very self-aware, especially at work," *Harvard Business Review,* March 12, 2015, https://hbr.org/2015/03/research-were-not-very-self-aware-especially-at-work.

52 **those with poor financial:** "Study shows link between self-awareness and company financial performance," Korn Ferry Institute, June 15, 2015, http://www.kornferry.com/press/korn-ferry-institute-study-shows-link-between-self-awareness-and-company-financial-performance/.

52 **more likely to derail:** PDI Ninth House. "You're not all that: Self-promoters six times more likely to derail," prnewswire.com, April 17, 2012, http://www.prnewswire.com/news-releases/youre-not-all-that-self-promoters-six-times-more-likely-to-derail-according-to-pdi-ninth-house-and-university-of-minnesota-study-147742375.html.

52 **underestimate their top performers':** David Dunning. "On identifying human capital: Flawed knowledge leads to faulty judgments of expertise by individuals and groups." *Advances in Group Processes.* Emerald Group Publishing Limited, 2015, pp. 149–176.

52 **Early successes give way:** Ulrike Malmendier and Geoffrey Tate. "CEO overconfidence and corporate investment." *Journal of Finance* 60.6 (2005): 2661–2700.

52 **executives more dramatically overvalue:** Fabio Sala. "Executive blind spots: Discrepancies between self-and other-ratings." *Consulting Psychology Journal: Practice and Research* 55.4 (2003): 222–229.

52 **experienced leaders:** Cheri Ostroff, Leanne E. Atwater, and Barbara J. Fein-

berg. "Understanding self-other agreement: A look at rater and ratee characteristics, context, and outcomes." *Personnel Psychology* 57.2 (2004): 333–375.

52 **older managers tend:** John W. Fleenor, et al. "Self-other rating agreement in leadership: A review." *The Leadership Quarterly* 21.6 (2010): 1005–1034.

52 **business students, compared:** Phillip L. Ackerman, Margaret E. Beier, and Kristy R. Bowen. "What we really know about our abilities and our knowledge." *Personality and Individual Differences* 33 (2002): 587–605.

53 **aren't reliable mechanisms:** Margaret Diddams and Glenna C. Chang. "Only human: Exploring the nature of weakness in authentic leadership." *The Leadership Quarterly* 23.3 (2012): 593–603.

53 **"walls, mirrors and liars":** Alison Boulton. "Power corrupts but it also plays with your mind: Lloyd George, Chamberlain, and Thatcher all suffered from 'hubris syndrome,'" independent.co.uk, September 21, 2013, http://www.independent.co.uk/life-style/health-and-families/health-news/power-corrupts-but-it-also-plays-with-your-mind-lloyd-george-chamberlain-and-thatcher-all-suffered-8831839.html.

53 **no one lets their packages:** Rachel M. Hayes and Scott Schaefer. "CEO pay and the Lake Wobegon effect." *Journal of Financial Economics* 94.2 (2009): 280–290.

53 **emotionally distant personal:** Per F. Gjerde, Miyoko Onishi, and Kevin S. Carlson. "Personality characteristics associated with romantic attachment: A comparison of interview and self-report methodologies." *Personality and Social Psychology Bulletin* 30.11 (2004): 1402–1415.

53 **overestimate the number of words:** Gary Wolf. "The data-driven life," *The New York Times Magazine*, April 28, 2010, http://www.nytimes.com/2010/05/02/magazine/02self-measurement-t.html?_r=0.

53 **great financial management:** Greenwald & Associates, Inc. Parents, youth, and money: Executive summary. 2001, https://www.ebri.org/surveys/pym-es.pdf.

54 **Two percent:** College Board. Student descriptive questionnaire. Princeton, NJ: Educational Testing Service. 1976–1977.

54 **whopping 38 out of 40:** Mark D. Alicke, et al. "Personal contact, individuation, and the better-than-average effect." *Journal of Personality and Social Psychology* 68.5 (1995): 804–825.

54 *least* **competent people:** Justin Kruger and David Dunning. "Unskilled and unaware of it: How difficulties in recognizing one's own incompetence lead to inflated self-assessments." *Journal of Personality and Social Psychology* 77.6 (1999): 1121–1134.

54 **skills like driving:** E. Kunkel. "On the relationship between estimate of ability and driver qualification." *Psychologie und Praxis* (1971).

54 **academic performance:** Beth A. Lindsey and Megan L. Nagel. "Do students know what they know? Exploring the accuracy of students' self-

assessments." *Physical Review Special Topics—Physics Education Research* 11.2 (2015): 020103; Douglas J. Hacker, et al. "Test prediction and performance in a classroom context." *Journal of Educational Psychology* 92.1 (2000): 160–170.

54 **job performance:** Daniel E. Haun, et al. "Assessing the competence of specimen-processing personnel." *Laboratory Medicine* 31.11 (2000): 633–637.

54 **incentivized to be accurate:** Joyce Ehrlinger, et al. "Why the unskilled are unaware: Further explorations of (absent) self-insight among the incompetent." *Organizational Behavior and Human Decision Processes* 105.1 (2008): 98–121.

54 **"blessed with inappropriate confidence":** David Dunning. "We are all confident idiots," psmag.com, October 27, 2014, http://www.psmag.com/health-and-behavior/confident-idiots-92793.

54 **series of ingenious studies:** Oliver J. Sheldon, David Dunning, and Daniel R. Ames. "Emotionally unskilled, unaware, and uninterested in learning more: Reactions to feedback about deficits in emotional intelligence." *Journal of Applied Psychology* 99.1 (2014): 125–137.

56 **Our first awareness:** Michael Lewis, et al. "Self development and self-conscious emotions." *Child Development* (1989): 146–156.

56 **despite repeated revelations:** Susan Harter. *The Construction of the Self: A Developmental Perspective.* Guilford Press, 1999, p. 318.

57 **"What am I like":** Ibid.

57 **predictable progression toward:** This finding is from our self-awareness research program. See also: Andreas Demetriou and Karin Bakracevic. "Reasoning and self-awareness from adolescence to middle age: Organization and development as a function of education." *Learning and Individual Differences* 19.2 (2009): 181–194.

59 **"they rated themselves":** Constantine Sedikides, et al. "Behind bars but above the bar: Prisoners consider themselves more prosocial than non-prisoners." *British Journal of Social Psychology* 53.2 (2014): 396–403, p. 400.

59 **"top-down thinking":** David Dunning, et al. "Why people fail to recognize their own incompetence." *Current Directions in Psychological Science* 12.3 (2003): 83–87.

60 **ESPN published the predictions:** Ira Stoll. "How the experts struck out on World Series baseball," nysun.com, October 28, 2013, http://www.nysun.com/national/how-the-experts-struck-out-on-world-series/88471/.

60 **experts are wrong:** S. Atir, E. Rosenzweig, and D. Dunning. "When knowledge knows no bounds: self-perceived expertise predicts claims of impossible knowledge." *Psychological Science* 26.8 (2015): 1295–1303.

60 **important role of experience:** Berndt Brehmer. "In one word: Not from experience." *Acta Psychologica* 45.1 (1980): 223–241.

61 **brains secretly and simplistically:** Daniel Kahneman. *Thinking, Fast and Slow.* Macmillan, 2011, p. 99.

61 **To illustrate Emotion Blindness:** Norbert Schwarz. "Stimmung als Information: Untersuchungen zum Einflufs von Stimmungen auf die Bewertung des eigenen Lebens" [Mood as information: The influence of moods and emotions on evaluative judgments]. *Psychologische Rundschau* 39 (1987): 148–159.

61 **students were asked two questions:** Fritz Strack, Leonard L. Martin, and Norbert Schwarz. "Priming and communication: Social determinants of information use in judgments of life satisfaction." *European Journal of Social Psychology* 18.5 (1988): 429–442.

63 **participants were given a series:** Wilhelm Hofmann, Tobias Gschwendner, and Manfred Schmitt. "The road to the unconscious self not taken: Discrepancies between self- and observer-inferences about implicit dispositions from nonverbal behavioural cues." *European Journal of Personality* 23.4 (2009): 343–366.

67 **we typically assume:** Chris Argyris. *Teaching Smart People How to Learn.* Harvard Business Review Press, 2008.

67 **simple, practical process:** Peter F. Drucker. "Managing oneself." *Harvard Business Review* 83.1 (2005): 100–109.

68 **overconfident poor performers:** Justin Kruger and David Dunning. "Unskilled and unaware of it: How difficulties in recognizing one's own incompetence lead to inflated self-assessments." *Journal of Personality and Social Psychology* 77.6 (1999): 1121. See also D. Ryvkin, M. Krajč, and A. Ortmann. "Are the unskilled doomed to remain unaware?" *Journal of Economic Psychology* 33.5 (2012): 1012–1031.

68 **"amusing yet accurate":** Bob Sutton. "Great Piece on Narcissistic CEOs in *The New York Times*," *Work Matters* blog, March 7, 2012, http://bob sutton.typepad.com/my_weblog/2012/03/great-piece-on-narcissistic-ceos -in-the-new-york-times.html.

68 **Great leaders have people:** Thanks to my friends Mike Herron and Chuck Blakeman for this point.

Chapter 4: The Cult of Self

72 **analyzed the names given:** Jean M. Twenge, Emodish M. Abebe, and W. Keith Campbell. "Fitting in or standing out: Trends in American parents' choices for children's names, 1880–2007." *Social Psychological and Personality Science* 1.1 (2010): 19–25.

72 **"Parents used to give":** Gina Jacobs. "Unique baby names not just a celebrity fad," newscenter.sdsu.edu, May 20, 2009, http://newscenter.sdsu .edu/sdsu_newscenter/news_story.aspx?sid=71319.

73 **Cult of Self is a fairly:** Roy F. Baumeister, et al. "Does high self-esteem cause better performance, interpersonal success, happiness, or healthier lifestyles?" *Psychological Science in the Public Interest* 4.1 (2003): 1–44.

73 **The seeds were first sown:** Stanley Coopersmith. *The Antecedents of Self-Esteem.* Consulting Psychologists Press, 1967.

74 **we didn't need to *become*:** Jean M. Twenge and W. Keith Campbell. *The Narcissism Epidemic: Living in the Age of Entitlement.* Simon and Schuster, 2009, p. 62.

74 **"profound consequences for every":** Nathaniel Branden. *The Six Pillars of Self-Esteem.* Bantam Dell Publishing Group, 1995, p. 5, as cited in Roy F. Baumeister, Laura Smart, and Joseph M. Boden. "Relation of threatened egotism to violence and aggression: The dark side of high self-esteem." *Psychological Review* 103.1 (1996): 5.

74 **"couldn't think of a single":** Nathaniel Branden. "In defense of self." *Association for Humanistic Psychology* (1984): 12–13, p. 12, as cited in Roy F. Baumeister, Laura Smart, and Joseph M. Boden. "Relation of threatened egotism to violence and aggression: The dark side of high self-esteem." *Psychological Review* 103.1 (1996): 5–33.

74 **"between self-esteem and teenage":** Andrew M. Mecca, Neil J. Smelser, and John Vasconcellos. *The Social Importance of Self-Esteem.* University of California Press, 1989, p. 105.

75 **"we all know in our gut":** Ibid.

75 **"the man who destroyed":** Will Storr. "The man who destroyed America's ego," medium.com, February 25, 2014, https://medium.com/matter/the-man-who-destroyed-americas-ego-94d214257b5#.dasai1u4q.

75 **military cadets' self-esteem:** Martin M. Chemers, Carl B. Watson, and Stephen T. May. "Dispositional affect and leadership effectiveness: A comparison of self-esteem, optimism, and efficacy." *Personality and Social Psychology Bulletin* 26.3 (2000): 267–277.

75 **College students' self-esteem:** Duane Buhrmester, et al. "Five domains of interpersonal competence in peer relationships." *Journal of Personality and Social Psychology* 55.6 (1988): 991–1008.

75 **Professionals with high self-esteem:** Julia A. Bishop and Heidi M. Inderbitzen. "Peer acceptance and friendship: An investigation of their relation to self-esteem." *Journal of Early Adolescence* 15.4 (1995): 476–489.

75 **boosting the self-esteem of the unsuccessful:** D. R. Forsyth and N. A. Kerr. "Are adaptive illusions adaptive." Poster presented at the annual meeting of the American Psychological Association, Boston, MA (1999), cited in Baumeister et al., 1996.

75 **neither "a major predictor":** Roy F. Baumeister, et al. "Does high self-esteem cause better performance, interpersonal success, happiness, or healthier lifestyles?" *Psychological Science in the Public Interest* 4.1 (2003): 1–44.

75 **"bemoan[ing] the lack":** Ibid.

75 **more violent and aggressive:** Baumeister et al. "Relation of threatened egotism to violence and aggression: The dark side of high self-esteem." *Psychological Review* 103.1 (1996): 5–33.

75 **When their romantic:** Caryl E. Rusbult, Gregory D. Morrow, and Dennis J. Johnson. "Self-esteem and problem-solving behaviour in close relationships." *British Journal of Social Psychology* 26.4 (1987): 293–303.

76 **more likely to cheat:** Thalma E. Lobel and Ilana Levanon. "Self-esteem, need for approval, and cheating behavior in children." *Journal of Educational Psychology* 80.1 (1988): 122–123.

76 **drink, and do drugs:** Meg Gerrard, et al. "Self-esteem, self-serving cognitions, and health risk behavior." *Journal of Personality* 68.6 (2000): 1177–1201.

76 **"special and unique.":** Richard Adams. "Headteacher whose praise for pupils went viral falls foul of Ofsted," theguardian.com, September 24, 2015, http://www.theguardian.com/education/2015/sep/24/headteacher-whose-praise-for-pupils-went-viral-falls-foul-of-ofsted.

76 **"robs the victim":** Zole O'Brien. "Children are never naughty, says head," express.co.uk, June 28, 2015, http://www.express.co.uk/news/uk/587459/Children-teachers-bad-behaviour.

76 **"You know I think you're wonderful":** Allison Pearson. "Sparing the rod has spoilt these teachers," telegraph.co.uk, June 30, 2015, http://www.telegraph.co.uk/education/primaryeducation/11707847/Allison-Pearson-Sparing-the-rod-has-spoilt-these-teachers.html.

77 **"you have emptied":** Ibid.

77 **"tried their best during":** "Barrowford school's KS2 'proud' letter to pupils goes viral," bbc.com, July 16, 2014, http://www.bbc.com/news/uk-england-lancashire-28319907.

77 **a "fantasy":** Jaya Narain. "Inspectors slam primary school where there's no such thing as a naughty child and teachers are banned from raising their voices—and give it Ofsted's lowest possible rating," dailymail.co.uk, September 25, 2015, http://www.dailymail.co.uk/news/article-3249078/Inspectors-slam-primary-school-s-no-thing-naughty-child-teachers-banned-raising-voices-Ofsted-s-lowest-possible-rating.html.

77 **"very positive and excited":** Ibid.

77 **hands out roughly 3,500 awards:** Ashley Merryman. "Losing is good for you," nytimes.com, September 24, 2013, http://www.nytimes.com/2013/09/25/opinion/losing-is-good-for-you.html?_r=0.

78 **banned all competitive sports:** Dilvin Yasa. "Has the self-esteem movement failed our kids," childmags.com.au, September 22, 2014, http://www.childmags.com.au/family/relationships/6766-has-the-self-esteem-movement-failed-our-kids.

78 **they're too "negative":** William Turvill. "School bans red ink—and

tells teachers to mark in green instead (and get pupils to respond in purple)," dailymail.co.uk, March 19, 2014, http://www.dailymail.co.uk/news/article-2584672/School-bans-red-ink-tells-teachers-mark-green-inst.

78 **"I Love Me" lessons:** Richard Lee Colvin. "Losing faith in self-esteem movement," latimes.com, January 25, 1999, http://articles.latimes.com/1999/jan/25/news/mn-1505.

78 **with 30 valedictorians:** Frank Bruni. "Common core battles the cult of self-esteem," dallasnews.com, December 1, 2013, http://www.dallasnews.com/opinion/latest-columns/20131201-common-core-battles-the-cult-of-self-esteem.ece.

78 **grade inflation:** Valerie Strauss. "Why grade inflation (even at Harvard) is a big problem," washingtonpost.com, December 20, 2013, https://www.washingtonpost.com/news/answer-sheet/wp/2013/12/20/why-grade-inflation-even-at-harvard-is-a-big-problem/?utm_term=.6b4ef3d0ee6d.

78 **grades awarded were A's:** Matthew Q. Clarida and Nicholas P. Fandos. "Substantiating fears of grade inflation, dean says median grade at Harvard College is A-, most common grade is A," thecrimson.com, December 4, 2013, http://www.thecrimson.com/article/2013/12/3/grade-inflation-mode-a/.

78 **72 percent of students polled:** Kristin Touissant. "Harvard class with A- average not worried about grade inflation," boston.com, May 27, 2015, http://www.boston.com/news/local-news/2015/05/27/harvard-class-with-a-average-not-worried-about-grade-inflation.

78 **"a more consistently excellent":** Robert McGuire. "Grade expectations," yalealumnimagazine.com, September/October 2013, https://yalealumnimagazine.com/articles/3735.

79 **college freshmen were overconfident:** Richard W. Robins and Jennifer S. Beer. "Positive illusions about the self: Short-term benefits and long-term costs." *Journal of Personality and Social Psychology* 80.2 (2001): 340–352.

79 **"guileful and deceitful":** C. Randall Colvin, Jack Block, and David C. Funder. "Overly positive self-evaluations and personality: negative implications for mental health." *Journal of Personality and Social Psychology* 68.6 (1995): 1152, 1156.

79 **"complex, interesting, and intelligent":** C. Randall Colvin, Jack Block, and David C. Funder. "Overly positive self-evaluations and personality: negative implications for mental health." *Journal of Personality and Social Psychology* 68.6 (1995): 1152–1162.

79 **entrepreneurs and founders tend:** Keith M. Hmieleski and Robert A. Baron. "Entrepreneurs' optimism and new venture performance: A social cognitive perspective." *Academy of Management Journal* 52.3 (2009): 473–488.

80 **"dead certain":** Arnold C. Cooper, Carolyn Y. Woo, and William C. Dunkelberg. "Entrepreneurs' perceived chances for success." *Journal of Business Venturing* 3.2 (1988): 97–108.

80 **Canadian Innovation Centre:** Thomas Åstebro and Samir Elhedhli. "The effectiveness of simple decision heuristics: Forecasting commercial success for early-stage ventures." *Management Science* 52.3 (2006): 395–409.

81 **"I believe that someone":** Daniel Kahneman. *Thinking, Fast and Slow.* Macmillan, 2011, p. 264.

84 **post the most selfies:** Laura E. Buffardi and W. Keith Campbell. "Narcissism and social networking web sites." *Personality and Social Psychology Bulletin* 34.10 (2008): 1303–1314.

84 **"moral shallowing hypothesis":** Paul Trapnell and Lisa Sinclair. "Texting frequency and the moral shallowing hypothesis." Poster presented at the Annual Meeting of the Society for Personality and Social Psychology, San Diego, CA. 2012.

84 **anyone who takes selfies:** Jesse Fox and Margaret C. Rooney. "The Dark Triad and trait self-objectification as predictors of men's use and self-presentation behaviors on social networking sites." *Personality and Individual Differences* 76 (2015): 161–165.

84 **narcissism increased, a full 30 percent:** Jean M. Twenge, et al. "Egos inflating over time: A cross-temporal meta-analysis of the Narcissistic Personality Inventory." *Journal of Personality* 76.4 (2008): 875–902.

84 **roughly 80 percent:** Cassandra Rutledge Newsom, et al. "Changes in adolescent response patterns on the MMPI/MMPI-A across four decades." *Journal of Personality Assessment* 81.1 (2003): 74–84.

85 **increase in self-focused:** William J. Chopik, Deepti H. Joshi, and Sara H. Konrath. "Historical changes in American self-interest: State of the Union addresses 1790 to 2012." *Personality and Individual Differences* 66 (2014): 128–133.

85 **maintaining our relationships:** Sonja Utz. "The function of self-disclosure on social network sites: Not only intimate, but also positive and entertaining self-disclosures increase the feeling of connection." *Computers in Human Behavior* 45 (2015): 1–10.

85 **11 percent less likely:** Sara H. Konrath, Edward H. O'Brien, and Courtney Hsing. "Changes in dispositional empathy in American college students over time: A meta-analysis." *Personality and Social Psychology Review* 15.2 (2010): 180–198.

86 **narcissists indeed use social media:** Eric B. Weiser. "# Me: Narcissism and its facets as predictors of selfie-posting frequency." *Personality and Individual Differences* 86 (2015): 477–481; Soraya Mehdizadeh. "Self-presentation 2.0: Narcissism and self-esteem on Facebook." *Cyberpsychology, Behavior, and Social Networking* 13.4 (2010): 357–364.

86 **spent 35 minutes online:** E. Freeman and J. Twenge. "Using MySpace increases the endorsement of narcissistic personality traits." *Society for Personality and Social Psychology* (2010).

86 **personality disorder characterized:** American Psychiatric Association.

Diagnostic and Statistical Manual of Mental Disorders (DSM-5®). American Psychiatric Publishing, 2013.

86 **overrate their performance:** John W. Fleenor, et al. "Self–other rating agreement in leadership: A review." *The Leadership Quarterly* 21.6 (2010): 1005–1034.

86 **dominate decision processes:** Robert Hogan, Robert Raskin, and Dan Fazzini. "The dark side of charisma." *Measures of Leadership* (1990).

86 **seek excessive recognition:** Carolyn C. Morf and Frederick Rhodewalt. "Unraveling the paradoxes of narcissism: A dynamic self-regulatory processing model." *Psychological Inquiry* 12.4 (2001): 177–196.

86 **show less empathy:** Seth A. Rosenthal and Todd L. Pittinsky. "Narcissistic leadership." *The Leadership Quarterly* 17.6 (2006): 617–633.

86 **behave unethically:** Michael Maccoby. "Narcissistic leaders: The incredible pros, the inevitable cons." *Harvard Business Review* 78.1 (2000): 68–78.

86 **lowest in effectiveness:** Timothy A. Judge, Jeffery A. LePine, and Bruce L. Rich. "Loving yourself abundantly: Relationship of the narcissistic personality to self- and other perceptions of workplace deviance, leadership, and task and contextual performance." *Journal of Applied Psychology* 91.4 (2006): 762–776.

86 **less responsive to objective:** Arijit Chatterjee and Donald C. Hambrick. "Executive personality, capability cues, and risk taking: How narcissistic CEOs react to their successes and stumbles." *Administrative Science Quarterly* 56.2 (2011): 202–237.

86 **measured the size of CEO:** Charles Ham, et al. "Narcissism is a bad sign: CEO signature size, investment, and performance." *UNC Kenan-Flagler Research Paper* 2013–1 (2014).

87 **overly favorable impression:** Shanyang Zhao, Sherri Grasmuck, and Jason Martin. "Identity construction on Facebook: Digital empowerment in anchored relationships." *Computers in Human Behavior* 24.5 (2008): 1816–1836.

87 **Facebook status updates:** Trudy Hui Chua and Leanne Chang. "Follow me and like my beautiful selfies: Singapore teenage girls' engagement in self-presentation and peer comparison on social media." *Computers in Human Behavior* 55 (2016): 190–197.

87 **dating profiles:** Nicole Ellison, Rebecca Heino, and Jennifer Gibbs. "Managing impressions online: Self-presentation processes in the online dating environment." *Journal of Computer-Mediated Communication* 11.2 (2006): 415–441.

87 **Twitter feeds of congresspeople:** David S. Lassen and Benjamin J. Toff. "Elite ideology across media: Constructing a measure of Congressional candidates' ideological self-presentation on social media." Unpublished manuscript (2015).

87 **fewer negative words:** Natalya N. Bazarova, et al. "Managing impres-

sions and relationships on Facebook: Self-presentational and relational concerns revealed through the analysis of language style." *Journal of Language and Social Psychology* 32.2 (2012): 121–141.

87 **goal of creating a favorable:** L. Bareket-Bojmel, S. Moran, and G. Shahar G. "Strategic self-presentation on Facebook: Personal motives and audience response to online behavior. *Computers in Human Behavior* 55 (2016): 788–795.

87 **shutting down her social:** Megan McCluskey. "Teen Instagram Star Speaks Out About the Ugly Truth Behind Social Media Fame." Time.com, November 2, 2015, http://time.com/4096988/teen-instagram-star-essena -oneill-quitting-social-media/.

88 **"Let's be Game Changers":** "Essena O'Neill invites us to 'Let's be Game Changers,' as she exposes the 'fakeness' of social media," mybody myimage.com, November 3, 2015, http://www.mybodymyimage.com/ essena-oneill-invites-us-to-lets-be-game-changers-as-she-exposes-the-fakeness-of-social-media.

88 **60 percent of our talking:** Robin I. M. Dunbar, Anna Marriott, and Neil D. C. Duncan. "Human conversational behavior." *Human Nature* 8.3 (1997): 231–246.

88 **whopping 80 percent:** Mor Naaman, Jeffrey Boase, and Chih-Hui Lai. "Is it really about me?: message content in social awareness streams." *Proceedings of the 2010 ACM Conference on Computer Supported Cooperative Work*. ACM, 2010.

89 **one of two categories:** Ibid.

90 **"a merchant":** Andrew Anthony. "Angela Ahrendts: the woman aiming to make Apple a luxury brand," theguardian.com, January 9, 2016, https://www.theguardian.com/technology/2016/jan/10/profile-angela-ahrendts-apple-executive-luxury-brand.

90 **impressive company turnaround:** Jennifer Reingold. "What the heck is Angela Ahrendts doing at Apple?" fortune.com, September 10, 2015, http://fortune.com/2015/09/10/angela-ahrendts-apple/.

91 **"executives . . . who are touching":** Tim Hardwick. "Angela Ahrendts says she views Apple Store staff as 'executives,'" macrumors.com, January 28, 2016, http://www.macrumors.com/2016/01/28/angela-ahrendts-apple-store-staff-executives/.

91 **"What the heck is Angela":** Jennifer Reingold. "What the heck is Angela Ahrendts doing at Apple?" fortune.com, September 10, 2015, http:// fortune.com/2015/09/10/angela-ahrendts-apple/.

91 **2015 marked the company's:** "Apple reports record fourth quarter results," apple.com, October 27, 2015, http://www.apple.com/pr/library/2015/10/27Apple-Reports-Record-Fourth-Quarter-Results.html.

91 **skyrocketed to 81 percent:** AppleInsider staff. "Angela Ahrendts treats Apple Store employees like execs, retained 81% of workforce in

2015," appleinsider.com, January 28, 2016, http://appleinsider.com/ articles/16/01/28/angela-ahrendts-treats-apple-store-employees-like-execs-retained-81-of-workforce-in-2015.

92 **teams with humble leaders:** Bradley P. Owens, Michael D. Johnson, and Terence R. Mitchell. "Expressed humility in organizations: Implications for performance, teams, and leadership." *Organization Science* 24.5 (2013): 1517–1538.

92 **humility is actually a necessary:** R. A. Emmons. *The Psychology of Ultimate Concerns: Motivation and Spirituality in Personality.* Guilford Press, 1999, p. 33, as cited in June Price Tangney. "Humility: Theoretical perspectives, empirical findings and directions for future research." *Journal of Social and Clinical Psychology* 19.1 (2000): 70–82.

92 **aren't dependent on external:** Kristin D. Neff and Roos Vonk. "Self-compassion versus global self-esteem: Two different ways of relating to oneself." *Journal of Personality* 77.1 (2009): 23–50.

93 **"really, really want[ed]":** Neff, Kristin D., Kristin L. Kirkpatrick, and Stephanie S. Rude. "Self-compassion and adaptive psychological functioning." *Journal of Research in Personality* 41.1 (2007): 139–154.

93 **also less creative:** Steven G. Rogelberg, et al. "The executive mind: leader self-talk, effectiveness and strain." *Journal of Managerial Psychology* 28.2 (2013): 183–201.

94 **"I am unconscious of intentional":** George Washington. *Washington's Farewell Address [1796].* First National Bank of Miami.

Chapter 5: Thinking Isn't Knowing

98 **enjoy stronger relationships:** Rick Harrington and Donald A. Loffredo. "Insight, rumination, and self-reflection as predictors of well-being." *Journal of Psychology* 145.1 (2010): 39–57.

98 **calmer and more content:** Anthony M. Grant, John Franklin, and Peter Langford. "The self-reflection and insight scale: A new measure of private self-consciousness." *Social Behavior and Personality: An International Journal* 30.8 (2002): 821–835.

98 ***thinking* about ourselves:** Paul J. Silvia and Ann G. Phillips. "Evaluating self-reflection and insight as self-conscious traits." *Personality and Individual Differences* 50.2 (2011): 234–237.

98 **the *less* self-knowledge:** Anthony M. Grant, John Franklin, and Peter Langford. "The self-reflection and insight scale: A new measure of private self-consciousness." *Social Behavior and Personality: An International Journal* 30.8 (2002): 821–835, p. 824.

98 **no more self-insight:** J. Gregory Hixon and William B. Swann. "When does introspection bear fruit? Self-reflection, self-insight, and interpersonal choices." *Journal of Personality and Social Psychology* 64.1 (1993): 35–43.

98 **Though chimpanzees:** David Premack and Guy Woodruff. "Does the chimpanzee have a theory of mind?" *Behavioral and Brain Sciences* 1.04 (1978): 515–526.

98 **dolphins:** Heidi E. Harley. "Consciousness in dolphins? A review of recent evidence." *Journal of Comparative Physiology* A 199.6 (2013): 565–582.

98 **elephants:** Joshua M. Plotnik, Frans B. M. De Waal, and Diana Reiss. "Self-recognition in an Asian elephant." *Proceedings of the National Academy of Sciences* 103.45 (2006): 17053–17057.

98 **even pigeons:** Robert Epstein, Robert P. Lanza, and Burrhus Frederic Skinner. "Self-awareness in the pigeon." *Science* 212.4495 (1981): 695–696.

99 **engaged in introspection:** Susan Nolen-Hoeksema, Angela McBride, and Judith Larson. "Rumination and psychological distress among bereaved partners." *Journal of Personality and Social Psychology* 72.4 (1997): 855–862.

99 **associated with poorer well-being:** Julie J. Park and Melissa L. Millora. "The relevance of reflection: An empirical examination of the role of reflection in ethic of caring, leadership, and psychological well-being." *Journal of College Student Development* 53.2 (2012): 221–242.

99 **have more anxiety:** Anthony M. Grant, John Franklin, and Peter Langford. "The self-reflection and insight scale: A new measure of private self-consciousness." *Social Behavior and Personality: An International Journal* 30.8 (2002): 821–835.

99 **less positive social experiences:** John B. Nezlek. "Day-to-day relationships between self-awareness, daily events, and anxiety." *Journal of Personality* 70.2 (2002): 249–276.

99 **more negative attitudes:** Daniel Stein and Anthony M. Grant. "Disentangling the relationships among self-reflection, insight, and subjective well-being: The role of dysfunctional attitudes and core self-evaluations." *Journal of Psychology* 148.5 (2014): 505–522.

99 **let's look at Karen:** I'd like to thank the clinical psychologist who shared this example with me, whose name I'm not mentioning to maintain the confidentiality of his patient.

100 **Timothy Wilson calls "disruptive":** Timothy. D. Wilson, *Strangers to Ourselves*. Harvard University Press, 2004.

100 **"belief in this image":** Tarthang Tulku. *Skillful Means*. Dharma Publishing, 1978, pp. 102–103.

101 **cleverly represses important:** Sigmund Freud. *An Outline of Psycho-Analysis*. W. W. Norton, 1949.

101 **excavate these sometimes:** Timothy D. Wilson and Elizabeth W. Dunn. "Self-knowledge: Its limits, value, and potential for improvement." *Psychology* 55 (2004): 493–518.

102 **"no other notable figure":** Todd Dufresne. "Psychoanalysis is dead . . . so how does that make you feel?," latimes.com, February 18, 2004, http://articles.latimes.com/2004/feb/18/opinion/oe-dufresne18.

102 **falsifying patient files:** Adopf Grünbaum. "Précis of the foundations of psychoanalysis: A philosophical critique." *Behavioral and Brain Sciences* 9 (1986): 217–284.

102 **worsened some of his patients':** Daniel Goleman. "As a therapist, Freud fell short, scholars find," nytimes.com, March 6, 1990, http://www.nytimes.com/1990/03/06/science/as-a-therapist-freud-fell-short-scholars-find.html?pagewanted=all.

102 **his life a "catastrophe":** Todd Dufresne. "Psychoanalysis is dead . . . so how does that make you feel?," latimes.com, February 18, 2004, http://articles.latimes.com/2004/feb/18/opinion/oe-dufresne18.

102 **we can't uncover them:** Timothy D. Wilson. *Strangers to Ourselves.* Harvard University Press, 2004.

103 **placebo effects may explain:** Bruce E. Wampold, et al. "A meta-analysis of outcome studies comparing bona fide psychotherapies: Empirically, all must have prizes." *Psychological Bulletin* 122.3 (1997): 203–215.

103 **relationship she has with her client:** Jennifer A. Lyke. "Insight, but not self-reflection, is related to subjective well-being." *Personality and Individual Differences* 46.1 (2009): 66–70.

104 **"hinder the search for":** Omer Faruk Simsek. "Self-absorption paradox is not a paradox: illuminating the dark side of self-reflection." *International Journal of Psychology* 48.6 (2013): 1109–1121.

105 **showed male college students:** Zoë Chance and Michael I. Norton. "I read *Playboy* for the articles." *The Interplay of Truth and Deception: New Agendas in Theory and Research* 136 (2009).

106 **hire men over women:** Michael I. Norton, Joseph A. Vandello, and John M. Darley. "Casuistry and social category bias." *Journal of Personality and Social Psychology* 87.6 (2004): 817–831.

106 **conducted a creative study:** Donald G. Dutton and Arthur P. Aron. "Some evidence for heightened sexual attraction under conditions of high anxiety." *Journal of Personality and Social Psychology* 30.4 (1974): 510–517.

107 **"so convenient a thing":** To see another excellent example of this phenomenon, check out this recent and fascinating study: Mitesh Kataria and Tobias Regner. "Honestly, why are you donating money to charity? An experimental study about self-awareness in status-seeking behavior." *Theory and Decision* 79.3 (2015): 493–515.

107 **most plausible answer:** Timothy D. Wilson, et al. "Introspection, attitude change, and attitude-behavior consistency: The disruptive effects of explaining why we feel the way we do." *Advances in Experimental Social Psychology* 22 (1989): 287–343.

107 **reasons why your relationship:** Timothy D. Wilson, et al. "Effects of analyzing reasons on attitude-behavior consistency." *Journal of Personality and Social Psychology* 47.1 (1984): 1–5.

108 **self-described basketball experts:** Jamin Brett Halberstadt and Gary M. Levine. "Effects of reasons analysis on the accuracy of predicting basketball games." *Journal of Applied Social Psychology* 29.3 (1999): 517–530.

108 **reduces our satisfaction:** Timothy Wilson et al. "Introspecting about reasons can reduce post-choice satisfaction." *Personality and Social Psychology Bulletin* 19.3 (1993): 331–39.

108 **negative impact it has:** Ethan Kross, Ozlem Ayduk, and Walter Mischel. "When asking 'why' does not hurt distinguishing rumination from reflective processing of negative emotions." *Psychological Science* 16.9 (2005): 709–715.

108 **write about *why*:** E. D. Watkins. "Adaptive and maladaptive ruminative self-focus during emotional processing." *Behaviour Research and Therapy* 42.9 (2004): 1037–1052.

108 **"sociability, likeability and interestingness":** J. Gregory Hixon and William B. Swann. "When does introspection bear fruit? Self-reflection, self-insight, and interpersonal choices." *Journal of Personality and Social Psychology* 64.1 (1993): 35–43.

109 **"rationaliz[ing], justify[ing], and explain[ing]":** Ibid.

110 **five minutes of *what*:** Timothy D. Wilson, et al. "Introspection, attitude change, and attitude-behavior consistency: The disruptive effects of explaining why we feel the way we do." *Advances in Experimental Social Psychology* 22 (1989): 287–343.

111 **that "an emotion, which is a passion":** R. H. M. Elwes. *The Chief Works of Benedict de Spinoza*, 1887, p. 248.

112 **act of translating our emotions:** Matthew D. Lieberman, et al. "Putting feelings into words affect labeling disrupts amygdala activity in response to affective stimuli." *Psychological Science* 18.5 (2007): 421–428.

112 **don't understand *why*:** James C. Collins. *How the Mighty Fall: And Why Some Companies Never Give In.* Jim Collins, 2009.

112 **Charley Kempthorne has been keeping:** Clare Ansberry. "The power of daily writing in a journal," wsj.com, January 26, 2016, http://www.wsj.com/articles/the-power-of-daily-writing-in-a-journal-1453837329.

113 **more self-reflection but *less* insight:** Anthony M. Grant, John Franklin, and Peter Langford. "The self-reflection and insight scale: A new measure of private self-consciousness." *Social Behavior and Personality: An International Journal* 30.8 (2002): 821–835.

113 **"deepest thoughts and feelings":** James W Pennebaker. "Writing about emotional experiences as a therapeutic process." *Psychological Science* 8.3 (1997): 162–166.

113 **distressing in the short term:** Brian A. Esterling, et al. "Empirical foundations for writing in prevention and psychotherapy: Mental and physical health outcomes." *Clinical Psychology Review* 19.1 (1999): 79–96.

113 **longer-term improvements:** James W. Pennebaker, Janice K. Kiecolt-Glaser, and Ronald Glaser. "Disclosure of traumas and immune function: health implications for psychotherapy." *Journal of Consulting and Clinical Psychology* 56.2 (1988): 239–245.

113 **and well-being:** Crystal L. Park and Carol Joyce Blumberg. "Disclosing trauma through writing: Testing the meaning-making hypothesis." *Cognitive Therapy and Research* 26.5 (2002): 597–616.

114 **have better memories:** Kitty Klein and Adriel Boals. "Expressive writing can increase working memory capacity." *Journal of Experimental Psychology: General* 130.3 (2001): 520–533.

114 **higher grade point averages:** James W. Pennebaker and Martha E. Francis. "Cognitive, emotional, and language processes in disclosure." *Cognition & Emotion* 10.6 (1996): 601–626.

114 **less absenteeism from work:** Martha E. Francis and James W. Pennebaker. "Putting stress into words: The impact of writing on physiological, absentee, and self-reported emotional well-being measures." *American Journal of Health Promotion* 6.4 (1992): 280–287.

114 **quicker re-employment:** Stefanie P. Spera, Eric D. Buhrfeind, and James W. Pennebaker. "Expressive writing and coping with job loss." *Academy of Management Journal* 37.3 (1994): 72-–733.

114 **help collegiate tennis players:** V. B. Scott, et al. "Emotive writing moderates the relationship between mood awareness and athletic performance in collegiate tennis players." *North American Journal of Psychology* 5.2 (2003): 311–324.

114 **stronger immune systems:** James W. Pennebaker, Janice K. Kiecolt-Glaser, and Ronald Glaser. "Disclosure of traumas and immune function: health implications for psychotherapy." *Journal of Consulting and Clinical Psychology* 56.2 (1988): 239–245.

114 **showed less personal growth:** Sonja Lyubomirsky, Lorie Sousa, and Rene Dickerhoof. "The costs and benefits of writing, talking, and thinking about life's triumphs and defeats." *Journal of Personality and Social Psychology* 90.4 (2006): 692–708.

114 **"Happiness is a mystery":** G. K. Chesterton. *Heretics.* Butler and Tanner, 1905, p. 103.

114 **"who talk about things":** Bridget Murray. "Writing to heal," apa.org, June 2002, http://www.apa.org/monitor/jun02/writing.aspx.

114 **writes "short narrative scenes":** Clare Ansberry. "The power of daily writing in a journal," wsj.com, January 26, 2016, http://www.wsj.com/articles/the-power-of-daily-writing-in-a-journal-1453837329.

115 **neither on its own is effective:** James W. Pennebaker and Sandra K. Beall. "Confronting a traumatic event: Toward an understanding of inhibition and disease." *Journal of Abnormal Psychology* 95.3 (1986): 274–281.

115 **True insight only happens:** Christopher D. B. Burt. "An analysis of a self-initiated coping behavior: Diary-keeping." *Child Study Journal* 24.3 (1994): 171–189.

115 **when journalers use more causal:** James W. Pennebaker. "Writing about emotional experiences as a therapeutic process." *Psychological Science* 8.3 (1997): 162–66; James W. Pennebaker, Tracy J. Mayne, and Martha E. Francis. "Linguistic predictors of adaptive bereavement." *Journal of Personality and Social Psychology* 72.4 (1997): 863–871.

116 **writing every few days:** James W. Pennebaker. "Writing about emotional experiences as a therapeutic process." *Psychological Science* 8.3 (1997): 162–166.

116 **"I'm not even convinced":** Jordan Gaines Lewis, Ph.D. "Turning Trauma into Story: The Benefits of Journaling," psychologytoday.com, August 17, 2012, https://www.psychologytoday.com/blog/brain-babble/201208/turning -trauma-story-the-benefits-journaling.

119 **we don't measure up:** T. Pyszczynski and J. Greenberg. "Self-regulatory perseveration and the depressive self-focusing style: A self-awareness theory of reactive depression." *Psychological Bulletin* 102.1 (1987): 122– 138. See also Ann G. Phillips and Paul J. Silvia. "Self-awareness and the emotional consequences of self-discrepancies." *Personality and Social Psychology Bulletin* 31.5 (2005): 703–713.

119 **related to lower grades:** V. B. Scott and William D. McIntosh. "The development of a trait measure of ruminative thought." *Personality and Individual Differences* 26.6 (1999): 1045–1056.

119 **impaired problem solving:** Sonja Lyubomirsky, et al. "Why ruminators are poor problem solvers: clues from the phenomenology of dysphoric rumination." *Journal of Personality and Social Psychology* 77.5 (1999): 1041–1060.

119 **worse moods:** Nilly Mor and Jennifer Winquist. "Self-focused attention and negative affect: a meta-analysis." *Psychological Bulletin* 128.4 (2002): 638–662.

119 **poorer-quality sleep:** Jacob A. Nota and Meredith E. Coles. "Duration and timing of sleep are associated with repetitive negative thinking." *Cognitive Therapy and Research* 39 (2015): 253–261.

119 **stuck in ruminative thought patterns:** T. Pyszczynski and J. Greenberg. "Self-regulatory perseveration and the depressive self-focusing style: A self-awareness theory of reactive depression." *Psychological Bulletin* 102.1 (1987): 122–138.

119 **survey of more than 32,000 people:** Peter Kinderman, et al. "Psycho-

logical processes mediate the impact of familial risk, social circumstances and life events on mental health." *PLOS One* 8.10 (2013): e76564.

119 **rumination can often masquerade:** J. Paul Hamilton et al. "Depressive rumination, the default-mode network, and the dark matter of clinical neuroscience." *Biological Psychiatry* 78.4 (2015): 224–230.

120 **ruminators are *less* accurate:** Joseph Ciarrochi and Greg Scott. "The link between emotional competence and well-being: A longitudinal study." *British Journal of Guidance & Counselling* 34.2 (2006): 231–243.

120 **miss the larger picture:** Rick Harrington and Donald A. Loffredo. "Insight, rumination, and self-reflection as predictors of well-being." *Journal of Psychology* 145.1 (2010): 39–57.

120 **effectively an avoidance strategy:** Steven C. Hayes, et al. "Experiential avoidance and behavioral disorders: A functional dimensional approach to diagnosis and treatment." *Journal of Consulting and Clinical Psychology* 64.6 (1996): 1152.

120 **correlation between rumination:** Rick E. Ingram. "Self-focused attention in clinical disorders: Review and a conceptual model." *Psychological Bulletin* 107.2 (1990): 156–176.

120 **ruminators were 70 percent:** Jay G. Hull. "A self-awareness model of the causes and effects of alcohol consumption." *Journal of Abnormal Psychology* 90.6 (1981): 586–600.

120 **avoid the people and situations:** S. Rachman, J. Grüter-Andrew, and R. Shafran. "Post-event processing in social anxiety." *Behaviour Research and Therapy* 38.6 (2000): 611–617.

120 **poor perspective-takers:** Jeffrey A. Joireman, Les Parrott III, and Joy Hammersla. "Empathy and the self-absorption paradox: Support for the distinction between self-rumination and self-reflection." *Self and Identity* 1.1 (2002): 53–65.

122 **help us combat rumination:** Carol I. Diener and Carol S. Dweck. "An analysis of learned helplessness: Continuous changes in performance, strategy, and achievement cognitions following failure." *Journal of Personality and Social Psychology* 36 (1978): 451–462; Carol I. Diener and Carol S. Dweck. "An analysis of learned helplessness: II. The processing of success." *Journal of Personality and Social Psychology* 39.5 (1980): 940–952.

123 **learn-well reps had significantly:** Don VandeWalle, et al. "The influence of goal orientation and self-regulation tactics on sales performance: A longitudinal field test." *Journal of Applied Psychology* 84.2 (1999): 249–259.

123 **I call *hitting pause*:** Allison Abbe, Chris Tkach, and Sonja Lyubomirsky. "The art of living by dispositionally happy people." *Journal of Happiness Studies* 4.4 (2003): 385–404.

124 **whatever ruminative thought came into:** R. S. Stern, M. S. Lipsedge, and I. M. Marks. "Obsessive ruminations: A controlled trial of thought-stopping technique." *Behaviour Research and Therapy* 11.4 (1973): 659–662.

Chapter 6: Internal Self-Awareness Tools That Really Work

129 **Harvard psychologist Ellen Langer:** Cara Feinberg. "The mindfulness chronicles," harvardmagazine.com, September/October 2010, http://harvardmagazine.com/2010/09/the-mindfulness-chronicles.

129 **"out of the Zen meditation":** Ibid.

129 **"the process of actively noticing":** Ibid.

129 **"The people I know won't sit still":** Ibid.

130 **"people prefer to be doing":** Timothy D. Wilson, et al. "Just think: The challenges of the disengaged mind." *Science* 345.6192 (2014): 75.

130 **celebrities like Angelina Jolie:** Alexia Bure. "Surprising celebrities who meditate," wellandgood.com, December 26, 2012, http://www.wellandgood.com/good-advice/surprising-celebs-who-meditate/slide/9/.

130 **Anderson Cooper:** "The newly mindful Anderson Cooper," cbsnews.com, September 6, 2015, http://www.cbsnews.com/news/the-newly-mindful-anderson-cooper/.

130 **Ellen DeGeneres:** "What Gisele Bundchen, Ellen DeGeneres & other celebrities say about meditation," choosemuse.com, http://www.choosemuse.com/blog/9-top-celebrity-meditation-quotes/.

130 **corporations like Google:** David Hochman. "Mindfulness: Getting its share of attention," nytimes.com, November 3, 2013, http://www.nytimes.com/2013/11/03/fashion/mindfulness-and-meditation-are-capturing-attention.html.

130 **McKinsey:** David Gelles. "The hidden price of mindfulness inc.," nytimes.com, March 19, 2016, http://www.nytimes.com/2016/03/20/opinion/sunday/the-hidden-price-of-mindfulness-inc.html?_r=2.

130 **Nike, General Mills, Target, and Aetna:** David Hochman. "Mindfulness: Getting its share of attention," nytimes.com, November 3, 2013, http://www.nytimes.com/2013/11/03/fashion/mindfulness-and-meditation-are-capturing-attention.html?_r=0.

130 **reaching more than 300,000 students:** Lauren Cassani Davis. "When mindfulness meets the classroom," theatlantic.com, August 31, 2015, http://www.theatlantic.com/education/archive/2015/08/mindfulness-education-schools-meditation/402469/.

130 **U.S. Marines and professional sports:** Associated Press. "U.S. Marine Corps members learn mindfulness meditation and yoga in pilot program to help reduce stress," January 23, 2013, http://www.nydailynews.com/life-style/health/u-s-marines-learn-meditate-stress-reduction-program-article-1.1245698.

131 **one-billion-dollar cottage industry:** David Gelles. "The hidden price of mindfulness inc.," nytimes.com, March 19, 2016, http://www.nytimes.com/2016/03/20/opinion/sunday/the-hidden-price-of-mindfulness-inc.html?_r=2.

131 **38 million Americans admit:** CashStar, Inc. "More than 38 million* online Americans shopped while on the toilet," prnewswire.com, November 19, 2012, http://www.prnewswire.com/news-releases/more-than-38-million-online-americans-shopped-while-on-the-toilet-179955401 .html.

131 **nearly half reported being distracted:** Matthew A. Killingsworth and Daniel T. Gilbert. "A wandering mind is an unhappy mind." *Science* 330.6006 (2010): 932.

131 **researchers asked dieters:** Todd F. Heatherton, et al. "Self-Awareness, Task Failure, and Disinhibition: How Attentional Focus Affects Eating." *Journal of Personality* 61.1 (1993): 49–61.

132 **who practice it are happier:** Kirk Warren Brown and Richard M. Ryan. "The benefits of being present: mindfulness and its role in psychological well-being." *Journal of Personality and Social Psychology* 84.4 (2003): 822–848.

133 **healthier:** Paul Grossman, et al. "Mindfulness-based stress reduction and health benefits: A meta-analysis." *Journal of Psychosomatic Research* 57.1 (2004): 35–43.

133 **more creative:** E. J. Langer, D. Heffernan, and M. Kiester. "Reducing burnout in an institutional setting: An experimental investigation." Unpublished manuscript, Harvard University, Cambridge, MA (1988).

133 **more productive:** Kwang-Ryang Park. An experimental study of theory-based team building intervention: A case of Korean work groups." Unpublished manuscript, Harvard University, Cambridge, MA (1990).

133 **more authentic:** Michael H. Kernis and Brian M. Goldman. "A multicomponent conceptualization of authenticity: Theory and research." *Advances in Experimental Social Psychology* 38 (2006): 283–357.

133 **more in control of their behavior:** Kirk Warren Brown and Richard M. Ryan. "The benefits of being present: mindfulness and its role in psychological well-being." *Journal of Personality and Social Psychology* 84.4 (2003): 822–848.

133 **more satisfied in their marriages:** Leslie C. Burpee and Ellen J. Langer. "Mindfulness and marital satisfaction." *Journal of Adult Development* 12.1 (2005): 43–51.

133 **more relaxed:** Ellen J. Langer, Irving L. Janis, and John A. Wolfer. "Reduction of psychological stress in surgical patients." *Journal of Experimental Social Psychology* 11.2 (1975): 155–165.

133 **less aggressive:** Whitney L. Heppner, et al. "Mindfulness as a means of reducing aggressive behavior: Dispositional and situational evidence." *Aggressive Behavior* 34.5 (2008): 486–496.

133 **less burnt-out:** E. J. Langer, D. Heffernan, and M. Kiester. "Reducing burnout in an institutional setting: An experimental investigation." Unpublished manuscript, Harvard University, Cambridge, MA (1988).

133 **even thinner:** Eric B. Loucks, et al. "Associations of dispositional mindfulness with obesity and central adiposity: The New England Family Study." *International Journal of Behavioral Medicine* 23.2 (2016): 224–233.

133 **mindfulness meditation can save us:** Chen Hemo and Lilac Lev-Ari. "Focus on your breathing: Does meditation help lower rumination and depressive symptoms?" *International Journal of Psychology and Psychological Therapy* 15.3 (2015): 349–359.

133 **intensive mindfulness training retreat:** Richard Chambers, Barbara Chuen Yee Lo, and Nicholas B. Allen. "The impact of intensive mindfulness training on attentional control, cognitive style, and affect." *Cognitive Therapy and Research* 32.3 (2008): 303–322.

133 **enjoy greater self-insight:** Kelly C. Richards, C. Estelle Campenni, and Janet L. Muse-Burke. "Self-care and well-being in mental health professionals: The mediating effects of self-awareness and mindfulness." *Journal of Mental Health Counseling* 32.3 (2010): 247–264.

133 *because* **it increases insight:** Yadollah Ghasemipour, Julie Ann Robinson, and Nima Ghorbani. "Mindfulness and integrative self-knowledge: Relationships with health-related variables." *International Journal of Psychology* 48.6 (2013): 1030–1037.

133 **"Mindfulness offers a strategy":** Personal communication.

135 **better control our behavior:** Shannon M. Erisman and Lizabeth Roemer. "A preliminary investigation of the effects of experimentally induced mindfulness on emotional responding to film clips." *Emotion* 10.1 (2010): 72–82.

135 **They asked students to write:** Whitney L. Heppner, et al. "Mindfulness as a means of reducing aggressive behavior: Dispositional and situational evidence." *Aggressive Behavior* 34.5 (2008): 486–496.

137 **only the mindfulness group:** J. David Creswell, et al. "Alterations in Resting-State Functional Connectivity Link Mindfulness Meditation with Reduced Interleukin-6: A Randomized Controlled Trial." *Biological Psychiatry* (2016).

137 **"the essence of mindfulness":** Ellen Langer. "The third metric for success," ellenlanger.com, 2009, http://www.ellenlanger.com/blog/171/the-third-metric-for-success.

139 **reframing our experiences:** I'd like to thank my superstar research assistant Lauren Tronick for spotting this interesting trend in the data.

139 **"going to the balcony":** William Ury. *Getting Past No: Negotiating with Difficult People.* Bantam Books, 1992.

142 **"But how to speak about":** Gustave Flaubert, translated by Lowell Bair. *Madame Bovary.* Bantam Books, 1959, p. 35.

143 **rarely take time to reflect:** Giada Di Stefano, et al. "Learning by thinking: Overcoming the bias for action through reflection." *Harvard Business School NOM Unit Working Paper* 14-093 (2015): 14–093.

143 **call-center trainees who took:** Ibid.

145 **"biographers of our lives":** Timothy D. Wilson. *Strangers to Ourselves.* Harvard University Press, 2004, p. 16.

145 **"Think about your life":** Note: I've adapted this slightly to serve the purpose of self-awareness. Dan P. McAdams, et al. "Continuity and change in the life story: A longitudinal study of autobiographical memories in emerging adulthood." *Journal of Personality* 74.5 (2006): 1371–1400.

146 **life stories are associated:** Ibid.

146 **Chase discovered his theme:** Jennifer L. Pals. "Authoring a second chance in life: Emotion and transformational processing within narrative identity." *Research in Human Development* 3.2–3 (2006): 101–120.

146 **achievement . . . relationships:** McAdams and his colleagues call these "agency" and "communion" respectively.

147 **struggling with their grades:** Timothy D. Wilson and Patricia W. Linville. "Improving the academic performance of college freshmen: Attribution therapy revisited." *Journal of Personality and Social Psychology* 42.2 (1982): 367–376.

147 **"I was dead, but the doctors":** Dan P. McAdams. "The redemptive self: Generativity and the stories Americans live by." *Research in Human Development* 3.2–3 (2006): 81–100, p. 90.

147 **even the most horrific experiences:** Dan P. McAdams, et al. "When bad things turn good and good things turn bad: Sequences of redemption and contamination in life narrative and their relation to psychosocial adaptation in midlife adults and in students." *Personality and Social Psychology Bulletin* 27.4 (2001): 474–485.

149 **less introspection and more self-awareness:** Anthony M. Grant. "The impact of life coaching on goal attainment, metacognition and mental health." *Social Behavior and Personality: An International Journal* 31.3 (2003): 253–263.

149 **people sustained this progress:** L. S. Green, L. G. Oades, and A. M. Grant. "Cognitive-behavioral, solution-focused life coaching: Enhancing goal striving, well-being, and hope." *Journal of Positive Psychology* 1.3 (2006): 142–149.

149 **solutions-mining is a powerful:** Edward R. Watkins, Celine B. Baeyens, and Rebecca Read. "Concreteness training reduces dysphoria: proof-of-principle for repeated cognitive bias modification in depression." *Journal of Abnormal Psychology* 118.1 (2009): 55–64.

150 **Solutions Focused Brief Therapy:** Steve De Shazer. *Clues: Investigating Solutions in Brief Therapy.* W. W. Norton & Co, 1988. Note that I've slightly adapted this question for brevity.

150 **produced dramatic improvements:** Jacqueline Corcoran and Vijayan Pillai. "A review of the research on solution-focused therapy." *British Journal of Social Work* 39.2 (2009): 234–242.

150   **populations such as parents, prisoners:** Wallace J. Gingerich and Sheri Eisengart. "Solution-focused brief therapy: A review of the outcome research." *Family Process* 39.4 (2000): 477–498.

150   **adolescents . . . struggling with their marriages:** Jacqueline Corcoran and Vijayan Pillai. "A review of the research on solution-focused therapy." *British Journal of Social Work* 39.2 (2009): 234–242.

150   **insight and psychological growth:** Wei Zhang, et al. "Brief report: Effects of solution-focused brief therapy group-work on promoting post-traumatic growth of mothers who have a child with ASD." *Journal of Autism and Developmental Disorders* 44.8 (2014): 2052–2056.

150   **reduce their putting yips:** Robert J. Bell, Christopher H. Skinner, and Leslee A. Fisher. "Decreasing putting yips in accomplished golfers via solution-focused guided imagery: A single-subject research design." *Journal of Applied Sport Psychology* 21.1 (2009): 1–14.

151   **college students were asked to write:** Jack J. Bauer and Dan P. McAdams. "Eudaimonic growth: Narrative growth goals predict increases in ego development and subjective well-being 3 years later." *Developmental Psychology* 46.4 (2010): 761–772.

Chapter 7: The Truth We Rarely Hear

157   **the words of a drunk:** Bruce D. Bartholow, et al. "Alcohol effects on performance monitoring and adjustment: affect modulation and impairment of evaluative cognitive control." *Journal of Abnormal Psychology* 121.1 (2012): 173–186.

161   **infinitely less accurate:** Timothy W. Smith, et al. "Hostile personality traits and coronary artery calcification in middle-aged and older married couples: Different effects for self-reports versus spouse ratings." *Psychosomatic Medicine* 69.5 (2007): 441–448.

161   **only the subordinates could:** Bernard M. Bass, and Francis J. Yammarino. "Congruence of self and others' leadership ratings of naval officers for understanding successful performance." *Applied Psychology* 40.4 (1991): 437–454.

161   **anticipate our future behavior:** Tara K. MacDonald and Michael Ross. "Assessing the accuracy of predictions about dating relationships: How and why do lovers' predictions differ from those made by observers?" *Personality and Social Psychology Bulletin* 25.11 (1999): 1417–1429.

161   **match for all but three:** David C. Funder, David C. Kolar, and Melinda C. Blackman. "Agreement among judges of personality: Interpersonal relations, similarity, and acquaintanceship." *Journal of Personality and Social Psychology* 69.4 (1995): 656–672.

163   **different aspects of who we are:** Simine Vazire and Erika N. Carlson. "Others sometimes know us better than we know ourselves." *Current Di-*

rections in Psychological Science 20.2 (2011): 104–108. Simine Vazire and Matthias R. Mehl. "Knowing me, knowing you: The accuracy and unique predictive validity of self-ratings and other-ratings of daily behavior." *Journal of Personality and Social Psychology* 95.5 (2008): 1202–1216.

164 **This clever experiment:** Sidney Rosen and Abraham Tesser. "On reluctance to communicate undesirable information: The MUM effect." *Sociometry* (1970): 253–263.

166 **"devised to keep people":** Herbert H. Blumberg. "Communication of interpersonal evaluations." *Journal of Personality and Social Psychology* 23.2 (1972): 157–162.

166 **jeopardize our social standing:** Charles F. Bond and Evan L. Anderson. "The reluctance to transmit bad news: Private discomfort or public display?" *Journal of Experimental Social Psychology* 23.2 (1987): 176–187.

166 **social rejection activates:** Kipling D. Williams, Christopher K. T. Cheung, and Wilma Choi. "Cyberostracism: Effects of being ignored over the Internet." *Journal of Personality and Social Psychology* 79.5 (2000): 748–762.

168 **asked them to evaluate:** Bella M. DePaulo and Kathy L. Bell. "Truth and investment: Lies are told to those who care." *Journal of Personality and Social Psychology* 71.4 (1996): 703–716.

168 **more successful and promotable:** Bernard M. Bass and Francis J. Yammarino. "Congruence of self and others' leadership ratings of naval officers for understanding successful performance." *Applied Psychology* 40.4 (1991): 437–454; Mike Young and Victor Dulewicz. "Relationships between emotional and congruent self-awareness and performance in the British Royal Navy." *Journal of Managerial Psychology* 22.5 (2007): 465–478.

168 **predictor of leadership success:** J. P. Flaum. "When it comes to business leadership, nice guys finish first," greenpeakpartners.com, http://greenpeakpartners.com/resources/pdf/6%208%2010%20Executive%20study%20GP %20commentary%20article_Final.pdf.

168 **less likely you are to be self-aware:** Fabio Sala. "Executive Blind Spots: Discrepancies Between Self-and Other-Ratings." *Consulting Psychology Journal: Practice and Research* 55.4 (2003): 222–229.

169 **labeled CEO *Disease*:** John A. Byrne, William C. Symonds, and Julia Flynn Silver. "CEO disease." *The Training and Development Sourcebook* 263 (1994).

170 **future for the automaker:** Richard Whittington. *What Is Strategy—And Does It Matter?* Cengage Learning EMEA, 2001.

170 **succeeded his father-in-law:** William Engdahl. "Who is Pehr Gyllenhammar, and what are the Aspen-Skandia networks?" larouchepub .com, August 31, 1982, http://www.larouchepub.com/eiw/public/1982/

eirv09n33-19820831/eirv09n33-19820831_043-who_is_pehr_gyllen
hammar_and_wha.pdf.

171 **"cheeky" and "provocative"**: "Volvo cars and Volvo museum exhibited Pehr G Gyllenhammar's cars," volvo.cars.com, April 15, 2014, http://www.volvocars.com/international/about/our-company/heritage/heritage-news/volvo-cars-and-volvo-museum-exhibited-pehr-g-gyllenhammars-cars.

171 **nickname "The Emperor"**: Robert F. Bruner. "An analysis of value destruction and recovery in the alliance and proposed merger of Volvo and Renault." *Journal of Financial Economics* 51.1 (1999): 125–166.

172 **"an impenetrable mess"**: Paula Dwyer. "Why Volvo kissed Renault goodbye," *Business Week*, December 19, 1993, http://www.bloomberg.com/news/articles/1993-12-19/why-volvo-kissed-renault-goodbye.

172 **upped the deal's projected savings**: Ibid.

172 **"We didn't realize Mr. Gyllenhammar"**: Ibid.

172 **"envious vendetta" against him**: Robert F. Bruner. "An analysis of value destruction and recovery in the alliance and proposed merger of Volvo and Renault." *Journal of Financial Economics* 51.1 (1999): 125–166.

173 **regularly solicit feedback**: The top performing leaders were the top 10 percent and the bottom performing leaders were the bottom 10 percent. Joseph Folkman. "Top ranked leaders know this secret: ask for feedback," forbes.com, January 8, 2015, http://www.forbes.com/sites/joefolkman/2015/01/08/top-ranked-leaders-know-this-secret-ask-for-feedback/#b958b9e608fe.

173 **socially and professionally rewarded**: Susan J. Ashford and Anne S. Tsui. "Self-regulation for managerial effectiveness: The role of active feedback seeking." *Academy of Management Journal* 34.2 (1991): 251–280.

174 **With a rich history**: David W. Bracken, et al. *Should 360-Degree Feedback Be Used Only for Developmental Purposes?* Center for Creative Leadership, 1997.

174 **anywhere from 30 percent**: David W. Bracken, Carol W. Timmreck, and Allan H. Church, eds. *The Handbook of Multisource Feedback*. John Wiley & Sons, 2001.

174 **to 90 percent**: Mark Robert Edwards and Ann J. Ewen. *360 - Feedback: The Powerful New Model for Employee Assessment & Performance Improvement*. AMACOM, 1996.

174 **higher-quality homework**: Jesse Pappas and J. Madison. "Multisource feedback for STEM students improves academic performance." *Annual Conference Proceedings of American Society of Engineering Education*. 2013.

175 **subordinates fear the repercussions**: Arthur Morgan, Kath Cannan,

and Joanne Cullinane. "360 feedback: a critical enquiry." *Personnel Review* 34.6 (2005): 663–680.

175 **"[If my 360 tells me] anything critical":** Ibid.

Chapter 8: Receiving, Reflecting on, and Responding to Difficult or Surprising Feedback

198 **performance of female chess players:** Hank Rothgerber and Katie Wolsiefer. "A naturalistic study of stereotype threat in young female chess players." *Group Processes & Intergroup Relations* 17.1 (2014): 79–90.

199 **dubbed *stereotype threat*:** Claude M. Steele and Joshua Aronson. "Stereotype threat and the intellectual test performance of African Americans." *Journal of Personality and Social Psychology* 69.5 (1995): 797–811.

199 **scored 12 percent lower:** Thomas S. Dee. "Stereotype threat and the student-athlete." *Economic Inquiry* 52.1 (2014): 173–182.

199 **women hold only 22 percent:** National Science Report, 2000, as cited in Joyce Ehrlinger and David Dunning. "How chronic self-views influence (and potentially mislead) estimates of performance." *Journal of Personality and Social Psychology* 84.1 (2003): 5.

199 **ability to reason about science:** Joyce Ehrlinger and David Dunning. "How chronic self-views influence (and potentially mislead) estimates of performance." *Journal of Personality and Social Psychology* 84.1 (2003): 5–17.

200 **"psychological immune system":** Daniel T. Gilbert, et al. "Immune neglect: A source of durability bias in affective forecasting." *Journal of Personality and Social Psychology* 75.3 (1998): 617–638.

200 **40-percent reduction:** Geoffrey L. Cohen, et al. "Reducing the racial achievement gap: A social-psychological intervention." *Science* 313.5791 (2006): 1307–1310.

200 **it reduces our levels:** J. David Creswell, et al. "Does self-affirmation, cognitive processing, or discovery of meaning explain cancer-related health benefits of expressive writing?" *Personality and Social Psychology Bulletin* 33.2 (2007): 238–250, p. 242.

201 **open to difficult feedback:** Clayton R. Critcher and David Dunning. "Self-affirmations provide a broader perspective on self-threat." *Personality and Social Psychology Bulletin* 41.1 (2015): 3–18.

201 **help us hear tough truths:** Brandon J. Schmeichel and Andy Martens. "Self-affirmation and mortality salience: Affirming values reduces worldview defense and death-thought accessibility." *Personality and Social Psychology Bulletin* 31.5 (2005): 658–667.

201 **"more open to ideas":** David K. Sherman and Geoffrey L. Cohen. "The psychology of self-defense: Self-affirmation theory." *Advances in Experimental Social Psychology* 38 (2006): 183–242.

203 **less likely to hold delusional:** Matthew Vess, et al. "Nostalgia as a resource for the self." *Self and Identity* 11.3 (2012): 273–284.

203 **reminiscing reduces rumination:** Sander L. Koole, et al. "The cessation of rumination through self-affirmation." *Journal of Personality and Social Psychology* 77.1 (1999): 111–125.

203 **increases well-being:** Fred B. Bryant, Colette M. Smart, and Scott P. King. "Using the past to enhance the present: Boosting happiness through positive reminiscence." *Journal of Happiness Studies* 6.3 (2005): 227–260.

203 *before* **getting threatening feedback:** Clayton R. Critcher, David Dunning, and David A. Armor. "When self-affirmations reduce defensiveness: Timing is key." *Personality and Social Psychology Bulletin* 36.7 (2010): 947–959.

Chapter 9: How Leaders Build Self-Aware Teams and Organizations

216 **lost a whopping 25 percent:** Sarah Miller Caldicott. "Why Ford's Alan Mulally is an innovation CEO for the record books," forbes.com, June 25, 2014, http://www.forbes.com/sites/sarahcaldicott/2014/06/25/why-fords-alan-mulally-is-an-innovation-ceo-for-the-record-books/#c35aeec779bb.

216 **"[Bill] Ford found himself":** B. G. Hoffman. *American Icon: Alan Mulally and the Fight to Save Ford Motor Company.* Crown, 2012, p. 3.

216 **"This company means a lot":** Ibid., p. 56.

218 **"We'll all be here again":** Ibid., p. 106.

219 **"nothing short of bovine scatology:** Ibid.

220 *Somebody has to figure out:* Ibid., p. 124.

222 **self-aware teams are:** Susan M. Carter and Michael A. West. "Reflexivity, effectiveness, and mental health in BBC-TV production teams." *Small Group Research* 29.5 (1998): 583–601; Michaéla C. Schippers, Deanne N. Den Hartog, and Paul L. Koopman. "Reflexivity in teams: A measure and correlates." *Applied Psychology* 56.2 (2007): 189–211.

222 **likely to stay MUM:** Susan J. Ashford and Anne S. Tsui. "Self-regulation for managerial effectiveness: The role of active feedback seeking." *Academy of Management Journal* 34.2 (1991): 251–280.

225 **constellation of behaviors as "authentic leadership":** Remus Ilies, Frederick P. Morgeson, and Jennifer D. Nahrgang. "Authentic leadership and eudaemonic well-being: Understanding leader-follower outcomes." *The Leadership Quarterly* 16.3 (2005): 373–394; Fred O. Walumbwa, et al. "Authentic leadership: Development and validation of a theory-based measure." *Journal of Management* 34.1 (2008): 89–126.

225 **more productive than those:** Joanne Lyubovnikova, et al. "How authentic leadership influences team performance: The mediating role of team reflexivity." *Journal of Business Ethics* (2015): 1–12.

226 **children were happier:** Heather K. Warren and Cynthia A. Stifter. "Ma-

ternal emotion-related socialization and preschoolers' developing emotion self-awareness." *Social Development* 17.2 (2008): 239–258.

226 **followers tend to imitate:** Albert Bandura and Richard H. Walters. "Social learning theory." General Learning Press, 1997.

228 **"a super-intensive getting-to-know-you":** Cathy Olofson. "GE brings good managers to life," fastcompany.com, September 30, 1998, http://www.fastcompany.com/35516/ge-brings-good-managers-life.

228 **better, more trusting relationships:** Steven V. Manderscheid and Alexandre Ardichvili. "New leader assimilation: Process and outcomes." *Leadership & Organization Development Journal* 29.8 (2008): 661–677.

231 **science of team self-awareness:** Amy C. Edmondson. "Learning from mistakes is easier said than done: Group and organizational influences on the detection and correction of human error." *Journal of Applied Behavioral Science* 32.1 (1996): 5–28.

231 **480 and 960 potential errors:** The average hospital patient received between 10 and 20 doses of medication each day with an average stay of 4.8 days. Amy C. Edmondson. "Learning from mistakes is easier said than done: Group and organizational influences on the detection and correction of human error." *Journal of Applied Behavioral Science* 32.1 (1996): 5–28.

231 **kill hundreds and injure:** "Medication error reports," fda.gov, October 20, 2016, http://www.fda.gov/Drugs/DrugSafety/MedicationErrors/ucm080629.htm.

232 **"The term," Edmondson explains:** Amy Edmondson. "Psychological safety and learning behavior in work teams." *Administrative Science Quarterly* 44.2 (1999): 350–383.

232 **reached a similar conclusion:** Charles Duhigg. "What Google learned from its quest to build the perfect team," nytimes.com, February 28, 2016, http://www.nytimes.com/2016/02/28/magazine/what-google-learned-from-its-quest-to-build-the-perfect-team.html?_r=0.

235 **create clear norms:** Vanessa Urch Druskat and D. Christopher Kayes. "The antecedents of team competence: Toward a fine-grained model of self-managing team effectiveness." *Research on Managing Groups and Teams* 2.2 (1999): 201–231.

237 **"leading by being self-aware":** Edwin E. Catmull and Amy Wallace. *Creativity, Inc.: Overcoming the Unseen Forces That Stand in the Way of True Inspiration.* New York: Random House, 2014. Print, xvi.

237 **"unhindered communication":** Ibid., p. 4.

237 **"The year is 2017":** Ibid., p. 283.

238 **"broke[n] the logjam":** Ibid., p. 292.

238 **"made it safer for people":** Ibid., p. 293.

238 **"collaboration, determination and candor":** Ed Catmull. *Creativity,*

Inc.: Overcoming the Unseen Forces That Stand in the Way of True Inspiration. Random House, 2014, p. 277.

241 **"radical truth" and "radical transparency":** James Freeman. "The soul of a hedge fund 'machine,'" wsj.com, June 6, 2014, http://www.wsj.com/ articles/james-freeman-the-soul-of-a-hedge-fund-machine-1402094722.

241 **a fireable offense:** Richard Feloni. "Ray Dalio explains why 25% of Bridgewater employees don't last more than 18 months at the hedge fund giant," businessinsider.com, March 23, 2016, http://www.businessinsider .com/biggest-challenges-new-bridgewater-employees-face-2016-3.

241 **"digital baseball card":** Eliza Gray. "Questions to answer in the age of optimized hiring," time.com, June 11, 2015, http://time.com/3917703/ questions-to-answer-in-the-age-of-optimized-hiring/.

241 **give one another "dots":** Ibid.

241 **"What we're trying to do":** Bess Levin. "Bridgwater associates truth probings are about to get turbo-charged," dealbreaker.com, July 18, 2011, http://dealbreaker.com/2011/07/bridgwater-associates-truth-probings-are-about-to-get-turbo-charged/.

242 **more money than any other hedge fund:** Nishant Kumar. "Bridgewater's Dalio trumps Soros as most profitable hedge fund," bloomberg.com, January 26, 2016, http://www.bloomberg.com/news/articles/2016-01-26/ bridgewater-s-dalio-trumps-soros-as-most-profitable-hedge-fund.

242 **And indeed, many employees:** James Freeman. "The soul of a hedge fund 'machine,'" wsj.com, June 6, 2014, http://www.wsj.com/articles/ james-freeman-the-soul-of-a-hedge-fund-machine-1402094722.

242 **"constant drumbeat of criticism":** Michelle Celarier and Lawrence Delevingne. "Ray Dalio's radical truth," March 2, 2011, http://www .institutionalinvestor.com/Article.aspx?ArticleID=2775995&p=3.

242 **"What you see at Bridgewater":** Michelle Celarier and Lawrence Delevingne. "Ray Dalio's radical truth," March 2, 2011, http://www.institutional investor.com/Article.aspx?ArticleID=2775995&p=3.

242 **30 percent of new hires:** Michelle Celarier and Lawrence Delevingne. "Ray Dalio's radical truth," March 2, 2011, http://www.institutional investor.com/Article/2775995/Channel/199225/Ray-Dalios-radical-truth.html?ArticleId=2775995&p=4#/.V04K15MrK8U.

249 **trying to conjure a name:** Elizabeth Brayer. *George Eastman: A Biography.* University of Rochester Press, 2006.

249 **"strong [and] incisive":** Kiplinger Washington Editors, Inc. "The story behind Kodak Trademark." *Kiplinger's Personal Finance,* April 1962, p. 40.

250 **85 percent of cameras:** Henry C. Lucas. *The Search for Survival: Lessons from Disruptive Technologies.* Praeger, 2012, p. 16.

250 **hurt their film business:** Ernest Scheyder and Liana B. Baker. "As Kodak struggles, Eastman Chemical thrives," reuters.com, December 24,

2011, http://www.reuters.com/article/us-eastman-kodak-idUSTRE7BN06 B20111224.

250 **"That's cute—but don't tell":** Paul B. Carroll and Chunka Mui. *Billion Dollar Lessons: What You Can Learn from the Most Inexcusable Business Failures of the Last Twenty-five Years.* Portfolio, 2008, p. 93.

250 **company filed for Chapter 11:** Reuters. "Kodak files for bankruptcy, plans biz overhaul." business-standard.com, January 19, 2012, http://www .business-standard.com/article/international/kodak-files-for-bankruptcy-plans-biz-overhaul-112011900119_1.html.

252 **"Take two of these":** B. G. Hoffman. *American Icon: Alan Mulally and the Fight to Save Ford Motor Company.* Crown, 2012, p. 248.

Chapter 10: Surviving and Thriving in a Delusional World

255 **just one unaware person:** Erich C. Dierdorff and Robert S. Rubin. "Research: We're not very self-aware, especially at work," *Harvard Business Review*, March 12, 2015, https://hbr.org/2015/03/research-were-not-very-self-aware-especially-at-work.

255 **unaware bosses have a detrimental:** Dan F. Moshavi, William Brown, and Nancy G. Dodd. "Leader self-awareness and its relationship to subordinate attitudes and performance." *Leadership & Organization Development Journal* 24.7 (2003): 407–418.

255 **asked 13,500 employees:** Sherri Dalphonse. "Washington's real-life horrible bosses," washingtonian.com, December 4, 2013, https://www .washingtonian.com/2013/12/04/real-life-horrible-bosses/.

256 **"suffer the severe disorientation":** William B. Swann Jr., Peter J. Rentfrow, and Jennifer S. Guinn. "Self-verification: The search for coherence." In M. R. Leary and J. J. P. Tangney, eds. *Handbook of Self and Identity.* Guilford Press, 2003, p. 376.

259 **appealing to their self-interest:** Erika N. Carlson, Simine Vazire, and Thomas F. Oltmanns. "You probably think this paper's about you: Narcissists' perceptions of their personality and reputation." *Journal of Personality and Social Psychology* 101.1 (2011): 185–201.

264 **cornerstone of narcissism:** John F. Rauthmann. "The Dark Triad and interpersonal perception: Similarities and differences in the social consequences of narcissism, Machiavellianism, and psychopathy." *Social Psychological and Personality Science* 3.4 (2012): 487–496.

264 **to identify one of the best ways:** Sander van der Linden and Seth A. Rosenthal. "Measuring narcissism with a single question? A replication and extension of the Single-Item Narcissism Scale (SINS)." *Personality and Individual Differences* 90 (2016): 238–241.

264 **view them as positive!:** Sara Konrath, Brian P. Meier, and Brad J. Bush-

man. "Development and validation of the single item narcissism scale (SINS)." *PLOS One* 9.8 (2014): e103469.

264 **"believe they are superior":** Mary Elizabeth Dallas. "Need to spot a narcissist? Just ask them," healthday.com, August 5, 2014, http://consumer .healthday.com/mental-health-information-25/psychology-and-mental-health-news-566/need-to-spot-a-narcissist-just-ask-them-690338.html.

265 **others are just too dim:** Erika N. Carlson, Simine Vazire, and Thomas F. Oltmanns. "You probably think this paper's about you: Narcissists' perceptions of their personality and reputation." *Journal of Personality and Social Psychology* 101.1 (2011): 185–201.

265 **rated lowest in effectiveness:** Timothy A. Judge, Jeffery A. LePine, and Bruce L. Rich. "Loving yourself abundantly: Relationship of the narcissistic personality to self—and other perceptions of workplace deviance, leadership, and task and contextual performance." *Journal of Applied Psychology* 91.4 (2006): 762–776.

271 **positive correlation between stress:** Delroy L. Paulhus, Peter Graf, and Mark Van Selst. "Attentional load increases the positivity of self-presentation." *Social Cognition* 7.4 (1989): 389–400.

276 **would prepare him to hear:** Geoffrey L. Cohen, Joshua Aronson, and Claude M. Steele. "When beliefs yield to evidence: Reducing biased evaluation by affirming the self." *Personality and Social Psychology Bulletin* 26.9 (2000): 1151–1164.

279 **it *is* often possible:** Leanne Atwater, Paul Roush, and Allison Fischthal. "The influence of upward feedback on self-and follower ratings of leadership." *Personnel Psychology* 48.1 (1995): 35–59.

279 **require repeated evidence:** Zoe Chance, et al. "The slow decay and quick revival of self-deception." *Frontiers in Psychology* 6 (2015).

282 **"a better and happier man":** Benjamin Franklin. *The Autobiography of Benjamin Franklin.* Garden City Publishing Company, 1916.

286 **Self-awareness transforms us into supernovas:** If you're reading this endnote, perhaps you're a science-minded individual. Yes, technically supernovas are dying stars, but I hope that you choose to remember the spirit of the quote!

Abbott, W. W., 10
Abuja, 194
    Unity Fountain in, 14
Accountability Conversations, 248
Aetna, 130
Age of Effort, 73
Age of Esteem, 73–74
aggression, 75, 133, 135, 177, 235,
    262
Ahrendts, Angela, 90–92
alarm clock events, 44–46, 158
    definition of, 44
    earthquake events as, 11, 45–46
    new roles and rules as, 44–45
alcohol abuse, 74, 75, 120
Alcoholics Anonymous, 204
Allen, Eleanor, 38–40, 167–68
Allen, Woody, 23–24
ambition, 10, 29, 49, 66, 90, 148,
    195–96
American Dream, 250
American Icon (Hoffman), 216
American Youth Soccer
    Organization, 77
anger, 34–35, 41, 64, 69, 135, 193, 267,
    268, 277–78
animals, 98, 100, 153
anxiety, 33–34, 74, 97, 99, 103, 104,
    113, 120, 136, 153
Apple, 91, 236, 238
Argyris, Chris, 67
Aron, Arthur, 106–7
Aronson, Joshua, 199
arrogance, 158, 160, 195
Asner, Ed, 265
aspirations, 24, 30, 151, 284, 290

assumptions, 66–68, 222, 236, 240,
    257, 295
Åstebro, Thomas, 80

Baby Boomers, 54n, 84
Bankable Leadership (Eurich), 306
Barrowford Primary School, 76–77
baseball, 59–60
Baseball America, 60
basketball, 108
Baumeister, Roy, 75
behavior, 131
    anticipation of, 161, 226n
    choices of, 34, 69
    cruel, 268–70
    decisive, 36–37
    destructive, 75–76
    evaluation of, 4, 27, 45–46, 56,
        62–66, 98
    impact of, 4, 6n, 24, 35, 37–42, 50,
        143, 263, 267–68, 284, 293
    improvement of, 42, 65, 68,
        158–59
    learnable, 58
    management of, 35, 133, 135
    nonverbal, 63
    outside perception of, 10, 16–17,
        23, 24, 40–43, 46, 63, 64–66, 98,
        159–62, 170, 176–77, 189, 192
    patterns of, 32–34, 103, 104
    rare, 108
    reasons for, 105–12
    self-assessment of, 88
Behavior Blindness, 62–63, 284
beliefs, 99, 107
    challenging of, 214

beliefs (*cont.*)
self-limiting, 198–200
shared, 232–36
Bell, Kathy, 168
Berg, Insoo Kim, 150
"Better Than Average Effect," 51
Bible, 6–7
Billings, Josh, 48
Billion Dollar Lessons (Carroll and Mui), 250
Blakeman, Chuck, 251
Blink (Gladwell), 182
Blumberg, Herb, 165–66
Bocas del Toro, 33–34
Boeing Commercial Airplanes, 214
Boorstin, Daniel J., 71
boredom, 27, 28, 62, 110
Boston Red Sox, 59–60, 130–31
Boulder, Colo., 132
Bradberry, Travis, 5–6
Branden, Nathaniel, 74, 75
Bridgewater Associates, 241–42
BringBackOurGirls movement, 13–14, 281
British Petroleum (BP), 223–25
Brown, Brené, 234
Buddhism, 22, 70, 100, 128–29
buildings:
construction of, 21, 48, 49
design of, 27–28
bullying, 30, 33, 50, 57, 261
Bushman, Brad, 265
business, 51, 140
CEO compensation in, 53
challenges in, 112
failure in, 28, 80
feedback in, 17
online, 91
retail, 91
risks in, 60, 79–80
startup, 28
survival in, 79–80
teams in, 215, 218–31

calendars, 21, 116
California Task Force to Promote
Self Esteem and Personal & Social Responsibility, 74–75, 76
Campbell, Keith, 72
Canadian Innovation Centre, 80
Candor Challenge, 242–49
Capilano River Regional Park bridges, 106–7
Carlin, George, 78
Carroll, Paul, 250
Catmull, Ed, 169–70, 180–81, 233, 237–41
Centre d'Etudes Industrielles, 171
CEO disease, 169
change, 81, 88, 93, 104, 110, 197, 257–62
lack of, 203–6
rejection of, 266–70
taking action for, 256, 272
cheating, 4, 76
chess, 198–99
Chesterton, G. K., 114
Chibok girls kidnapping, 12–14
children, 50, 122, 194, 226
adoption of, 99–100, 104
demands of, 55–56
dreams of, 90
infant, 55–56, 72
naming of, 71–72, 86
praise of, 76–77
punishment of, 76
raising of, 4, 7, 27, 51, 53–54, 60, 76, 187–88
"special," 76–78
testing and grading of, 77–78
vocabularies of, 53
see also students
Chödrön, Pema, 70
Churchill, Winston, 213
Cicero, 26
C. JoyBell C., 286
Cohen, Geoffrey, 200
collaboration, 5, 50, 52, 249
Collapse (Diamond), 22
college professors, 51, 90, 105, 145, 183, 191–93

colleges, 62, 78, 79, 84, 85, 90, 105, 147
Collins, Jim, 112
Colorado, 35–36
"come to Jesus" moments, 65, 161
communication, 5, 44, 175, 180, 187, 204, 225
   avoidance of, 164–70
   of bad news, 164–65
   of clear boundaries, 269
   experiments in, 164–65, 188–89
   inner, 93
   of needs, 268–69, 285
   risks vs. benefits of, 274–80
   style of, 35, 39
   see also feedback
community, 36, 58–59, 174
companies:
   CEOs of, 53, 86–87, 90–91, 121, 134, 148–49, 151, 167–71, 214–17
   financial returns of, 52, 111
   grading of, 80
   merger and acquisition of, 82
   publicly traded, 52
   selling of, 110–11
   start-up, 141, 205
compassion, 58, 272, 280
   without judgment, 260, 285
competition, 31, 78, 235
computers, 135, 141, 169, 224, 233–34, 236
"confirmation bias," 107
conflict, 40–41, 52, 203, 257
   avoidance of, 243
   working through, 37, 40
Congress, U.S., 10
consciousness, 98
Construction of Self, The (Harter), 57
Cook, Tim, 91
Cooper, Anderson, 130
cooperation, 54, 207
Costa Rica, 33
courage, 2, 18, 65, 70, 81, 137, 173, 197, 209, 249
creativity, 4, 126, 133, 135
Creativity Inc. (Catmull), 237

crime, 58
criticism, 64–66, 78, 86, 93, 196, 213–14, 258–59
   loving, 179–86, 285
   unloving, 178–79
Cult of Self, 70–88, 264–65, 284, 296, 297
   resistance to, 88–94
curiosity, 27, 28, 88, 104

Dalai Lama, 23
Dalio, Ray, 241–42
Daring Greatly (Brown), 234
decision making, 61–62, 64, 68, 69, 88, 94, 108, 116, 124, 132, 135, 208
Deepwater Horizon oil rig, 224
defensiveness, 45–46, 134, 135, 183, 193
Delphi, Temple of Apollo at, 22
delusion. *See* self-delusion
Denver, Colo., 35–37, 127, 140, 157
DePaulo, Bella, 168
depression, 74, 97, 103, 104, 108, 119, 133
Descartes, Rene, 98
de Shazer, Steve, 150
Detroit News, 251, 253
Diamond, Jared, 22
Diener, Carol, 122, 151
Dinner of Truth, 186–90
Disney Animation Studios, 169, 233
distraction, 130, 131–32
divorce, 7, 81, 87, 99
Donziger, Marcia, 116–18, 121–22
Dreyfuss, Richard, 282
drinking, 34, 76, 120, 238
driving, 51, 54, 270–71
drug abuse, 74, 75
Dufresne, Todd, 101–2
Duke University, 147
Dunning, David, 54–55, 59, 68, 199
Dunning-Kruger Effect, 54
Dutton, Donald, 106–7
Duval, Shelley, 23
Dweck, Carol, 122, 151

earthquakes, 21
Eastman, George, 249–50
Edmondson, Amy, 231–33
ego, 91–92, 135, 217
ego defense, 79
egotism, 265
Ehrlinger, Joyce, 59, 199
electric shock, 130
Elhedhil, Samir, 80
e-mail, 34, 38–39, 191–92, 233–34,
    238
embarrassment, 56, 159
Emeryville, Calif., 236–37
emotional intelligence (EQ), 5–6,
    55, 269
Emotional Intelligence (Bradberry),
    5–6
Emotion Blindness, 60–62, 64, 284
emotions, 32, 40, 45, 56, 102, 105,
    159, 201
    being in touch with, 8, 98, 99, 101,
        133, 135, 136
    expression of, 163
    management of, 5, 35, 111, 226
    monitoring of, 131
    naming of, 112, 185
    sensitivity to, 197
    upsetting, 100, 120
empathy, 5, 40, 52, 86
energy, 31, 32, 47, 49, 80, 88, 120,
    236, 256
England, 58, 76–77
environment, 8, 112, 169, 284, 291
    work, 31, 32
ESPN, 60
Eurich, Abby, 127–28, 132, 153
exercise, outdoor, 136
exhaustion, 28, 116
experience:
    comparing and contrasting of,
        139–43, 148, 285
    daily check-ins of, 143–44
    looking at multiple angles of,
        139
    near-death, 147
    reframing of, 137–44, 285

expressive writing, 113–15
extroverts, 232
eye contact, 63, 64

Facebook, 85, 87, 131
    "likes" on, 89, 93
fear, 3, 41, 64, 69, 74, 93, 173, 263
feedback, 8, 17, 38–39, 42–44, 64–66,
    68–69, 81, 86, 120, 135, 150,
    158–63, 166, 170–90, 227–31
    accuracy of, 180, 196
    candid, 238–39
    difficult or surprising, 193–94, 198,
        201, 203–9
    free resources for, 306
    ground rules of, 246–47
    helpful, 179–80
    mental preparation for, 189
    need for, 190
    organizational, 253
    patterns of, 197
    questioning of, 182–83, 188–89
    reflecting on, 191–209
    rejection of, 193, 258–59
    responding to, 180, 188, 190–209,
        230–31, 258–59
    right kind of, 176–86, 190
    seeking of, 178, 181–83, 192, 251,
        304–5
    Start/Stop/Continue Model of,
        182–83, 235
    team, 244–49, 257–59
    3R Model of, 190–209, 246n, 285
    360-degree feedback, 174–77, 183,
        190, 203–5
    understanding of, 196
    see also criticism
Feel Good Effect, 78–79, 80–81, 201,
    284
Fenigstein, Allan, 23
Fielding, Lara, 103
Fields, Mark, 215, 219–21, 253
fight-or-flight response, 112
Fischer, Bobby, 198
fit, 24, 31–32, 44, 284
Fitzgerald, F. Scott, 105, 107

Five Cornerstones of Collective Insight, 222–23, 225–26, 228, 240
Five Dysfunctions of a Team, The (Lencioni), 242n
Flaubert, Gustave, 142
Florence Ozor Foundation, 14
Forbes, 90
Ford, Bill, 216–17
Ford Motor Company, 15, 214–23, 226–27, 251–53
  Business Process Review (BPR) at, 218–21, 223, 252
  financial turnaround of, 216–17, 221–22
Fort Necessity, Battle of, 9–10
Fortune, 13, 90, 91
Franken, Al, 200
Franklin, Benjamin, 24–27, 107, 143, 191, 208, 280
  inventions of, 26
  personal principles of, 25–27, 42, 282
Franklin, James, 24–25
Freud, Sigmund, 101–4
fulfillment, 74, 75
fun, 157, 226n
Funder, David, 161
future, 118n, 129, 148, 150, 153, 161
  planning for, 28–29, 99, 103

General Electric, 228
General Mills, 130
generosity, 59
Gen Xers, 84
Georgia, University of, 164
Germany, 110
Gilbert, Daniel, 131
Gladwell, Malcolm, 182
goals, 121, 223, 228, 280
  achievement of, 30, 31
  listing of, 28–29, 30
  pursuit of, 29–30, 134, 151, 235, 262–63
Goldman Sachs, 134
Goldsmith, Marshall, 134

Good Man Project, 186
Google, 130, 234
  People Operations Department of, 232
Grant, Anthony, 23n, 97–98
Great Stupa of Dharmakaya, 127, 152–53
Greece, 225
  ancient, 22
Gulf of Mexico, 224
Gyllenhammar, Pehr, Jr., 170–72
Gyllenhammar, Pehr, Sr., 171, 172

Ham, Charles, 86–87
Hamilton, J. Paul, 119n
happiness, 4, 18, 31–32, 44, 74, 88, 133
  choices in service of, 8, 14, 22, 24, 134
  introspection and, 97, 98, 143
  mystery of, 114
  roadblocks to, 8, 65
  studies of, 60–61
Hardinge, Frances, vii
Harter, Susan, 57
Harvard University, 67, 78, 129, 131, 231, 241
  Business School of, 105
Hawaii, 82
Hayward, Tony, 224
Heath, Chip, 150
Heath, Dan, 150
Heppner, Whitney, 135
Herbert, Frank, 21
Hindenburg, 43
Hixon, J. Gregory, 108–9
hockey, 71–72
Hoffman, Bryce, 216, 219, 251–53
Hollywood, 169
Homo sapiens, 4–5
  needs of, 74, 76
  survival of, 166
Honduras, 33
honesty, 58, 70, 79, 163, 181–82, 193, 215, 237–39, 242–49, 267
Hong Kong, 41

hope, 94, 126, 147, 153
How the Mighty Fall (Collins),
    112
hubris, 3, 7, 171, 172
Hughes Aircraft, 37
Huh, Ben, 28–30
human brain, 61, 108, 153, 166
    amygdala of, 112
    development of, 4
    prefrontal cortex of, 119n
    scanning of, 137
humanities, 52n
humiliation, 9, 33, 117–18, 256
humility, 10, 26, 73, 91–92, 94, 197,
    216, 297–98
    cultivation of, 88, 90
humor, 54, 205, 265–66, 285
hydrogen, 43

I Can Has Cheezburger website,
    29–30
Icarus myth, 65
ignorance, 51, 70, 259
    blissful, 65, 80–82, 160–61
illness, 80, 116–17, 161, 269
"I Love Me" lessons, 78
incompetence, 62
Increasing Leadership Effectiveness
    (Argyris), 67
information technology (IT), 27–28,
    144
"Informers," 88, 89
initiative, 37
insight, 5, 16–18, 32, 98, 100, 159,
    195, 198
    acting on, 148, 195–96, 281
    from blindness to, 64–70, 94, 279
    cultivation of, 33, 64–70, 114, 115,
        153, 162, 190, 193
    everyday, 46–47
    lack of, 51, 79–80, 94, 104, 264–65
    potential for, 271
    rewards of, 215
    seven pillars of, 16, 24–47, 103,
        140, 283–84
Instagram, 85, 131

intelligence, 51, 55, 79, 103, 262
    testing of, 108
interleukin 6 levels, 137
intimacy, 40
    fear of, 74
introspection, 23, 56, 97–126, 133,
    143, 149
    approaches to, 100, 102, 103–4
    definition of, 129
    four follies of, 100–126
    happiness and, 97, 98, 143
    motivation for, 104
    "normal," 119n
    rumination as the evil twin of,
        118–26
    self-awareness and, 100
    time spent on, 98
    why and what questions in,
        105–12, 285
introversion, 12–13, 27, 34, 146, 167,
    232
intuition, 23
inventions, 26, 67
Islam, 22

jobs, 146, 159, 160
    applying for, 138
    interviews for, 93
    loss of, 137–38, 167
    quitting of, 213–14, 270
    see also work
Jobs, Steve, 233, 290
Johns Hopkins University, 165
jokes, 62, 183
journaling, 16, 57, 112–16, 143
    benefits of, 113–15
    exploring the negative in, 114
    self-help, 26–27
    traps of, 113, 115
Judaism, 22
Judeo-Christian tradition, 73
Jupiter, 144
justice, 25

Kahneman, Daniel, 51, 55, 61, 81
Kansas, University of, 214

Kardashian Kim, 74
Keillor, Garrison, 50, 76
Kempthorne, Charley, 112–13, 114, 116
Kentucky Derby, 57
Kenyon College, 23
Kets de Vries, Manfred, 53
Killingsworth, Matthew, 131
kindness, 32, 58, 116, 261
King, Levi, 203–5, 208, 233–34
Klein, Gary, 67–68
Kneff, Kristin, 93
knowledge, 34, 54, 56, 98, 192
Knowledge Blindness, 59–60, 64, 284
Kodak, 249–51
Kruger, Justin, 54, 68

"Lake Wobegon," 50, 53, 76
L'Amour, Louis, 127
Langer, Ellen, 129, 131, 137
Lasseter, John, 233, 238
laugh tracks, 265–66, 285
Leader Feedback Process, 227–31, 244, 281–82
leadership, 39, 44–45, 46, 91, 103n, 126, 160, 170, 206–8
    creating clear norms by, 235–36
    delusional, 49–50, 52–53
    effective, 4, 230
    ineffective, 55, 68, 86
    military, 1–3, 9–10
    organizational, 138, 213–15, 217–31
    philosophy of, 49–50
    qualities of, 4, 5
    rebellion against, 3
    rising to, 52
    seniority and experience in, 52–53
    skills of, 49
    style of, 49–50, 51, 66, 161, 169, 204
    teaching of, 33, 93, 124–25
    team, 257–59
Lean In (Sandberg), 199
learning, 68
    commitment to, 66
    double-loop, 67
    single-loop, 67

learn-well mindset, 122–23
    do-well mindset vs., 303
Lencioni, Patrick, 242n
"Let's be Game Changers" website, 88
Life Story, 102n, 145–48, 153
    complex narratives of, 146–48
    "contamination sequences" vs. "redemption sequences" in, 147
    thematic coherence in, 146–47
LinkedIn, 85
love, 29, 116, 187
    marital, 40
    uncritical, 179
Lucas, George, 169
Lucasfilm, 169
Lund University, 171
lying, 4, 63, 166–68
Lyke, Jennifer, 103
Lyubovnikova, Joanne, 225

McAdams, Dan, 145–47
McCall, Morgan, 45–46
McKinsey, 130
Madame Bovary (Flaubert), 142
Mad Men (TV series), 101
magnetic resonance imaging (MRI), 137
Marcus Aurelius, Emperor of Rome, 196–97
Marines, U.S., 130
marriage, 31, 99, 139, 142–43, 144, 161
    conflict in, 40–41
    satisfaction and love in, 40
Mary Tyler Moore Show, The (TV show), 265
Maslow, Abraham, 73–74
Matrix, The (film), 102
maturity, 54, 151
Mayans, 21–23
meditation, 8, 127–36, 152, 153
    walking, 132
    see also mindfulness
"me" focus, 84–85, 88–89
"Meformers," 89

memory, 114, 116, 133, 140, 202
mental health, 108, 119–33
"midlife" career crises, 28–30
military combat, 1–3, 9–10
Millennials, 54n, 84
Milton, John, 118
mindfulness, 127–44, 152
    definition of, 129, 137
    non-meditative, 136–44, 148, 153
    relaxation vs., 136–37
    self-awareness and, 133
    tools of, 136–44, 145, 148, 260–61
    training in, 133
    see also meditation
mirrors, 56, 98, 104, 115, 120, 162
Misner, Josh, 186–89
mistakes, 60, 76–77, 93, 94, 99, 105,
        122, 123, 138, 151, 234
    forgiveness for, 236
    medical, 231–32
modesty, 73
money, 61, 63, 242, 278–79
mood, 31, 56, 111, 113, 127, 143, 193,
        201
Moore, Mary Tyler, 265
morale, 39, 50, 99
morality, 42, 58, 256
"moral shallowing hypothesis," 84
Moran, Seana, 45
Morris, Jim, 240
Mui, Chunka, 250
Mulally, Alan, 15, 214–15, 217–21,
        223, 225–27, 251–53, 281
    Working Together Principles and
        Practices credo of, 226–27
MUM Effect, 165–68, 170, 175, 221,
        222, 227
Murray, Bill, 282
music, 69, 153
MyLifeLine.org, 117
MySpace, 85, 86

names:
    conventional, 72
    unique, 71–72, 86
narcissism, 83–88, 120, 264–65

National Register of Historic Places,
        37
Nature Conservancy, 133–34
neighborhood organizations, 36–37,
        174
"New Leader Assimilation Exercise,"
        228
New York, N.Y., 12, 13, 241, 266
New York Institute of Technology,
        169
Nigeria, 12–15, 194–95
Nike, 130
No Asshole Rule, The (Sutton), 260
Nobel Prize, 51
North Sea, 223–24
nostalgia, 202

O'Neil, Essena, 87–88
opportunity, 36, 44, 138–39, 140, 192,
        234, 257
optimism, 79–80, 111, 258, 259
Oracle Corporation, 91
Osment, Haley Joel, 50
Ostrich Trinity, 170–74, 178
Ozor, Florence, 12–15, 194–97, 198,
        203, 208, 281

Panama, 33–34
Pankejeff, Sergius "The Wolfman,"
        102
parenting, 4, 7, 27, 45, 51, 53–54, 60,
        72, 76, 99–100, 186–89
Parents Magazine, 72
passions, 24, 27–30, 32, 37, 40, 111,
        284, 289
    exploring of, 28, 140
    listing of, 28, 29
patterns, 24, 284
    of behavior, 32–34, 103, 104
Pearson, Allison, 77n
Pennebaker, James, 113–14, 116
Pennsylvania, Great Meadows in,
        9–10
Percy, Walker, 157
perfectionism, 87–88
persistence, 80–81

personality, 32, 44, 204, 232
 characteristics of, 53–54, 56–57,
  58–59, 134, 158, 160, 165–66,
  273–74
 self-rating of, 79
 Type A, 92, 129–30, 153
personality tests, 32–33, 63
perspective, 40–43, 115, 137, 139, 159,
  194, 197
Philadelphia, Pa., 25
philosophy, 22, 147, 266
Pixar, 169, 180, 233, 237–42
 "Notes Day" at, 237–40
 Peer Pirates program of, 240–41
placebo effect, 103
Plato, 3, 22
Plotinus, 22
Pokémon GO, 131
politeness, 54, 63, 168, 233
power, 52, 65, 86, 234
 challenge of, 53
 knowledge as, 34
 truth and, 69, 275
praise, 76–77, 92
prayer, 136, 152
"pre-mortems," 67–68
Presbyterian Church, 25
pride, 1–2, 42
Prince, Bob, 241
prisoners, 58–59
privacy, 13
problems, 224, 235, 239, 242
 awareness of, 275
 Miracle Question approach to,
  150–51, 283
 reframing of, 260–61
 solutions-mining approach to,
  149–51
 solving of, 38, 66, 119, 122, 149–50
Proverbs of Solomon, 26
"psychological immune system," 200
psychological safety, 232–36
psychology, 32, 58, 63, 67–68, 75, 79,
  97, 106, 113, 149–50, 182, 191
 child, 122
 clinical, 60, 103

 humanistic, 73
 organizational, 23, 140, 232, 243,
  244
Psychology of Self-Esteem, The
  (Branden), 74
psychotherapy, 8, 16, 74, 100–103,
  109, 115, 150
public relations (PR), 53
public speaking, 36–37, 62–63, 110,
  117, 121, 167, 181
Puerto Rico, 38–40

racism, 51
Ramachandran, V. S., 3–4
Rao, Hayagreeva, 68
reality, 79, 120
 acceptance of, 65–66, 80
 checking of, 124–26
 inner, 148
 objective, 92
"recency effect," 108
Reingold, Jennifer, 91
relationships, 79, 97, 146–47
 alienation in, 7, 64–65, 81, 82, 169
 building of, 5, 38–40, 47, 151, 175
 failed, 142
 focusing on others in, 88–90
 healing of, 279–80, 286
 insensitivity in, 8, 38
 lasting, 18, 31–32
 loss of, 99–100
 maintenance of, 85
 online, 83–88
 peer, 222
 personal, 4, 32–33, 53–54, 139,
  187–88, 265
 professional, 4–5, 30–31, 34–35,
  37–40, 44–45, 48–55, 62, 64–65,
  69, 81, 139, 150, 164–68, 176–86,
  213–15, 253
 questioning of, 107–8
 reframing of, 137–39, 142–43
 romantic, 45, 61, 68, 75, 142–43
 strong, 98
 trusting, 31, 39, 40, 69
 walking away from, 269–70, 285

relaxation, 136–37
religion, 22, 114
resilience, 5, 73, 77, 80, 226n
respect, 70, 93, 226n, 234, 246
responsibility, 54
Rochester, N.Y., 249
Rogelberg, Steven, 93
Rogers, Carl, 73
Roosevelt, Franklin Delano, 173
Roosevelt National Forest, 127
Rosen, Sidney, 164–65
Rothgerber, Hank, 198–99
rumination, 104, 117–26, 123, 142,
    143, 301–2
  as avoidance strategy, 120
  combating of, 121–26, 149
  definition of, 129
  hitting pause in, 123–24, 126
  learn-well mindset and, 122–23,
    125–26
  post-decision (PDR), 124
  reality checks in, 124–26
  shutting down of, 123, 126
Rumsfeld, Donald, 68, 294

St. Louis Cardinals, 59–60
Sandberg, Sheryl, 199
San Francisco Bay, 51
Sasson, Steven, 250
Saturday Night Live, Stuart Smalley
    character on, 200–201
Schön, Donald, 67
Schwartz, Norbert, 61
Schweitzer, Louis, 171
science, 75, 102
  gender gap in, 199–200
  physical, 52n
  "publish or perish" world of, 80–81
  social, 52n
scientific method, 75, 102
Seattle, Wash., 29
Sedikides, Constantine, 58–59
self-absorption, 83–84, 86, 88, 97,
    115, 120
self-acceptance, 88, 92–94, 98
self-actualization, 74

self-affirmation, 198–203, 277
self-assessment, 6, 7, 88
  age and accuracy of, 52n
self-awareness, 3–18, 100, 105, 151,
    163
  anatomy of, 21–47
  boosting of, 284–85
  building blocks of, 4, 16, 24–27,
    42–47, 92, 94, 223–42
  capacity for, 55–56
  collective, 231
  commitment to, 236–49
  definitions of, 5, 7–8, 23–24
  development of, 4, 8–9, 10–17, 54,
    55–58, 64–70, 88, 222
  distortion of, 83–84
  emotional intelligence vs., 6n
  external, 8, 11, 17, 42–46, 135–36,
    155–209, 285
  as foundation to a life well lived,
    17–18
  high, 11
  importance of, 12
  improvement in, 10–12, 16, 24,
    113, 151, 167
  inherent, 11
  internal, 6n, 8, 11, 16, 42–44, 58n,
    73, 97–153, 159, 284–85
  lack of, 4–7, 11, 49–55, 172,
    254–86
  Life Story approach to, 102n,
    145–48, 153
  misconceptions about, 94
  moderate, 11
  myths and truths of, 16–17, 42
  need for, 272
  organizational, 249–53
  process of, 280–86
  roadblocks to, 16, 17, 43, 47–94,
    157–74, 284
  selecting spheres of, 283
  skills of, 52
  strengthening of, 47
  study of, 10–11, 15–16, 22–24, 42,
    58–63, 81, 133
  team, 213–53

three blindspots in, 58–63, 64, 68, 295

tools of, 126–53, 284–85

transformative power of, 15

virtues and benefits of, 4, 15–18

self-awareness unicorns, 15, 24, 26–27, 30, 33, 35, 44–47, 58, 70, 80, 81, 83, 88, 89, 94, 104, 121, 255

diversity of, 11–12

self-compassion, 92, 93n, 94

self-confidence, 1–4, 17, 38, 51, 54, 59, 65, 86, 105, 143, 196, 197, 207

excess of, 7, 52, 53, 54, 60, 64, 68, 79, 169, 177

loss of, 87

self-consciousness, 23, 93

self-control, 59

self-criticism, 93

self-delusion, 2–3, 5–7, 9–10, 17, 49–55, 64–66, 78–79, 81, 83, 254–86

Aware Don't Care, 256, 260, 263–69, 270

leadership and, 49–50, 52–53

Lost Cause, 256, 259–62, 263–64, 270

Nudgable, 256, 270–80

rewards of, 53

survival of, 285

self-discipline, 116

self-discovery, 209

self-esteem:

achievement of, 73–74

benefits of, 80

boosting of, 75–79

expected consequences of, 74–75

inflated, 56, 71–94

low, 35, 57, 74, 75, 92

obsession with, 6, 76

rising levels of, 75

study of, 75–76

success and, 74–75

unconditional, 73

self-examination, 145

self-exploration, 153

selfies, 82–84, 86

Selfie Syndrome, 82–84, 284

self-image, 50, 71, 79, 163

self-improvement, 22, 64, 81, 183, 280–81

self-involvement, 8

self-knowledge, 22, 98, 104, 126, 137

self-love, 75

self-perception, 79

self-pity, 116

self-presentation, 85

self-promotion, 12, 86, 87, 89

Seven-Day Insight Challenge, 17, 282–83

Seven Pillars of Insight, 16, 24–47, 103, 140, 283–84

Seven Years' War, 10

Shambhala Mountain Center, 127–28, 132, 153

Sheldon, Oliver, 54–55

Sherman, David, 201

shyness, 35–36, 57, 81

silence, 25, 65, 153, 166, 169, 219

Silent Generation, 73

Simon, Paul, 250

Simsek, Omer, 104

Sixth Sense, The (film), 50

Skandia Insurance, 171, 172

smartphones, 130, 131

Smith, Timothy, 161

Snapchat, 85, 87

social media, 83–89, 115, 131, 251

social skills, 51, 75, 108, 204–5

Socrates, 22, 26

software design, 27, 28

Solution Focused Brief Therapy, 150

South Korea, 29

space exploration, 104

Spinoza, Benedict de, 111

spiritual practices, 4

sports, 51, 71–72, 77–78, 105–6, 130–31, 199

Sports Illustrated, 60

Stanford University, 45, 54, 68, 260

State of the Union addresses, 84–85

Steele, Claude, 199, 200

stereotypes, 198–99
"stereotype threat," 199
Steve Disease, 51–55, 64
Storr, Will, 75
stress, 31, 34–35, 49, 97, 101, 120, 129
    management of, 5, 35, 93, 112, 137
students, 61–62, 76–79, 84, 85, 99,
        105–6, 108–9, 122, 130, 135,
        191–93
    academic performance of, 54–56,
        77–79, 147, 199–200, 202
    African American, 199–200
success, 14, 15, 17, 23, 30, 47, 51, 65,
        66, 80, 169
    career, 99
    fear of, 74
    motivation for, 151
    odds of, 80
    personal, 146
    prediction of, 74–75, 103
    stagnation vs., 148
    subjective views of, 53
supernovas, 286
Suttles, Doug, 223–25, 227, 234
Sutton, Bob, 260
Swann, William, 108–9, 256
Sweden, 171
Switch (Heath and Heath), 150
Switzerland, 171
Sydney, University of, 97
sympathy, 164

Target, 130
teaching, 33, 51, 53, 66, 76–78, 81,
        141, 206, 208
Team Feedback Exchange, 244–49
technology, 51, 251
TED talks, 168
teenagers, 56–57, 68, 74
telescopes, 144–45
Telltale Brain, The (Ramachandran),
        3–4
Tercek, Mark, 133–35
terrorism, 14
Tesser, Abraham, 164–65
thinking, 32, 67, 105, 191

    control of, 131
    disruptive, 100
    fast vs. slow, 61n
    flexible, 104
    of learning over performance,
        122–23, 125–26
    positive, 134
    superficial, 84
    top-down, 59–60
    see also introspection; meditation;
        mindfulness; rumination
Thinking, Fast and Slow (Kahneman),
        61n
Thomson, James, 26
Thoreau, Henry David, 27
time, 31, 39–40, 88, 89, 98, 149, 236
    free, 141–42
    measurement of, 21, 255
    past, 145, 148, 153
    present, 129–30, 140, 145, 148
    see also future
Tomlinson, Rachel, 76–77
tranquility, 25
travel, 31, 137
    airline, 41
    world, 30
trust, 31, 39, 40, 58, 69, 181, 193, 227,
        228, 230, 234, 243
truth, 2, 5, 7, 23, 31, 160, 163, 213,
        217, 253
    absolute, 104, 146, 159, 299–300
    absorption of, 46, 65, 88, 193
    avoidance of, 164–70
    blindness to, 79
    expectation of, 231–36
    fantasy vs., 10, 77
    inconvenient, 75
    need for, 104, 146, 299–300
    painful, 189
    as power, 69
    seeking of, 16, 22, 65, 104, 170, 174,
        186–90, 209, 241
    spoken, vii, 64, 158–59, 233, 235,
        275
    unheard, 157–60
Tulku, Tirthang, 100

Tumblr, 87
Twenge, Jean, 72, 84
Twitter, 85

Uganda, 33
unconscious, 101–5
United Kingdom, 225
United States:
    economic crises in, 73, 221
    founding fathers of, 9–10, 24–27
United States Chess Federation, 198
"unknown unknowns," 68, 294
Upanishads, 22
Usman, Hadiza Bala, 13
Utah, University of, 169, 180

values, 24, 26–27, 32, 37, 103, 148,
    284, 287–88
    challenging of, 45
    commitment to, 27, 57
    Judeo-Christian, 73
Vancouver, 106
Vasconcellos, John, 74–75
Vess, Matthew, 202
victim mentality, 109, 110
violence, 75
virtues, 25–26, 42
Volvo, 170–72
vulnerability, 234–35, 286

Walpole, Horace, 10
Warner, Megan, 133
Washington, D.C., 13, 255
Washington, George, 15, 24–25, 281
    farewell address of, 94
    heroic reputation of, 10
    military leadership of, 9–10
    presidency of, 10, 94
    single military defeat of, 10
Washingtonian, 255
Water for People, 40, 168
weaknesses, 204–5, 217, 281–82
    strengths vs., 292
Weissbourd, Richard, 41

well-being, 98, 99, 113, 130, 151
West, Kanye, 89
Western Hockey League, 71–72
What About Bob? (film), 282
What Not Why, 109–12
Wickland, Robert, 23
Williamson, Marianne, 209
Willis, Bruce, 50
Wilson, Timothy, 100, 130, 145, 147
wisdom, 16, 29, 98
Wolsiefer, Katie, 198–99
work, 51, 82, 137, 194
    cutthroat culture at, 44
    entrepreneurial, 28, 79–80, 89,
        116, 141, 203
    fulfilling, 35
    hard, 73, 80, 91, 175, 213
    high-stakes, 38, 49
    morale and productivity at, 39, 50
    promotions at, 138, 148–49, 165,
        207
    self-assessed vs. objective
        performance at, 51–52, 54, 119
    success at, 55
    team performance at, 50, 52, 91,
        92, 150
    see also jobs
work ethic, 216
World Series of 2013, 59–60
World War I, 73
World War II, 32, 73, 77n
worry, 118n
Wundt, Wilhelm, 98
www.insight-book.com, 17
www.Insight-Challenge. com, 283,
    286
www.Insight-Quiz.com, 283
www.TashaEurich.com, 63n

Yale University, 78
    Medical School of, 133
YouTube, 87

"Zoom In, Zoom Out," 41–42